AF333352

ROBERTSON

ROBERTSON

THE PULPIT AND THE POWER

ARTHUR FREDERICK IDE

American Atheist Press
Austin, Texas 1988

American Atheist Press, P O Box 140195
Austin, TX 78714-0195
©1988 Arthur Frederick Ide. All rights reserved.
Published January 1989.
Printed in the United States of America

Ide, Arthur Frederick.
    Robertson! : the pulpit and the power : plotting, planning,
pretending — Pat's putsche for the presidency / by Arthur Frederick
Ide.
        p.   cm.
    Includes bibliographical references and index.
    ISBN 0-910309-46-9 (pbk.) : $5.00
    1. Robertson, Pat.   2. Church and state — United States.
3. Christianity and politics.   4. Southern Baptist Convention —
— Clergy — Biography.   5. Baptists — United States — Clergy —
Biography.
6. Presidential candidates — United States — Biography.   I. Title.
BX6495.R653134 1987
269' .2'0924 — dc19
[B]
                                                        87-28998
                                                        CIP

ISBN 0-910309-46-9

Table of Contents

Chapter 1
Pat: The Man & His Ideas on The Family

Marion Gordon "Pat" Robertson was born 22 March 1930. His natal appearance occurred in Lexington, Virginia, a sleepy village nestled in the soft, misty beauty of Virginia's Shenandoah Valley. Its population generally stabilized at four thousand inhabitants.

Even in this small southern town, at the beginning of Pat Robertson's life, there were shadows in his past for he was born of an incestuous marriage. His father, A. Willis Robertson, married his first cousin, Gladys Churchill Willis, in 1920. In most states liaisons within such a close degree of bloodline consanguinity are not legally tolerated.

Although Pat claims that his mother was the driving force who brought him to a realization of Jesus Christ, he says little or nothing else about her in his official works.

The only picture he has ever placed of her in any of his biographies is a single outdoor snapshot from 1922 in which her facial features are not distinguishable. But the mother treasured a picture of the son in which we clearly see Pat with tresses, twisted into soft, long curls that cascade to his waist. One can only wonder what kind of boyhood he had.

But, here we are almost sixty years later when Pat Robertson appears to many Americans as a man of stability, piety, and objectivity, who thinks only of "the mission of god," and cares not for "the things of the flesh." He possesses none of these attributes.

William Riley, a former Yale Law School classmate of Pat, who was with him in business in New York, declared that Pat had only two goals in life. One goal was "to make a lot of money." The other was "to go into politics."[1] Nothing else mattered.

Born into wealth, Robertson grew accustomed to luxury and self-indulgence at an early age. He grew up in a mansion, a two-story home with hardwood floors throughout, ten rooms, and three baths. He knew a life of unparalleled ease and comfort. His family was patronized and honored, since his father was a United States Senator. In his youth he attended the McCallie School in Chattanooga, Tennessee, a private school for the wealthy and the upcoming heirs of the South's finest families. He went from there to the equally expensive Washington and Lee University in Lexington, Virginia. Each year his father, a United States senator for over twenty years, was able to find well-paid and prestigious summer employment for his son. After Pat graduated from the university his father treated him to several tours of Europe, where he developed a taste for the Riviera. Spoiled by his father, he went on to law school at Yale, where tuition costs are astronomical. While at that Ivy League university, his father gave him summer employment with the U. S. Senate Appropriations Committee.

Robertson took a degree in law at Yale — but failed to pass his New York bar examination.[2] Having thus flunked out as a prospective attorney, he went to work for the W. R. Grace Company, training for an executive position. It would not be unrealistic to assume that his father also obtained this position for his son through his senatorial and business connections, the elder Robertson having been, for years, chairman of the powerful U. S. Senate Banking and Currency Commission. Robertson claims he was a "troubleshooter" in South America for the W. R. Grace Company, but apparently he was in its Foreign Service School to study economic conditions in that part of the world. The reputation of this company as an exploitive American "pirate" firm has caused it to be well-hated in South America. Its current president, J. Peter Grace, has an unrivaled reputation as a fanatical anti-communist who has done much to assist not only the Contras but other repressive groups. (*The Wall Street Journal* [8 May 1987] pp. 1, 12.)

This adventure into the world of business brought Pat little personal success, however, and only a minor sense of accomplishment.

During this period, Robertson was living the jet set life internationally, and when back in New York the *haute mode* — after all, who in New York City can afford to dine at the Stork Club or other such luxury bistros nightly?

When Pat left the Grace Company, he entered the electronic component business, the Curry Sound Corporation, with two of his

Yale classmates. It was hardly a shoestring affair considering those who were involved. He did not find, however, the get-rich-quick reward he expected. He could not discipline himself to be a private entrepreneur working tirelessly to build on a long term-basis, not just to enrich himself immediately. Immediate money — and a lot of it — was then, as it remains to Robertson now, everything.

By his own admission, Pat Robertson found life distressing, and at one time this self-confessed "swinger" had "contemplated suicide."[3] Before that, he disguised his suicidal nature with alcohol. His classmates remember him as a "poker-playing, fun-loving student." His business associates remember a high rider. Robertson was adept at drinking away his frustrations, but alcohol was only a temporary escape.[4] Yet, no one anticipated that Pat would be the mogul of a gigantic irrational religious television ministry; that he would claim to have the power to perform miracles; that he would even be in direct communication with the lord; or that he would push himself into the national political arena.[5]

Even when Pat became involved in a shotgun wedding, and subsequent married life, the high life continued. Yet he often felt keen anguish and agonized over his chosen lot in life. His marriage, however, was not the alkahest he sought for his problems.

His seeming "futility of life"[6] appeared to Pat to be more than he could bear. His only escape was to occupy himself on a golf course. Golf was more than the sport of leisured lords — it became Pat's paradise on earth. As if golf had a divine commission, or as if Jesus had played a good game in the low 50s, Pat determined that it would be a form of spiritual reward for himself. To surrender this fetish was anathema. Golf he would never give up.[7] Golf was never futile. Futility existed in "other things."

Robertson defined this "futility of life" which obsessed him as over-indulgence, yet he dined at the most expensive bistros in New York, wore silk suits, drank good whiskey, and toted fine leather briefcases. From food to clothing, his tastes were expensive. Even when he later condemned luxury enjoyed by others around him, he never gave up his own. To this day, Robertson retains his own stockbroker. Craftily he plays Wall Street securities, watching over his investments as if he were the Old Testament god watching over the Israelites.[8]

Pat's alleged "suffering" when he was a seminarian and early minister is not true. His wealthy parents were always there, or his wife's parents were, a prosperous Roman Catholic family from Columbus, Ohio, where Dede's father was a vice president of the Hanna Paint Company.

Pat simply could not bring himself to a position of self-support; Daddy had taken care of him too long. His wife, Dede, exposed the nature of the financial impoverishment when she declared in tired resignation, "If it weren't for the generosity of your parents, we'd be in the poorhouse."[9] It was, of course, her parents who bought the young couple an automobile. And, in 1957 Senator Robertson claimed Pat, Dede, and their babies as dependents on his tax return.

Later, the future televangelist would-be-presidential-candidate's life-style escalated to a lavish display of conspicuous consumption as he built up his television empire. Rather than saving souls as a pastor of a poor parish, Pat determined to sell salvation on the tube, which was both more fashionable, more ego-satisfying, and more profitable. Pat quickly fashioned himself into a fast-service, convenient, readily available televangelist for those of low income.[10]

Finding himself to be a natural in show biz, using hortatory skills he had not known he had, Pat discovered it was extraordinarily easy to coax monies from believers. Yet, while regularly promising them spiritual hamburgers, he dined on the filet mignon of reality, garnished with all the good things in life that their money would buy. The double-faced exercise, of course, was accomplished by exhorting in the name of Jesus while banking as a Virginia scion of wealth.[11]

Historically, Pat has been a dreamer.[12] Work has always been unpleasant for him. He prefers to let others do for him what he would not do for himself. Turning to the vast mass of religious folk who watch him on their tube, he constantly seeks their assistance and their money in the name of his Jesus so he can avoid any hard labor or personal energy investment. Much like the parasites of the past, Pat feeds his greed on the deflating pocketbooks of his victims. He prefers to con money out of men and women by promising spiritual rewards in heaven in exchange for earthly goods given to him here and now. It proves easier and more financially rewarding than toiling.[13]

More comfortable around the affluent[14] than the poor and hungry, Pat needed a god-gimmick that would fund his extravagances and — later — his political aspirations. Fundamentalist religion would be the key to opening the vaults of earthly wealth and power. He was to gain it all by selling spiritual favors, prayerful healings, and promised rewards in heaven. Not waiting for castles in the sky himself, Pat built his mansion on earth, filled his stables with riding horses, provided himself with tennis courts and a swimming pool, and covered any potential health problems with medical insurance for himself and his family.

The use of the idea of Jesus would become his bankbook and the foundation of his fortune. He was right in his estimate of the gullibility of the religious in our nation: Pat has never known want or poverty since he cashed in on Jesus.

Jesus could build Pat an empire, the preacher argued. This prophecy came to fruition for him as he skillfully incorporated into his team those who would advance the career of himself and his mentor, Jesus.

Pat's evangelical empire erupted like a volcano, offering a temporary shower of molten messages that burned into those who longed for respite of sorrows and surcease of suffering. Very quickly the televangelist Robertson spanned the airwaves, and his television territory grew, engorged with monies milched from the mindless, the lonely, the sick, the poor, the aged — all those who, unlike him, actually labored for their money.

As his finances grew, Robertson could afford more of the good things in life. Like other fundamentalists from coast to coast, Pat proudly proclaimed, "I found it!"

"It" allowed Pat to live palatially — in stark contrast to those who supported him. He found comfort and justification for his life-style and his lack of concern for those who struggled to sustain and expand his empire in his Bible: "The poor you shall have with you always" (Matt. 26:11). There was no need to worry about the lot of the masses. Poverty tested the faithful, thus proving the mercy, goodness, and justice of his god.

While many of the poor, the children, the unemployed, and the elderly ate at soup lines, stood in line for food stamps, ate cans of dog food, or rummaged in garbage pails and bins, Pat dined on fresh seafood and steak. Justifiably, he could offer up the prayer, "God is good."

The goodness of Pat's god exceeded human understanding. Not only would Pat ride in luxury on the ground and speed in his own jet in the air, live in a mansion, wear the finest of clothes, eat superb food, and find time his all-important golf games, but Pat would have headquarters fitting his station in life as the spokesman for his deity. Robertson built a command base in Virginia Beach, Virginia, that would equal the palaces of times tipped back to the past — where his own thinking would feel at home.

Pat Robertson's home base in Virginia — once he had achieved the notoriety of being a popular televangelist — is the ultimate expression of his being in favor with his deity. Among its accoutrements is a magnificent broadcast studio from which he spawns his daily sermons of covert hate interlaced with pleas for money, news distortions, and his prophetic political aspirations. Yet the actual filming is done in a cozy living room setting, the entrance to which requires security coded cards to unlock doors.[15] This seemingly innocuous setting was the power base from which he could plot the overthrow of basic civil rights and liberties, all in the name of the lord. CBN became a brothel in which the intellectual whores of the religious right would transmogrify the Constitution into what they would have, and rewrite our nation's history into a transposed and distorted revisionist Christian treatise. Science would be viewed as the enemy in the secular educational system he aspired to undercut. All of this was to be done in the name of Jesus and the monarchy-theocracy he plotted to yoke upon the bent back of a subservient United States citizenry.

Robertson claims that his "King" is Jesus.[16] His life commitment to himself alone, his begging-for-Jesus business, his ability to shrewdly manipulate fear, guilt, and hope to gain monetary gifts for which he gives nothing — really — in return, demonstrate that he sees "the Lord" as a shill for his own profit. The kingdom of Jesus becomes the business-theocracy of Pat Robertson.

Pat claims he has studied diligently the sacred writings concerned with his shill. But Pat's real passion has not been for the scriptures of the Christian Bible. Rather he burns the midnight oil over books on management and investment theories, as he longs to add the elusive element of respectability to his operations.

To assure his empire of having a lucrative and everlasting economic existence, Pat discharges anyone he feels might cause the smallest ripple, even the most loyal "Christian man," or servant of god. He only needs his imagined god to whisper in his ear and the luckless employee's job is terminated.[17] There is no need for proof of public wrongdoing, misappropriation of CBN funds or material, or incompetency to back up the discharge. Pat needs only to "understand the offense" before he speaks to his angry and capricious god about what he should do with the culprit.

Until he resigned from CBN on 29 September 1987, Robertson made all business decisions but refused to accept any blame for uncharitable, unwise, or inhumane treatment of employees. Once in a while, he has felt that he had to take the stand of Ezekiel blasting those who "erred," whether the sinner was a member of his own televangelic empire,[18] a politician, or a fellow evangelist.

Let's take a look at one of Robertson's cohorts. Jimmy Swaggart brings in $140 million a year in his television crusade for Jesus. Where this goes is anyone's guess. No religious group needs to make public how its income is spent. So, it is not unusual that it is alleged, that during one campaign to raise monies for overseas missions, Swaggart collected $13 million, but only $1 million found its way to its originally stated destination.

Jimmy Swaggart inflates both statistics and his Bible. While it is estimated that he has an audience of 8 million in the United States, he claims he has in "excess of 500 million people" worldwide in 145 countries.

Swaggart was initially reluctant to back Robertson's bid for the presidency but then came out for Pat, predicting that the Virginia Beach televangelist would win "the Pentecostal and charismatic vote" — claimed to be 30 million in the United States. Swaggart believes that Christians could better stand up for the Constitution than Jews or "anyone else." Christians, according to Swaggart, have a near-monopoly on faith and patriotism. For whom else would they vote but a fellow Christian like Pat Robertson.

Anti-Catholic, anti-Jewish, and anti-freedom, Swaggart has condemned everyone and everything, even himself, if that person differs with his myopic and narrow religious vision. He has publicly broadcast his anti-Jewish position. On the Roman Catholic church he has regularly declared it to be "a false cult," the doctrines of which are "of devils." He has issued a veritable condemnation, declaring that the Mormon church is "contrary to the Word of God," and chortled that Seventh Day Adventists will "die lost."

Swaggart prophesies death, doom, and gloom universally. "Soon" two-thirds of Israel is to be slaughtered. Those Jews who aren't slain are to become Christians and will become "the most evangelizing," with Israel becoming the "premier" Christian state.

Desiring privacy, Swaggart lives in a palace that is estimated to be worth more than $2 million, sprawls over 9,337 square feet, and boasts a "four-columned, step-up Jacuzzi with a gold-colored swan faucet," and has "No Trespassing" signs posted everywhere.

A life of poverty is anti-Christian and anti-god, according to Swaggart. If you can wheedle money from people, that proves your election into god's chosen circle. The more impoverished and the older the person milked for Jesus, the more blessed is the taker.

Swaggart has been especially effusive about Pat's stand on "moral values" and the "traditional family." Nothing has been said against his own adulterous pornographic relations with Louisiana prostitutes at the Travel Inn. Swaggart made a full confession of a moral problem to the officials in his denomination, the Assemblies of God, on Saturday, 20 February, 1988. Swaggart has been the leading voice in protesting the moral problems of Jim Bakker and the strong supporter of President Reagan's quest to restore morality to the United States.

Robertson pledges that as president, should he win the GOP nomination and the general election, *this is the man to whom he will turn for advice.*[19]

Further, Pat does not have to take a stand against his enemies, he argues, Jesus can do that for him. (We need Norman Lear here.)

Jesus is Robertson's henchman. Jesus is Pat's heavy. Jesus is the bully. Jesus is the muscle, the blackguard, the insensitive slob that curses those who don't agree with Robertson or don't meet Robertson's immediate or long-range needs. To quote Gerard Straub, a man who worked with Pat intimately for years, "It's bad enough to be fired by an insensitive boss, but imagine being fired by God!"[20]

Jesus has many roles which he plays for Pat. Jesus is not only Robertson's "buddy," but serves as his banking partner and financial adviser. His wife, Dede, has always been second. His children take an even smaller role — as if they were children of a lesser god.

As long as you believe in Jesus, Robertson commands, everything "is wonderful" and everything "wonderful will occur." Yet when "everything wonderful" does not occur, hopeful converts to Robertson's Jesus blame themselves and sink down into the spiral of self-doubt.[21] They forget that they have to accept Robertson as well as Jesus — as if Jesus had twinned with Pat, and the two men had merged together body and soul into one super being. Yet, his own mother believed that Pat never knew Jesus. Pat writes that his mother noted that her son "never mentioned his [Jesus'] name"[22] when he was at home.

Pat's wife saw him as a fanatic when he turned religious suddenly — almost overnight.[23] Then, as her Christian husband, the head of the family, Pat was given to forcing his ideas, values, and interpretations on her against her wishes and interests.[24]

Pat's life, goals, requirements, and restrictions were paramount. As he told it, he was the head; Dede (whose full name is Adelia Elmer[25]) Robertson was but the foot, the hand, the laborer. She was without equality or rights in his autocratically controlled family. The Christian castigation with which Pat whipped Dede would be the same belt that he would wield as the televangelist star of the "700 Club."

Chasing the money changers *into* his temple, Pat pounded out the tin sword of his attack on gender equality. It is a weapon he carries to the nation and to the world. No one may die from its initial blows, but once contaminated the wound will fester until the richness of liberty has turned into the poison of mental slavery.

Robertson has regularly prated against woman's equality on his "700 Club," time and time again. The message has always been the same. Men, because of their sexual organs, are supreme. Women, because of their gender apparatus, are to subject themselves to the dictation of the male. To force obedience to this injunction, Pat preaches to solidify and strengthen "the family," by which he means the dependent group each male controls.

Pat, however, showed little regard for his own family while he was "finding Jesus." He never said how Jesus got lost, but he knew he had to find him. Buddies don't let each other down.

When Pat found the lost Jesus, he embraced him on behalf of his family. His discovery of Jesus the family man, an unmarried, childless, Jew who had died two millenium ago, strengthened Pat's determination for male rule of the contemporary family, which finally became Pat's hallmark.

The "family" became a centerpost in Robertson's public statements. He declares that he "backs" the family and insinuates that "liberals," "Atheists," "non-Christians," Democrats, and others who voice opposition to his stand[26] are "anti-family." This message he carries into his 1988 campaign for the presidency.

Exactly what is "family" in Robertson's thinking? His perspective on the "family" is narrow at best. He claims that his conceptualization of "the family" is found in *his* Protestant Bible.

Again the family is defined in sexual gender terms. Pat is convinced that "the family" is to be headed by the male of the human species. He implies that the female is not mentally capable. Frequently, the televangelist has said on his "700 Club" that woman was never meant by his god to lead, guide, guard, or rule over the family, since, because of her gender, woman has only the "lock" while man has the "key." It is this key that opens the gates of a pulsating paradise in which his god determines who will come and who is to be denied.

Robertson implies that the male of the species is, by means of his genitalia, more intelligent, more astute, and more knowledgeable than a woman — because of her genitalia. Pat sees the woman as "receiving the man." He fails to consider that the woman may be the one who engulfs the man.

Pat's maudlin gynephobia is more in keeping with "Christian" thinking in the first two hundred years of the current era[27] than today's. Robertson has no faith in or acceptance of current psychological discoveries, nor with the present consensus on women's rights and inalienable equality.

Robertson's misogyny goes further than mere gynephobia. This televangelist is a proto-terrorist who strikes out at any liberated woman. Still hanging on to the dusty myth of a first woman (Eve) who caused the downfall of generic man, Pat argues that woman is the source of sin and is to be subject to the man so that sin will be curtailed through her husband's prayers.

Robertson is utterly convinced that the woman is incapable of maintaining a family or contributing to the advance of the commonweal. Archaically, Robertson argues that laboring in the open market workplace is "intolerable" to women. The televangelist pontificates that when a woman is forced to compete in the sphere of business and labor, her commercial or industrial labor leads to the breakdown of the family structure, the lessening of the male's authority, and ultimately to divorce.

Taking a catchphrase from feminist groups, Robertson further fulminates that the disintegration of the family is the result of the "feminization of poverty." At the same time he is against any governmental assistance to women who earn less than men.

Determined to keep women chained to the stove, or supine in bed, Robertson argues against working welfare mothers. He states, as if it were fact, that:

> The average woman . . . takes home something between $1,600 and $1,800 a year after taxes, clothes, cosmetics, transportation, lunches, and child care.

Bristling, he concludes "it's hardly worth it."

Robertson doesn't bother to ask the woman who allegedly makes between "$1,600 and $1,800" a year take-home pay whether her toil is "worth it" or necessary, or even if she has a choice. He doesn't feel she has enough intelligence to make a decision about her well-being since she has agreed to this "minimum wage." And Robertson doesn't tell his audience from what source he has taken his absurd and preposterous "facts."

Antipathetic toward women who make "something between $1,600 and $1,800 a year," Pat Robertson is equally against government subsidies for child-care that could ease the economic plight of the impoverished, underpaid woman. If child care centers could be closed, women would return to the home, marry a man who could economically keep her in exchange for her producing babies for him who would be subject to him as "the mediator of Jesus," according to the Gospel of Pat.

Government subsidies for child care, the televangelist thunders, are "anti-family" since they "permit" women to leave the home in quest of a job. Not only does Robertson distort the child-care "subsidy" issue, as well as the amount of money the average woman takes home, but Pat angrily argues that employment outside of the home makes women lackluster in their duties as wives and mothers, as well as boring in bed. Far better it would be for women, the preacher pronounces, if the government gave the husbands a tax deduction so that their wives could stay at home to be mothers, wives, homemakers, and *Kaffee-klatschers*.[28]

Pat's ideas and statements on the "family" have met with applause and congratulations. The televangelist found most "support" when he declared that "the Bible tells us" that his interpretation was correct. The majority of those who concur are men who have a vested sexual interest in keeping women both subordinate and supine. It is in his reading of Christian scriptures that Pat found points that prove his ideas, interests, and judgments. Those who eagerly seek an absolute criteria, an absolute rule, and a totally controlled way of life jumped onto the Robertson bandwagon. Robertson and his new faith-fooled flock of gospel geese happily become slaves to the Bible.

Many of Robertson's claims concerning the family are drawn from Old Testament references. However, the Old Testament books required thousands of years to hallucinate, compile, and write down. Many times certain stories within those books were recognized as having appeared at earlier times in other cultures and in other languages, which made early Christian thinkers question their value as early as the third century of the current era. To argue that the *Torah* (a Hebrew word meaning "instruction"), or the *Pentateuch* (a Greek word meaning "five scrolls"), both terms used to describe the first five books of the Old Testament, were written by Moses is a problem. Not only are there contradictions within the existing texts, but the events are out of order, a fact noted by a Greek writer, teacher, and Christian church "father" of the third century, Origen. He raised objections to the unity and Mosaic authorship of the books in question. The duplicity of stories in the Old Testament can be seen with the doubling of the story of The Flood in Genesis 6 and 8; the differing accounts of "creation" in Genesis 1, 2, 3; the "golden calf's" story; the proper name for god; etc.[29]

Without flinching, Robertson stoically surrendered his intellect, his ability to reason, his own interests to follow the scribblings of this Bible. Pathetically, he confessed:

> I . . . began devouring my Bible, morning, noon, and night. I read it aloud to Dede after we went to bed. Often she would just turn over and go to sleep, but I read it until I couldn't read any more.[30]

Robertson was hypnotized by the absurdities on the printed pages. He thought of nothing else. His life had devolved to a state of meaninglessness. Now he had found a friend — albeit it a pulp story. Still, this new friend spread out her riches more quickly than any wife could — and this new friend never argued back — only instructed. It quickly became his mistress, an uncompromising taskmaster who could not be moved, lurking between the lines of ink-cover words and cloth-covered boards. By his own admission, Robertson had little interest in anything other than himself, his own relationship with Jesus Christ, and his time to read about it all.

> I am a Christian, and that means my relationship with the Lord Jesus Christ is the most important in my life; that my life belongs to the Lord; and, that my desire is to please Him in all that I do.

Pat showed little consideration for his wife. Since Dede was, in Pat's eyes, inferior to him, he would control her, read to her, admonish her — regardless of her interest, wishes, and beliefs. What Dede wanted, needed, or sought was secondary to that which Pat insisted on having.

Pat's consistent chauvinism crossed common sense. He sent a message of dominance, preeminence and supremacy to Dede. He savagely slashed out at any concept of equality between husband and wife.

Dede could not escape the fact that Pat meant to dominate, control, and enslave her to his will. Realizing the limited extent of her new lot in life, she mourned, "I know you think a woman is supposed to submit herself to her husband."[31]

Dede told her mother, "I take orders only from my husband and from the Lord." Yet her acknowledgement of the fact of her subordination to Pat was difficult.

Later, when penning his autobiography, *Shout It from the Housetops*, Robertson rejoiced that Dede ultimately became "willing . . . to submit herself to my spiritual leadership."[32] He was elated that his wife stopped thinking for herself and recognized what he termed his superiority on earth over her.

The recognition of male supremacy came late and only with difficulty for Dede. For several years she fought for her self-identity. Only after years of marriage, and after having given birth to and caring for several children, did she surrender her mind to the televangelist.

Until that fateful moment of ultimate capitulation to Pat, Dede Robertson stood up for herself. Her independence and self-actualization were finally completely surrendered as she put her mind under the dominance of the man who would thenceforward control her destiny, provide her a home and food, give her clothes to wear, and children to rear. She sold her own potential for a pot of surreal porridge, and surrendered the faith in which she had been reared to her husband, Pat, who would give her shallow solace in exchange for a lifetime of subjection.

Before her final collapse to the pressure of the man she married, Dede Robertson angrily argued for her rights as an equal. She demanded respect as a human.[33] Pat refused to recognize or give her either.

In spite of Dede's tears, and her plaintive plea, "Please, Pat, consider someone besides yourself,"[34] the would-be minister tartly turned thumbs down on her supplication, as he reached toward the day he would be heralded as a new savior. Pat had started to become a spiritual *Führer* who would command an unquestioning allegiance to his interpretation of scripture and law. It was but a short time — twenty years — until he would begin to dream of the day when he would be president of our nation.[35]

Psychologists today argue that those who have delusions of grandeur are of danger only to themselves. But the same psychologists qualify their statement: they could well become a danger to others if the delusion is a "Napoleonic" complex that the individual will attempt to make real, riding roughshod over the rights of others.[36]

Until an delusion is acted out, there is little danger. But when an delusion becomes a vital driving force in the psychology of an individual to the point that it diverts the individual's attention from traditional duties that are expected, the delusion becomes a form of schizophrenia.[37]

Was Pat Robertson schizophrenic? He appeared to have developed a dual personality: the one of the "swinging single,"[38] and the other of being "god's prophet."[39] He was to take charge not only of his wife's life,[40] but the lives of others[41] — a task for which he believed he was divinely commissioned when he talked to a god[42] who lived in the trees around him.[43]

Dede Robertson judged him "schizoid." She declared, drenched in tears:

> I'm a nurse. I recognize schizoid tendencies when I see them, and I think you're sick. It's just not normal for a man to walk out on his wife and leave her with a small child when she's expecting a baby any minute — while he goes off into the woods to talk to God. God doesn't tell people to do things like that.[44]

But, Pat's god commands people to do irrational acts without question. He therefore responded that he was only obeying this god who lived in the woods.[45]

Morality is negotiable.

Love is less important than hate.

War is more valuable than peace — especially when war swells religious fervor in the hearts of men and anticipates the ultimate Armageddon prophesied by John the First Beloved — and Pat the Second Beloved.

While in the woods, Pat learned that his Jesus was about to return to earth with the sword. Jesus was a military leader in Robertson's eyes — more powerful and commanding greater allegiance than the United States Joint Chiefs of Staff of the Armed Forces.

Although a tough commander in chief, Robertson saw his Jesus also as a tender daddy who disciplined only those who did not hear his word — or the word of Pat — and keep it. Robertson's Jesus is also a jungle-dwelling aborigine who is intolerant of all who disagree with him or Pat. Pat's Jesus is quick to threaten to cast into the fiery pits of hell those mortals who dare to raise questions of Pat or question this deity's universality, omniscience, omnipotence, and omnipresence.

Questioning Pat is unacceptable to the televangelist's god. Pat made this clear not only in his attack on Norman Lear, but in his hatred of Federal Judge William R. Overton, who had sagely declared Arkansas law 590 of 1981, which mandated creation science be taught in public schools, as violative of the First Amendment.[46] Pat's libel of the judge was not exclusionary or selective; similar soundings shot down anyone who opposed him[47] — and all in the names of Jesus.

In the 1982 fracas the attorney general of Arkansas, Steve Clark, was attacked by Robertson as "crooked" when he made a donation to an action sponsored by the ACLU, which was fighting the case. He also charged the ACLU with attempting to destroy the Judeo-Christian heritage of the nation. Clark sued for slander; Robertson sent a written apology and settled out of court. (*Arkansas Gazette*, 12/9/82; 10/14/83.) It was in March 1986 that Robertson also accused Paul Kirk, Democratic National Committee Chairman, of "virulent anti-Christian bigotry" when Kirk referred to Robertson as a "radical right" leader trying to seize control of the Republican party. (*Courier-Journal*, 3/2/86, p. A5; *Syracuse Herald American*, 3/2/86, p. A10.)

After Pat's act of excommunication of any disbeliever, questioner, or opposer is completed — in the name of Jesus, Pat, while sitting comfortably in aristocratic wingback chairs in his living room/television studio[48] remounts quickly his mission to milch more money for this same laconic lunatic masquerading as a deity. The carefully appointed room is a symbol of Pat's spirit, psychology, and interest in the things of this world.

Pat preaches poverty of spirit for others, but personally likes the gusto of dictating, the macho of spirit, as well as the lush luxury of the good life. As a "Jesus follower" like Swaggart, Falwell, Schuler, Scott, Roberts, and other televangelists who have reaped millions of dollars from the savings of the poor and middle class, Pat is convinced that he deserves rich rewards.[49] Yet for all of the power Robertson attributes to his god, this Jesus is in a constant state of economic emergency, demanding more and more money to carry on his cavorting career of badgering and bashing unbelievers, promising to feed hungry multitudes, and bring surcease of sorrow, while always keeping a sizeable "residual" of money for Robertson to maintain his electronic ministry, mansion, and way of life of conspicuous consumption.[50]

Quick to condemn, pointing out other people's "sins," in spite of the fact that the Christian Bible details that "not even God is a respecter of persons"[51] and that the Jesus of the Greek New Testament forbade any of his followers from making value judgments on the quality, merit, situation, position, or morality of another,[52] Robertson places himself and his god above and superior to the god of the Greek New Testament.[53] Robertson judges, as does his god, who has little relationship to the Jesus of the New Testament.

Not only has this crafty cleric concerted his attacks upon the unknown "enemies of Christ," but he has taken pains to denounce them as "ungodly" and "profane." Unbelievers, who include Jews, Atheists, agnostics, "secular humanists," non-Christians, and those outside of his charismatic pentecostal Southern Baptist confession are to be "educated" or "cast out."[54] To help him in this Herculean task would require Robertson's god to have a giant computer in the sky. This giant computer would not only have to keep records on each mortal but maintain a running total of all sins committed by all people at all times in all places.

The great machine of Pat's god must run by a clock, for Robertson called on one of the strangest lines in Scripture, Revelations 8:1: ". . . there was a silence in heaven about the space of half an hour."[55] This half-hour was to be a sneak preview of the ultimate terror of a merciless god winging to earth to slash at those who had done him, or Pat, wrong[56] — be the sinner a viewer, an apostate, an unbeliever, or even Pat's wife.

Dede's god was not, at first, Pat's god. Pat's illusion of god was more in keeping with the phenomenon fantasized for centuries by frigid fundamentalist fanatics.[57] Pat's immortal required slavish devotion, draconic demonstrations of filial piety and obsequious obedience. A singular god has become the repository of the polytheism of past periods: the burning bushes that talked, the whirling winds that preached, the clouds that thundered, terrorizing sermons of hate, and the ubiquity that ordered Abraham to slaughter his son in testimony to his faith.[58]

Pat was ordered to abandon his wife to minister to the deity's desires. Like an Old Testament prophet, Pat felt justified in deserting her. The spirits of the woods, like the god of the bush, demanded total allegiance. Even a letter begging Pat to come back to her did not move the would-be "man of God,"[59] who had become subservient to superstition. Calling on the god who ruled the fates, Robertson's inquiry was mystically marginal. Rather than proceeding to a hermeneutic analysis, utilizing methodological principles of interpretation that have been accepted as primary and scholarly tools, Robertson turned to chance. He said, "I let my Bible fall open,"[60] as if a glance at a printed page was a method of divinition similar to stirring and "reading" the entrails of slaughtered fowl, sacred to mythological deities. The passage he chanced upon, 1 Corinthians 7:32,[61] gave him justification for putting himself and his "ministry" before his wife or family.

Pat's wife, child, and family became inconsequential to his god and to himself. Unlike Augustine of Hippo who found masochistic justification in a scriptural passage enjoining him to be celibate — and who prayed "Lord, let me be chaste — but not yet"[62] — Robertson flew to his spiritual release from mortal, emotional ties to his wife and child, by isolation, reading, writing, praying, and psychological self-flagellation.

When Pat did finally respond to Dede's request that he leave his new interest to remain with her until the birth of their second child, he wrote, "I can't leave." He justified his denial of familial responsibility with the narcissistic, Augustinian apology, "God will take care of you."[63]

Like most "converts," Robertson became a zealot. Confirming his "election" as a "chosen one of god," he was determined to prove to himself and to others that, like an Old Testament prophet, he had acquired special, divine powers.

To prove his election Pat promised a miracle. He prayed for rain. Later Pat explained his storming of heaven with prayers petitioning for rain to a coreligionist. His prayers were answered; it rained "in torrents," he squealed with joy; and, as that rain fell, Robertson felt himself to be an equal to the omnipresent. From that moment he would turn his faith and prayers into a constant attuning with the godhead.[64]

It would only be a matter of time until he would declare that he would be able, through his prayers, to turn a hurricane around in the middle of the ocean — as it raced towards his televangelistic empire in Virginia. Controlling the elements of nature would be lesser miracles. Greater miracles were promised.

If enough was given to his god in faith, the "law of reciprocity" would bring back in greater quantities[65] to the believer who gave. Reciprocity, put simply, means one gets back that which one gives — or more. Much of his justification for this "principle of reciprocity" is gleaned from Luke 6:31-38, with a special emphasis on verses 36-38. The context of this text is actually concerned with attitudes and spontaneous giving, as defined in Matthew 6:33. Robertson's concept of tithing to reach and be fulfilled by the "law of reciprocity" is taken primarily from the Old Testament book of Malachi (especially 3:7-10), a reference which is not unique to the Malachi or the Jews, but rather to their numerous Near Eastern ontological antecedents. Interestingly, Robertson does have an "exclusionary clause" in his concept. "Renegades" defined as those who "oppose him and those belonging to him" won't merit reciprocity no matter how much they give to Jesus or give in any similar situation.[66]

"Miracles" play a significant role in the law of reciprocity, according to Pat. Giving money to a holy cause can generate a miracle of good health, vocational or occupational promotion, or other physical needs, such as peace of mind — rather than produce a financial return on a financial investment.[67]

From his confrontation with heaven to his ministrations on earth, all with limited benefit of formal education, or a foundation in ontology, or in theological hermeneutics,[68] Robertson proceeded to preach. He declared that all he needed was his Bible.

Like a raving John Knox, denouncing Mary of England, or a wild-eyed John Calvin of Geneva, blasting false body ornamentation, Pat's sermons are based on a literal interpretation of Scriptures — utilizing crass editions that give a popular translation to messages penned at first in Greek, a language of which he shows little understanding. Yet he believes blindly, unquestioningly, irrationally, in a translation that may well be described as beautiful literature but which has only a modicum of exactitude towards "the original" Greek.[69]

Irrational actions and misplaced resolve were commonplace with Pat. He could not decide what he wanted to do. He repeated himself. He confronted imaginary enemies. He told unheard stories. He became, even more so, a contradiction in terms, life-styles, and experiences. His exasperated Roman Catholic wife, Dede, sighed in asking, "Can't you ever make up your mind about anything?"[70]

Charismatic Christianity was to give Pat Robertson power, purpose, and a sense of organization.[71] Suddenly, Robertson believed he had been called to save all non-Christian people: Koreans, Chinese, "and others." Salvation was to come by means of self-denial, self-abuse, self-rejection — by those to be saved, not by Pat. The future talk-show host would carry his cross only by reading and preaching his Bible.

For those who would follow Pat to the pearly gates, hours were to be spent in unnatural self-torture; staying day and night on one's knees "in prayer," going without food or drink, comdemning one's self for imaginary sins, lamenting one's past as if the lamentation could undo it, crying out for a second chance to be granted by some divine, yet capricious, hand. Prayers, "crying and travailing in the Spirit for many hours at a time," became a passport to inward peace and spiritual fulfillment[72] — while homes went uncleaned, food was not prepared, hygiene was ignored, and families abandoned. Hallucinations were excused as holy inspirations and questions multiplied about the fantasies that filled the heads of the faithful: was this a foretelling of the Second Coming of Christ, the Last Judgment, or the Revival?[73]

When Robertson was confronted with adversities, the problems that he experienced were "caused" by the Devil:

You are allowing Satan to dissipate my zeal through the pressure of stupid things like housework and cooking. . . . I am forced to stay home and take care of my wife and children. I want to fast and pray. . . . I am tied down to a sinkful of dirty dishes and a pailful of messy diapers.

It was as if Robertson had been born again — this time as a Messiah, who underwent a torturous turmoil of spiritual thought which ultimately brought him into direct communion with the godhead.

When those around him objected to his self-mortifications, Pat lashed out that they were "doing the Devil's work." Like St. Anthony of the Desert, another wild-eyed fanatic who delighted in placing scorpions and insects upon his body, inviting lice to infest his hair, and who dined meagerly in anticipation of gaining "the beatific vision" and seeing his "lover" Jesus Christ "face to face," Robertson flagellated his spiritual flesh and his mind with an abrasive raking by the Bible — ever in his hand.

His prayers for those who spoke against him, or issued "unkind remarks," went unanswered, and their remonstrances and protests tortured his own thoughts. In a self-inquisition, he resorted to the Bible for answers but that brought only stinging retort. He observed, "Unkind remarks . . . drain[ed] all my spiritual zeal in a matter of seconds."[74]

When Dede could no longer fight Pat's "insanity,"[75] she joined him.[76]

Although a Southern Baptist, Pat and his wife, a Roman Catholic, quickly became "spirit-filled" charismatics. Shouting Christianity became their reason for living. Choruses of "Glory!" and "Hallelujah!" punctuated their verbal communication when they were not busy reading religious polemics against reason, believing blindly that they would receive gifts — of empty promises.[77]

Pat broke out in garbled language. He claimed to be "speaking in tongues." But the tongues in which Pat spoke were not the "speaking of tongues" detailed in the Book of Acts.

In Acts 2:3-11,[78] the "tongues" in Greek (*qlossa, glutta, glussan nomizein* — meaning "commonly understood languages") in which the early followers of the crucified Jesus spoke were the foreign languages of the various nationalities assembled, so that they could understand what the disciples were saying. As the writer of Acts noted, the various nationalities, upon hearing the message, each in his own tongue, commonly questioned,

> And how hear we every man in our own tongue, wherein we
> were born? Parthians, and Medes, and Elamites, and the dwellers
> in Mesopotamia, and in Judea, and Cappadocia, in Pontus, and
> Asia, Phrygia and Pamphylia, in Egypt, and in the parts of Libya
> about Cyrene, and strangers of Rome, Jews and proselytes,
> Cretes and Arabians, we do hear them speak in our tongues
> . . . .

The "tongues" to which the disciples referred in this instance were
definitely not the gobbledygook of contemporary pentecostalism —
and emphatically not the language distortions and vocal exercises
forced from Robertson's tortured throat.

But the nonsensical guttural speech reenforced the televangelist's
determination to be someone different. It was different all right! And,
Robertson was, at last, on his way to become the showman, which
would raise him to stardom on his own television station. There,
unchecked and unopposed, he could brutalize genuine "biblical
literalism" and biblical scholarship, while bastardizing reality and
biblical exegesis for the glorification of what became his self-created
cult.

At the same time, being a Southern Baptist, Robertson laid the
groundwork for the radical right in the Southern Baptist Convention
to rally against members of their own denomination who could not or
would not accept a literal interpretation of their very fallible Bible. Thus,
the Southern Baptist Convention would, under Paige Patterson,
Wallace A. Criswell, Richard Land, and other fundamentalists, strangle
not only individual freedom of choice concerning biblical interpretations
and adherence but intellectually assault those who disagreed with
them.[79] Patterson,[80] and his equally determined prophets of
fundamentalist fratricide, now promise to take over the existing
Southern Baptist seminaries and turn them into cells for rigid rote
memorization — forbidding disagreement, and denying the possibility
of allegories in the Bible they hold to be absolute.[81] The literal word of
their god is not to be challenged — as if the deity had sat personally
before a computer and punched keys to compose a book that could
never be changed.

Robertson was so thrilled with his "miracle" of being able to speak
in tongues[82] — he believed that his first encounter gave him the power
to speak in "some kind of African dialect"[83] — he questioned how he
could use this special "gift." In his biography, however, he did not
bother to elaborate on how he knew his speech was "some kind of

African dialect," nor did any colleague or family member, a significant fact since none of their official *vitae* include any formal or informal study in any African language.

Adding even more spice to this overseasoned porridge of perfidious piety is Robertson's announcement that not only did he listen to a unique "gift" of speaking in tongues that a friend (Harald Bresdesen, pastor of the Reformed Church in Mt. Vernon) executed, but that after the minister would "speak a short phrase in tongues," he would "give the interpretation in English," and then repeat the process "as if a heavenly teletype machine had mysteriously been activated."[84]

Many who witnessed Robertson's "gift of tongues" were so impressed that they flew to their checkbooks to write out various sums to further his ministry.

Mrs. Ruth (Norman Vincent) Peale was one of those who were willingly included in this illusion. The inheritor of the magazine *Guideposts*, Mrs. Peale told her staff of her experience. John Sherrill, a staff member, saw a story in it — and Pat's career was launched. Pat became "desperate" for a mission. He couldn't wait. His debut in Ruth Peale's *Guideposts* was just a beginning. Pat's god had to hurry up. Like most converts of unbridled zeal, Pat pulsed, "It seems a tragic waste for us to just sit around twiddling our thumbs."[85]

When it was suggested that he might not be the "chosen one" of his god, Robertson reacted savagely. He didn't take kindly to the idea that maybe "god" hadn't called him. That kind of god he would not accept. His god would obey him. He would be the god of god.

At this point, Robertson talked himself into believing that he had been "called" to the "worst black slum in America."[86] In such surroundings, Pat was convinced he would win the godhead's interest, respect, and ultimate rewards. Dede wasn't excited about moving to the slums of New York. She wanted to hold out for a fancy parsonage position pastoring in Tucson.

To counter his wife's ministrations, Pat turned to the Bible for an answer. Robertson began basing all of his life on passages found in the Bible by random selection. To whatever page the Bible fell open and his finger or eye glance happened first to chance upon — that became his answer for any problem and his menu for direction in life and living. The Bible spelled out every act he was to contemplate or commission.[87]

Dede had no choice, if she was to stay married to Pat. She had to follow his example.[88] Fortunately for Dede, Pat's mission in New York was brief. There was no money among the very poor. They could not exchange dollars for prayers. Thus it was that his sojourn as a preacher to the poor was but a temporary stop along the way in his real quest — for power and empire.

He had learned how to win the ear and open the pocketbooks of important and powerful people, those with whom he had associated in his youth and young manhood. He simply went back to his own. He attended a presidential prayer breakfast at which his father, Senator Robertson, spoke. He volunteered to serve as counselor for the Billy Graham Crusade in New York City.[89] He spoke to William Randolph Hearst and now boasts that his conversation catapulted Billy Graham into "worldwide fame."[90] Robertson's ego soared.

Now it was time to trot with turkeys and turn the world into his breadbasket. This he would do by means of initiating, ultimately owning, and thoroughly controlling his own television network.

What came to be known in the United States as televangelism would prove more lucrative than conducting any tent or stadium crusade for Christ. It would dwarf the efforts of any cathedral or mammoth church. It would reach more persons in one hour than an entire denomination could touch in a year.

When a television station in Portsmouth, Virginia, became available for "$250,000 [to] . . . $300,000," the enterprising evangelical entrepreneur Robertson was ecstatic. According to Robertson, he had received the encouragement that "the Lord" would help him to beat the price requested. His mother had initially heard of the station through a friend, and advised Pat of its availability. Although she initiated the idea and had financial resources enough to obtain the station for her son, suddenly she drops from the narrative.

As the story is told, with consummate cunning, Robertson himself bartered, pleaded, and promised prayers and other intangibles in a desperate effort to lower the price tag to one with which "the Lord" would be happier. God had become a real estate broker and began bargaining for the lowest price.[91] He was selective with whom Pat would do business. Robertson's god did not want *just any Christian* to profit from his entrepreneurial enterprises:

> "I don't want some Christian to get it," God said in my heart,
> "I want *you* to have it."[92]

Robertson allegedly secured the bankrupt UHF station for only $37,000. Of that figure, Robertson claims only $70 was his own cash.[93] But with the help of god and mother, anything can happen, for God was no longer objective, but a selector of persons, a deity playing favorite with Pat, who now became a chosen one after Jesus — possibly even the next Jesus?[94] Robertson argues that his god has determined exactly what properties the deity designated as being exclusively for Robertson, along with the usual quibble over how much this Omniscient would permit Robertson to pay for the property. It is interesting to note, however, that as far as is recounted, God never *gave* Robertson property or other real estate outright.[95] But, in this instance, Robertson and his god were successful brokers. Their financial coup — the purchase of the television station — would only be the beginning. From this initial endeavor, Robertson would quickly learn how to milk money from millions of the pious. And Robertson milked that market well, as if it were a cow pastured for a week with no hand willing to squeeze its teats.

Meanwhile, mass religious hysteria, speaking in tongues, and outright buffoonery became the staple diet for those who became Robertson's coreligionist club members,[96] with Robertson lecturing god on when "the right time" had come. Then, resignedly, suggesting that maybe the "right time" hadn't come for god.[97]

With stardom beckoning, Pat became increasingly more involved with demons[98] and demonology.[99] Uttering the name "Jesus" became a panacea: getting rid of lice, rats, mice, various vermin, bedbugs, and roaches. Deliverance from these creatures is strictly a Christian trick. In part the antipathy, the hostility, toward natural beings, such as rats and vermin, is the Christian response to paganism that had prized all things which evolved.[100]

The demonic plagues with which Robertson was confronted were not, however, physical phenomena. Instead, most of the "demons"[101] with which the "afflicted" were infested were psychological, illusionary incubi (evil spirits): chimeric, unreal, and unsubstantiated. Most were "visited" upon poor, uneducated Blacks ("Carolina Negroes") who had turned to a life of prostitution and crime in order to scratch out a basic existence in the Christian society in which they lived — a Christian society which gave more to war than to the poor.

Like St. Anthony of the Desert, Robertson has described himself awakening and being "under demonic attack." He ended this hallucination by crying out, "Satan, in the name of Jesus, I cast you forth." His ideas on demons and demonology, Robertson declares,[102] come from a unique reading of Revelation 12:11, 1 John 4:4, and 1 Thessalonians 5:23, yet these passages do not support his theses. 1 Thessalonians 5:23 reads on the sanctification of the body and soul "to be preserved blameless" until Jesus's assumed Second Coming;

demons are not mentioned. Nor are demons mentioned in 1 John 4:4, or in Revelations 12:11 (the "Devil" is mentioned in verse 9 and is a reference to the "great dragon . . . that old Serpent, called the Devil" being cast out "into the earth" along with the "angels" of the "Devil" who were given dominion over the earth.) Cf. Job 2:1.

Interestingly this same demon infestation befell Dede Robertson, who awakened one evening hallucinating that she was covered with rats.[103] Robertson's response to his wife' traumatic *delirium tremens* was that "It's just Satan's trick to scare you." Yet when his friend Dick Simmons complained of satanic attacks, Robertson sloughed it off, claiming that Simmons' red welts were the result of a vitamin A deficiency.[104]

Demonology and demon dances became the Christian cudgel[105] to hold over the heads of those individuals Robertson determined he would control or use in the development of his ministry.

Robertson is quick to lace his language with prophecies of doom and gloom to be heard by both family and outsiders. He is equally agile in brightening his banal barrage when approached by colleagues and coworkers.[106]

Robertson was especially worried about any independence that his wife Dede would show. He confessed that "Dede's rebellion bothered me." Too much rebellion could cost him his plot in the pages of history, and such an attack on his aspirations could not be tolerated.[107] Hysterics became a daily part of his life. Robertson is given to tears, cries of anguish, and exultation repetitively.[108]

Joy comes when Robertson gains property and other tangible forms of wealth. Tears of desperation follow any realization that he will not always have his way.[109] Robertson has had a difficult time accepting the fact that "god" did not always share his views, nor did his god always work toward Robertson's personal goals.[110] When things failed, it was a failure of faith, or a misunderstanding of the will of god, for Robertson would never say that god failed him.[111]

All longings for wealth and fame have been excused as being the goals and determinations of the YHWHistic god of the Old Testament.[112] Robertson considers himself nothing less than the instrument of bringing this YHWH into agreement with the New Testament Jesus.

God is to take an active part in American life, politics, rules and regulations, commerce, and education. Robertson's god is to exercise his authority over the FCC, contributors, news commentators, jurists, educators, politicians, business people, craftspersons, and general citizens.

God's advent into the American political arena is to be at Robertson's request. Pat is to become the Protestant pope of this god. He is to be the new Charismatic vicar of Christ and have dominion over all things.

Robertson is to be the instrument of god's pleasure and god's wrath.[113] God even established a bank account on earth. In many ways this new divine bank account is like the Treasury of Merit developed by wayward monks, greedy prelates, and corrupt popes in the Middle Ages.[114] God's bank account, which he set up for Pat, was to be styled "The Christian Broadcasting Network, Inc."[115] When god established this account, Jesus was overdrawn by three dollars. His indebtedness multiplied from the start.[116]

Jesus' being in debt didn't bother Robertson. He was, according to his own admission, soon to receive checks from god. The father could not let down the son; that had happened once in history, and god recognized his mistake — at least Robertson thought so.

In return for the checks for god, Robertson would prepare financial reports and statements.[117] These reports, however, were to be for god alone. The reports were not to be opened to the IRS or any other taxing authority.[118]

But with some of Pat's organizations, their tax status is questionable. The IRS has had a difficult decision to make: can the IRS audit god? Using controversial fund-raising methods unique in national politics, Robertson pushes the theme of "contributions" to a "holy cause," which is, in reality, more a promise of a *jihad* or holy war against the infidel than a quest for funds to aid the sick, poor, and homeless. Robertson has raised millions of dollars to finance the mobilization of the United States into a new Christian nation. The IRS remained uncertain as to whether or not such pledge solicitation constitutes partisan politics and maneuverings, yet Robertson's revitalized Freedom Council continues to muster a concerted assault on the Constitution and the American way of life — as currently understood.

To say that the monies raised in Robertson's religious calls are being used for nonsecular interests and goals is ludicrous. Robertson's Freedom Council, nationwide, spent more than $4 million in 1986 to "encourage" fundamentalist Christians to participate in politics in 1986 — as candidates or prospective candidates. The Freedom Council funded fourteen staff people — nine hired specifically to recruit Republican precinct delegates for the 5 August 1986 primary in Iowa.

Faced with the possibility of being exposed as a man who used sacred funds for secular causes, Robertson continued the agreed-upon lie that the money was used for "educational purposes." Even when he completed lecturing at a political fund-raiser, he noted that his "traditional values" have to be financed in order to become the mainstay of present politics.

Memorandums put out by Robertson not only call for increased contributions to his "holy" cause but ask for donations to overthrow the existing cultural order in the United States. This call for funds became especially aggressive during Robertson's initial campaign for support to run for the presidency of the United States. It was unfurled throughout the nation, with special attention directed towards the fundamentalist block of voters in Michigan.

Notes

1. The incestuous marraige of Pat's parents is detailed in David Edwin Harrell, Jr. *Pat Robertson: A Personal, Religious, and Political Portrait,* (San Francisco: Harper & Row, 1987), p. 17. Gladys was ten years younger than Absalom Willis Robertson. John J. Fialka and Ellen Hume, "Pulpit and Politics: TV Preacher, Possibly Eyeing the Presidency, Is Polishing His Image," *Wall Street Journal* CCVI.77 (17 October 1985), p. 23.

2. *Des Moines* [Iowa] *Register* (10 June 1986), sec. A, p. 8. Michael Kramer, "Are You Running with Me, Jesus? Televangelist Pat Robertson Goes for the White House," *New York* (18 August 1986), p. 25.

3. Pat Robertson with Jamie Buckingham, *Shout It from the Housetops* (Plainfield, NJ: Logos International, 1972), p. 21, cf. p. 13.

4. See: Larry Fruhling, "Robertson: Religious Zealot or New Force in U.S. Politics?" in *Des Moines Register* (9 August 1987), sec. A, pp. 1, 4.

5. Robertson, *Shout It from the Housetops,* p. 26.

6. Robertson, *Shout It from the Housetops,* p. 49.

7. Robertson, *Shout It from the Housetops,* p. 122.

8. Dudley Clendinen, "Ordained of God: Surge of Christians See Pat

Robertson as God's Candidate," *Chattanooga* [Tennesee] *Times* (25 June 1986).

9. Robertson, *Shout It from the Housetops*, p. 82. Any suffering was preplanned. He wrote that he was a saint (p. 20) and thus had to have the image of one.

10. Cf. Jay Ambrose, "No TV Preachers Wanted at the Bully Pulpit," *Rocky Mountain* [Denver, Colorado] *News* (6 October 1986).

11. "Painful Scrutiny for Pat; Mounting Questions about the Political Preacher," *Newsweek* (13 October 1986), p. 48.

12. Robertson, *Shout It from the Housetops*, p. 82.

13. Robertson, *Shout it from the Housetops*, pp. 119, 121, 123, 128, 130-31, 144-45, 146, 147, 173, in which he is given a house rent-free; p. 179 discusses "volunteers" pp. 226-34; in which Pat "began secretly to pray" for $100 million; p. 242 discusses his "negotiations" with defense-contractor LTV of Grand Prairie/Dallas, Texas, with the final pages detailing Pat's praying like a medieval monk for the afflicted.

14. April Witt, "Pat Robertson," The *Virginian-Pilot/The Ledger-Star* (1 June 1986), sec. C, pp. 1, 2. Pat delights in eating with Nelson Bunker Hunt, a Texas investor, and Cory SerVass, publisher of the *Saturday Evening Post*.

15. *Time* (February 17, 1986), p. 65.

16. Robertson, *Shout It From the Housetops*, pp. 21-22. Gerard Thomas Straub, *Salvation for Sale: An Insider's View of Pat Robertson's Ministry* (New York: Prometheus Books, 1986), p. 35.

17. Straub, *Salvation for Sale*, p. 35

18. See Robertson's account of the ministry of Jim and Tammy Bakker in his *Shout It From the Housetops*, pp. 204ff, when the Bakkers hosted their first show on the "700 Club."

19. See Lloyd Grove, "Jimmy Swaggart: Wonders of the Lord and TV," *Washington Post* (29 September 1986), sec. C, pp. 1, 8.

20. Straub, *Salvation for Sale*, p. 35.

21. William F. Fore, *Christian Century* (7 July 1981).

22. Robertson, *Shout It from the Housetops*, p. 18.

23. *Robertson, Shout It from the Housetops*, p. 27.

24. *Robertson, Shout It from the Housetops*, p. 28.

25. Dede was originally from Columbus, Ohio, and is the mother of Pat's four children: Tim (born ten weeks after they were married), Elizabeth, Gordon, and Ann, and grandmother of four.

26. *Washington Post* (9 September 1986).

27. See my *Woman as Priest, Bishop and Laity* (Mesquite, TX: IHP, 1984), chap. "Male Collaboration Against the Female Sex in the Early Christian Church," pp. 61-102. Pat's misogyny is similar to that articulated by Clement of Alexandria, *Paedaqoqus* III.3, in which this clerical sexist said, "his beard . . . is the badge of a man and shows him unmistakably to be a man. It is older than Eve and is the symbol of the stronger nature. By God's decree, hairiness is one of man's conspicuous qualities, and at that, it is distributed over his whole body. Whatever smoothness or softness there was in him, God took from him when he fashioned the delicate Eve from his side to be the receptacle of his seed, his helpmate both in procreation and in the management of the home. What he had left (remember, he lost all traces of hairlessness) was manhood and reveals that manhood. His characteristic is action; hers, passivity. For what is hairy by nature is drier and warmer than what is bare; therefore, the male is hairier and more warm-blooded than the female; the uncastrated, than the castrated; the mature than the immature. Thus it is a sacrilege to trifle with the symbol of manhood [the penis]." Clement, like Robertson, sees women as "castrated," "immature," "cold-blooded," and passive — in need of being kept, maintained, guarded both from others and from herself by a man. She is to be the "receptacle" [toilet?] of his seed, since she is too weak to refuse him. And since she is "hairless," the "hairy" man is to keep her warm.
Neither Robertson nor Clement fully addressed the issue of the

dominant woman and the passive man. They imply that such characteristics are satanic, and that society should control the fates of such "ill-tempered" individuals. Heinrich Himmler had a similar policy — in dispatching those who did not measure up to his standards of what a true "man" or "woman" was to be.

28. "Pat Robertson and Politics," *Christian Life Magazine* (August 1986), p. 45.

29. A popular reference work on this point in the Old Testament is by Richard Elliott Friedman, *Who Wrote the Bible* (New York: Summit Books, 1987). On the creation story, see my *Woman in Ancient Israel Under the Torah & Talmud: with a Critical Commentary and Parallel Translation (Greek, Hebrew, English) of Genesis 1-3* (Mesquite, TX: IHP, 1982). On the issue of Moses, see: Jean Astruc, *Conjectures sur les memoires origine/aux dont il parait que Moyses s'est servi, pour composer le livre de la Genese* (Paris, 1753). On Deuteronomy, see Martin North, *Uberliefenunqsqeschichtliche Studien* (Tubingen: Max Niemeyer Verlag, 1957), and Hans Walter Wolff, "Das Kerygma des deuteronomistischen Geschichtswerks," *Zeitschrift Für die alttestamentliche Wissenschaft* 73 (1961), pp. 171-86; with the full problem of the Pentateuch discussed by Rolf Rendtorff, *Das überlieferunqsqeschichtliche Problem des Pentateuch (Beihefte zur Zeitschrift für die alttestamentliche Wissenschaft* p. 147 (Berlin: Walter de Gruyter, 1977).

30. Robertson, *Shout It from the Housetops*, p. 29.

31. Robertson, *Shout It from the Housetops*, p. 129, cp. 90.

32. Robertson, *Shout It from the Housetops*, p. 92.

33. Robertson, *Shout It from the Housetops*, p. 28.

34. Robertson, *Shout It From the Housetops*, p. 31.

35. An interesting study on non-traditional goal setting, see: Malca K. Aleksandrowicz, "The Little Prince: Psychotherapy of a Boy with Borderline Personality Structure," *International Journal of Psychoanalytic Psychotherapy* 4 (1975): pp. 410-25. Cf. O. Kernberg, "Structural Derivatives of Object Relationships," *International Journal of*

Psychoanalysis 47 (1966): pp. 236-53.

36. Mardi J. Horowitz, "Sliding Meanings: A Defense against Threat in Narcissistic Personalities," *International Journal of Psychoanalytic Psychotherapy* 4 (1975): pp. 167-80. A. Adler, *The Neurotic Constitution: Outlines of a Comparative Individualistic Psychology and Psychotherapy*, trans. B. Gluck and J. Lind (New York: Moffat Yard & Co, 1916). Sigmund Freud, "On Narcissism: An Introduction" in his *Standard Edition*, vol. 14 (London: Hogarth Press, 1957), pp. 69-102. M. Mahler, *On Human Symbiosis and the Vicissitudes of Individuation* (New York: International Universities Press, 1968).

37. Cf. N. S. Cameron, "Experimental Analysis of Schizophrenic Thinking," *Language and Thought in Schizophrenia*, ed. J.S. Kasanin (Berkeley, CA: University of California Press, 1946), pp. 50-64. E. H. Erickson, "Identity and the Life Cycle," *Psychological Issues* 1: Monograph 1. H. Guntrip, *Schizoid Phenomena, Object Relations, and the Self* (New York: International University Press, 1969).

38. Robertson, *Shout It from the Housetops*, p. 20.

39. Robertson, *Shout It from the Housetops*, pp. 198, 191, 255.

40. Robertson, *South It from the Housetops*, pp. 82, 70, 27.

41. Robertson, *Shout It from the Housetops*, pp. 203-08, 192.

42. Robertson, *Shout It from the Housetops*, pp. 82

43. Robertson, *Shout It from the Housetops*, pp. 31-33ff.

44. Robertson, *Shout It from the Housetops*, p. 31.

45. Robertson, *Shout It from the Housetops*, pp. 34, 36, 37.

46. *Arkansas Gazette* (6 August 1983).

47. *Arkansas Gazette* (6 August 1983). Cp. George Wells, "Clark Sues Evangelist, Alleges Libel," *Arkansas Gazette* (9 December 1982. and 11 December 1982), for follow-up reports on the suit launched and later dropped by Arkansas Attorney General Steven Clark, stemming

from Robertson's 9 December 1981 telecast of the "700 Club" that was carried on KARK-TV and two channels on the Little Rock cable. Cp. Robertson's remarks concerning Democratic National Committee Chairman Paul Kirk, in The *Atlanta Journal and Constitution* (2 March 1986), p. 6. Kirk hurled back the charge that Robertson is a "radical right-wing leader" who wants to "abolish public education." See Phil Gailey, "Evangelist and Democrats' Chief Trade Fire," *New York Times* (2 March 1986), p. 22; and, *Syracuse* [New York] *Herald American* (2 March 1986), sec. A, p. 10.

48. Darrell Yates Rist, "A Sinner's Guide to the TV Evangelists," *The Village Voice* (3 September 1985), pp. 37-38. On Pat's opulent life-style and utilization of his ministry for increasing his wealth, see David H. Van Biema, "Heaven Only knows; TV Evangelist and Self-styled Prophet Pat Robertson Awaits the Divine Go-ahead for His Run at the Presidency," *People* [Weekly Magazine] (11 August 1986), pp. 27-31.

49. Jim Bakker, "Servant 'Of Lord' Lives Lush Life," *Buffalo Courier-Express* (2 June 1980), pp. 1, 4. By 1986, Robertson was paying out more than $20 million to appear on broadcast outlets in 185 cities. The studio generates an annual $233 million income. While boasting on the airwaves that a widow donated her entire $7,000 savings to him and his "ministry," he acknowledged that her contribution could make him "the biggest fool and idiot and con man in the world. . . ." Cf. Power, Glory — And Politics: Right-wing Preachers Dominate the Dial," *Time* (17 February 1986), pp. 62-69, with especial attention to pp. 62, 65, 67.

50. Straub, *Salvation for Sale*, p. 124.

51. Acts 10:34:᾽Ανοίξας δὲ Πέτρος τὸ στόμα εἶπεν,᾽Επ᾽ ἀληθείας καταλαμβάνομαι ὅτι οὐκ ἔστιν προσωπολήπτης ὁ θεός. The early Christian community held that all individuals were of equal character and worth, and rejected the concept of an immediate clergy. Thus most of the meetings of the catacumens was based around a sharing of the day's events. It was only after A.D. 67 that a clergy was elected by local congregations to meet the needs of conducting memorial services for the dead Nazarene. These services were based upon Jesus' instructions "do this in memory of me" (Luke 22:19: καὶ λαβὼν ἄρτον εὐχαριστήσας ἔκλασεν καὶ ἔδωκεν αὐτοῖς λέγων, Τοῦτό ἐστιν τὸ σῶμά μου τὸ ὑπὲρ ὑμῶν διδόμενον· τοῦτο ποιεῖτε εἰς τὴν ἐμὴν ἀνάμνησιν.). Note, this is not the account in Matthew, which ignores the "last supper" being

a memorial (Matthew 26:29-30: λέγω δὲ ὑμῖν, οὐ μὴ πίω ἀπ' ἄρτι ἐκ τούτου τοῦ γενήματος τῆς ἀμπέλου ἕως τῆς ἡμέρας ἐκείνης ὅταν αὐτὸ πίνω μεθ' ὑμῶν καινὸν ἐν τῇ βασιλείᾳ τοῦ πατρόςμου.), as does Mark (Mark 14:25-28: ἀμὴν λέγω υμῖω ὅτι οὐκέτι οθ μὴ πίω ἐκ τοθ γενήματος τῆς ἀμπέλου ἕως τῆς ημέρας ἐκείνης ὅταν αθτὸ πίνω καινὸν ἐν τῇ βασιλείᾳ τοῦ θεοῦ. Καὶ υμνήσαντες ἐξῆλθον εἰς τὅ Ορος τῶν Ελαιῶν. Καὶ λέγει αθτοῖσ ὁ' Ινσοθς ὅτι Πάωτες σκανδαλισθήσεσθε, ὅτι γέγραπται, **Πατάξω τὸν ποιμένα, καὶ τὰ πρόβατα διασκορπισθήσονται**. ἀλλὰ μετὰ τὸ ἐγερθῆωαί με προάξω υμᾶσ εις τὴνΓαλιλαίαν.). In light of the Bible, the "memorial" is contingent on a single gospel, and that gospel is not universally considered to be authentic.

52. Matthew 7:1: Μὴ κρίωετε, ἵνα μὴ κπιθῆτε., cf. Luke 6:37; Καὶ μὴ κπίνετε, καὶ οθ μὴ κπιθῆτε. καὶ μὴ καταδικάζετε, καὶ οθ μὴ καταδικασθῆτε. ἀπολύετε, καὶ ἀπολυθήσεσθε.,, 12:57, which is an admonition against surreptitious judging of others on any grounds. The key word, in Greek, is *Krino*: κπίνω

53. Matthew 7:1: Μὴ κρίωετε, ἵνα μὴ κπιθῆτε.

54. Robertson, *Shout It from the Housetops*, p. 29.

55. Καὶ ὅταν ὕνοιξεν τὴω σφπαγῖδα τὴν εβδόμαν, ἐένετο σιγν̀ ἐω τῶ οὐραωῶ ως ημιώριοω..

56. Straub, *Salvation for Sale*, pp. 128-29.

57. Cp. James G. Frazer, *The Golden Bough: The Roots of Religion and Folklore* (New York: Avenel Books, 1981; reprint of 1980 edition published by Macmillan of London). Morton Smith, *Jesus the Magician* (San Francisc: Harper & Row, 1978). Much of Robertson's claims for his god can be traced to *Papyri graecae magicae*, 2d ed., ed. K. Preisendanz and A. Heinrichs (Stuttgart, 1973-1974), although it is uncertain if Robertson reads, much less alone understands, Greek; cf. ibid., IV:3205f, for faith healing, VIII:75ff for contemporary prophetship, and XII:134ff for casting out demons.

58. Genesis 17-25, especially 22:4-11 for Abraham; Exodus 3:2-4 for burning bushes; Job 38:1, and 40:6, Jeremiah 30:23 on whirling wind gods that speak and have other human attributes. Monotheism was not

an attribute of early Judaism, nor was it a part of the period of Jesus, nor did Jesus accept a monotheistic god. Genesis specifically and distinctly uses the plural "*elohim*" in declaring that the world was created by *gods* (Genesis 1:1-11, 14, 16, 17, 20, 21, 24, 26, 27 etc.), with "*el*" less frequently used as a singular object of worship. Even Ruth acknowledged the existence of numerous gods "your people and your gods are my gods" (Ruth 1:16). Jesus' expiration on the cross called on the gods in questioning why he was forsaken (Matthew 27:46). Later theological apologists transmogrified "*elohim*" and "*eli*" into "*theos*" to give the primary paganism of biblical passages a homogenous harmony by harping on monotheism. This "one-god" defense cannot bear close scrutiny or investigation, for even Isaiah addressed god as a rock (*tsur*; in Isaiah 44:8), while the early apostles considered the existence of several demonic gods ("*daimonion*" δαιμόνιου in the Greek; see Acts 17:18) to be a part of earthly reality as well as a point of faith. In all cases this "god" had "eyes" (Deuteronomy 11:12), is the "god of gods" (Deuteronomy 10:17) who enjoys camping out in the mountains (Exodus 24:13f), walks (Numbers 23:4), fights (Joshua 10:42), sends in "evil spirits" (Judges 9:23, I Samuel 10:18), and leaps over walls with mortal men (II Samuel 22:30), when not busy having sons (Job 1:6), who takes numerous brides (Isaiah 62:5).

59. Robertson, *Shout It From the Housetops*, ibid.

60. Robertson, *Shout It from the Housetops*, pp. 33, cf. 40.

61. 1 Corinthians 7:32 θέλω δὲ θμᾶς ἀμερίμνοθς εῖναι. ο ἀγαμος μεριμνᾷ τὰ τοῦ κθπίου, πῶς ἀπέση τῷ κθία. As is customary in Robertson's elastic exegesis, the line is taken out of context. The full text is an admonition to respect differences in life. In the line above, which reads καὶ οιχρώμενοι τν κόσμον ως μὴ καταχπέμενοι. παράγει γὰπ τὸ σχῆμα τοῦ κόσμου τούτοθ., the comment is that the "unmarried [man] cares [more] for the things that belong to the Lord" since he is not encumbered with the obligations to make certain that his wife and family are cared for (v. 32) — a direct contradiction to Robertson's interpretation. This contradiction is carried out even further in subsequent verses, such as the 34th: καὶ μεμέρισται. καὶ ἡ υθωὺ ἡ ἀγαμος καὶ ἡ παρθένος μεριμνᾷ τ τοῦ κυπίου, ἵνα ἦ ἀγία καὶ τῷ σώματι καὶ τῷ πνεθματι. ἡ δὲ γαμήσασα μερμνᾷ τὰ τοθ κόσμοθ, πζς αἰρέση τῷ αἰνδρί., which differentiates between the single (virgin) woman and the married woman; the *married* woman's obligation is to "please her

husband." Although the rank chauvinism of Saul of Tarsus (St. Paul) is apparent, the entire text urges unmarried men to work for the Lord; there is no comment against marriage, and in fact, in verse 39: Γυνὴ δέδεται ἐφ ὃσον χπόνον ζῖ ὁ ἀνὴπ αθτῆς. ἐὰν δὲ κοιμηθΖ ο) ἀνήρ, ἐλεθθέρα εἰστὶν ᾧ θέλει γαμηθῆναι, μόνον ἐν κυπίῳ., the writer of this letter to the congregation at Corinth declares emphatically that a widow is at liberty to marry a second time. There is no insistence of spouse abandonment or the taking of a vow of celibacy. Chastity is an elective matter that is to be privately determined by the individual, as read in verse 37: ὃς δὲ ἕστηκεν ἐν τῇ καρδίᾳ αθῖτοθ ἑδραῖος μὴ ἒ χων ἀνάυκην, ἐξοθσίαν δὲ ἒχει περὶ τοῦ ἰίου θελήματος καὶ τοῦτο κέκρικεν ἐν τῇ ἰδίᾳ καρδίᾳ, τηρεῖν τὴν ἑαυτου παρθένον, καλῶς ποιύσει.

62. Augustine of Hippo [Saint, 354-430, church father], *Confessions* 8:7; he left one mistress for another that was "less creditable" but certainly better sexually (see: Augustine of Hippo, *Confessions*, 6:150). Like previous, and later, Christian apologists, Augustine would attempt to show Christianity as antedating Jesus, as when he declared that he found the Christian god while reading *Hortensius* written by the pagan Cicero of Rome; see: Augustine of Hippo *Confessions*, 3:4. His final acceptance of Christianity, pushed on him by his mother Monica and friend Alypius, came when he heard the preaching of Ambrose of Milan, but then the conversion was not complete, for it came as a result of Augustine's quest for a single authority; see, Augustin of Hippo, *Adversus Manicheus*, 5 — quite in keeping with the psychology of those who flock to the staff held by Robertson.

While Robertson "wrestled" with temptations, Augustine accepted their inevitability. See: Augustine of Hippo, *Confessions*, 8:8. The two men have similar paths, however, for both wallowed in self-condemnation and self-pity, ultimately took up their Bibles, and allowed random selection ("fate") to determine their destinies — quite in keeping with the superstition of stirring entrails, watching the flight of sacred geese, and offering burnt sacrifices to see which way the wind would blow, common with Augustine, but not in keeping with twentieth-century realism. See: Augustine of Hippo, *Confessions*, 8:12, where he states he chanced across the passage in Romans [13:13-41], which "told" him to give up the "sins" of the flesh: wine, good foods, etc. Pat, unlike Augustine, has not made public his attitude on this line in his Bible, and his life-style does not deny it.

63. Robertson, *Shout It from the Housetops*, 33.

64. Robertson, *Shout It from the Housetops*, 34-35.

65. Pat Robertson, *The Secret Kingdom; A Promise of Hope and Freedom in a World of Turmoil*, with Bob Slosser (Nashville, TN; Thomas Nelson, 1982), 103-20.

66. See: Robertson, *The Secret Kingdom*, 119.

67. See: Robertson, *The Secret Kingdom*, 182-85, 187-90, 191-95.

68. He received a Masters of Divinity degree from New York Theological Seminary. Later, Pat was awarded an honorary doctor of divinity degree from Tulsa, Oklahoma-based Oral Roberts University without benefit of course or seminar work.

69. Robertson, *Shout It from the Housetops*, 36-37. Robertson would go on to study "Bible" at Biblical Seminary in downtown Manhattan, New York. His education was an inductive course. He had decided against training at the accredited Gordon Divinity School outside of Boston. Robertson, historically, cites the King James 1611 version of the Protestant Bible. In part, the King James Version (KJV) was a response (the only response) to the Puritan's "Millenary Petition" presented to King James in April 1603 while he was on his way to London. The conservative Puritans, who were strict biblical literalists and fundamentalists, did not approve nor did they endorse this Bible which they considered to be too "high church." There exists numerous errors in the translation of the KJV, and it does take a decidedly monarchistic overtone towards subject development.

70. Robertson, *Shout It from the Housetops*, 39.

71. Robertson, *Shout It from the Housetops*, 44ff.

72. Robertson, *Shout It from the Housetops*, 48.

73. Robertson, *Shout It from the Housetops*, 51.

74. Robertson, *Shout It from the Housetops*, 57.

75. Robertson, *Shout It from the Housetops*, 32.

76. Robertson, *Shout It from the Housetops*, 58.

77. Robertson, *Shout It from the Housetops*, 62-63.

78. Acts 2:3-11:καὶ ὠφφθησαν αὐτοῖς διαμεριζόμεναι γλῶσσαι «σει πυρὸω καὶ ἐκαωισεν ἐφ ε.να εκαστον αυτώ, καὶ εῖπλησωησαν πάντες πηεύματος ἁγίου καί η.ρξαντο λαλειν ἑτέπαις γλώσσαις καθὼς τὸ πνευμα ἐδιδου ἁποφθεγγεσθαι αὐτοις. Ησαν δὲ εἰς″Ιερουσαλὴμ κατοικουητεζ″Ιουδαιοι, ἂνδπες ευλαβεις ἀπὸ παντὸς ἔθνους των ὑπὸ τὸν οὐρανὸν. γεομὲνης δὲ της φωνης ταὐτης συηλθεν τὸ πληθος καὶ συνεχὺθη, ὃτι ἦκουον εις ἒκαστος τη ἰδια διαλὲκτω λαλουντων αυτων. εξισταντο δὲ καὶ ἑθαυμαζον λὲγοντες, Οὐχ ἰδοὺ ἆπαντες ουτοὶ εἰσιν οἱ λαλουντες Γαλιλαιοι· καὶ πως ὺμεις ἁκουομεν ἒκαστος τη ἰδια διαλεκτω ἡμὼν εν ἦ ἑγεννηηθημεν· Πάπθοι καὶ Μηδοι καί΄Ελαμιται καὶ οἱ κατοικουντες τὴν Μεσοποταμίαν, Ιουδάιαν τε καὶ Καππαδοκιιαν, Πόντον καὶ τὴν΄Ασὶαν, Φπυγίαν τε καὶ Παμφυλίαν, Αἰγμπτον καὶ τὰ μέπη της Λιβύς της κατὰ Κυπηνην, καὶ οἱ ἐπιδημουντεσ΄Πωμαιοι, ᾿Ιουδαιοί τε καὶ προσήλυτοι, Κρητεςς καὶ″Αραβες, α:κούομεν λαλουντων αυτωνν ταις ημέτραις γλωσσαις τὰ μεγαλεια του θεου.

79. Dan Martin, "Patterson Brands Charges 'Fascism,' Asks for Debate," *Baptist Standard* 96.36 (5 September 1984): 3, 20.

80. Paige Patterson is determined to weed dissent out of Southern Baptist seminaries, stifle freedom of speech, and squash any form of academic liberty. See Dan Martin, "Pressler, Patterson Are 'Encouraged'," *Baptist Standard* 99.4 (28 January 1987): 5. Cp. Toby Druin, "Carter Nomination at Seminary Withdrawn," *Baptist Standard* 99.14 (8 April 1987) 5: a discussion on the nomination of an "unacceptable" who ordained women as deacons and ministers, and whose theology was questioned as not being in line with strict evangelical fundamentalism in spite of his credentials. Cp. "Leavell: Trying to 'Aim' Seminary Graduates," *Baptist Standard* 99.12 (25 March 1987): 9.

81. " 'Holy War' Is Declared on SBC 'Hijackers,' " *Baptist Standard* 96.36 (5 September 1984) 3, 8.

82. Robertson, *Shout It from the Housetops*, 95.

83. Robertson, *Shout It from the Housetops*, 64.

84. Robertson, *Shout It from the Housetops*, 65f.

85. Robertson, *Shout It from the Housetops*, p. 71.

86. Robertson, *Shout It from the Housetops*, 73.

87. Robertson, *Shout It from the Housetops*, 77, 75, 33, 61, 126-27, 145, 182, 228, 255.

88. Robertson, *Shout It from the Housetops*, 77-78.

89. Robertson, *Shout It from the Housetops*, 49-50.

90. Robertson, *Shout It from the Housetops*, 53.

91. Robertson, *Shout It from the Housetops*, 81, 97-98.

92. Robertson, *Shout It from the Housetops*, 98

93. Cf. p. 100, 170-71,

94. Cp. p. 105, 148-149f, 153, 164.

95. Cf. p. 165,

96. (pp. 165-166)J. Cf. Fialka and Hume, "Pulpit and Politics," 1, 23.

97. Michael Barone, "Pat Robertson's 'Noble Cause'," *The Washington Post* (3 June 1986), A19.

98. Cf. The Annamite belief in demons inhaling the breath and soul of man, as presented by Landes, "Contes et le'gendes annamites," No. 76 in *Cochinchine Francaise, Excursions et Reconnaissances*, No. 23, p. 80. On the abduction of the soul, see: Perelaer, *Ethnographische schrijving der Dajaks*, 26 sq., which is either taken by a hostile demon or a friendly angel, or supplicants are to petition with the prayer for the soul's release from invading demons. See: Van Schmidt, "Aanteekeningen, nopens de zeden gewooten en gebruiken, benevens de vooroordeelen en bijgelovigeden der bevolking van de eilanden Saparoea, Haroekoe, Noessa Laut, en van een gedeelte van de

zuidkust van Ceram," in *Tijdschrift voor Neerland's Indie*, 1843, dl. ii, 511 *sq.*, for the former, and for the later: Fr. Valentyn, *Oud en nieuw Oost-Indien*, iii, 13 *sq.* All of these works cite and discuss non-Christian phenomena which has been incorporated into the Christian *corpus.*

99. Robertson, *Shout It from the Housetops*, p. 85ff.

100. See E. Krause, "Aberglaubische Kuern und sonstiger Aberglaube in Berlin," *Zeitschrift für Ethnoloqie* 15 (1883), 93. Cp. R. van Eck, "Schetsen van het eiland Bali," In *Tijdschrift voor Nederlandsch Indie*, N.S. 8 (1879), 125., and Grohmann's *Aberqlauben und Gebräuche aus Bölmen und Mähren* 405.

101. Cf. Pat Robertson, *Answers to 200 of Life's Most Probing Questions* (New York: Bantam Books, 1984), 120-21.

102. Robertson, *Shout It from the Housetops*, 85-86ff.

103. Robertson, *Shout It from the Housetops*, 87.

104. Robertson, *Shout It from the Housetops*, 88.

105. Cf. L'Abbé Lecanu, *Histoire de Satan, sa chute, son culte, ses manifestations, ses ouvres, etc.* (Paris, 1861). M. Hagen, *Teufel im Lichte der Glaubenensquellen* (Berlin, 1899). Devil and demon are used interchangeably in Christian commentary. The antecedents to the devil and demons are pre-Christian and pre-Judaic; both are universal in nature and theology, but adapted to Christianity to give a special tool to control the faithful out of fear that was crystallized into a hell that did not exist in Judaic records or primitive Christian accounts. The Hebrews had a *Shoel* (translated as "place for the dead"), with the concept of resurrection not occuring until late (cf. Psalm 16:10) in Jewish lore. While the contemporary vision of hell holds it to be a place of fire, the writers of the gospel saw it as "outer darkness" (Matthew 25:30: καὶ τὸν ἀχρειον δουλον ἐκβὰλετε εἰς τό σκότος τό ἐξώτερον. εκει ἔσται ο κλαυθμὸς καὶ ο βρυγμὸς τςν ὀδὸτων, cf. 13:42: καὶ βαλουσιν αὐτοὺς εις τήν κὰμινον του πυρός εκει ἔσται ὁ κλαυθμὸς καὶ ὁ ο βρυμὸς των ὀδόωτων). The "unquenchable fire" stated in Mark 9:43 is a reference to the destruction of that which already is useless: the corpse (cf. Isaiah 66:24: *Gehanna*). This same destruction is the context found in 2 Thessalonians 1:9 (ὀιτινες δίκην

τίσουσιν ὄλεθρον αἰώνιον ἀπὸ προσώπου του κυρίου καὶ ἀπὸ τῆς δόξης τῆς ἰσχύος αὐτου), and Philemon 3:19. Later exegeses have argued that hell is a permanent place where god can destroy both the body and the soul (life-spirit), but this is not in keeping with the earliest records.

106. Robertson, *Shout It from the Housetops*, 88f.

107. Cf. p. 92.

108. Robertson, *Shout It from the Housetops*, 94.

109. Robertson, *Shout It from the Housetops*, 102-3f, 106-7.

110. cf. p. 140.

111. cf. pp. 142ff.

112. Robertson, *Shout It from the Housetops*, 110f, 141, 173.

113. Robertson, *Shout It from the Housetops*, 112ff.

114. Robertson, *Shout It from the Housetops*, pp. 115ff. Cf. Albrecht of Hohenzollern, *Instructio Summaria* in *Dokumente zum Ablasstreit von 1517*, ed. Walther Köhler (Tübingen, 1934), 104-16, discussed in my *Unzipped: the Popes Bare All: A Frank Study of Sex and Corruption in the Vatican* (Austin: American Atheist Press, 1987), 53ff.

115. Robertson, *Shout It from the Housetops*, p. 116f.

116. Robertson, *Shout It from the Housetops*, 119-21, 125. Sam Twohig of RCA in New York had a difficult time appreciating the business practices of god, although he, according to Robertson, acknowledged that Pat was "acting for the Lord" (p. 125-26); cf. pp. 128, 130, 133.

117. Robertson, *Shout It from the Housetops*, p. 177.

118. Failka and Hume, "Pulpit and Politics," p. 23.

Chapter 2
Going after The Presidency

It takes money to run a campaign. Even when god called on Pat to run for the presidency of the United States, human coffers had to be filled, since it was beyond his god to personally fund the cost of Pat's race.

To gain the necessary finances to pay for his political try, Robertson gave a series of speeches nationwide, urging American voters to cast out the devil — liberals and Democrats — and restore "traditional values" of intolerance and censorship to the nation. To finance this, Robertson issued a plea, printed on cards and fliers in red, white, and blue. The patriotism of the requests encouraged many to contribute to Pat's political posturings. Those who were uncertain how to word their dedication and contribution to the political arm of the televangelist had it spelled out for them. All they needed to do was to sign the pledge card, and give money — "until it hurts."

Donors were not to concern themselves with their own welfare. It was far more important to Pat for donors to consider *his* needs and *his* campaign costs.

Throughout fundamentalist cults in Michigan, donors were given special "Pat Robertson for President" cards. The cards instructed the donors to declare: "Yes, Pat! I will try to become a delegate in my precinct. Yes, Pat! Have someone contact me from the Freedom Council. I want to volunteer. Yes, Pat! I want to help pay for Operation Michigan."[1]

Overnight, Michigan politics degenerated into cult politics.[2] Vile hatred was flung like cow chips by Christian fundamentalists and other religious right radicals at incumbents who did not endorse strict biblical justice and advocate an end to civil liberties.[3]

In an act of Christian celebration, they gave most heavily to Robertson's campaign chest. From this treasury the televangelist vowed to pay the freight of Christianizing America.[4]

As if he were a reincarnated fifteenth-century Johann Tetzel, Robertson pledged that each gift of money would bring the contributor a special blessing. This blessing would come with a pentecostal descent of a "holy spirit" and the ability to speak in undecipherable tongues. Those who contributed heavily to the televangelist's war chest could also anticipate an increase in their personal economic gain — possibly even to the extent that the giver would receive as much a bounty as Robertson, who has used congregational contributions to buy a twenty-four-seat jet as his campaign vehicle.[5]

Pat's promise was an initial embarrassment to some. The more he spoke of it, the less support he realized. When he pushed his pentecostalism, he did not find an initial hospitable reception. Many fundamentalists joined ranks with their enemy, the feared and hated "liberals," for neither group would accept all of Pat's charismatic interpretations and practices.

Robertson faulted the conservatives for not adhering to a strict biblical literalism. He chided the liberals, who wished to disassociate themselves from his ministry, for lack of faith, implying that liberals were neither Christians nor capable of understanding salvation. One political analyst points out that the conservative views the liberal as an instinctively "evil" man and believes that all men need to be restrained. The classic liberal sees man as essentially good, and with unlimited capabilities, which if allowed to be realized, can increase the quality of life and the celebration of thought and effort. The conservative is narcissistic, selfish, and wanting to maintain the *status quo* so that he or she can ultimately reign, and command; the liberal, however, is more oriented to humanitarian concerns, has a world view, and sees order coming from the equalization of factors and people without regard to race, creed, sex, sexual preference, national origin, or other external criteria.[6]

Robertson denounced exegeses.[7] Although his rantings continue partly to be laced with many exegetical fulminations and misreadings, he rants with such sincerity that those he fleeces flock to his staff.

Followers of Robertson believe blindly. His form of Christianity is paramount. To maintain Robertson-type Christianity, the followers of his new faith, his cult members, send him money to sustain a special membership association for spiritually select souls: the "700 Club." The club's purpose is to buy up UHF stations — especially in major metropolitan centers so that Robertson's financial empire can spread like a cancer through the community, devouring all disbelief and unbelief.[8]

Robertson's financial empire is enormous. It consists of three television stations and one radio station and the Christian Broadcasting Network (CBN). This cable network is the fifth-largest in the United States. The empire itself sits on 685 acres of prime real estate in Virginia Beach. It includes CBN University, a graduate school with about 750 students; a television station which has state-of-the-art production facilities; a $13 million library; a huge chancellor's residence occupied by Robertson and his wife that is worth over one-half million dollars; a $4 million student housing complex; and an $18 million hotel and conference center. Beyond this there is the CBN headquarters building, which is a towering Georgian mansion with tiled marble floors, polished woodwork and exquisite early American antiques — not a bad advance for a man who claims that he began his empire on three dollars that Jesus lent him.[9]

Robertson had little difficulty in becoming one of the top ten television charismatics.[10] Winning the allegiance and financial support of millions of Americans who hunger for an absolute authority, a definite director in their lives, the desperate found it easier to follow the judgment and pontifications of one man rather than to rely on their own wisdom and strength. The abdication of self-identification and self-determination among those who joined early resulted in the "700 Club" — a continued indication of a growing mental malaise causing insecurity and desperation to grow in American minds.[11]

Grasping at empty promises of false security, "700 Club" members flooded and continue to flood Robertson's treasury with their coins and bills. In 1985, Robertson had an estimated annual budget of $233,000,000. This sum was raised from approximately 16,250,000 households, making Robertson "No. 1" with the religious television audience.

As a true actor, Robertson blends his Ivy League polish with Southern gentility — while reaching ever-deeper into countless pockets to pay his bills. He has mastered the tube and his ever-present, intimate daily appearances in his club member's homes have bonded them to him.

The news media has had a field day reporting how the money gathered in by the televangelists in the United States is spent. The bills that are paid are not for debts incurred for spreading the gospel. Less than one percent of the monies received is spent in that exercise. Approximately 57 percent of the money taken in from appeals is spent on private evangelistic educational institutions — in Robertson's case, on CBN University.[12] A sizeable budget is given to CBNU's film department, which is styled the School of Communication. Its purpose is to train Christian cameramen and other technicians to "combine spiritual principles of communication with the best insights, practices, theory and research in all pertinent areas of communication," so that video and audio works can be censored and/or adapted to spreading the Christian message.

Robertson's Christian Broadcasting Network has spawned a $40 million facility on the southern fringe of his Tidewater empire. Average tuition to the School of Broadcasting is $3,200 per quarter and the courses are centered on "biblical studies." Twenty-four percent is spent on buying additional television airtime to launch yet additional appeals for cash.[13]

Televangelists' appeals for additional funding are as regular as their utilization of Hollywood stars who claim that they have been "born again" — quick to run for an interview or guest appearance, or as the one-time actor in gothic romances, Pat Boone, declared, should their "agreeability" to take over televangelistic ministries if vacancies or scandals occur. Others, such as the Bakkers (Jim and Tammy Faye), Ben Moore, and Jerry Falwell,[14] make Christianity a commercial commodity that is packaged, pasteurized, and marketed. Video and audio tapes, records, books, key rings, dolls, and other "Christian goods" are for sale. The sale of these religious artifacts enables today's televangelists to live "the good life" of exceptional ease, comfort, and venal decadence.[15] In turn, this "good life" enables the Bakkers, Robertsons, Swaggarts, and other religious scions of the screen to come into the home of Joe Average, who stays tuned to their Bible thumpings, dais demonstrations, and pulpit preachings.

Falwell originally endorsed George Bush for the GOP nomination. As Robertson's star rose, Falwell, with customary lackadaisicality and mercurialism, hesitated. Finally, in a private breakfast meeting in Robertson's palatial home in Virginia Beach, Falwell reached an *entente* critical to Robertson's presidential aspiration. Falwell revealed, after the breakfast, "I told Pat that I'm for Bush by conviction. But I can support Pat if he wins the nomination." Oral Roberts endorsed Robertson for president the third week in September, joining Rex Humbard, Jimmy Swaggart, and two past presidents of the Southern Baptist Convention.

Televangelists are eagerly joined by such office seekers as Jeane Kirkpatrick and Jack Kemp, neither of whom has made a pretense about their own political aspirations and low estimate on human rights. Kirkpatrick shares the views of Robertson closely in regard to Nicaragua and has been an avid war hawk screaming throughout the White House during her advisory term and as U.N. ambassador for the United States.

To entrench the "good life," televangelists such as Robertson have taken to commercial avenues: spawning an entire religiously related industry, sponsoring media expositions, and coordinating "Holy Land Tours." Beauty queens (such as Rhonda Cullison, Miss National Teenager, 1986), bluenose censors, including the insensitive and reactionary Tipper Gore (wife of Senator Albert Gore of Tennessee), and congressional luminaries have sought them out to participate in their ever-expanding media empire — a "spiritual" empire that Robertson hopes to turn, by political advantage, into his own holy land. This holy land is to be an earthly paradise. In it he will walk as the new god, the Reverend President of the United States. He will spy out the nakedness of those around him. He will punish those who have eaten of the forbidden fruit of knowledge from the tree of liberty.

When Robertson's political aspirations crystallized, change came over many of his coterie. They saw his political aspirations as a golden calf before which fundamentalists would bow down. In response to the Robertson horn on which he blasts his spiritual messages, they raced into the Republican party to aid in capturing the GOP nomination for him. Among the politicians who have tied themselves to Robertson is Herbert Ellingwood, a personal longtime friend of Attorney General Edwin Meese III, who worked in the United States Department of State, as director of the Office of Liaison after serving a term as head of the Office of Legal Policy, which screens candidates for federal judgeships. Ellingwood reportedly held prayer meetings in his office during working hours at taxpayer expense. Ellingwood joined the Robertson *putsch* as director of administration.[16] At the same time, other of Robertson's followers labored with little rest until they had amassed, at ground level, as much political clout with Republicans as the AFL-CIO has had with Democrats. Republican officials privately estimated that 15 to 20 percent of the GOP delegates to the 1988 Republican Convention will come out of the Christian movement, gluing together a coalition that could ramrod Robertson into the White House.[17]

New, "born-again" Republicans gathered at such meeting places as

The Jesus People Church in Minneapolis and Temple Baptist Church in St. Paul. Beneath the shadow of the cross on which their god was crucified, they discussed politics mixed with religion over wine and cheese. They chided the Democrats who didn't "have it so good," and sneered that the Democrats were meeting in union halls, drinking beer, and eating pretzels.

So strong has the Christian Right been in Minnesota Republican politics and policy-making that the Minnesota GOP appointed a special liaison, Doug Shaddix, to work specifically with the evangelicals. The Minnesota GOP is especially interested in maintaining a strong alliance with the religious right. To curry the favor and support of the radical right, the Republican party in Minnesota has gone on record supporting the teaching of the Bible's version of creation in public schools and has drafted a "creation-science" plank in its platform, even though only 40 percent of the state GOP convention-delegate slots are filled with Christian fundamentalists.[18] The minority, a sizeable number, would control the majority. The interests, beliefs, aspirations, and consensus of the other 60 percent of GOP adherents in Minnesota didn't matter to the Old Guard, who had formerly guarded and guided Republican maneuverings in the state which once gave many political luminaries to the nation.

Notes

1. Thomas B. Edsall, "Evangelist's Tax Status, Gifts Raising Questions," *Washington Post* (15 June 1986).

2. Thomas B. Edsall, "Pat Robertson and the Power of GOP Activists; He's Scared Bush and Kemp; Will He Scare Voters?" *Washington Post* (1 June 1986), sec. C, p. 4.

3. George Weeks, "Cult Politics Hit State; Blanchard Scoffs while GOP Woos Rightists," *Detroit News* (16 April 1986), sec. A, pp. 3, 9.

4. Jacob V. Lamar, Jr., "Michigan's Holy Confusion," *Time* (9 June 1986):31. On the Jewish concern over Robertson's pledge to Christianize the United States, see J. Michael Parker, "City Jews Consider Robertson Meeting," *San Antonio* [Texas] *Express-News* (13 December 1986), sec. B, p. 2.

5. Sandy Grady, "Preacher Covets the Big Pulpit," *Syracuse* [New

46

York] *Herald-Journal* (22 August 1985), sec. A, p. 4.

6. Cf. J. Alexis Burland, "Conservativism and Liberalism: A Psychoanalytic Examination of Political Belief," *International Journal of Psychoanalytic Psychotherapy* 5 (1976):369-93. Cp. Sigmund Freud, "Aggression in Relation to Emotional Development: Normal and Psychological," in *Psychoanalytic Study of the Child* (New York: International Universities Press, 1949), pp. 3-4: 37-42, also Freud's work "On Narcissism: An Introduction," in *Standard Edition* (London: Hogarth, 1957), vol. 14, pp. 67-102. H. Girvetz, *The Evolution of Liberalism*, 2d ed. (London: Collier-Macmillan, 1963). J. Sandler, "On the Concept of the Superego," *Psychoanalytic Study of the Child* 15 (1960), pp. 128-62.

7. Robertson, *Shout It from the Housetops*, pp. 137-38.

8. Robertson, *Shout It from the Housetops*, pp. 178-79.

9. Doug Hill, "Pat Robertson: A Serious Presidential Contender," *TV Guide* 34.11 (15 March 1986), p. 36.

10. On the growth of charismatics, see Dudley Glendinen, "Pat Robertson Looks to South and Evangelicals as Key to 1988," *New York Times* (24 June 1986), p. 8.

11. Wesley Jackson, "Poll Names Top 10 charismatics," *The* [Baton Rouge, LA] *Times-Picayune/The States-Item* (31 August 1985), sec. C, p. 7. Russell Chandler, "Christian Right Advancing, Scholar Says," *Los Angeles Times* (2 November 1985), pt. 2, p. 7.

12. See: Lewis Beale, "Lights, Camera . . . Amen," *Detroit News* (16 April 1985), sec. 13, pp. 1, 3.
See: Lewis Beale, "The Apostles of Christian Film-Making," *Los Angeles Times Calendar* (7 April 1985), pp. 17, 18.

13. Steven Simpler, "God-given: For TV evangelists, Money Means Power to Preach," *Arizona Republic* (19 October 1985), p. F4.

14. See: *Newsweek* (29 September 1986), "Periscope."

15. Bob Dart, "Nation's TV Evangelists Share Pulpit as Religious

Broadcasters Congregate," *Atlanta* [Georgia] *Constitution* (6 February 1986), sec A, p. 4. Perry Deane Young, *God's Bullies: Power Politics and Religious Tyranny: Native Reflections on Preachers and Politics* (New York: Holt, Rinehart and Winston, 1982), especially pp. 195f. On the unscrupulous policies of Kirkpatrick, see my *Tomorrow's Tyrants: the Radical Right and the Politics of Hate* (Dallas: Monument Press, 1985), index.

16. Liberal GOP United States Senator Lowell Weicker, Jr., of Connecticut, has noted, "You're damn right he [Pat Robertson] could win the nomination," and thus many politicos tied their life-support systems to his political star. See: Malcolm Gladwell, "Evangelicals Cool to Robertson Bid," *Insight* (10 November 1986), p. 22.

17. For a dissenting view, see Frank Jennings, "Does God Vote for President?" *Detroit Free Press* (28 December 1985).

18. Michael D'Antonio, "The Politics of Religion: Evangelicals, Fundamentalists Labor to Reshape America to Their Vision," *The Stockton* [California] *Record* (27 December 1985), sec. A, pp. 10, 11.

Chapter 3
Robertson's Invasion of The GOP

Michigan

By 1986 the lunatic fringe of the radical right "born-again" Christian fundamentalists gained control over several Congressional districts in Michigan. Although evangelical forces, "new conservatives," who have styled themselves "Independent Republicans," understate their purpose to turn Michigan politics into theological testimonies in keeping with Old Testament "justice" and New Testament revelations,[1] they pose a powerful threat to democracy as Michigan residents have experienced.

Robertson told his Michigan evangelical supporters to unite[2] "like a mighty army" and exert their political influence to "bring about moral renewal" in the United States. Robertson's militancy was explained by both Robertson and his supporters as a testimony of "God Almighty . . . saying to us all, 'You have come into the kingdom for a time like this.' "

Not only had Robertson become a new Samuel to preach against sin, but a reincarnated Saul anointed to rule and slaughter those who would not believe as he.[3] Michigan was to be but one of the battlegrounds for the Robertson forces.

Virginia

In Virginia, the Christian right dominates the Republican party in the area surrounding Robertson's CBN empire: Norfolk and Virginia Beach. It remains a minority political power statewide. Virginia is Robertson's home state, as it is the home of Jerry Falwell, another televangelist.

For Virginia politicians not to be subservient to Robertson is viewed as heresy. Money is flooded regularly into evangelical Virginia political coffers not only to change the political spectre in the state but to change the minds of those Virginians who still see Robertson as a significant threat to liberty, personal freedom, and democracy.

Oregon

In Oregon, Christian conservatives battle traditional moderates for control of the GOP. Baptist minister Joe Lutz, although poorly financed, won 43 percent of the vote against incumbent Republican Senator Bob Packwood in the Oregon Republican Senate primary in 1986.[4] Lutz's showing has been an encouragement for others who have vowed to delete from Oregon politics those men and women who do not confess Jesus Christ as their personal savior, who reject a literal interpretation of the Protestant Bible, and who hold out for freedom of choice not only in the area of abortion, but personal life-style, economic determination, and the issue over an individual's right to end his or her own life when suffering an incurable, irreversible, debilitating disease, or being maintained on a life-support system. Total control of the individual by the evangelicals is not only a stated goal, but a plank many have pushed to be included in the state GOP's platform.

Alaska

In Alaska, Falwell's Moral Majority took over statewide GOP politics in 1980. Born-again evangelicals promise to turn Alaska into a Republican theocracy.

Falwell's anticipated Alaskan theocracy is to be ruled by the Christian Bible at the expense of all non-fundamentalists and non-believers.[5] Christian Fundamentalists, like any other group of religious fanatics, from the Shiite Moslems who blindly obey the Ayatollah Khomeini to the fundamentalists of Sri Lanka and India, have historically argued that their bible is "the only absolute, objective, final test for all truth claims and the clearest verbal picture of reality that has ever come into the hands of mankind. By it, and it alone, are all philosophies, books, values, actions, and plans to be measured as to their consistency with reality, visible and invisible, . . . Whatever statements or values are in opposition to the statements and values of the Bible err to the degree of their opposition."[6] The Protestant fundamentalist Bible is to become the constitutional determination of law in Alaska, and crime is to be defined from Old Testament passages, with punishment determined from the same Scriptures. Thus, if a woman should touch the penis of any man, her hand is to be cut off. Those who would work on the Sabbath are to be punished — although not necessarily by being stoned to death. Those who oppose strict Christian fundamentalism and biblical literalism are to have no right to a job, a home, a family, a life.[7]

Pat won all GOP delegates in the Alaska caucus in February, 1988. Many who voted for him vowed his campaign was but the beginning of a new Christian crusade against "the unchurched."

Texas

Texas fundamentalists are as backward-thinking and religiously self-righteous as the evangelicals of Alaska. Texas is also Robertson's target, a fertile ground in which he can easily sow his seeds of hate. From this soil he hopes to reap the singular grain that will give him a homogenized society void of differing opinions, actions, and directions.

Texas is increasingly becoming a Republican state — a state which has the narrow thinking of numerous radical-right politicians. At one end of the spectrum are politicians such as Bill Clements, who laughed at an oil spill his company created which washed across the Gulf of Mexico, ruining numerous sea-dependent businesses as well as tourist trade. Clements gaffawed that he wasn't worried about Texas fishing and shrimping since he procures his seafood from Louisiana. At the other end is Mary Lassiter, who styles herself an authority on United States history while diligently distorting primary documents in favor of Christian misinterpretation and overstatement — an academic abuse loved by the Metropolitan Republican Women's Club of Tarrant County, which sees any form of scholarship that disagrees with its interpretation of what should have been as tantamount to consorting and copulating with Beelzebub in the bowels of hell.[8] Evangelical evaporators of ideas have a heavy hand.

Robertson is supported by most members of the lunatic fringe of the radical right, born-again, and fundamentalist cult systems in Texas. Among his champions are Wallace A. Criswell. An historic segregationist,[9] and pastor of the First Baptist Church, Dallas, Criswell is convinced that the separation of state and church[10] is "the figment of some infidel's [i.e., Thomas Jefferson who based the United States Constitution on Virginia's Religious Freedom Bill] imagination."

Robertson has applauded Criswell. Together they have styled the expression "separation of state and church" to be an "Atheistic Communist" idea.[11]

51

In Houston, Texas, Christian activist Steven Hotzel[12] put up a "Straight Slate" opposed to an ordinance promoting equal rights for gays. Not only was Hotzel supported by Christian fundamentalists, but he was joined by Nazis and the Christian Knights of the Ku Klux Klan, who paraded their hate and bigotry before the vote — a vote which the radical right won.[13]

The Klan and Nazis are fundamentalists, historically.

A similar phenomenon occurred in Bexar County (San Antonio). The religious right organized a massive write-in vote for the positions of precinct chairs. A record 125 write-in votes were cast on 30 April 1986, a critical factor since there were 221 vacancies on the Bexar County Republican Executive Committee.

The Bexar County write-in paid off. During the precinct conventions held directly after the voting had been concluded, a large number of resolutions were passed endorsing Christian involvement in government. A resolution in one precinct convention urged endorsement of Robertson as president.

Some Robertson supporters not only went to the polls with Robertson-sanctioned election slips on who was a good Christian and acceptable to the fundamentalist movement, but also carried pre-printed resolutions that dealt with "Christian" issues. One of the "Christian issues" which was approved during the balloting encouraged elected officials of the GOP to be supportive of Christian ideals "and wrest . . . control of the party from the [Republican] liberals currently in office."

A liberal Republican, by classic definition, does not exist in Texas. The Texas evangelicals are determined to see that such an "abomination" does not occur during their lifetime.

The "liberals" to which the fundamentalists were referring include Texas State Party Chairman George Strake, an outspoken homophobe and anti-Semite. He barely retained his job as the evangelical onslaught washed before him, but by careful Machiavellian maneuvering, Strake won a heatedly contested race. Fearing for his own political aspirations, Strake quickly learned the extent of the Christian vote. His only apparent salvation was to out-Christian the Christians.

One man on whom Strake had counted was GOP boss Knox Duncan, an Anglican clergyman. Duncan zealously supports the new Robertson religious tribunal. A priest quick to damn and judge those around him, Duncan takes comfort in the fundamentalist surge towards autocratic theocracy.[14]

Fundamentalist theocracy is guided by several Texas clergy. Among the most radical and hate-filled Bible preachers is Fort Worth's W. T. Otwell. Otwell not only has prayed for the death of the Texas Attorney General Jim Mattox, who confirmed a court order to have Otwell's Community Baptist Church Boys Home for the "wayward"[15] inspected for fire hazard violations and other sanitation scrutinies, but has staged a mock trial on the steps of a local courthouse. After suitable prayers calling on the near-sleeping god who had somehow missed the destruction of his Fort Worth medieval school, Otwell found Mattox guilty of "the murder of religious freedom in Texas." The "religious freedom" Otwell opted to orchestrate was "freedom" to be a Southern fundamentalist Baptist and to be above the law of the state, to endure no secular holds over parochial education, and to allow unlicensed homes to operate under any condition — provided that they were staffed by good Christian fundamentalists.

Rural Granberry, Texas, Pastor Ray Allen, past president of the Christian Voice,[16] a far-right fundamentalist movement that issues moral "report cards" on members of Congress, chortled, "The Republican Party cannot elect a presidential candidate without the evangelicals." In 1984, the fundamentalist faction fostered hysteria to the point that the evangelicals were victorious in defeating five Democratic congressional representatives. Puffing up like Japa the Hut, Allen bragged, "We are everywhere." His odious message was seconded by the executive director of the Christian Voice Moral Government Fund and chief lobbyist for Christian Voice. This despotic doomsayer gloated that Texas would fall the way of Michigan and other states. Prophetically he declared, "We are going to swamp the caucuses in Iowa."

Iowa

The political posturings of the Robertson camp in Iowa were clandestine for the most part. Robertson's Freedom Council[17] had advised Iowa Robertson supporters to:

> Give the impression that you are there [in the Republican party] to work for the party, not to push an ideology. . . . Try not to let on that a close group of friends are [sic] becoming active in the party together. . . . Hide your strength.[18]

It was done. Dramatically.

Robertson forces took over the GOP apparatus in Des Moines[19] and nearby counties with barely a struggle.[20]

The drive to oust traditional Republicans who had a more universal and charitable perspective was coordinated by Steven Scheffler. Scheffler promised the media that the Robertson *putsch* was just the beginning of a fundamentalist new order that would revolutionize the United States. It is possible to see Scheffler's prediction as reminiscent of the pledge made in a beer hall in Munich in the late 1930s by another devotee of a similar demagogue.

Dudley Rutherford, pastor of the Exciting West Side Church, a fundamentalist cult center, boasted that the Robertson phenomenon is "just the tip of the iceberg." The promise was made: darker days for freedom lay ahead. For those who believe in individual liberty, if the Robertson tidal wave swirls its intellectual refuse upon the shores of American freedom, they are to be swept away.[21]

Like garbage collectors, the evangelicals in Iowa hauled off reason, and without authority promised "an end to abortion, pornography and the U.S. Department of Education." Prayer is to be in schools, and *"homosexuals and lesbians are to be denied housing and employment rights."*[22]

Ian Binnie, a long-time GOP activist, rightfully acknowledged that Robertson was the Republican's Lyndon LaRouche.[23]

The promise of darker days was realized quickly. In May 1986 Robertson's Iowa local Freedom Council Inc. chairman helped engineer a fundamentalist Christian takeover of the Republican party in the 4th Congressional District. Being anything other than a worshiper of Robertson and his brand of Christianity was tantamount to foresaking any aspiration to political office and social acceptability.[24] Established politicians in the GOP trembled as if YHWH was about to turn their hair into burning bushes.

The sleepy little town of Cedar Falls, Iowa, which boasts of being the home of the University of Northern Iowa and such intellectuals as feminist-historian Glenda Riley,[25] erudite aviation historian Donald Whitnah,[26] and scholars of the stature of Donald Howard[27] and John Eiklor,[28] is also the base of reactionary-fundamentalist Leroy D. Corey, chairman of the Mid-America Conservative Political Action Committee. He also sits on the national board of the American Conservative Union and Christian Voice/Moral Government Fund.

Corey makes no pretense of his solitary interest in promoting "Christian morality," "Christian values," and "Christianity." Barely disguised anti-Judaism flows in his speeches, defiling the values held by our founding fathers to sustain, support, and protect differences of opinion and expression.

Corey laments that 15 percent of Iowa does not believe that Jesus rose from the dead. He is determined to change this around through a "conservative Christian agenda." Corey's conservative agenda is to come into being by electing conservative *Christians* to political offices from local to statewide races. When this "special happening" occurs, Jesus will return in glory to rule over city, county, state, and national interests — and Pat will be in the White House.

Like Robertson, Corey pines for a Christianized Supreme Court. To obtain his goal, Corey prizes and seeks political contributions for such nondescript Iowa politicians as Don Sundquist, who equally thrives on anticipating the Christianizing of schools.

Fearing that his true ideas and intents of this Christianizing will be discovered and subsequently exposed, Corey is quick to offer the *caveat* to his coterie that "they should be careful not to sound like they are against public schools."[29]

Corey loathes public education. He is convinced that the public school system is run by secular humanists, Jews, Atheists, and other "nonbelievers." If this form of education is allowed to survive, prevail, and progress, Jesus will be most disheartened. His displeasure will be far more wrathful upon the survivors of his impending holocaust than the fires of Auschwitz, the camps in Siberia, the Trail of Tears of the American Indians, or the blood baths of the Crusades.

It is in the public schools that "Christianization" of the United States is to take place. Christian prayers are to be said. Christian hymns are to be sung. The Christian god is to be worshiped. And with the advent of Christianity into the Iowa public school system, Judaism, Islam, Buddhism, and other faiths as well as Atheism, agnosticism, and human secularism are to be routed. The children "who have been disadvantaged" by not having "met Jesus" are to be "introduced" to Corey's god. Once Corey's Jesus has been forced upon them, the children of Iowa are to be converted to the faith of Robertson. A new meaning is to be given to the biblical injunction: "Suffer the little children to come unto me," for the children will suffer far more as their learning is abridged, their expression curtailed, and their independence limited.

One political tactic that bought votes in the past, Robertson has mastered as if he were a party boss a hundred years ago. Hungry people want food. For food, hungry people will steal. They will also kill or vote — according to the wishes of whoever feeds them.

To influence debt-ridden Iowa farmers, Robertson pledged $100,000 to provide food, clothing, and shelter. His move was disguised as a charitable act. It came under, and from, his Operation Blessing.

Iowa farmers, especially those in Polk[30] and surrounding counties, dutifully repaid their benefactor. Praising the name of Pat and pledging support for his candidacy, these desperate men and women turned unwittingly into yet another tentacle of the evangelical octopus.[31]

Iowa was not unique. The same ploy was practiced in other states. A vote for Robertson meant a full stomach that night.

In a GOP preference poll, taken Saturday, 12 September, 1987, Robertson's tactics of winning over voter allegiance paid off. Robertson scored 33.7 percent of the votes. These votes, representing 1,293 voters, were cast by strict fundamentalists disenchanted with the pluralism in American democracy. Robertson placed first, over George Bush,[32] with Kansas Senator Robert Dole[33] finishing third. It was a repeat of his Michigan coup.

The significance of this straw vote, held in the Iowa State University basketball arena at Ames, Iowa, cannot be ignored. Although in some ways the Iowa straw vote was a "beauty contest," it primarily tested the candidates and their ability to generate a turnout of their backers. As the wire services pointed out, Robertson "appeared to have the loudest and possibly the biggest contingent in the hall," who made themselves known with more fanfare than substance. It was immediately apparent that Robertson could not only pack but control the Iowa caucuses.

George Bush questioned the extent of Robertson's victory, when Marc Nuttle, a Norman, Oklahoma, lawyer who is president of Robertson's Committee for Freedom, said, "It is now clear that Bush has suffered a major setback in Michigan, and that Bush's earlier claims of 54 percent of the Michigan delegates were at best an example of the Bush campaign's inability to count and at worst a deliberate attempt to mislead members of the Republican Party, the citizens of Michigan and the national [news] media." Bush's optimism, however, was not shared with David Bugay, a Bush supporter and delegate from Mt. Clemens, Michigan, who lamented, "Basically, we're about to see the plowing under of the whole [Macomb] party by the [Pat Robertson] Freedom Council. . . . I don't see any effort to build harmony and unity. I see an effort to take over the party." State Republican Representative of Clinton Township, Robert Perakis, a Kemp supporter, accused the evangelicals of "exclusionary politics," by sending newcomers to the state convention and preventing longtime activists from going to the convention: "You can just feel the animosity," he sighed.[32]

Bush had relied on his endorsement and support of Jerry Falwell.

However, when Robertson captured a significant majority of votes in the Michigan primary, Falwell's support wavered. Of course, as one former Falwell aide noted, "He [Falwell] could have backed Attila the Hun. I don't think anyone who has ever worked for Jerry or who works for him now ever knows his real motivation."[33]

This "beauty contest" was not a part of Pat's original plan for running for president as he detailed to the news media, at which time he claimed that his candidacy came at his god's request to "combat a flood tide of social problems" that he claims are "a direct result of moral decay" as seen in excessive government spending and the U.S. trade deficit — both of which have occurred, according to Pat, when women demanded equality with their husbands and would not submit themselves to the stand-in for Jesus of their husbands' autocratic rule over them; when gay people began to be granted civil rights; and when education deemphasized Jesus, and Christianity was not supreme.[34]

Robertson scored heavily in Iowa when he insisted that "little children" should pray in school.[35] In a fervent flurry of rhetoric, Robertson took up the school prayer battle of his god and charged against the infidels who crowded hotly in his mind as the angry theme of "Rocky" played in the background.[36]

Robertson stepped on the stage of the arena as a new savior — a father figure for a nation torn apart. He was greeted by boisterous demonstrations. A new order was at hand, several zealots squealed.

Robertson's devotees cried out loudly for a new order once the Virginia Beach führer raised his hand saluting intolerance and promised the wrath of his god upon the heads of those who would not kneel.

Bordering on hysterics, the freshly scrubbed and image-conscious fundamentalists pledged themselves to tear out the viper of the unbeliever from the bosom of a Christian United States. Some wondered how much longer they would have to wait in their cornfields and factories until they could lay the foundations for punishment of those who disagreed with Robertson.[37]

Robertson does not tolerate those who disagree with him. This became his hallmark at Ames, Iowa. Those who tangled with him felt the wrath of Robertson's supporters who saw him as if he were a god. Following in their master's footsteps, Robertson's faithful promised opponents that they will be crushed by god for disagreeing with Robertson.[38]

Universally, Robertson styled himself a vicar of Christ, the voice of god, and a prophet of the same deity. Iowa fundamentalists ate it up.

Iowa was pledged to return to the age of superstition and fear, a flight back to the days when individual faith had to be publicly expressed.

Surprisingly, Iowa secularists and the Iowa Chapter of American Atheists[39] discounted the full weight Robertson would bring to bear upon Iowa, by flexing fundamentalist muscle. Robertson appeared, at first, to be a "non-event" to such an extent that the *Des Moines Register* failed to cover him. Time and circumstances changed this miscalculation of the Robertson strength. As time elapsed, those who believed that Robertson was but a fluke, learned the strength of the Robertson threat.

The Monday night (1 February 1988) rout of George Bush by Pat Robertson in the Iowa caucuses proves the extent of the Southern Baptist preacher's strength, organization of religious zealots, and determination to win the GOP nomination and the presidency of the United States. He disclaimed his past as a televangelist to Tom Brokaw on NBC network 8 February 1988, and thereby contradicted his own admission of clerical grounding to the National Religious Programmers Convention on 30 January 1988,[40] but it was precisely Robertson's clerical credentials that pushed him ahead of the Vice President.

Although a Gallup Poll the previous week showed Robertson only in fourth place with a possible 9 percent of "likely" caucus-goers, Robertson was able to amass 25 percent of the caucus strength by getting the strict fundamentalists out who traditionally neither voted nor opted to speak to pollsters. Robertson had said all along his "invisible army" would surprise everyone.[41]

Robertson surprised everyone at the end of the Iowa caucuses. His silent army routed the "enemies of god." In Iowa's corn fields and among the machinery of its industries, Iowa evangelicals fought. On 9 February 1988, Robertson pulled out 25 percent of those who traveled by car, bus, and truck to the schools, churches, and cafes where the caucuses were held. They took up his psalms and paraded for a new right wing to take over United States politics.

New Hampshire

Robertson was not seen as a threat to the fundamentalists in New Hampshire, any more than he was in any of the other forty-nine states. Evangelicals see the threat to the United States as coming from "liberals," "Jews," "Atheists," and "non-believers." These terms are used interchangeably, for Robertson's brand of political Christianization is more popular than is the traditional GOP stand and rhetoric.

Paul Young, executive director of the New Hampshire Republican

State Committee, admitted that the donor base of 20,000 claimed by Robertson was more than double the base of the state GOP. The majority of the 20,000 are newcomers. They are first-time political activists.

Kerry Moody, the New Hampshire-based northeast regional coordinator for Robertson's Freedom Council, estimated that the evangelical political newcomers[42] would make up 95 percent of Robertson's strength. Like converts in nearly every situation, they were almost willing to die for the televangelist if they could not secure his election into a power greater than that of his pulpit.[43]

Many of the New Hampshire evangelicals are young. Their education is above high school. They are concerned with jobs, spread advancement, and keeping the United States "safe for democracy." They have prospered under Reagan — at face value, for they don't see the growing deficit, the expansion of foreign trade into American markets, and the rising number of elderly as a plausible or possible threat to themselves and their posterity. Republican Robertson advocates a continued escalation in the birth rate, demands greater autonomy for states at the expense of federal cohesion, and argues for increased military spending, even though the military budget is the greatest this country has known.

Robertson was not as successful in New Hampshire as he had been in Iowa. Because of George Bush's popularity, for being Reagan's vice president than for having any personal backbone or plan to improve conditions in the United States, Robertson took only 9 percent of the popular vote.

Louisiana

A similar phenomenal growth of evangelicals in the political structure in the United States is found in microscopic format in Louisiana. Robertson's Freedom Council Coordinator, University Baptist Church of Shreveport's Pastor Billy McCormack, a man of unusual intolerance and lacking general objectivity, has recruited "Christians" to run for public office "to check the steep slide into total secularization."[44]

Like most contemporary Southern Baptists, McCormack longs for a theocracy in the United States. All human life is to be based on the Bible. From rising in the morning, through the labor of the day, to going to bed at night, every action, word, and thought is to be controlled and determined by the Bible, as if the prophets of perdition were resurrected from dust to dance demonically on the grave of our

Constitution, which has been crucified on a cross of capricious clerical callousness, and self-righteousness. The Ten Commandments are to be returned to the school wall. Sex education programs are to be banned. Christian prayers are to be recited in public schools. History is to be distorted and falsified to agree with the Christian fundamentalist interpretation of the past — an interpretation which includes the argument "that the laws of our forefathers were drafted straight from the [Christian] Bible, that this nation has been declared to be a Christian nation — except by the Supreme Court — and . . . Americans should be God-fearing and hard-working people."[45]

Although Robertson continues to distress traditional mainstream leaders in the GOP,[46] his popularity has soared, especially among the unemployed and those looking for quick, unquestionable answers.[47] Robertson has become the "thinker" for those too tired to think for themselves. Voting for Robertson promised to be easier than thinking for oneself.

Because society has become more open, more spontaneous, free-wheeling, and informal, there are those who are startled by change. They are opposed to change since it forecasts impermanence. They are unwilling to, or psychologically incapable of, making decisions for themselves.

The economic growth under Kennedy and Johnson, followed by the recessions under Nixon, Ford, and Reagan, have been unsettling. The change was too abrupt.

As the United States plunges deeper into debt, a debt that will be passed on from our generation to generations yet unborn, the change is terrifying. Equally startling is the growing fear that another candidate, like Ronald Reagan, who promised to balance the national budget but who increased it every year since his initial inauguration, will win the White House. Not only did Reagan make the national debt the highest it has ever been, but it now exceeds the combined budgets of all previous presidents.[48] While Reagan and his administration condemned the Democrats as "tax and spend," he followed a policy of "borrow and spend," raising the national debt from $6,750 to $16,562, per worker per annum, taking those who labor to a second-class economic station in life not experienced since the Great Depression.

Lyndon Baines Johnson was the last president of the United States to recognize a surplus — of $3.2 billion in 1969. The total deficit during the five years of Richard Milhous Nixon's presidency was $68.7 billion. Gerald Ford's twenty-seven-month presidency saw a deficit of $124.6 billion, with Jimmy Carter's four-year presidency being only $181 billion. Ronald Reagan's deficit is more than one trillion, with his first five-year deficit amounting to $728 billion. At the same time during the Reagan administration, corporate income declined, as seen in tax returns: In 1980, $64.6 billion in corporate income tax was collected; only $37 billion was collected, of which 6.2 percent came in the form of federal budget receipts. Those who felt the greatest pinch were the laborers who were displaced or discharged from employment. The low figures for unemployment in 1987 do not account for the number of people, many now homeless, who have given up looking for a job.

As generations of numerous marginalized and closeted people, from women, Blacks, Mexican-Americans, Orientals, the aged, gays, Atheists, and others, to the propertyless, homeless, unemployed, underemployed, and hungry, have increased, "liberation" theology[49] and new political ideas have challenged traditional theology, charitable works, and the status quo.[50] It appeared to many that it was inevitable that there would be a backlash against the movements towards greater freedom and experimentation. It was known as early as the 1960s that such a backlash would come from the religious community that had previously, albeit belatedly, assisted civil rights demonstrations and peace marches. Robertson found the opportunity and the money necessary to cash in on it.[51]

The unemployed and underemployed seldom vote. Robertson is attempting to change this, as those who vote tend not to trust preachers.

Robertson became the demagogue[52] for those whose lives had become more difficult, whose concepts of a deity had paled, whose prayers went unanswered. Although Robertson has disclaimed demagoguery, declaring that he, as a Protestant minister, is no different in facing a hostile United States than was Roman Catholic John Kennedy when he faced an anti-Roman Catholic, Protestant America, his protestations are transparent.

In spite of Robertson's rhetoric, the situation is not the same — nor are the candidates. John Kennedy openly declared that he would never be subject to the Roman Catholic church, its pope, or any priest or bishop within the Roman Catholic ecclesiastical structure. In 1960, John Fitzgerald Kennedy addressed the Greater Houston Ministerial Association, affirming that:

I believe in an America . . . where no Catholic prelate would tell the president, should he be Catholic, how to act, and no Protestant minister would tell his parishioners how to vote. I believe in a[n] America that is officially neither Catholic, Protestant nor Jewish . . . where no religious body seeks to impose its will directly or indirectly upon the general populace or the public acts of its officials.[53]

Pat Robertson, unlike Kennedy in his aversion[54] to mixing religion and politics,[55] openly confesses that he will tie church to state. Repeatedly Robertson rallies religious rightists to his tent of theopolitical revival with testimony that he will be guided by the views of his church. In the same sour speeches, he spears spiritual heretics.[56]

Robertson has pledged to impose the views of one segment of the Christian community as government policy on all non-Robertson-affirming Christians, all non-Christians — whom Pat calls "termites"[57] — all agnostics, all Atheists whom he lumps together under the title of "Communists"; in short, his brand of Christianity is to become the credo, confession, and catechism for an entire nation.[58]

For any political candidate to argue that his policy is directed by and comes directly from god leaves no room for debate or compromise if all candidates and the electorate affirm the same deity. It becomes stagnatingly simple: Believe or be labeled heretic and perish like the non-believers did in medieval Spain,[59] Calvin's Geneva,[60] at Smithfield in England, in the Vatican cellars (especially in the late nineteenth century),[61] and during internal opposition to World War I in the United States,[62] and the Red Scare that swept the United States in the 1920s,[63] leading to the great Age of Fear under Joe McCarthy and Richard Nixon in the United States of the 1950s.

While the sinister shadow of state church control looms menacingly on the United States horizon, not everyone is afraid of it or even considers it to be a threat. It does not seem real to many Robertson followers, and doesn't seem "plausible or possible" to many other electors, who "merely want a return to morality" and general prosperity. This type of thinking is especially found in Indiana.

Indiana

The demonic demagoguery[64] of Robertson dramatically developed in that state. Robertson's Hoosier followers pledged a "new beginning" and a "new world" for those "true believers" who vowed themselves, their posterity, and prosperity to Pat. The only task that stood between them and economic blessings of Jesus was the incumbency of traditional politicians. These political figures had to be removed. Then Jesus would come again. Once they were removed, those who bowed before the Robertson altar would know the good things in life.

Robertson's adherents turned to their evangelists. Promising to obey blindly their commands, evangelical fundamental Hoosiers begged for direction. "Tell us how to vote," appeared the common cry.

Together the evangelicals poised for revolution. Although Jesus had not take the sword to defend his own life, certainly, it was reasoned, the Nazarene would take up arms to fight for his buddy, Pat — after all Jesus did establish Pat's bank account, told him to enter politics, and promised that the righteous would reign unopposed after a bloody holocaust waged in the name of peace.

A small but united front, Indiana evangelicals scored major upsets against non-fundamentalists. James Butcher, a "born-again" Christian, defeated state Treasurer Julian Ridlen for the Republican nomination in the Fifth Congressional District primary. Ridlen was a veteran Republican loyalist and had been endorsed by thirteen of the fourteen district Republican chairmen in which the race was fought.

Ridlen's defeat loomed menacingly over the traditional GOP structure. Suddenly traditionally moderate party chairmen of the GOP learned how fragile was their own hold over their party members and party action. The fundamental tidal wave was about to erase all past tradition in its drowning wake.[65]

Butcher received support from fellow fundamentalists. The majority of Indiana's fundamentalists had come out — for example, Greg Dixon, an Indianapolis pastor and a former national secretary for the Moral Majority — to blast non-fundamentalists. Together they not only rallied against local "liberals," and "Atheists," but assorted "non-believers."

When Dixon flew to Fort Worth, Texas, to become involved in W. T. Otwell's struggle with the "satan" of the state capitol, Attorney General Jim Mattox, Dixon became like a god to his coreligionists. Distressed by what he saw as the state of Texas' "intrusion" into "church affairs," Dixon not only "sentenced" the Texas attorney general for crimes against the god of Dixon, but placed Mattox at the top of his rather unique prayer "hit list."[66]

Dixon prayed that god remove Maddox by "whatever method, whether it be illness or death."[67] Dixon's reputation glowed the praise layered on him by the evangelicals at home in Indiana. He would return to a hero's welcome that forbode little good for those who did not share his sentiments or hostilities.

Fundamentalists, especially fundamentalist ministers, rushed to take over the GOP in Indiana. The power struggle with the state that Dixon exemplified became their model. Brother Don Lynch, associate pastor of the fundamentalist church Independent Nazarene, for a seat in Congress, willingly sought to give up his canvas cathedral which sits in a grassy field that slopes to the creek where his church holds baptisms. As a soldier of Christ, Lynch prayed that he would be granted an opportunity to wield the swift sword of Christian justice, by representing Indiana's second congressional district.

World War III would be a blessing. The nuclear destruction of the enemies of Christ was enough to make the evangelicals sing. Their choirs voiced the popular praise: "Kill a Commie for Christ," and end the satanic rule of the liberals. Pat was definitely their boy. He would lead them on to victory, as a Christian soldier, carrying a cross of religious intolerance and life-style predetermination.

The machinations and political pronouncements promising a rise of a new Christian crusade concerned those who did not share Lynch's heated views on cleansing the United States of those who were not followers of his Jesus. His coreligionist, Brother Stafford, admitted "We may be fanatics," but testified that only "the devil" could defeat good Christians — such as Brother Lynch.[68]

Either the "devil" was exceptionally active on election day, or the god of Lynch and Stafford had gone on vacation, for the godly were confused, abandoned, and ignored. The evangelical "God's Squad" lost several legislative seats in Indiana — in spite of the Robertson drive. Republican Speaker J. Roberts Dailey of Muncie was defeated. James Butcher of Kokomo fell in the Senate. Lynch was also the victim of defeat, even after spending the $90,000 he raised in his congressional campaign to unseat the enemies of Jesus.

To regroup, the Indiana evangelicals began broadcasting every Saturday night a half-hour show known as "Indiana Salt and Light Co."[69] Indoctrination, propaganda, distortions, and cajolery became the order of the day. News was reported slanted to religious biases; Israel was praised, Palestinian fighters were condemned. The economy was in a disarray because of "godless elements" in Congress, while at the same time Reagan was lauded as being "stalwart" and the "champion of traditional Christian values."

The Indiana Salt and Light Co. discusses political issues from a Christian perspective. It hits hard on those who are either non-Christians or do not uphold a rigid biblical literalism in their political maneuverings, votes, and propositions. The stated goal of this Christian station in Noblesville is to "explain" the "Christian message more clearly," and to silence Jewish and non-Christian opposition to the Robertson agenda.

Georgia

Indiana's religious experiment drew admirers and imitators. Its fame spread like wildfire. Little time lapsed until Georgia evangelicals took up the cudgel of the Robertson camp and began to swing out at religious dissenters around them.

John Birch Society radical Joe Morecraft, the pastor of the Chalcedon Presbyterian Church in Dunwoody, Georgia, was elected the Republican nominee to challenge Seventh Congressional District Representative Buddy Darden. Evangelicals were delighted.

Sparing little effort to distort his opponent's record, Morecraft made every effort to bring about an immediate return of Jesus to the earth. Convinced that he would be another soldier in Joshua's army, Morecraft's campaign launched a prayer petition to the fundamentalists' god to remove the majority of the Supreme Court justices "in any way He sees fit" so that constitutional interpretations by the remaining justices would be more in line with the pastor's thinking.

Morecraft's maneuvers surprised and delighted many fundamentalists. Pat was even more ecstatic.

Robertson counts on the support of Morecraft, who has pledged his "army of god" to fight for Robertson's election, even if it is necessary to travel outside of Georgia.

Colorado

Colorado Republicans have been less hospitable to Robertson. Many are afraid that the religious right will monitor and censor textbooks. They read the numerous accounts of the Gablers' and Mary Lassiter's attack upon classroom text books in Tennessee, Alabama, and Texas. This brand of fundamentalism was unconscionable. Yet this same practice is a goal which Pat has approved.

Pat's endorsement of censorship escalated following the evangelical-sponsored lawsuits against "humanist" literature and core study books in Alabama and Tennessee.[70] How wonderful it would be, Colorado evangelicals whispered, if the same censorship would weed out non-Christian books in Colorado's public schools and libraries.

While many Colorado citizens worry about Robertson's stand in favor of censorship and church interference in public education, other Coloradoans see Robertson's claim that Jesus wants him to be president as a joke. Others see the Robertson candidacy as a sign of mental instability. Many see his quest for the White House as a combination of lunacy and as a means to control the United States and its citizens under an iron glove more crushing than the torturous glove of Inquisitorial Spain.

Colorado Republicans have acknowledged that they are more easily embarrassed by Robertson's revelations that he has been receiving signs from god to run[71] for president than they are angered about Jesse Jackson's relations with Cuban dictator Fidel Castro. They have reason to be afraid, as Congressional Representative Bob Stephenson learned when he lost a Republican primary in 1982. His seat had been considered safe. He served the conservative Colorado Springs district. Yet his defeat was assured when he asked school districts to "submit copies of textbooks to me to analyze for evidence of secular humanism."

Stephenson's censorial quest was intolerable. Coloradoans prefer to keep private matters private and church denominationalism out of the school and the state.

Stephenson was not the only one to lose after he came out in favor of censorship. Former Representative Frank Randall, the only lawmaker who supported Stephenson on this issue, lost a Republican primary the same year in an equally conservative Colorado Springs district.

Colorado Republican national committeewoman Kay Riddle declared that the right would never dominate her party. She intoned that it would be difficult for a religious "kook" to get in.[72]

Pennsylvania

The same is not true in conservative Pennsylvania. It is even less accurate in Philadelphia, the legendary City of Brotherly Love.

Fundamentalists in Philadelphia promise to "change America back" to its "Christian beginnings." Ignoring the realities of history, the evangelicals distort history by proclaiming that "the signers of the Constitution were Christian men who meant to establish a Christian government." Philadelphia evangelicals have vowed, therefore, to remove suffrage from those who do not adhere to the same traditions and principles. Those "who are not Christians have no right to a voice in American politics."

Philadelphia's evangelicals' determination to erase the names of non-fundamentalists from voter registration is in keeping with the covert comments of Robertson, usually found in his less popular works, such as his *Answers to 200 of Life's Most Probing Questions*. The United States is to become a haven for Christians and fundamental Jews. No one else is to be tolerated. The far-right wing of Jewish Orthodoxy has announced an accord with Robertson on matters of male-dominant family ties, anti-abortion, anti-birth control, mandatory prayers in schools, and a pro-Israel position.[73]

Pat's mindset on the presidency has endeared him to many in Pennsylvania, a state traditionally conservative. Some political pundits, such as Marc Nuttle, president of Robertson's Committee for Freedom, are convinced that Pat can win the state. To this end Robertson's Committee for Freedom has established thirty chapters throughout the state and appointed Thomas Bowman, a Potter County supervisor, as director.

Although Pat declared himself a convert to the Republican party and announced that he would run as a Republican candidate for the party's nod, the Pennsylvania Republican party resented that it had heard nothing of Robertson's campaign efforts in the state. Once more Robertson's penchant towards clandestine, covert actions carried him into waters yet uncharted. As is customary, Robertson looks to a coup in Pennsylvania with little support or input from the established politicians.[74] Traditionally, Robertson has had no loyalty or interest in any allegiance to anyone or any organization other than himself and the empire that he controls.

Pat's fairy-tale plans for the United States have been praised by the intellectual trolls who trek beside him. Eager to enlist all able-bodied men and women whose purse strings lay loose, Philadelphia pastor Harold Bredesen introduced Robertson as "a man whom God has anointed," who, like the Old Testament Samuel, is "the only man [who] can lead us in this hour."[75] Repeatedly, as if he were in a hypnotic trance, or was under the spell of a mind-altering drug, Bredesen bleated, "Only God . . . only God . . . Only a man whom God has anointed, only a man who fears God . . . at whatever cost obeys God . . ." Packed into Constitution Hall, Bredesen's gaggle of gospel geese honked back, "Amen!" "Amen!" "Amen!" for more than two hours waiting for Robertson to reveal the latest word from his god that only he was specifically privy to hearing.[76] Robertson took the assembled fundamentalists by storm basking in "wild cheering." He summoned his followers to sign his petition as "registered voters who love America and believe in the traditional moral values upon which our founding fathers established this nation,"[77] which also came with the signing of a "gift form" to contribute by cash, check, Visa, or MasterCard.[78] After all, Robertson's god started Robertson's first ministerial bank account,[79] and in 1988 he wants a return on his investment.

Mississippi

Pat's dreams have not fully crystallized in Mississippi. Only late in 1987 did Robertson realize the urgency of capturing the conservative evangelical vote in that state — a vote which traditionally supported the white-sheeted Christian Knights of the Ku Klux Klan, sang the praises of the John Birch Society, and boasted about "running Jews out of these here parts."

Part of the problem that Robertson knew he would face in Mississippi was the Black voter. Most Black voters wanted a Democratic candidate, Black Baptist preacher Jesse Jackson who was popular in Mississippi. Since both men professed the same denominationalism and spirituality, Robertson had little to gain by lauding his own Southern Baptist roots.

To win Mississippi, Robertson would have to paint the Democrats in general, and Jackson in particular, as being soft on morality. This was easily done by subtle, nearly unveiled racist overtones. "Black parents deserve better education for their children," Robertson officially declared. His call artfully articulated white supremacist's ideas of education for Black children being best if it were separate — but equal. Robertson was able to capitalize on both white and Black desires: white interest in segregation and Black needs for quality education.

Robertson's initial step into the brackish waters of Mississippi politics was not totally successful. Not only Black, but mainline politicians saw through his smiling facade.

The cherubic-faced leader of the Christian Broadcast Network was received hospitably enough, but the hospitality was a veneer. Some GOP leaders in Mississippi openly grumbled that the televangelist was not their choice to head their party, which was only beginning to emerge in the state as a power force to be considered. Their action was in keeping with the local psychology, for local churchmen drew the line on Pat's political pandering and activism. With few exceptions these men of the cloth did not approve of Robertson's *modus operandi*. They saw it as too much a mixture of state and church[80] — in an area where the line of demarcation between things spiritual and things temporal is still finely drawn.

Clay County GOP Chairman Gaines Hawkins blasted Robertson publicly, contending that Robertson's candidacy "is going to bring on a blood bath in the party." Even more was said on what Robertson's effect would be on the nation as a whole — a nation already deeply divided over the demonstrations against and the denunciations of democratic principles of equality and choice by the televangelist.[81]

In the Gulf States, especially in Mississippi and then in Alabama, Robertson gained a determined following of born-again zealots. Once more he played to local fears concerning school curriculum and immorality. Revisiting the state in January 1988, this time he promised to pump massive federal dollars into "creative and uncharted techniques" to make Mississippi a model state for education.[82] Like the wild-eyed Amos of the Old Testament, Robertson reiterated what he saw as the ever-present danger of "secular humanism." He vowed that his administration, if he were elected, would "purify society" and make the United States "a Christian nation again."

Televangelist Robertson was quick to force religion into the circus of Gulf states' politics. With local evangelicals in tow, Pat came across as a twentieth-century savior, twisting the cross into a shield behind which he would stand. The faithful fundamentalists in the Gulf region ate it up — especially those who lived in the five sister cities along the coast.

In Ocean Springs, Mississippi, faithful Robertson cultists huddled in "prayer circles" around their television sets as the televangelist postponed his official bid for the presidency of the United States on 18 September 1986. Many Ocean Springs citizens declared Robertson as the incarnate of god on earth.

Crying out, with a united voice that sounded like the blare of Joshua's trumpet before the walls of Jericho, the loudest and most prolonged applause for the preacher Robertson by the citizens of the Gulf cities came when Robertson raged, "There can be no education without morality and there can be no lasting morality without religion. For the sake of our children, we must bring God back to the classrooms of America."[83] Robertson's words echoed Hitler's "*Gott und Kinder und Vaterland.*" The response was the same.

He enchanted their hearts. He promised to purge all "unChristian elements." Those who did not agree — or who failed to sign the "personal gift form"[83] were trumpeted out of the convention hall.

Fundamentalists in other cities along the Gulf Coast share the same enthusiasm and religious ideology found among evangelicals in Ocean Springs. Virginia Slush of Biloxi, Mississippi, cooed her confidence in the pulpit pounder from Virginia, eager for "this campaign to get rolling."[84]

California

The hypnotism of Robertson's rhetoric spilled beyond the Gulf

Coast. At one point it washed up into San Jose, California.

Caught up in the "hellfire and brimstone" sermonizing of Robertson, senior citizens swooned with delight, anticipating an immediate return of Jesus — unless, as some felt — he had already come back to earth in the form and shape of preacher Pat. Robertson's smooth performance demonstrated his polish as a televangelist host.

Robertson's words electrified the members of this fundamentalist San Jose flock. They appeared eager to be fleeced by a minister who stood for the totalitarian theology that they had trucked miles to hear. They heard their shepherd's song and followed meekly to their intellectual slaughter. Raucous applause and foot-stomping more reminiscent of a hillbilly barn dance than a political soirée were enhanced with fanatical cries of "Amen!" and resounding shouts of "Hallelujah!" by the approximate four hundred men and women who crowded into the downtown exhibit hall.

In a crazed frenzy, the fundamentalists swayed to gospel music with their arms uplifted. Yet they felt neither inspiration, perspiration, or rain. Instead they felt drained "by his [Robertson's] presence" as if he were a deity determined to dip the United States in earth-centered torments of his grey tomorrows.

When it was all over, California Christian fundamentalists who had held court for Robertson's "almost" announcement of his presidential bid left weary. Their hands smarted, reddened by clapping to folk songs. Their throats were parched by shouting patriotic hymns. Their checkbooks and purses were drained "for the Lord's cause."

Like their spiritual brethren in Atlanta, Biloxi, Ocean Springs, Dallas, and elsewhere, San Jose evangelicals exited the hall clutching envelopes that ushers passed out as if they were sacred relics, thin pieces of wood from the True Cross, or tears from the seamless garment of Christ. In these envelopes the faithful could send Robertson additional cash and signatures.[85] Prosperity surrounded the preacher, who promised his faithful that if they gave, they would receive rewards back.[86] Few realize the magnitude of income that Robertson enjoys.

San Jose was but one of the Robertson enclaves. Los Angeles heralded an even bigger contingency of men and women willing to lay down their lives to establish a fundamental government in the United States.

In Los Angeles, the fundamentalist faction is fratricidal in its opposition to those who disagree with Robertson's god. Pastor Robert Hymers of the Fundamentalist Baptist Tabernacle delights in neo-Fascist denunciations of his opponents and those who counter his god.

Launching his own death-prayer campaign against the "Hitler-like" Supreme Court, he gutturalizes his animosities, like the Nazi Klaus Barbie of France.

Lyman, appearing like a Michaelangelo godhead with flowing white hair, paid for an airplane to buzz over Justice William Brennan while the jurist was delivering a commencement address in Los Angeles. From the plane trailed a banner that read, "Pray for Death: Baby-Killer Brennan."

Not content with this irrational and display, Hymers led his congregation in other "Christian" prayers beneath a banner that shouted in raw color: "Pray for the Death of Pro-Death Court." Mercy, forgiveness, charity, and understanding are as foreign to Hymer as is justice, truth, honesty, and the American way of tolerance, acceptance, and accommodation.[87]

Nebraska

A similar fever swept across Nebraska. Robertson activists quickly took over the Republican party in Douglas County, which includes Omaha. They nearly repeated the same *coup* in Lancaster County, which includes Lincoln, violating the interests of those traditionally active in the GOP and pledging to dump the non-believers by the wayside as their lord marched onward to victory against "the Establishment" in Washington, D.C.

Most of Nebraska's population is located in Douglas and Lancaster counties.[88] There, the common sentiment was to "clean up America" and to make the United States "Christian." Non-Christians, seen as "humanists, Atheists, Jews, and perverts," would no longer be welcomed. At times all of these judgments were applied to the same individual.

Anti-Jew, anti-intellectualism, and anti-freedom became the key words, keystone, and heartthrobs of Nebraska's born-again[89] religious fundamentalists who openly worshiped televangelist Robertson. With religious fervor, Nebraska evangelicals pledged themselves, their monies, and their time to spread the Robertson revolution against non-Christians.

The Nebraska evangelical pledge became the vow of fundamentalists from coast to coast: from the City of Brotherly Love to the City of the Angels,[90] from Norfolk, Virginia, and Washington, D.C. — to the great beyond.[91] Like the Old Testament firebrand general, Joshua, Robertson's army had come fully grown into stunted intelligent but shining glory, replete with fundamentalists who willingly split open their heads to receive Pat in.

Florida

At the Florida Republican convention on 13-14 November 1987, a straw vote gave Robertson 37 percent of the delegates although the vote was rigged in Bush's favor since 42 percent of the delegates were chosen by old-line party officials. Robertson's forces saw this travesty and cried foul. Robertson prepared to make hay over the rift and fill his theological barn with new souls to battle for the remaining fight — if not in 1988, then in 1992.

Robertson likes to structure his speeches around a repetitive phrase — what a jazzman might call a "riff." During the speech at the November rally, he used a populist refrain, "The people have been telling me." At a rally held the night before, Robertson's meeting reflected a camp meeting atmosphere. A woman sang, "This Is My Country," "This Land Is Your Land," and "My Country, 'tis of Thee." Robertson summoned up Americanism as a religion, the flag his sacreant, and the patriotic songs his hymns.

His message was moral rather than political. He promised redemption in the form of a "second American Revolution."

Robertson's rhetoric was classic. "You are here because we are going to restore the greatness of American through moral strength."[92]

Those who listened to the televangelist agreed. They would have the "second American Revolution" in order to stem the tide of secular humanism and to suppress all thought that differed from the preacher's.

Hawaii

Robertson's "Invisible Army" marshalled its forces in Hawaii to win a surprising 80 percent of the GOP vote in its preliminary beauty contest. Determined to bring "morality" to the islands, Preacher Pat pounced on what he saw as sin. Those who lusted to control the lives of others choired in unison, and while singing the praises of their newly found savior marched to the fields of "war" and voted out the expected winner while crowning Robertson with laurels of adulation, praise, and electoral strength.[93] As has been the case often, Robertson's Christian coup may have been the result of a growing sense of inadequacy among today's youth and first-time voters who look for an authority figure — an absolute answer — who want to be a part of something bigger than themselves. They see "God [as] the ultimate bigger thing," and thus rush blindly, unquestioningly towards religion and those who pretend a closeness to a god who, allegedly, speaks directly through these pretenders to the rest of humankind.[94] For many, "get involved with God," to means voting for Pat and a possible theocracy like Iran. Many of today's youth long for a state where their morals are dictated and those who do not believe as they do, who do not have a life-style according to their "Koran" — the Christian Bible — will simply be disenfranchised. Thus Sergio Villareal, sixteen, a junior at Lloyd V. Berker High School in Richardson, Texas, wears a small cherrywood crucifix he takes off only when he bathes, and endures such "personal sacrifices" as giving up "cuss words and carbonated drinks."[95] Others carry around Bibles and intimidate those who do not share their life-style.[96]

When Hawaii held their preference vote on 5 February 1988, Robertson walked away with 81 percent of the strawpoll. The "Second American Revolution" had begun.[96]

Notes

1. Phil Gailey, "From Crusade to Campaign in Michigan," *New York Times* (25 May 1986).

2. Portions of the following information are taken from Pat Robertson's newsletters, published under the banner "Americans for Robertson," which has a publication address of P.O. Box 37002, Washington, D.C. 20013. A complete collection, available to scholars, is in the Charles E. Stevens American Atheist Library, in Austin, Texas, which has generously loaned me use of the collection. The American Atheist Library has one of the finest collections of fundamentalist and religious writings, from the works of early Christian saints to the tomes of current Christian apologists and fundamentalists. Contrary to Robertson's *dicta* that "Atheists and unbelievers" only have to "read the [Christian] word of God" to "believe and be saved," their articles, books, diaries, and other writings have not converted any Atheists associated with the library.

3. Steve Maynard, "Television Evangelist Calls Fundamentalists to Rise Up," *Houston* [Texas] *Chronicle* (1 May 1986), p. 4.

4. Phil Gailey, "From Crusade to Campaign in Michigan," *New York Times* (25 May 1986).

5. Thomas B. Edsall, "Onward, GOP Christians, Marching to '88," *Washington Post* (30 June 1985), sec. C, pp. 1, 5.

6. David E. Anderson, "Bible Has Answers to All Issues, New Conservative Group Says," *Flint* [Michigan] *Journal* (4 April 1986), sec. A, p. 6.

7. See my forthcoming *Twisting the Cross: Unholy Rollers in Christian Fundamentalism.*

8. Unlike most Protestant Christian fundamental-evangelicals, Robertson has resurrected and accepts the concept of a *purgatory* which he defines as "an intermediate place, as opposed to the final establishment of a new heaven and a new earth, where little unbaptized babies go"; see Robertson, *Answers to 200 Questions*, pp. 88, 89. As for his hell, Robertson argues that it will "last forever" (his, *Answers,* p. 36), which he sees as a "lake of fire," which is filled with "worms, maggots, fire, and trouble," and from which "there will be no exit from hell, no way out, no second chance" (his, *Answers,* p. 160). He claims that this is the judgment of Jesus, citing Mark 9:43-48; yet in this reference the only "torment" listed is the worm. The actual passage is a part of the Codex Vaticanus and was copied sometime in the fourth century of the current era. The text has no punctuation, division, or capitalization of words or accents, and thus is open to textual criticism. Officially the "Gospel of Mark" has been referred to as "Peter's Memoirs" since Peter probably was its author, and Mark the scribe who wrote down what was dictated at least a generation after the actual occurrences of what is related. As a scribe, Mark was quick to put in Old Testament references to buttress the commentary issued by Peter, and thus *Gehenna* became a part of the story of what awaited those after their death. *Gehenna* is the ancient Israeli/Hebraic legend of a "fiery place" and appeared later in Matt. 10:28, with a quasi-metaphorical mention in Heb. 10:27, with Revelation seeing it as more of a symbolic cutting off from knowledge: Rev. 21:8, 19:20, 20:10.

Robertson uses the test of "hell" to win converts to his political posturings, especially in fulminating against literature of all variations, politics that are socially conscious, and individual ontological speculations. See: Lisa Ellis, "Evangelist Tests Politics in Texas," *Dallas Times-Herald* (4 March 1986), sec. A, pp. 9, 11. For further details on Mary Lassiter's unusual interpretations of United States history, see my *Unholy Rollers,* index; she is a strong supporter of the

Gablers of Texas who have made a full-time profession out of censoring textbooks that disagree with their rigid Christian fundamentalism.

9. Jim Schutze, *The Accommodation: The Politics of Race in an American City* (Secaucus, NJ: Citadel Press, 1986), pp. 91, 98.

10. Cf. *Virginian-Pilot* and *The Ledger-Star* (11 August 1985), sec. A, p. 16. Robert Maddox, the White House liaison for religious affairs during the Carter administration (1972-1976), and executive director for Americans United for Separation of Church and State, headquartered in Maryland, "deplores" Robertson's desire for "state-supported religion" and his "apocalyptic worldview." ibid.

Criswell, like Robertson, is a strict Southern Baptist who believes that Southern Baptists should control the political destinies of all people. Southern Baptist "morality" is to be the "morality" of all people. Freedom of thought, action, and expression are to be prohibited. See: Toby Druin, "Effort Can Stop Gamblers, Says Strickland," *Baptist Standard* 99.11 (18 March 1987): pp. 3, 5: in reference to a proposed Texas State lottery, which is buttressed by Presnall H. Wood, "Anti-Gamblers Organize," ibid., p. 9. Correlated articles and editorials are to be found in other issues, such as: "Compulsive Gamblers Present Sad Picture," *Baptist Standard* 99.7 (18 February 1987): p. 6; Ken Camp, "Battle Expected in Legislature on Lottery," *Baptist Standard* 99.1 (7 January 1987): pp. 3, 5; Ken Camp, "CLC Asks Action Now to Head Off Lottery," *Baptist Standard* 99.6 (11 February 1987): p. 9.

11. *Forum* (Fall 1986): 8. Cp. Bruce Buursma, "Separation of Church and State Erodes," *Chicago Tribune* (7 October 1986), pp. 1, 2.

12. Cf. Jim Simmon, "Christian Right, Other Elements May Clash; Some Fear Evangelist's Bid Would Split Texas GOP," *Houston Post* (14 September 1986), sec. A, p. 24.

13. D'Antonio, "The Politics of Religion," sec. A, p. 10.

14. James McCrory, "Fundamentalists Try GOP Grab," *San Antonio* [Texas] *Express-News* (7 May 1986), sec. E, p. 1.

15. *Forum* (Fall 1986): p. 12.

16. In 1986, the director of Texas' Christian Voice was Tommy

Garrett, who predicted "a lot of potential for tensions to arise at the county level" between newcomers on the Christian Right and the more pragmatic, "traditional" elements in the GOP. *See:* Jim Simmon, "Christian Right, Other Elements May Clash," *Houston Post* (14 September 1986), sec. A, p. 24.

17. Hugh McDiarmid, "Good-by to a Fiction: Freedom Council," *Detroit Free Press* (30 September 1986), sec. B, p. 1.

18. Robert S. Boyd, "Evangelical-for-Robertson Infiltrating Republican Ranks," *Houston Chronicle* (11 May 1986), sec. 1, p. 16.

19. Robert S. Boyd and Angelia Herrin, "Evangelicals-for-Robertson Infiltrating Republican Ranks," *Houston* [Texas] *Chronicle* (11 May 1986), sec. 1, p. 18. Steve Newton of Grace Reformed Presbyterian Church in Des Moines, "Criticizes Liberal View of Evangelicals," *Des Moines* [Iowa] *Register* (10 May 1986), sec. A, p. 21.

20. Elizabeth Flansburg, "Evangelicals Seen Dominating GOP District Convention," *Des Moines* [Iowa] *Register* (2 May 1986), sec. M, pp. 1, 7.

21. Thomas B. Edsall, "Evangelicals Take on GOP Regulars," *Washington Post* (29 May 1986), sec. A, p. 1.

22. Elizabeth Flansburg, "Evangelicals Seen Dominating GOP District Convention," sec. M, p. 7.

23. Elizabeth Flansburg, "Evangelicals Seen Dominating GOP District Convention," loc. cit.

24. Thomas B. Edsall, "High-Stakes Fund-Raiser Benefits Robertson," *Washington Post* (17 May 1986), sec. A, p. 6.

25. Among her many published works is the insightful *Frontierswomen: The Iowa Experience* (Ames, IA: Iowa State University Press, 1981). Her focus is narrow state identification, as seen in her classic, "Is Clio Still Sexist? Women's History in Recent American History Texts," *Teaching History: A Journal of Methods* 1.1 (Spring 1976); and her *Women on the American Frontier* (St. Louis, MO: Forum Press, 1976). She debunks numerous myths concerning women pioneers, as in her

"Images of the Frontierswoman: Iowa as a Case Study," *The Western Historical Journal* 8.2 (April 1977): pp. 189-202; and, her "Women in the West," *Journal of American Culture* 3.2 (Summer 1980): pp. 311-29.

26. Dr. Whitnah's research has culminated in many published works, including *Safer Skyways* (Ames, IA: Iowa State University Press, 1967); *Government Agencies* (New York: Greenwood Press, 1983); and *History of the United States Weather Bureau* (Urbana, IL: University of Illinois Press, 1961).

27. Since his retirement as professor of history at the University of Northern Iowa, Dr. Howard has been regularly contributing articles to the *Des Moines Register* and *Waterloo Courier* in Iowa. Dr. Howard is my premier professor, having taught me the value of diligent research, writing, rewriting, and writing over and over until scholarship had married composition. Dr. Howard is, in my estimation, Iowa's greatest teacher and the best example of a genuine thinker.

28. A Near East specialist and *l'uomo universale* who conducts many of his courses via telecommunications.

29. Leroy D. Corey, "How Christian Right Won and Can Keep GOP Power," *Des Moines* [Iowa] *Register* (1 May 1986), sec. A, p. 15. Having grown up in Cedar Falls, and taking my first degrees from the University of Northern Iowa, I recall well the strict Christian xenophobia that existed in the 1950s and 1960s between Christian denominations, Christian churches within denominations, and their unbridled hatred of Jews, agnostics, Atheists, and other "non-Christians." Professor Joseph Fox, an outstanding *illuminati*, was libeled as an "Atheist" by Lutheran minister G. E. Melchert of Trinity Lutheran Church (Waterloo), and Homer C. Larson damned me for entering his Lutheran church when he learned I had converted to Catholicism. Jew-baiting was common when John F. Kennedy, a Roman Catholic, ran for president in 1960. The issue of religion was constant, and Roman Catholics were badgered, bashed, and branded as Antichrists with Christian fundamentalists in the area of Waterloo-Cedar Falls detailing horror stories of nuns who killed their babies, priests who attacked little boys, and how the pope would rule the United States. When it was no longer kosher to crunch Roman Catholics, intradenominational feuding broke out again, each church

preaching that it had the "soul's sole route to heaven," either from the many pulpits or in the Bible campground that is situated west of Cedar Falls. Corey fits snugly into this molding mode of microscopic mentality.

30. Des Moines, the capital of Iowa, is in Polk County. The "dowager duchess of the Iowa Republican Party" has been Mary Louise Smith, who led an anti-Reagan guerrilla theater at the Republican National Convention in Dallas in 1986. She has made a stand on the evangelicals that has led Ian Binnie, senior vice president of Economy Forum, to unveil his pro-fundamentalist choice which he sees as tearing down the "elitist assumptions" of traditional Iowa Republicans. See: Ian Binnie, "Does Evangelical Might Make Political Right?" *Des Moines* [Iowa] *Register* (2 April 1986), sec. A, p. 11.

31. Associated Press wire, printed in the *Northwest* [New Jersey] *Daily Record* (16 December 1985), sec. B, p. 7.

32. See: Remer Tyson, "Bush, Robertson Claim Precinct Election Win," *Detroit Free Press* (15 August 1986), sec. A, pp. 3, 14. See: Malcolm Gladwell, "Falwell-Bush No Longer a Political Duo," New Jersey *Home News*, sec. A, p. 17.

33. Robert Dole has his own difficulties, especially in line with his tie to the tobacco industry. See: David Corn, "Bob Dole and the Tobacco Connection," *The Nation* 244.12 (28 March 1987): pp. 381, 396-99. On his record concerning freedoms experienced in the United States, see my *Tomorrow's Tyrants: The Radical Right and the Politics of Hate,* index.

34. *Fort Worth* [Texas] *Star-Telegram* (13 September 1987), sec. 1, p. 5.

35. "Republican Activists Split over Impact of Robertson Victory," *Waterloo* [Iowa] *Courier* (14 September 1987), p. 1. This headline article suggested that Robertson was strong, but that the reader of his margin must be cognizant with his emotional tactics.

36. *Cedar Falls* [Iowa] *Record* (14 September 1987), p. 1. *Fort Worth* [Texas] *Star-Telegram* (13 September 1987), loc. cit. Cf. Robert Shogan, "TV Evangelist Offers Bid for Presidency; Robertson to Join

GOP Race if 3 Million 'Pray' [Work and Give]" *Austin* [Texas] *American-Statesman* (18 September 1986), sec. A, p. 14; Dudley Clendinen, "Robertson Sets Conditions for Making a Run in 1988," *New York Times* (18 September 1986), p. 16, which runs the text of Robertson's arguments that "we have taken the Holy Bible from our young, and replaced it with the thoughts of Charles Darwin, Karl Marx, Sigmund Freud and John Dewey"; "Robertson Seeks Backing to Fight 'Moral Decay,' " Virginia Beach, Virginia *Star-Ledger* (18 September 1986), and, "Pat Robertson Vows to Run if Given Support; TV Evangelist Hoping for 3 Million Followers." *Atlanta Constitution* (18 September 1986), sec. A, p. 19.

37. From various wire reports: AP, UPI, Knight-Rider, etc. 12-13 September 1987.

38. Myra MacPherson, "The Pulpit and the Power: '700 Club's' Pat Robertson, Preaching Gospel & Eyeing the White House," *Washington Post* (18 October 1986), sec. D, p. 8.

39. Letter from the director of the Iowa Chapter, in the files of the American Atheist GHQ, Austin, Texas, graciously loaned to this author by Madalyn O'Hair for purposes of research.

40. Jackie Koszczuk, "Robertson Returns to Religious Roots among Ex-Peers," *Fort Worth* [Texas] *Star Telegram* (31 January 1988), sec. 1, p. 21.

41. *Dallas* [Texas] *Times-Herald* (9 February 1988), sec. A, pp. 1, 6.

42. David Yepsen, "Evangelicals in Politics? Why Not? New People Keep the System Fresh," *Des Moines* [Iowa] *Register* (31 March 1986), sec. A, p. 17.

43. Marcus Stern, "Robertson Run Could Split Christian Right," *San Diego* [California] *Union* (21 July 1986), sec. A, p. 6.

44. Marcus Stern, "Robertson Run Could Split Christian Right," *San Diego Union* (21 July 1986), sec. A, p. 6.
Letter from the director of the Iowa Chapter, in the files of the American Atheist GHQ, Austin, Texas.

45. Marcus Stern, "Robertson Run Could Split Christian Right," *San Diego Union* (21 July 1986), sec. A, p. 6.

46. Mary McGrory, "Clergy-Politicians Quietly Irritate Top People of Both Major Parties," *El Paso* [Texas] *Times* (6 June 1986), sec. A, p. 4. David Broder, "The Pat Robertson Pattern," *Modesto* [California] *Bee* (2 June 1986), sec. A, p. 19. Michael McManus, "The '700 Club' Candidate," *Modesto* [California] *Bee* (7 June 1986), sec. A, p. 19.

47. See: George Skelton, "Voters Are Religious, But Don't Favor Preachers as Politicians," *Toledo*, Ohio *Blade* (27 July 1986), sec. B, p. 5.

48. See my *Tomorrow's Tyrants: The Radical Right & the Politics of Hate* (Dallas: Monument Press, 1985), pp. 104-15.

49. Thomas Morton, "Theology Reflects Liberals' Roots," Butte, Montana, *Enterprise* (10 April 1986); cf. *Christianity & Crisis*.

50. Jon Margolis, "Robertson Appeals to People Upset by Rapid Social Change," *Chicago Tribune* (7 October 1986), sec. 1, p. 15.

51. Phoebe Courtney, "Pat Robertson for President?" "Tax Fax No. 214" issued by *The Independent American,* a national conservative newspaper in Littleton, Colorado. Her argument is that Pat is the only hope of those who "wish to oppose the Communist-appeasing Eastern elitists, such as Jack Kemp of New York and George Bush of Maine. (For political posturing, Bush claims his state of record to be Texas, but his sole claim to residency is a rented room in a Houston hotel.)

52. One-time Robertson associate, and author of *Salvation for Sale,* Gerard T. Straub, argues that Pat had presidential fantasies as early as 1979. Straub worked at CBN for two and one-half years, was the producer of the "700 Club" for nine months, and programming administrator before that. For a detailed discussion on Pat's developing demagoguery, see John Dart, "Ex-Aide Says Robertson Had 'Presidential Fantasy' 7 Years Ago," *Los Angeles Times* (23 August 1986), pt. II, pp. 6, 7.

53. Quoted by Jim Castelli, in "Robertson Could Learn from Kennedy," *Kokomo* [Indiana] *Tribune* (3 October 1986), p. 8.

54. Cf. Edwin M. Yoder, Jr., "Pat Robertson Flaunts a Tarnished Halo," *Los Angeles Times* (12 August 1986), p. 8.

55. Cf. David S. Broder, "Religion in Politics: An American Tradition," *Pittsburgh* [Pennsylvania] *Post-Gazette* (24 December 1986), syndicated by the *Washington Post.*

56. Jim Castelli, "Robertson and Religious Intolerance," *Trenton*, New Jersey, *Times* (29 September 1986).

57. Michael Kramer, "Are You Running with Me, Jesus? Televangelist Pat Robertson Goes for the White House," *New York Magazine* (18 August 1986): p. 22.

58. *Chicago Sun-Times* (23 September 1986), p. 32. Cf. Jody Powell, "Direct Discourse with God: The Pat Robertson Difference," *Denver Post* (28 September 1986), sec. F, p. 5.

59. Yitzhak Fritz Baer, *Die Juden in Christlichen Spanion* (Berlin: Shocken Verlag, 1936). Juan Antonio Llorente, *A Critical History of The Inquisition in Spain* (Williamstown, MA: John Lilbrune Co., 1967). Henry C. Lea, *A History of The Inquisition in Spain* (New York: Macmillan, 1906).

60. Jean Calvin, *Ordonnances Ecclésiastiques* (Geneva, 1537).

61. See my *Unzipped: The Popes Bare All: A Frank Study of Sex and Corruption in the Vatican* (Austin, TX: American Atheist Press, 1987).

62. H. C. Peterson and Gilbert C. Fite, *Opponents of War, 1917-1918* (Seattle: University of Washington Press, 1957).

63. National Popular Government League, *Report on the Investigation of the United States Department of Justice,* given in part in *Twentieth-Century America: Contemporary Documents and Opinions,* ed. John A. Garraty and Robert A. Divine (Boston: Little, Brown and Co., 1968), pp. 222-32.

64. Cf. [Editors] "Fundamentalism a Millstone for GOP," *The*

Atlanta Constitution (6 October 1986), sec. A, p. 10. Cp. Russell Baker, "Criticism Comes Hard in Parson's Campaign," *San Antonio* [Texas] *Express-News* (3 October 1986), sec. B, p. 9.

65. Phil Gailey, "From Crusade to Campaign in Michigan," loc. cit.

66. "Politics of Religious Right Draws Fire," *St. Louis* [Missouri] *Post-Dispatch* (30 August 1986); cp. Toby W. Deone, "Religious Invasion," ibid.

67. Anthony Podesta, "Radical Preachers Out to Win — Even if It Costs Opponents' Life," *Homestead* [Florida] *Leader* (29 August 1986), sec. A, p. 16.

68. Marsha Blakemore, "Religion Shows Clout in GOP," *St. Petersburg* [Florida] *Press* (24 August 1986), sec. B, p. 1.

69. David Dawson, "Religious Right Regroups after Losing Mandate," *Lafayette Journal and Courier* [West Lafayette, Indiana] (16 November 1986).

70. U.S. District Judge W. [illiam] Brevard Hand ruled that forty-five textbooks used in the Alabama public classrooms promoted secular humanism, a philosophy that he ruled to be a religion. Robertson claimed that the books promoted an alliance with the Soviet Union. Hand was ultimately overruled on appeal. Robertson continues his denunciation of the books in keeping with his stated goal of ultimately confronting the Soviet Union in a nuclear war, dropping bombs on Russian cities, and annihilating Soviet people from the earth. See the *Escondido* [California] *Times Advocate* (6 March 1987), sec. A, p. 3, and my notes below on Robertson's quest for nuclear holocaust.

The books Hand banned from the classrooms are: *Caring, Deciding and Growing* by Helen McGinley (Ginn and Co., 1983 ed.); *Contemporary Living* by Verdene Ryder (Goodheart-Wilcox Co., 1981, 1985); *Homemaking: Skills for Everyday Living* by Frances Baynor Parnell (Goodheart-Wilcox, 1981); *Teen Guide* by Valerie Chamberlain (McGraw-Hill Book Co., Webster Division, 1985); *Today's Teen* by Joan Kelly (Bennet & McKnight Publishing Co., 1981); *Person to Person* by [no first name listed] Bennett, publisher unlisted, 1981; *America Is* by Frank Freidel (Charles E. Merrill Publishing Co., 1978); *The American Dream* by Lew Smith (Scott,

Foresman and Co., 1980); *Exploring Our Nation* by Sidney Schwartz (Globe Book Co., 1984); *History of a Free People* by Henry W. Bragdon (Macmillan Publishing Co., 1981); *History of Our American Republic* by Glenn M. Linden (Laidlaw Brothers, 1981); *Our American Heritage* by Herbert J. Bass (Silver Burdett Co., 1979); *People and Our Country* by Norman K. Risjord (Holt, Rinehart & Winston, 1978); *Rise of the American Nation* by Lewis Paul Todd (Harcourt Brace Jovanovich, 1977); *These United States* by James P. Shenton (Houghton Mifflin Co., 1981); Rand McNally Series (1980 edition) of the following social studies books: (1) *You and Me, Here We Are,* (2) *Our Land,* (3) *Where On Earth,* (4) *Across America,* and (5) *World Views;* Scott Foresman series of six books entitled *Social Studies* (1979 ed.); 1981 editions of the Speck series: (1) *Our Family,* (2) *Our Communities,* (3) *Our Country Today,* (4) *Our Country's History,* (5) *Our World Today,* and (6) *Our Neighbors;* 1981 editions of the Laidlaw series: (1) *Understanding People,* (2) *Understanding Families,* (3) *Understanding Communities,* (4) *Understanding Regions of the Earth,* (5) *Understanding Our Country,* (6) *Understanding the World;* and, the Houghton Mifflin 1981 series: (1) *At Home,* (2) *At School,* (3) *In Our Community,* (4) *Ourselves and Others,* (5) *Our Home, the Earth,* (6) *America: Past and Present,* and (7) *Around Our World.*
On Robertson's view of the action of Brevard Hand, see *St. Petersburg* [Florida] *Times* (6 March 1987), sec. A, p. 20.

71. Cf. Michael Kramer, "Are You Running with Me, Jesus? Televangelist Pat Robertson Goes For The White House," *New York Magazine* (18 August 1986): pp. 22-29.

72. Berney Morson, "Dems See Religious Right as GOP's Own Albatross," *Rocky Mountain* [Denver, Colorado] *News* (5 October 1986), p. 26.

73. Gary A. Warner, "TV Preacher Aims President Campaign at Pennsylvania," *Pittsburgh Press* (20 July 1986), sec. A, p. 12.

74. Dudley Clendinen, "For Robertson's Followers, Candidacy Is Divine," *Orange* [County, California] *Register* (21 September 1986), sec. A, p. 26.

75. Ronald Brownstein, "Robertson: The Politics of Religion," *Los Angeles Times* (28 September 1986), pt. 5, pp. 1, 3.

76. Dudley Clendinen, "For Robertson's Followers, Candidacy Is Divine," loc. cit.

77. James R. Pierobon, "Robertson Promises . . ." loc. cit.

78. Pat Robertson, *Shout It from the Housetops,* pp. 114-23.

79. Cf. Cal Thomas, "Religious Right's Priorities Changing," *Syracuse* [New York] *Herald American* (9 February 1986), sec. D, p. 4.

80. W. F. Minor, "Pat's Foray Stirs Little GOP Disarray," *Mississippi Press* (8 June 1986), sec. A, p. 13.

81. Donald M. Rothberg, "Robertson Outlines Candidacy Conditions," *Biloxi and Gulfport* [Mississippi] *Sun Herald* (18 September 1986), sec. A, p. 3.

82. *The* [Hattiesburg] *Mississippi Press*(12 January 1988), sec. A., p. 3.

83. Donald M. Rothberg, "Robertson Outlines Candidacy Conditions," loc. cit.

84. Steve Brunsman, "Coast Followers Support Robertson Bid for President," *Biloxi and Gulfport* [Mississippi] *Sun Herald* (18 September 1986), sec. C, p. 1.

85. Mark Z. Barabak, "Robertson to Run — God and 3 Million Fans Willing," *San Francisco Chronicle* (18 September 1986), p. 5.

86. Jim Jones, "Prosperity Preachers: Give and Ye Shall Receive Big Money Back," *Montgomery* [Alabama] *Journal and Advertiser* (4 October 1986), sec. B, pp. 5, 8. Cf. Donald M. Rothberg, "Robertson — Pray and Give and I Will Run." *Muskogee* [Oklahoma] *Chronicle* (18 September 1986), p. 5.

87. Anthony Podesta, "Radical Preachers out to Win — Even if It Cost Opponents' Lives," *Homestead* [Florida] *Leader* (29 August 1986), loc. cit.

88. Robert Walters, "Christians Quietly Take Over," *Kokomo* [Indiana] *Tribune* (3 October 1986), p. 8.

89. The issue of those "born-again" — Christian fundamentalists — is discussed in Kevin Phillips, "The Classes of '86," *Los Angeles Times* (17 August 1986), pt. V, pp. 1, 3.

90. Personal interview with Jerry Rucker of Omaha, and Linda Johnson of Lincoln.

91. Ellen Whitford, "Hometown Crowd among the Converted," *Norfolk* [Virginia] *Ledger-Star* (18 September 1986), sec. A, pp. 1, 3. and April Witt, "Robertson Wants 3 Million Pledges; Signatures Would Spur Him to Run," ibid., sec. A, pp. 1, 3. Dudley Clendinen, "Robertson: If Prayers and Support Are There, I'll Run," *Chattanooga* [Tennessee] *Times* (18 September 1986), sec. A, pp. 1, 3. The Robertson declaration was not universally popular. San Antonio, Texas, clergy declared that Robertson's candidacy "would isolate Christianity and make it subject to ridicule because certain things Pat believes would be held up by the press to ridicule." *San Antonio Express-News* (19 September 1986), sec. A, p. 9.

92. John B. Judis, "Republican Consternation and Aversion in Orlando," In These Times (25 November/8 December, 1987), pp. 6-7.

93. *Austin* [Texas] *American Statesman* (6 February 1988), sec. A, p. 1; *Dallas* [Texas] *Times-Herald* (6 February 1988), sec. A, p. 11.

94. Michele Weldon, "Today's Teens Get into The Spirit of Religion," *Dallas* [Texas] Times-Herald (6 February 1988), sec. F, p. 1.

95. Weldon, "Today's Teens," Sec. F, p. 3.

96. *Dallas* [Texas] *Times-Herald* (18 April, 1985), sec. A, p. 32.

Chapter 4
The GOP à la Robertson

Robertson enjoys using such words as "honesty," "fairness," "the American way," "decency," "hardwork," "family," and "morality" as if he invented them. He has invested them, in fact, with religious significance. He does not have a monopoly on these words, although he issues them in his campaign so that they float like confederate currency to the top of the mire of insinuations, hyperbolizations, lies, and deceits that are ever a part of the wash that floods from his fantasies. In the debris that surrounds Robertson are the dead, discarded ideas of civil liberties guaranteed by the Bill of Rights, the promise of economic, racial, sexual, and educational opportunities, and justice for all,[1] as well as the United States' unique religious and cultural pluralism. His ideas build a public pantheon for panderers preaching Armaggedon.

Robertson is a revivalist. He preaches to the mental equivalent of tent people, limiting his constituency with every word he utters. His language attracts the easily aroused, the hate-filled, and the designing.

Interestingly, what Robertson pledges to his faithful followers, the words he uses to stir up religious emotions, is opposite that which he uses with secular crowds.[2] Instead of claiming to be an evangelist or preacher, Robertson told "CBS Morning News," "Well, you know, really what I am is a morning talk-show host."[3] God doesn't come up very often, doesn't have much of a say in the televangelist's economic prophesying when Pat is addressing strictly business crowds.[4]

Two-faced hypocrisy is only the tip of the Robertson iceberg[5] as it moves menacingly toward the ship of state. Freedom lovers on board have only the Constitution as their life jackets, yet most are afraid to signal the captain of the danger moving toward them.

Robertson would deny that life jacket of the Constitution to the majority of the citizens of the United States. He believes that the current interpretation of the Constitution is not "Christian" enough. For that reason, he treats it as a mere scrap of paper to be ignored by those who are not pleased with its doctrines, as he interprets them.

A bleak existence is promised to non-fundamentalists, non-Christians, and Atheists in a Robertson reign.[6] Those outside the pale of fundamentalism are to be left by the wayside as emerging evangelicals emasculate the democratic process and cut the Constitution to shreds.[7]

The evangelicals make no pretense but that they will wing their way to power through television. They see themselves, alone, as speaking for Jesus. Their collective Christian intelligence is to become the stamp of orthodoxy for the land. Christianity is to be the only party in the United States, and ultimately, Robertson hopes, the only faith and organized religion.

Pluralism, secularism, humanism, and a plethora of other opinions, options, convictions, persuasions, and their means of human expression are to be first corralled, then censored, and eventually erased. This aspiration of limiting and ultimately destroying the melting pot of a heterogeneous society is to be known as Intelivote — the doublespeak of a future 1984.

Intelivote is a Texas phenomenon. During elections local ministers sent questionnaires to both incumbent and aspiring candidates to test their religious orthodoxy. The questions were directed to the candidates' private lives and their opinions on moral and religious issues. Questionnaires returned were rated on a point system, information from which was distributed to prospective voters.[8]

Intelivote workers are to come from within the Robertson camp. A national functioning intelivote is to be the "Christian Voice" of the nation and it will be the voice of an intolerant god.

Robertson's god will speak on everything from abortion[9] through refinancing the national debt, to relations with Zimbabwe.[10] The Christian Voice will carry, live, the conferences between Robertson and his god — on every televison and radio network.[11]

The Christian Voice is adept at terroristic tactics — all actions being justified as "the will of Jesus." No atrocity, no miscarriage of justice, no inhumane act is to inhibit it. All are approved as "necessary" by Robertson's god.

The Christian Voice's national efforts are disguised by a long list of organizations with patriotic and religious sounding names. Nearly all of these power bases are headed by preachers. Their budgets range in the millions, with Falwell's Moral Majority — a.k.a.[12] The Liberty Foundation — having an annual purse of more than $6 million.

The purpose of Christian Voice god-squads is to target legislators in various states for defeat. This is to be done by networking in fundamentalist churches, registering church members to vote and watching their voting patterns closely. Behind it all is a determination to make the GOP "God's Own Party."

An exclusive party, it does not even recognize the plurality and diversity within its own ranks. Those who go against Pat's concepts of normality are to be weeded out.

The warfare of the Christian Voice has already netted evangelicals major blocks of delegates to state and national conventions.

The evangelicals are determined to erase homosexuality from the face of the earth, calling homosexuality not only a "sin" but also a "perversion" or "abomination." The anomaly of this is that a large number of gay men and lesbians in the United States are pentecostal, charismatic — and surprisingly, Republican. Consequently, a near-majority of the homosexuals in the United States vote Republican, adding to the GOP strength to ultimately deny gay men and lesbians the limited civil rights and liberties they currently enjoy.

Although a "good cry with Jesus" may cleanse the soul, no number of tears can put out a fire lit under the feet of a sexual heretic. Even these Republican sexual heretics are not safe. They too must be sacrificed on the altar of Robertson's god.

Adherence to, support for, and membership in the GOP by gays is especially prevalent in Dallas, Texas. Not only was Phil Gramm, an ardent opponent to gay rights, popular there among gay men and lesbians, but so, too, is Ronald Reagan, and other homophobes.

Dallasite J. Jacobs argued passionately in 1984, for gay men and lesbians to vote Republican.[13] They did. In less than two years what few freedoms they had won from lower courts in Texas concerning gay rights they lost in the United States Supreme Court with the judges appointed by the man for whom they cast their ballots.

Conversely, although Texas evangelicals are firmly opposed to gay and lesbian rights, they rejoiced in the number of gays and lesbians who supported them. And, the gays and lesbians continue to send the same men and women whom they style as "abominations" in their state GOP platform, invitations to contribute to future GOP gay-lesbian bashings.

Gay-lesbian bashing is only one of the sports of the Texas GOP. With the advent of the evangelicals into GOP politics, trials are judged on who can oppose what book the loudest as being "un-Christian." The winners of the book burnings and classroom censorship usually are Mel and Norma Gabler of Longview, Texas. Arch-reactionary Mary Lassiter of Mesquite, Texas, is running a close second.

Texas Republicans labor under two very strong anti-rights spokespeople: State Republican Chairman George Strake,[14] who became immortalized in Texas literature for decrying lesbians as "dykes on bikes" during the 1984 Republican Convention,[15] and Southern Baptist Bill Price, whose anti-choice crusade has pushed confrontation over freedom of choice to a near-eruptive point. The Texas GOP, according to an analysis released by Price, "will have Christian Right stamped all over it." Strake argued that the religious right "feels comfortable" within the GOP because of "philosophical similarities" on such issues as abortion and defense. Strake's staunch homophobic stand was another issue that the fundamentalists were quick to appreciate. Freedom of choice is to be abolished when the evangelicals take power. Gays are to be quarantined. A woman is to lose control over her own body. Education is to become the stepchild of religious intolerance.

To celebrate the advent of the fundamentalist voting block, preacher Sam Hoerster of Austin, Texas, rushed to establish a "Solemn Covenant Republican Platform" that would link the GOP to "the advancement of the kingdom of our Lord and Saviour Jesus Christ."[16] Congressional representatives and contenders are informed that they will get the support of the Christian Voice, Robertson and other televangelists, only if they declare themselves "born-again" Christians.[17]

In Fort Worth, Texas, Robertson cultists have not only held political "revivals" inside "a huge air-conditioned tent at the Circle T Ranch"[18] (reminiscent of the ghost of Elmer Gantry when salvation was openly for sale by psuedo-religious fundamentalists) but hired an airplane to circle the ranch, trailing a sign that read, "Go For It, Pat."[19] Fort Worth Republican women began to wear their hair styled like Dede, practiced praying emotionally, and flocked to see the new televangelist when he was in town.

The idolatrous worship of Robertson is especially keen among evangelicals who live in Michigan. Michigan fundamentalist Christians are zealously anti-Judaism and see the Robertson candidacy as a way to erase the "curse of the Jews" who live around them. To support the Robertson candidacy and their own anti-Judaism, Michigan biblical-literalists have formed a voting block that has become a founding block of the Freedom Council's grassroots movement.

The unwritten line among Michigan evangelicals is the volatile, yet non-violent anti-Judaism of fundamentalist organizations and their members.

Their anti-Judaism is seen most frequently in the numerous attempts of the conservative Christian fundamentalists to unseat Michigan congressional representative Howard Wolpe. While Robertson was praying for a "miracle" in Michigan,[20] Christian Congressional Representative Mark Siljander wrote to the pastors of Wolpe's district soliciting for their votes to unseat Wolpe, who is Jewish. Siljander objected to Wolpe's presence in Congress, not only because Wolpe is Jewish, but because the representative allegedly "vot[ed] against traditional American values which have helped build this country into the evangelistic arm that it has become." Siljander ended with a plea to help "send another Christian to Congress."

Siljander pushed his Christian "response" to Wolpe's Jewry to every political action committee he discovered. He sent messages to local Christian clergy to "pray and fast" with him so that the god of the fundamentalists could clear the way for a Christian revolution throughout the United States to bring the nation "back into the Christian camp." From there it would be only a short distance until a Christianized America[21] accepted its responsibility to launch a holy war against non-Christian states,[22] fighting with all of its arms and armaments until the world was made safe for Christ and every mouth breathed the word "Jesus."

A three-term congressman from Three Rivers, Siljander's baiting Christian rhetoric filled the front pages of the *Herald-Palladium* of St. Joseph — one of the largest daily newspapers in Siljander's 4th Congressional District. At one point, the St. Joseph *Herald-Palladium* carried the complete text of Three Rivers Christian Fellowship congregant Siljander. As a Christian, Siljander declared:

> We must look at Satan in the face and the humanism that faces our nation and the social destruction that's before us. . . . We cannot afford to rest now that the church (has woke up) [*sic*] from the slumber and sleep. . . . It's time to wake up. The days are growing shorter. The times are more desperate than ever. . . . Pornography has been thrown out of the convenience stores and drug stores and gas stations all over America. Playboy [enterprises] has been forced out of the nightclub and casino business. Anti-

sodomy laws are being reinforced by our courts. Pornographic bookstores are being shut down as public health violations. . . . God has now cleared the way for a pro-life chief justice of the Supreme Court and for the appointment of Judge [Antonin] Scalia, another pro-life judge. . . . We need to break the back of Satan and the lies that are coming our way.

The "back of Satan" was the back of his opponent Fred Upton of St. Joseph, an aide to David Stockman when he was budget director. No person was safe from Siljander's rhetoric. Siljander's denunciations knew no bounds. They had no limits.

In flaming demagoguery, Siljander perjured the human race, spat upon the concept of fairness, and libeled those who opposed him,[23] all the while keeping in strict goose step with Pat Robertson.[24] Siljander, an evangelical, is determined to put an evangelical in the White House and in all other offices of government.

Republican Senator Paul Laxalt of Nevada is equally vitriolic. He wrote to 40,000 Christian pastors to urge them to support Ronald Reagan's re-election,[25] arguing that "As leaders under God's authority, we cannot afford to resign ourselves to idle neutrality in an election that will confirm or silence the president" who supported Christian goals.[26] Now he supports Robertson's plan for the United States, and favors Robertson's mouthpiece: the Christian Voice.

The Christian Voice has frightened many a Jew who sees its actions as similar to the preparations to receive the little Austrian into German politics at the end of the 1930s. Rabbi David Saperstein of the Religion Action Center of Reform Judaism explained:

> As a Jew, I know that when leaders rise to power based on the notion that one brand of politics is accepted by God that it's the beginning of the end for minorities such as Jews. . . . These people have a vision of America being based on conservative Christian values. Along with that is the belief that it is the government's role to strengthen those values. That would leave a society based solely on the will of the majority with no alternatives for the minority. That's anathema to America as a pluralistic society. The result, no matter what the intent, is anti-Jewish.[27]

What makes the anti-Judaism of evangelical fundamentalists even more dangerous to American democracy is that they have an immediate access to the people by means of the tube. Through the use of the televison air waves, evangelical fundamentalists can enter into every home. More than sixty-one million households in America (representing 40 percent of all homes that have televison sets) watch one or more of the top ten charismatic televangelists. Robertson claims 28.7 million of these viewers. Jeffrey K. Hadden, past president of the Society for the Scientific Study of Religion, argues that Robertson uses his "religious televison role to demonstrate to the world his political acumen and to build a following for his political views."[28]

Notes

1. Cf. A. James Rudin, "Pat Robertson and 'Our America'," *New York Times* (21 September 1986), p. 25.

2. Cf. Otis Pikes's appraisal, "What if Pat Robertson Won?" (syndicated by Newhouse News Service, 1986).

3. Dudley Clendinen, "For Robertson Followers, Candidacy is Divine," loc. cit.

4. Andrew Mollison, "Robertson Accents Business Side; It's More Presidential," *Atlanta Constitution* (14 September 1986), sec. A, pp. 1, 22, 23.

5. Cf. Russell Baker, "That Awesome Cloth," *New York Times* (20 September 1986).

6. David E. Anderson, "Bible Has Answers to All Issues, New Conservative Group Says," *Flint* [Michigan] *Journal* (4 July 1986), sec. A, p. 6.

7. Edsall, "Onward, GOP Christians," p. 5

8. See my *Evangelical Terrorism* (Irving, TX: Scholars Books, 1986), pp. 112-13.

9. Robertson, *Answers*, pp. 175-76.

10. Allan J. Mayer, *et al.*, "A Tide of Born-Again Politics," *Newsweek* (15 September 1980): pp. 28-32, 36.

11. John Buchanan, "Waiting for God's Guidance," *The Modesto* [California] *Bee* (5 November 1985), sec. A, p. 13. Buchanan is an ordained Southern Baptist minister and a former eight-term Republican congressman from Alabama who has been consistently targeted by the Robertson group to be silenced since Buchanan is chairman of People for the American Way.

12. "Also Known As."

13. Cf. my *Tomorrow's Tyrants*, pp. 288ff.

14. *Austin* [Texas] *American-Statesman* (30 May 1986), p. 32.

15. See my *Tomorrow's Tyrants*, p. 291.

16. Dave McNeely, "Christian Right Groups Endorse State GOP Chairman's Re-election Bid," *Austin* [Texas] *American-Statesman* (27 June 1986), sec. B, p. 2.

17. Cf. David Matustik, "Christian Activism Built U.S., Politicking Robertson Says," *Austin* [Texas] *American-Statesman* (14 December 1986).

18. Juan R. Palomo, "From Pulpit to Politics? Robertson's Followers Await Word," *Houston* [Texas] *Post* (14 September 1986), sec. A, pp. 1, 24.

19. *Austin* [Texas] *American-Statesman* (3 August 1986), sec. B, p. 2.

20. Larry Eichel, "Robertson Wants 'Miracle' in Mich[igan]," *Philadelphia* [Pennsylvania] *Inquirer* (31 July 1986), sec. A, p. 5.

21. Cf. "Question: 'Who Will Win Americans to Christ?'," *Baptist Standard* 99.9 (4 March 1987): p. 6.

22. Cf. Ralph Woerner, "Reasons Why People Turn Christ Aside," *The Good News Messenger* 12.2 (March 1987): pp. 1, 3.

23. Jon Margolis, "Michigan Primay Results Show A GOP Religious Problem," *The Orange County* [California] *Register* (10 August 1986),

sec. A, p. 22. Cp. Ken Fireman and Remer Tyson, "GOP Finds Religious Right Voters Can Stray," *Detroit Free Press* (10 August 1986), sec. A, pp. 1, 10. It must be noted that Robertson won only 37 percent. Cf. United Press International accounts on 10 August 1986.

24. Ken Fireman, "Siljander Asks Prayers for Victory over Satan," *Detroit Free Press* (2 August 1986), sec. A, pp. 1, 7.

25. "Laxalt Tells Evangelicals They Are Welcome in the GOP," *Washington Post* (1 October 1986).

26. D'Antonio, "Politics and Religion," p. 11.

27. D'Antonio, "Politics and Religion," p. 11.

28. Russell Chandler, "Christian Right Advancing, Scholar Says," *Los Angeles Times* (2 November 1985), pt. 2, p. 5.

Chapter 5
Robertson on "Other Religions"

Those who pledge themselves to work for Robertson do so to bring about his political goals and implement his ideas. Many of those who work at CBN work for minimal wages — according to Robertson, as both "a favor" and an act of faith. He declares that their work is considered by the godhead to be an act of charity to the non-Christian (meaning anyone who is not a charismatic fundamentalist who mimics Robertson's brand of bastardized Christianity), and for this act of charity the laborer will win for himself or herself a special place in the heart of Jesus and a promise of eternity.[1]

To insure his place at the head of the table of tomorrow's theological tyrants, Robertson has issued a call against "Satanic worship," labeling dissident elements of other religions to be "cults," and any non-fundamental practice or belief to be false and heretical.[2]

Robertson is especially critical of "denominational people" expressing a belief in reincarnation. He labels their prayer groups as believers in "Satanic doctrine." These "denominational people" — whom Pat condemns — include the Spiritualist Church and some Episcopal parishes.[3]

Pentecostalism is fine. Spiritualism is taboo.

Rather than accept various forms of religious expression, Robertson has determined to root them out. What is important to Robertson's theology is emotionalism.

To support emotional pentecostalism, Robertson introduced Jim and Tammy Faye Bakker to the world. They made their first appearance on the "700 Club" as "people of God" since "Jim and Tammy made a good team."[4] They became a television success story overnight. The Bakker speciality was the ability which they had to raise money — something which endeared them to Pat Robertson's heart. It would be a short while, however, until they would have their own television empire, the "PTL (Praise The Lord, or People That Love, which after the sex scandal involving Jim Bakker, was renamed 'Pay The Lady') Club." From the PTL Club they would take in millions of dollars to build a Christian Disneyland, a lavish home for the Bakkers, complete with gold-plated faucets and an air-conditioned doghouse, and pay for lavish trips and sumptuous hotel accommodations for those the Bakkers would entertain.

Meanwhile, back at the "700 Club" faith-healing "miracles" were claimed,[5] although none were medically proven or scientifically substantiated. Robertson, until recently the "TV Healer" of the "700 Club," is a showman at best, passing off carnival magic acts as "miracles" so that he and other famed televangelists can con millions of dollars out of gullible faithful followers, according to the Committee for the Scientific Examination of Religion (CSER).[6] At worst, Robertson is a charlatan persuading people to pass over genuine physicians in favor of cult healing and mystery superstition clothed in the rotting fabrications of Bible literalism.

In fact, the primary danger of the healing charades put on by Robertson and other televangelists, who claim that they have the power to heal, is that many afflicted people do substitute "faith healing" for legitimate medical practices.[7] Robertson has no concern for any tragic result from the choice which he urges the ailing to make.

Robertson lauds "miraculous cures" as testimony to individual belief that the "Second Coming" of Christ is imminent.[8] He cites scriptural passages boasting of the "powers of faith healing" that appear in both the Old and the New Testament.[9]

Robertson's ritual of faith healing is dramatic, colorful, theatrical — and unproved. He never has immediate testimonials or medical verification of his absurd claims of his power to work for god in the field of health.[10] Instead, as occurred in 1981 at a Full Gospel Business Men's Fellowship Conference in Philadelphia, Robertson shouts "Satan be gone!" and cures are allegedly wrought. He squinches his eyes tightly and then announces, "God has just healed *somebody.*" He doesn't say who the lucky recipient of the miraculous cure is.

Not only does Robertson speak in generalities concerning those healed "by faith," but he makes a point to be ambiguous as he declares, "A hernia has been healed. If you're wearing a truss you can take it off.

It's *gone!*"

In a hushed voice, he theatrically he turns to yet another medical problem area, "*Several people* are being healed of hemorrhoids and varicose veins. Thank you, Lord. . . . Many people, their eyesight is being opened right now. You're seeing. You couldn't see well before. Your eyes, your vision, is being restored to you." When he opens his eyes, Robertson earnestly declares, "In the center section here, somebody's just been healed of an ulcer."

Those elusive "somebodies" never appear. They never testify. They never verify Robertson's cure, for they are never examined. They are just phantoms in Pat's rhetoric calculated to push adrenaline higher in the veins of his listeners, escalating a "spiritual fever" that makes his adherents willing to walk to the closest post office to send in their money or pledge for a Robertson holy war.[11]

Robert S. Alley, a professor of humanities at the University of Richmond (a conservative, Baptist-affiliated school where Alley has taught religion and social ethics for more than twenty years), calls Robertson's charade of faith healing "a disgrace. It's a use of people, playing on their emotions."[12]

The sad truth about Robertson's "faith healing" is that it is no better, and sometimes worse, than the "faith healing" of other quacks and charlatans. Not only are those "healed" left anonymous, but the unfortunate few who believe in this religious voodoo ritual find themselves either not cured, in a worse medical state than they had been before the "cure" — or dead. One woman, who was told during a faith-healing service to discard her brace and run across the stage, suffered a backbone collapse the following day; four months later she was dead.[13]

Robertson's faith healing spills over into "helping" people to lose weight, stop drinking alcohol, curb drug abuse, end mental depression, become free from fear, moderate manic-depression, and cancel the compulsion to gamble; see: Robertson, with the support of scriptural passages, nearly always taken out of context. Nowhere in the Christian Bible is a person's weight discussed as being a sin or mark of salvation; the "sin" of "gluttony" was a medieval invention by ascetics who deliberately attempted to punish their bodies in quest of social recognition as "specially marked by god" and thus a "holy" individual. Drinking alcohol is not condemned; the Bible rejects "drunkenness" (Prov. 20:1, Hab. 2:15, Rom. 14:21; Pat ignores the fourteenth verse which reads: "I know, and am persuaded by the Lord Jesus, that there is nothing unclean of itself: but to him that believes something to be unclean, it is unclean to him alone.")

Despite modern medical advances, superstitions and belief in "miraculous cures" still exist — and persist, as people yearn for a magic cure,[14] a therapeutic happening that is coupled with raw emotions and a positive message.[15] The "faith healer" not only gives the desperate a good show, but hope, although there has never been a recorded case of any one thing cured by faith.

No other Christian denomination dares to chastize Robertson, Oral Roberts, or any other "faith healer" for each programs aid through prayer into their belief sets. The Roman Catholic Church relies heavily on the miraculous healings at Lourdes and has even canonized an American woman, Elizabeth "Mother" Seton, for her documented healings of cancer scores of years after her death. Mary Baker Eddy's Church of Christ Scientist not only practices healing through prayer but the practitioners of the art receive payments through Medicaid for their services. The hypocrisy of these religions is as great as that of Robertson.

The hypocrisy of Robertson's alleged "faith healing" is that he performs for god these "miraculous cures" only when it is to his advantage — either as a preacher pandering to gullible guests or when he needs to raise money from equally impressionable and compassionate congregations.[16]

Robertson has no time for those who would challenge his fake cures. He does not accept "challenges" from the doubting, even if their challenges would bring him greater fame, prosperity, and power, as is the case detailed by former Reagan assistant Ed Rollins, who turned down the chance to head the Robertson-for-President drive.

Ed Rollins drove to Virginia Beach to visit Pat at his lavish home, where he and his wife, Dede, live sumptuously. His visit coincided with Hurricane Gloria. As Rollins told it later:

> I saw Pat in Virginia Beach at about the time of the hurricane last fall. One of the first things I noticed was that he'd ordered a big statue of the Four Horsemen of the Apocalypse taken indoors for fear that the storm would trash it. And I was hurting pretty bad with a hernia. I said to him, and not totally in jest, "If you heal my hernia, I'll do your campaign." He looked at me like I was crazy.[17]

Unfortunately the tent-show healers are still here. Like Robertson, they claim their phoney cures are a part of a spiritual revival. Yet

Robertson and other similar con men fail to note the psychological repercussions that afflict and affect their faithful believers who are not cured. If a sick "believer" is not cured, he may feel a deep guilt, a sense of being forgotten or foresaken by the god that allegedly works for the faith healer. Under such circumstances, suicide is sometimes the only out, and a life is lost — but not before the faith healer has reaped the rewards of public adulation and the gain of greater contributions through his telethonic faith program which is usually linked to his telephonic religious network, be it Robertson's "700 Club" or Oral Roberts' House of Power.

What is especially tragic is the despair and guilt those who do take their lives feel up to the moment of the act. Casting away all thoughts of hope or any recognition of their own self-worth, they condemn themselves for a plethora of sins which range from "impure thoughts" to "impure acts." These "sins," in most cases, are those dreamed up by the unusual tunnel-vision minds of the televangelists who thrive on discussing a penitent's sexual and private life — acts which are no strangers to Robertson and are customarily aired on his "700 Club" soap opera.[18]

To confront the medical and scientific unprovability of "faith healing,"[19] an Atheist organization offered a $10,000 challenge to any religious faith healer who could restore a missing part of the outward body — such as a nose — but not intestines or a brain which so many practitioners and their followers seem to be lacking anyway. The only requirement to win the $10,000 purse was for the faith healer to find someone without a nose, a leg, a finger, a toe, an ear, an eye, or a hand and, by means of song, prayer, and laying on of hands, bring the nose, the leg, finger, toe, ear, eye, or hand back to where it belonged and all of this before a live audience. Of course, the nose must be fully functional when restored.[20] Robertson, who has "shouted from the housetops" that he can perform miracles,[21] didn't accept the challenge. He can't cure acne — nor can his god.

Although Robertson's god can't cure anything, Robertson witnesses that the same deity cures cancer.[22]

However, when his wife, Dede, was diagnosed by Dr. Charles Warne, the Robertson family physician, as having breast cancer, Robertson decided not to call on god. Dede's fate was decided apparently only by Pat. A mammogram on July 8, 1986 revealed a suspicious mass, and Pat's first impulse was to splash a few drops of oil from a vial into his palm as he laid his hand on Dede's head, anointing her and praying for divine healing. The anointing did not work, as two weeks later, a biopsy of tissue from her right breast revealed that the mass was cancerous.

Robertson's faith in god's healing power was put to a test.

When, some years prior to this, his youngest son, Gordon, had become ill with a staph infection in a New York City hospital, he recalled, "I turned to that seemingly empty room and I said in a tone of command, 'Virus, in the name of Jesus Christ of Nazareth, I take authority over you. Get out of here.' "[22] However, with a presidential race in the offing he could ill afford to let Dede die if Jesus Christ of Nazareth did not respond to the oil in his hand and prayer in his mouth.

He therefore took Dede for a two-week vacation in New Hampshire's White Mountains, the thought of cancer having sent "an awful chill" through him. By the time they returned to Virginia the cancer had spread and it was obvious that a complete mastectomy was needed.

He wavered with indecision, as he waited on god. His campaign was in need of money and he had arranged a fund-raising trip. Whenever any choice for Robertson includes one of money — his response is always the same: he goes for the gold. Dede's appearance was needed at two back-to-back fundraisers: the lavish party at the Texas ranch of Nelson Bunker Hunt on August 1 and at a huge dinner at the Anaheim, California, convention hall on August 2.

Dede resorted to pain pills to keep herself going, breaking down into tears after the fund-raisers were completed, with an August 8 surgery confronting her. But Pat had scheduled a major series of public appearances and it was touch and go if he would remain with his wife for the surgery. But, this time Dede was not alone in her complaints that Robertson should remain by her side. His children also "let him have it," Dede later explained. And thus it was that god having failed, Robertson chose a surgeon's knife to remove all of Dede's cancerous tissues.[23]

Other life-threatening diseases that Robertson's god does not cure are AIDS or any other communicable disease. Robertson follows the rigid Southern Baptist line unkindly iterated by Southern Baptist Convention president Charles Stanley. AIDS — like other viruses — is "god's punishment for homosexuality (or any other form of sin)" — despite medical evidence that AIDS is an equal opportunity virus that afflicts heterosexuals, hemophiliacs, intravenous drug users, and others in addition to gay *men*. There is no record of AIDS ever being contracted by a lesbian. This means, if we use the Southern Baptist criterion as elucidated by Bailey Smith, Charles Stanley, and other homophobes, gay women are god's chosen people. And, all of this is an avouchment that Jesus "is coming soon."

Robertson's seething hatred for homosexuals is far beyond any rational position. Distrusting and then misusing medical evidence, Robertson has fanned the flames of hatred against gay men and women by declaring that homosexuality is itself a disease. This category of "disease" is not accepted by any respected medical or psychological/psychiatric authority, yet Pat declares that "Doctors at the Center for Disease Control are now projecting 40,000 cases of this disease [will appear] *next year* [emphasis his]."[24] The CDC has never issued this "warning" of the progress of the "disease" of homosexuality spreading to 40,000 uninfected people. But twisting fact into fiction is nothing new to Pat.

Pat continues his gay-bashing on a regular basis. He has argued that if a boy should see two "*naked* (emphasis his) men in bed at once [together]" the youth would be mentally impaired. Robertson then lamented that such is "One of the *shocking* miscarriages of justice."

Offering spiritual lamentations to his punishing god who does not tolerate homosexuality — a god too weak to erase it from the earth as Pat would wish — Pat declares that this "injustice" must be undone. He hesitates. Then, lowering his eyes in mock humility, he intones, as if his comments were a medieval *Te Deum,* "This injustice will only be corrected" when either Pat reaches the White House, or Jesus "Comes Again!"

The immediacy of the alleged "Second Coming" has political promise. Robertson could use it as leverage for increasing America's political might, increasing armament appropriations, and escalating military numbers in a mad rush towards an American Armageddon.

Notes

1. Robertson, *Shout It from the Housetops,* p. 179f.

2. Cf. Jody Powell, "GOP Had Better Believe It: True Believers Spell Trouble," *Los Angeles Times* (19 June 1986), pt. 2, p. 7.

3. Robertson, *Shout It from the Housetops,* pp. 180, 185-86.

4. Robertson, *Shout It from the Housetops,* pp. 186-87.

5. Pat Robertson with Bob Slosser, *The Secret Kingdom: A Promise of Hope and Freedom in a World of Turmoil* (Nashville: Thomas

Nelson, 1982), pp. 180-97.

6. John Jones, "TV Healers Pass Off Carnival Acts as Miracles," in *Globe* (22 April 1986).

7. Michael Kramer, "Are You Running with Me, Jesus? Televangelist Pat Robertson Goes for the White House," *New York Magazine* (18 August 1986): p. 27.

8. Robertson, *Shout It from the Housetops,* pp. 191-93.

9. Pat Robertson with William Proctor, *Beyond Reason: How Miracles Can Change Your Life* (New York: William Morrow, 1985), p. 37, citing Isa. 53:5, Matt. 21:21, John 14:13, and 3 John 2, before claiming that "medical tests showed that healing had begun," but offering no verifiable evidence for such a claim and giving neither the clinic nor the practitioner's name or address.

10. Robertson, *Answers,* pp. 41, 102-5.

11. Robertson, *Answers,* pp. 186-88, 201.

12. Myra MacPherson, "The Pulpit and the Power: '700 Club's' Pat Robertson, Preaching Gospel & Eyeing the White House," *Washington Post* (18 October 1985), sec. D, p. 8.

13. *Answers,* pp. 221-30.

14. Cf. Robertson, *Answers,* pp. 217-19. Robertson, *Beyond Reason,* pp. 48-52, 73-74, 89, 94, 99-110, 137-38, 148-50.

15. Lisa M. Krieger, "TV's 'Faith Healers' Harm More Than Heal, Critics Say," *San Francisco Examiner* (10 August 1986).

16. Robertson, *Answers,* pp. 103-105, 268-69, 275-78.

17. Michael Kramer, "Are You Running with Me, Jesus? Televangelist Pat Robertson Goes for the White House," *New York Magazine* (18 August 1986): pp. 26, 29.

18. Lisa M. Krieger, "TV's 'Faith Healers' Harm More Than Heal,"

loc. cit. On Robertson, see Straub, *Salvation for Sale,* p. 275; and my comments below. Jan Ziegler, "Scientists Take Aim at Faith-Healers," *St. Petersburg* [Florida] *Times* (15 September 1986), sec. A, p. 3.

19. Al Martinez, "I Doubt That You'll See Pat Robertson Restore A Body Part," *Los Angeles Times* (11 August 1986); Valley Edition, pt. 2, p. 7.

20. Robertson, *Shout It from the Housetops,* pp. 191f, and below. Cf. Pat Robertson, *The Secret Kingdom,* pp. 180-98.

21. Robertson, *Beyond Reason,* pp. 53-54.

22. David Edwin Harrell, Jr., *Pat Robertson A Personal, Political and Religious Portrait* (San Francisco: Harper & Row Publishers, 1987) p. 119.

23. Lee Bandy, "Wife's Cancer Challenges Robertson's Deepest Values," *St. Paul* [Minnesota] *Pioneer Press* (3 January 1988): pt. D, pp. 1, 6.

24. Rist, "A Sinner's Guide to The TV Evangelists," p. 36.

Chapter 6
Pulling The Mote out of His
Brother's Eye

Lyndon Baines Johnson, one-time Texas senator and then president (1963-1968) of the United States, was personally judged by Robertson as guilty of "taint[ing] the federal government with the easy morality and arrogance of the Texas wheeler-dealer."[1] In a CNN interview, Robertson said he agonized over whether or not to pray for Lyndon Johnson. Pat's god told him not to do so.[2] Instead, Johnson's "tainting" of the federal government was to be stopped by the hand of Robertson's god, who would arbitrarily and impatiently guide the hand of Robertson's faithful followers to help Pat "rid the high places on the earth for I have heard your prayer, your conflict, your worry and concern about this project; and I, the Lord, will build it for my glory."[3]

Pat's revelation is beyond all orthodox canons of scripture. Not only is it unbiblical, but it is contrary to, and in opposition of, the literal lines and injunctions of his Bible which declares: ". . . If any man shall add unto these things, God shall add unto him the plagues that are written in this book."[4]

As has been Pat's custom over the years since he began to preach, Robertson supplements scripture. Regularly Robertson records new messages from his god in the manner of a prophet or apostle. Many of the messages Robertson receives concern the sins of others whom the televangelist is ordered to correct.

Robertson saw "sin" in Norman Lear's attack on fundamentalists who attempted to breach the separation of state and church in the United States. He called the founder of People for the American Way an "Atheist,"[5] and rebuked the television award-winning director and producer of such popular series as "All In The Family," for defying him — in direct contradiction of his Bible's prohibition against bearing false witness against one's neighbor.[6] Robertson pronounced himself an agent of god and warned Lear that he was in over his head: "Your arms are too short to box with God."[7]

The televangelist's attack on Norman Lear was assailed by University of Chicago church historian Martin E. Marty. A friend and confidant of Lear, Marty publicly accused Robertson — along with Jimmy Swaggart and Jerry Falwell — of violating the biblical commandment of bearing false witness against one's neighbor. Marty termed Lear a spiritual pilgrim-in-progress who "struggles mightily and sincerely with God and the meaning of life."

An ordained Lutheran, Martry chastized Robertson for pretending that he had a monopoly on civic virtue. Indeed, the professor responded, Robertson was using Lear as his "primary Atheist" foe and bogeyman to win over others to his way of thinking.

Robertson questioned Secretary of Education William S. Bennett's "patriotism, love of God, love of country, and support of the traditional family."[8] The televangelist's attack on Secretary Bennett was placed in a fund-raising letter, claiming that "the Christians" had "won . . . What a breakthrough for the Kingdom."

Robertson criticized Bennett for not backing Christianity and proselytizing in his official capacity. Robertson has wanted the Office of Education to become an instrument to indoctrinate Christian fundamentalism into every course in every class in every school within the United States. Robertson believed it was Bennett's spiritual obligation since the Democrats had "forgotten" their religious heritage.

Overwhelmed by Robertson's hostile harangue, Bennett measured his response crisply. "This sort of invidious sectarianism must be renounced in the strongest terms," Bennett declared publicly.

Bennett noted that Robertson was coupling state and church together in every arena and at every stop along his political trail. Such action was never the intent of the original Founding Fathers of the United States.

Later, when Robertson was attempting to clarify his misstatement of fact, the televangelist claimed that he was arguing against the Democratic Party's platform. At no time did he mean to attack another Republican. The Democrats, Robertson weasled, lacked support for "God, country, and traditional family values."

Robertson predated Ollie North's plea that he loved "god and country" more than those around him. As did Ollie North, Robertson found those who opposed him distasteful and unacceptable.

To be acceptable to Robertson, a person had to be like Robertson. To be like Robertson required the individual to be a Christian patterning himself or herself after Pat's interpretation of the life and ministry of Jesus.

Alcohol is wrong. Sex outside of marriage is evil. Education has to be Christ-centered. Democrats are of the Devil. God is a Republican.

Once a believer in Jesus has accepted Pat as the final prophet of the deity, the United States would flourish. Pat would be in the White House. The Supreme Court would be transmuted into a religious tribunal. And, the name of Jesus would be on everyone's lips. Pornographic magazines, books, movies, videocassettes, pamphlets, pictures, slides, sexual paraphenalia, and non-Christian works concerning, endorsing, or teaching evolution or the equality of all religions as well as the absence of religion, would all be burned on an open pyre flamed with the torch of intolerance. The Christian Protestant Bible would become the final authority on all subjects.

To save the United States, Pat would need access not only to the pulpit but to the power. If he could not change the direction of a hurricane, he could not change the hearts of the people of the United States, and if he could not change the hearts of the people of the United States, Pat could not change the hearts, thinking, and emotions of the people of the world. If such would occur the only solution was to let go the terror of a nuclear holocaust that would rush those few saved fundamental evangelicals into the arms of god, while the rest of the world, like the people drowned by the jealous god in the days of the legendary Noah, perished from the earth in balls of nuclear fire.

He would gain his goal by increasing the acceptability and visibility of his televangelistic ministry by way of the "700 Club"9 and by achieving the office of the president of the United States.

Robertson was worried that his ordination would be a stumbling block with voters. He decried what he saw in the United States as religious bigotry. Feeling that he could best serve his god by resigning his ordination commission, Robertson vowed that he would run as a businessman and corporate executive.

Robertson's knowledge concerning the Constitution of the United States is equally marginal in this area. There is no prohibition in the United States Constitution against any minister of any faith running for public office. On 19 April 1978, the United States Supreme Court unanimously ruled a provision in the Tennessee Constitution written in 1796, prohibiting ordained ministers from serving in political positions, was unconstitutional.[10]

The Founding Fathers of the United States were sensitive about ministers of religion serving in civil capacities. Many of the early Constitutional signers were opposed to the clergy running for public office or having positions in government. They took this stand in order to assure the success of a new and innovative political experiment: the separation of state and church.

Members of the early congresses who sat to chart a course for the emerging states were painfully aware of Anglican control of the British government. Many were personally confronted with denominational control of the colonies. Still, they believed in the right of all people to be treated equitably and fairly.

In pursuit of equality our Founding Fathers argued that all men should be treated the same — regardless of any individual belief or lack of the same. Clergy in the collective thirteen states were to be guaranteed the same rights and protection as all other white men; the Founders only expressed hope that the clergy would treat those who were not in clerical orders with the same justice and civility.

Since organized religion is totally subjective it cannot serve to minister to the objectivity of reality, a sentiment expressed forcefully by Voltaire. Good government cannot be subject to that which is not objective, yet Robertson is determined to parade religious subjectivity across the United States and put regressive biblical precepts in place where advanced egalitarian progressivity exists.

To fashion himself as a "man of the people," the televangelist gave up his ordination papers on 27 September 1987. He had been ordained a minister at the Freemason Street Baptist Church in Portsmouth, Virginia, in 1961. What few citizens in the United States know is that Southern Baptist preacher Pat Robertson never served in the capacity of full-time pastor anywhere. Could his ordination have been only a rue to cover his real intent? Was it a prospect toward an easy life that would afford him the leisure to plot his own political *putsch*?[11]

Notes

1. Robertson, *Shout It from the Housetops*, p. 196.

2. *TV Guide* (25 October 1986) "Cheers and Jeers."

3. Robertson, *Shout It from the Housetops*, p. 197.

4. Rev. 22:18. Note the key word "add," which in Greek is *epitithemi, reflecting the Hebrew yasaph* ("increasing") which appears in the Old Testament prohibition found in Deut. 4:2 and 12:32. This is but another example of Robertson's transmogrification of the Bible and basic theological literature in his quest for power. Cp. Robertson, *Shout It from the Housetops,* 197, 199, 203-204, 215, 226, 230, 255.

5. *Washington Post* (9 September 1986).

6. Bruce Buursma, "Evangelist's Attacks on Lear Are Unfounded, Cleric Writes," Little Rock *Arkansas Gazette* (24 January 1987), p. 15.

7. Richard Cohen, "Politically, Robertson Is Fair Game," *Detroit Free Press* (29 September 1986), sec. A, p. 12. *The Orange County* [California] *Register* (2 October 1986), sec. A, p. 18. Cf. Associated Press (19 September 1986).

8. *The Sun-Herald* (19 September 1986), sec. A, p. 7.

9. Robertson, *Shout It from the Housetops,* pp. 197ff.

10. *McDaniel vs. Paty* U.S. 618, 98 S.Ct. 1322; 55L.ED. 2d 593 1978.

11. Madalyn O'Hair, "Believers Are Ill Prepared to Govern," *USA Today* (16 February 1988), sec. A, p. 6.

Chapter 7
Economics, The Hunt Connection, and
The I.R.S.

Robertson's goal is to make the Southern Baptist faith the universal faith of mankind.[1] It is to surpass, supplant, and then replace all other faiths. Roman Catholicism, Islam, and other Protestant denominations faiths are opposed to Pat's Protestant interpretation and, therefore, are unacceptable to his god.[2]

Robertson has declared that he will take his ministry to Buddhists and Atheists. His god is to convert them through Pat's personal preaching.[3]

If he is to be "stopped" in his quest to conquer the world for Christ, it would only occur by the power of Satan[4] which has become the "counterforce" to his god. Robertson's deity has devolved into the classic yin and yang: an Ahura Mazda fighting demons of darkness. Robertson is equally determined to convert the Jews and works to establish an electronic ministry in Israel,[5] planning for a super-powered station to be located near the Dead Sea.[6] Africa is to fall under his sway by similar means.[7]

Pat Robertson hoped that he would pay for these encroachments on the human mind by dipping into the pockets of Herbert and Bunker Hunt of Dallas, Texas.[8] The Hunts, the sons of H. L. Hunt, who died of brain cancer, were among the wealthiest people in the United States. As members of First Baptist Church of Dallas, they are subservient to Wallace A. Criswell and his brand of Christianity. Collectively, Robertson believed, the Hunts promised to give Robertson's CBN a gift of $10 million, and promised, through the alleged illegitimate daughter of H. L. Hunt, Lucy, that the sum would be increased to $40 million.

Lucy wanted CBN to receive $100 million. This gift was to come in the form of stocks and cash. The stocks were, supposedly, kept in Denison, Texas, while the money remained in the Republic National Bank of Dallas. There was confusion, however, if this "gift" would ever take place. Ultimately Herbert Hunt informed Robertson that there was no "illegitimate daughter of H. L., by the name of Lucy," and the bequest and gift of money did not materialize. After this incident "in betrayal," Pat recalled that he had received a message from his god that said "a woman is going to deceive you," closely similar to the admonition found in Revelation: 20:2.

He discovered that the Hunt brothers, who funded the anti-Semitic organization "Christ for the Nations," had tied too much of their personal wealth up in other adventures and they would use their monies in a plot to corner the silver market.

To raise the monies which did not materialize from the Hunts of Dallas, Pat changed his message. In addition to healing the sick, he began promising to save the lives of others, but when his mother lay dying, Pat discovered that he could not save her life.[9] He had no power over life and death, a claim that became more popular with Oral Roberts of Tulsa, Oklahoma. He had not become god — yet — and some of his empire pulled away from him to go with the even more charismatic Jim and Tammy Faye Bakker, ". . . who began to get happy in the Lord . . . virtually screaming with joy."[10] (This joy, however, was not necessarily totally "in the Lord," for Jim would find greater pleasure in the mouth of a church secretary [getting there what most would find on top of a bear: head] and Tammy Faye would revel in cosmetics, body toning, and surgery — spending tens of thousands of dollars for breast enlargements while at the same time putting other contributions from faithful Pentecostalists into a plan for melting off unwanted poundage on her body. Meanwhile, she created a personal cult complete with dolls, records, and posters. Screams of "We love you! God loves you!" between members of this cult replaced courteous hellos and other salubrious salutations.[11] The "PTL Club" promised to rival Pat's "700 Club.")

Although Robertson colored himself as a religious man of great honesty and piety in an effort to rewin the hearts and cash of those who had drifted over to the PTL Club, researchers have discovered that, like the popes and other powerful potentates and ecclesiastics, Pat is neither honest nor pious. An assiduous double-speak artist who delights in distortion of fact, he has made himself appear to be an enlightened economist who studied at the London School of

Economics, taking an undergraduate degree in economics.[12]

At one point he boasted of his education in economics, claiming on CBS's "Face the Nation" that "I have ten years of higher education. . . . I've been to school, in graduate school at the University of London," a claim that appeared even in the prestigious *Wall Street Journal*.[13] The deliberately made impression was that he had studied in post-graduate economic classes at the London School of Economics. The University of London confirms only a three-month summer study course in 1950, a course that focused on British art and architecture, aimed primarily at visiting American students, not a course in economics. Spokesmen at the London School of Economics have no recollection of Pat Robertson as a student and he certainly never took a degree from that prestigious institution.[14]

Robertson's understanding of economics is at best amateurish. His economic prognostications and proposals are Bible-based[15] and outside mainstream economic thought.

What bothers most economists about Robertson's proposals is their inadequacy to meet contemporary needs and their potential threat to economic stability and enhancement. For instance, Robertson told the viewing audience of his "700 Club" that debts should be universally canceled every fifty years.[16] In January 1981, Robertson proposed that the United States follow an Old Testament Jewish practice and adopt a constitutional amendment that would read: "At the end of every forty-nine years would be a fiftieth year of Jubilee. In the year of Jubilee, all debts would be canceled."[17]

At the same time Pat proposes that the federal government cancel all debts, the televangelist proposes that the Federal Reserve[18] and the Social Security systems should be abolished. "Funds placed in God's kingdom will prosper regardless of the business cycle," Robertson wrote, even if the American economy went bankrupt.[19]

In 1979, Robertson predicted, "The odds are about 85-15 that we will experience a major worldwide depression in the early 1980s." This depression[20] in the United States and throughout the world would be followed by a Soviet attack on the Middle East and a nuclear war "on an awesome scale" that would "probably [occur] by 1982."[21]

As more people discovered Robertson's flights of fancy (predictions based on biblical prophecy), many began to question Robertson's sanity. To stop "leakage" of information from the Robertson camp, officials of Robertson's empire offered former employees $100 to sign a confidentiality agreement[22] barring them from discussing the Freedom Council in the future should they be approached by reporters.

The Confidentiality Agreement is a seventeen-page document pledging the signer not to disclose, without prior approval of council officials, "records, files, data, and all information about the council."

Such silence is seen as essential. Jerry R. Curry, past president of the council made this clear when he stated the council in the past made false statements to the Internal Revenue Service (IRS) about its activities.[23]

It is instructive to tread the trail of the Freedom Council for the exercise gives an insight into Robertson's corporate and financial manuevering.

The Freedom Council, Inc. first set up in Virginia in 1981, was founded "to increase participation by Christians in the political process." Robertson was the president and the stated purpose was to be obtained through "prayer, education and action." At that time the group had a 501(c)(4) federal tax exemption which permitted it to lobby for conservative issues, but it could not support individual candidates in any political elections, in any way.

The significance of an IRS tax exemption action is that contributors to Robertson, under whatever corporate name, can deduct their contributions from their taxable income at time of filing their individual 1040 tax returns. Since this encourages gift giving all "cause" organizations, left, right or center, seek out this status with Internal Revenue Service.

The initial financing for the Freedom Council came from the Christian Broadcasting Network (CBN) which helped to staff the council, gave it offices, and provided payroll money. Yet, the first tax return that it filed showed no income, no expenses, and no donation of either services or money from CBN. It also showed that it had no officers or directors in common with any other groups. This was a flat misrepresentation since Pat Robertson was president of both CBN and the Freedom Council. CBN was in fact "paying the freight" for the Freedom Council as a part of CBN's budget. Additionally, the Freedom Council continued to be listed as one of the network's project — Project 0015, to be exact. In a February 10, 1986, review of CBN's "engineering maintenance division" expenditures alone, the internal budget indicated $5,688.96 spent on Project 0015.

The problem is that CBN's tax exemption is under Section 501(c)(3) of the Internal Revenue Code, which prohibits the exempt group (in this case CBN) from donating to a group that operates under a restrictive political purpose exemption (in this case the Freedom Council).

Former officers of the Freedom Council state that CBN gave tens of thousands of dollars a month in the first years and later as much as $200,000 to $250,000 a month by late 1985. The council's finances were handled exclusively by Robertson, who also set its policies.

CBN's budget did not list any grants, payments, donations of money or of services to the council from 1982 through March, 1985. However, in 1984 it did list a loan of $821,000 to the council — although the former officers said no loan existed. The council's 1984 tax return showed no loans payable. It showed no donations over $5,000, no affiliation with CBN, and no "flow through" of funds.

But, the Freedom Council was passing on $35,000 a month to an organization known as the Freedom Council Foundation, Inc. Pat had set up this group in 1982 "to litigate religious issues" and, of course, it also received a tax exemption that year. During the years 1982 to 1985 this corporation filed no tax returns. It operated until June 1985 when it was dissolved and immediately reorganized with exactly the same name, according to state records. The documents filed with the state of Virginia gave no reason for the actions taken. A reporter seeking out information found simply that "changes of name and incorporation status were frequent in the Robertson organizations . . . ."

In January 1986, the Freedom Council Foundation changed its name to the National Freedom Institute, Inc.

On the exact same day, a new Freedom Council, Inc. was organized by all of the officers of the old Freedom Council and again, the Internal Revenue Service was petitioned for a tax exemption under 501(c)(3). This Freedom Council claimed in its application papers that it had not grown out of another organization, and had no relationship with any other organization as a result of common directors. In fact, the old and the new directors were the same, and many of the affairs of the old council were handled by the new one. Are you following all of this? There will be a short quiz at the end of the chapter.

The new Freedom Council wrote to the I.R.S. in April 1986 and asked for a quick approval (by May 1986) since two big donations were hinging on such approval. The two big donations were said to be an anticipated $500,000 from the Aldolph Coors Foundation and $150,000 from the (Penfield, NY) Kiwanis Club. Spokesmen for both organizations later denied such contributions had been promised.

The council was to be run by political specialists with strong ties to Paul M. Weyrick, who founded the conservative Heritage Foundation. Its stated goal was said to be to increase participation by Christians in the political process, and it was to operate under 501(c)(4) of the Internal Revenue Code, as indicated, that section which permits political activity but prohibits intervention in behalf of any candidates if the tax-exempt station is to be retained. The tax-exemption status was granted on Saturday, 7 June, 1986 — the actual action having taken place in Baltimore, Maryland, on 28 May.

What is instructive here is that the Freedom Council, on May 27 (the day before), succeeded in persuading more than 4,500 people to run for the offices of precinct delegates in the August 5 Michigan primaries. Everyone in the nation agrees that this resulted in a clear boost for Robertson's Michigan campaign. The cost of the effort was approximately $300,000 spent by the Freedom Council.

On May 16, 1986, Robertson held a fund-raising, $25,000-per-couple, dinner at the Washington Sheraton Hotel. Twenty-four persons were in attendance, one of which was H L. Hunt, of course. He was asked by Robertson to pay for his dinner with two checks. One for $5,000 (the largest donation allowed under federal campaign finance law) was to be written to the Committee for Freedom, Robertson's political action committee. The second, for $20,000 was to be written to the Freedom Council, for that "educational" organization had no prohibitive top cap put on any contribution. Robertson maintained to the end that the Freedom Council in Michigan had simply encouraged "people who care about traditional values" to enter "the political process." This was done, he alleged, "on a non-partisan basis," and the entire operation was simply one of educating.

The actual Robertson material distributed in Michigan asked donors to declare:

> Yes, Pat! I will try to become a delegate in my precinct. Yes, Pat! Have someone contact me from the Freedom Council. I want to volunteer. Yes, Pat! I want to help pay for Operation Michigan. Enclosed is my one-time gift. All gifts are fully tax-deductible. Make checks payable to: The Freedom Council.

How, indeed, could any message be more impartial, more non-partisan?

Speaking for those his council had recruited, he claimed:

> Christians in Michigan can say we stand for values, we stand for family, we stand for God and country, we stand for liberty and freedom.

In July, Robertson wrote a letter to his supporters boasting how he "educated, trained, and motivated" his private army all with the funds of this Freedom Council.[23]

Dear Friend,
    THE CHRISTIANS HAVE WON!

Your support of the Freedom Council has helped to make it possible.

You've probably already heard — it's been heralded by the media since the day after it happened. [Reference is to the May 27 filing deadline for precinct delegate candidates] . . . We went into the State of Michigan, we gave believers the tools they needed to file as precinct delegates all over the state — and thousands responded! . . .

Our work was most dramatically demonstrated by the fact that, on the Republican side of the response, the delegate applicants that we educated, trained, and motivated outnumbered the delegate applicants registered through the efforts of both Vice President George Bush and U.S. Congressman Jack Kemp combined!

This effort was significant because once precinct delegates have been elected, they have within their grasp the power to select nominees for numerous major offices in the state — including candidates for State Supreme Court, *the entire Michigan school board* [original emphasis] and delegates to the 1988 National Convention.

What a thrust for freedom! What a breakthrough for the Kingdom! . . . And as believers become involved in this process, they will be able to turn this nation back to its traditional moral values. That's my prayer. And that's what we've begun to see in Michigan. . . .

We know it can happen elsewhere. We saw the hand of God going before us in Michigan, affirming our every step. We went to city after city, and everywhere I found thousands of believers jumping to their feet, ready to work, ready to pray, ready to give — thrilled that their time had finally come. . . .

Your friend
/s/ Pat Robertson, Founder

The Freedom Council Institute was dissolved on October 1, 1986.

At the time of its dissolution, a written statement was issued that the council's mission had been misunderstood and misstated by the press, and the public. No other statements were ever made. Robertson's Freedom Council had an annual budget of about $4 million for its nationwide activities — in keeping with the "poverty of Jesus."[24]

Very little can be said of these shenanigans by other aspirants to political office. Sen. Gary Hart, D-Colo., Rep. Jack Kemp, R-NY, and Arizona Gov. Bruce Babbitt have set up tax-deductible "think-tank" foundations to pick up the tab for their political groundwork. Hart's is the Center for a New Democracy and Kemp's is the Fund for an American Renaissance. Vice President Bush has set up a Fund for America's Future, which accepts non-deductible contributions — since he has never felt a need for money for his overfinanced campaign.

Robertson may well have patterned his Freedom Council after them, for the "think-tanks" are creatively described as organizations which "examine issues and encourage public participation" in politics. They have been called "the new twilight zone of campaign politics." While federal tax laws prohibits any such tax-exempt group from endorsing candidates or campaigning on their behalf, they are permitted to advocate economic and political points of view. The groups cheerfully pay for research staffs, voter recruitment, direct mail lists — and even sponsor political "issue" seminars if media coverage is likely to be achieved.[25]

The Internal Revenue Service, instead of moving against Robertson, since obviously he had fractured, if not broken, the I.R.S. regulations, does nothing. One cannot alienate the fundamentalist religious vote of the nation by going after a king pin such as Robertson, such an action could well unsettle the Republican radical right. Therefore, the I.R.S. has initiated an "investigation" into the activities of politically active tax-exempt foundations, and has ordered the Federal Election Commission to check into their actions.[26]

James Ellis, a former consultant to Robertson's Michigan organization, noted, "I'm sure there's going to be an I.R.S. inquiry. There would almost have to be." But such an audit would have a devastating impact on the Robertson presidential bid and likely it will be put off until the millenium.[27]

Notes

1. For a history of the Baptist attack on personal civil liberties, see my *Evangelical Terrorism*, pp. 1-68.

2. Robertson, *Shout It from the Housetops*, pp. 209-25.

3. Robertson, *Shout It from the Housetops*, see: pp. 208.

4. Robertson, *Shout It from the Housetops*, see: p. 212.

5. Robertson, *Shout It from the Housetops*, see: p. 230.

6. Robertson, *Shout It from the Housetops*, see: p. 232.

7. Robertson, *Shout It from the Housetops*, see: p. 229.

8. Robertson, *Shout It from the Housetops*, p. 235-36.

9. Robertson, *Shout It from the Housetops*, p. 213.

10. Robertson, *Shout It from the Housetops*, p. 215-16.

11. Robertson, *Shout It from the Housetops*, p. 222.

12. Howard Phillips, "Pat Robertson Adds Perspective," in *Conservative Digest* (January 1986): pp. 93, 95. Robertson gives *U.S. News & World Report* as his source on the power of the chairperson of the Federal Reserve System and argues that the agency needs to be "brought under the control of the elected officials of this country" — which it already is.

13. 17 October 1985. This same distortion of Robertson's educational background is given by his publisher, Thomas Nelson of Nashville, as seen on the back cover/dust jacket of Robertson's *The Secret Kingdom*, which lists Pat as an economist. Pat's economic education, like this economic knowledge, is marginal and primarily based on Old Testament writings, as discussed below in this paper.

14. John L. Fialka, "Robertson's Presidential Bid Invites Scrutiny of His Economic Credentials," in *Wall Street Journal* (26 December 1986), p. 26.

15. Robertson, *Answers*, pp. 32, 196, 262-63, 231-32.

16. Pat Robertson in his *Perspectives*, now found only in the rare book room of the library of his CBN University and not made available to the general public which has been told since 1982 that the *Perspectives* are "unavailable."

17. Robertson, *Answers*, p. 196.

18. For a humorous view on Robertson's plan, see Kirk in the *Toledo* [Ohio] *Blade* (30 May 1986), p. 14.

19. Robertson, *Answers*, pp. 262-63.

20. Cf. Robertson, *Answers*, p. 32.

21. Fialka, loc cit.

22. Jeff Gerth, "Robertson and Confidentiality," *New York Times* (19 March 1987).

23. Hugh McDiarmid, "Robertson's Letter Strips away Myth," *Detroit Free Press* (17 July 1986).

24. *See Washington Post* (8 June 1986), p. A17. For an analysis of the rising phenomenon of religious political action committees, see William Schneider, "Amen to Politics: Ministers Move the Parties, Left and Right," *Los Angeles Times* (22 June 1986), pt. V, pp. 1, 3; Angelia Herrin, "Tax-Exempt Foundations Pick up Political Tab." *Knight-Ridder Service, San Antonio Light* (8 June 1986). sec. K, p. 4.

25. See: "Painful Scrutiny for Pat; Mounting Questions About the Political Preacher," *Newsweek* (13 October 1986), p. 48; Thomas B. Edsall, "Evangelist's Tax Status, Gifts Raising Questions," *Washington Post* (15 June 1986); Jeff Gerth, "Robertson Groups May Have Filed Faulty IRS Papers," Tacoma, WA *News Tribune* (11 December 1986) sec. A, p. 11; Thomas B. Edsall, "Pledge Made to IRS to Avoid Campaign," *Washington Post* (21 June 1986) sec. A, p. 4; April Witt, "Robertson Unit Faces IRS Audit," *The Virginia Ledger Star* (18 October, 1986); George Weeks, "IRS Audits Robertson Group," *Detroit News* (19 October 1986), sec. A, p. 19; . Jeff Gerth, "Robertson Groups' Tax Records Scrutinized," *The Orange County* California *Register*, (10 December 1986) sec. C, p. 1; Jeff Gerth, "Tax Data of Pat

Robertson Groups Are Questioned," *New York Times* (10 December, 1986).

26. *New York Times* 20 May 1987. Curry replaced Robertson as the council's president in late 1985. In May 1986 he was replaced by a former editor of *The New York Times*, Bob G. Slosser, a longtime associate of Robertson who co-authored *The Secret Kingdom: A Promise of Hope and Freedom in A World of Turmoil* (Nashville: Nelson, 1983; paperback: New York: Bantam, 1984).

27. Richard N. Ostling, "Power, Glory — And Politics," *Time* (17 February 1986): 62, 67. Robertson's Southern Baptists have a special "mission" to the poor, to "win them for Jesus," and keep them impoverished. See Mary Calvert, " 'Backpack' Evangelism Wins Streets," *Baptist Standard* 96.35 (29 August 1984): p. 4.

Chapter 8
Abortion

Robertson has unique and unorthodox designs on, and ideas concerning, the Constitution and the enforcement of constitutional provisions and judgments of law in the United States as defined by the Supreme Court. Pat's ideas are most strong on the issue of freedom of choice concerning abortion.

Robertson, as a Republican presidential candidate,[1] declared his firm opposition to abortion[2] before 250 people at the Memphis, Tennessee, Public Affairs Council luncheon at the Radisson Hotel on 17 June 1987. Robertson "made it clear [that] he would not honor a request to send federal marshals to enforce a hypothetical pro-abortion Supreme Court decision if state officers blocked abortion clinic doors. 'I would respectfully decline,' Robertson said," to enforce such a pro-abortion ruling by the United States Supreme Court[3] — in spite of the fact that the presidential oath of office of the United States requires all presidents to "uphold and defend" the Constitution which, of course, includes Supreme Court rulings interpreting contemporary laws by the criteria set in that Constitution.

In Denver in the summer of 1986, Robertson told anti-choice activists that abortions were the work of "despots." These "despots," he declared, were the "liberals" on the Supreme Court who had ruled in favor of choice in the landmark case *Roe v. Wade*.[4]

Coupling his arguments against the "killing of unborn babies," with promises, Robertson declared that the "liberals" of the Supreme Court would be killed by his god in retribution for the "slaughter of babies [sic: fetuses]."

125

In 1986, Robertson's Old Testament wrath rose to a fevered pitch when he talked of the "five old men" who had voted pro-choice. He delighted in the thought of the deaths of one or more of the Supreme Court justices:

> With the wonderful process of the mortality tables, only one more seat is needed for reversal.

And his neo-fascist adherents cheered him on.

The evangelical candidate accused the justices who composed the majority in *Roe v. Wade* of committing "runaway excesses" by allowing no "surcease in the inexorable, the wanton, slaughter of innocents in this nation."[5] Robertson was even more angry when the Supreme Court later, but by a more narrow margin, voted to uphold the hated *Roe v. Wade*. Instead of blasting the Supreme Court in general Robertson aimed again at the "five old men." Passionately, Pat claimed that an option to abort, given to a pregnant woman, was a disguise for cold-blooded murder.

Although Robertson's opposition to freedom of choice flowed freely from him, he was outdone by the demagoguery of one-time football player Jack Kemp of New York who blasted pro-choice advocates, argued "America needs more children" and promised that he would introduce into Congress a bill that would deprive women of limited or moderate means of obtaining a medically safe abortion of unwanted fetal matter. Without protective laws the same women would need to resort to back alley butchers and probable death in discharging the unacceptable cells attached to their uterus. George Bush, another leading candidate for the GOP nomination to the presidency of the United States, also favors an amendment to the Constitution that would severely limit a woman's freedom of choice. Bush is most adamant on not permitting victims of rape and incest to terminate the product of their violation from their bodies. This, of course, is diametrically opposed to his stand in 1980, but Bush, as a *politique*, is quick to change sides when such action might bring him votes, for, like Ronald Reagan, he has no ethics and no firm stand on anything but seeing himself elected and being written into the pages of history.[5]

Is abortion the murder of innocent "babies"? Medical evidence does not agree with the radical religious right's interpretation of abortion. Dr. Michael Bennet, chairman of the neuroscience department of the Albert Einstein School of Medicine in New York City, emphatically declared in 1986 that the brain does not exist at the time of conception.

A fetus without a brain can no more be considered a human being, than it can be thought to be a fish, a dog, a cat, or anything else. Without a brain a fetus cannot function above cell stage activity.

Conception does not give personhood to a fetus, as Robertson claims. Conception only generates a union of cells with the potential of being a human being having a brain and the promise of a possible evolution of the cells necessary to reach probable personhood — if generation is normal and all cellular matter is within the union structure.

Without a brain there is neither "humanity" nor activity. The brain is the organ of consciousness. Consciousness is the ability to perceive sensations, perception, and conscious experience.

Without a brain a fetus cannot withdraw from a painful experience, as Bernard Nathanson has falsified in his spurious and medically inaccurate film, *The Silent Scream*. Not only can a fetus *not* withdraw from a possible painful experience, it cannot perceive that it is going to be hurt or even destroyed. As the chair of neuroanatomy at the Yale University School of Medicine noted in a detailed letter to the *Washington Post* (9 February 1985), a twelve-week-old fetus cannot move independently at will seeking to thwart an abortion for it cannot sense an attempted abortion.[6]

A twelve-week-old fetus (the average age of a fetus that is aborted) cannot scream or utter any form of speech since it does not have synapses of the cortex, which do not develop in a fetus until its last months — definitely not in the first three months!

The twelve-week fetus is not able to feel pain since the brain is not fully developed. It has no cognitive reason(s) to "scream."This is because well-formed nerve endings/fibers which can transmit pain impulses along the spinal cord to the brain and chemical neurotransmitters capable of carrying the signal from neuron to neuron indicating pain or the presence of discomforture (as well as pleasure and other sensations) are not developed and the neural pathways which transmit impulses are not mature enough to function until mid-pregnancy or later. There is no record of any such necessary neurological development in a fetus in the first trimester of human generation.[6]

Not only is fetal material without a brain at the point of conception, but there are no brain neurons prior to four weeks into the fetal development. The cerebral cortex — that portion of the brain needed for thought processes, feelings, and conscious awareness and motor skill motivational actions — is the last part of the brain to fully develop.[7] The brain has never been found to have fully developed — with all essential facets as discussed above — in a twelve-week-old fetus — a medical fact that disproves the emotionally charged literature of Nathanson, Robertson, Falwell, and other anti-choice terrorists, as well as the wishful thinking of women and men who want to see all pregnancies terminate only through full development of the fetus and its normal.[8]

Dr. Dominick Purpura, former dean of the Stanford University School of Medicine, and present (1987) dean at the Albert Einstein School of Medicine in New York City, has gone on record testifying that the development of the cortex with sufficient axions, dendrites, and synapses to sustain the process of thought, feeling, and awareness that Bernard Nathanson argues in his distortion of fact, the fantasy movie *The Silent Scream*, to be necessary for personhood does not exist before the twenty-eighth week. Thus Nathanson's twelve-week-old fetus — which in *The Silent Scream* was only a plastic doll[9] — is nothing but cell matter. It is not an infant. It is not a fetus. It is not even a protofetus. It is not a human being. Women who are concerned about the fetal development but have little opportunity to study neuroscience and appreciate the plethora of medical knowledge frequently hallucinate that the fetus is "talking," "moving" independently, "seeing" through the uterus into the world, and similar audio/visual/motor functionings.[10]

For personhood to begin, a variety of gradual evolutionary steps is required. These "steps in evolution" do not offer the minimal, limited, or even boundary conditions for personhood until after the fetus is no less than seven months old. This fact by itself not only discredits Nathanson's *The Silent Scream*, but puts the lie to the Robertson rhetoric.

In spite of medical evidence, Robertson continues to lead the radical religious right in the GOP movement against freedom of choice for abortion by pregnant women. Robertson, the televangelist, has labeled the Supreme Court justices who voted for the right of women to terminate a pregnancy "despots"[11] who had, in his myopic thinking, turned the Constitution into a "sentence of death." He urged a gathering of Denver anti-choice activists to become more involved in politics to help "rid this country of the runaway excesses of five unelected men in black robes on the Supreme Court," and saw hope only in the mortality of the judges.[12]

Robertson in his television ministry brought the issue of choice into mainstream discussion. He has given those opposed to abortion in the United Statees a trumpet to use against the constitutional walls protecting the right of choice, and heralded the advent of one of the most bitter opponents of human freedom, Antonin Scalia, to the Supreme Court. Sitting at the bench of justice, Scalia has removed the bandage from the eyes of liberty, and has hurled the scales of justice to the floor where his personal feelings march against the rights of the oppressed. It is in the Supreme Court chamber that Scalia darts daggers into the very bosom of liberty in his mad quest to enslave dissenters to this own parochial mentality.[13] Fitting Robertson's mold for a "good justice," Scalia has brought his personal, narrow, religious ideas into a court which in the past has considered the general good of the commonwealth without reflecting upon personal considerations. No longer, with Scalia on the Supreme Court, is there "liberty and justice for all," for leagued with Sandra Day O'Connor and William Rehnquist, Scalia offers liberty and justice only to those who agree with him and worship his god.

The disintegration of the Supreme Court is one of the focuses of his book *America's Dates With Destiny*. In this book, Robertson styles fetal cells "unborn children,"[14] contrary to all medical fact on embryology and neurological understanding.[15] The "unborn child" is repetitively used to define the fetus — even though the fetus cannot suckle, experience pain, laugh or cry, and cannot sustain itself.

Robertson cites the Fourteenth Amendment as his defense for attacking abortion and the women who seek to avail themselves of a medically safe discharge of fetal matter. Justice Blackmum did not, and does not, agree, writing, "A fetus is not a person under the Constitution and thus has no legal right of life."[16]

For an individual who allegedly has studied law, as Pat Robertson's credentials bear witness, it is unusual to cite the Fourteenth Amendment as supporting anti-choice tactics and opposition to a woman's freedom of choice. The Fourteenth Amendment was a product of Reconstruction following the Civil War. It does not mention the fetus.

Section 1 of the Fourteenth Amendment declares that all persons born or naturalized in the United States are citizens of the United States and the states of their residence. This clause was the first time in our nation's history that the Constitution defined citizenship. The words grant citizenship only to those who have been *born* — not those who are in a state of evolving to a point in time that might lead to their birth — and those who are naturalized, having been born and migrating to the United States. Those individuals who are born in the United States, as well as those who are naturalized, having been born in some nation other than the United States, are, next, guaranteed the right to life, liberty, and property — again the Fourteenth Amendment says nothing about the *unborn*. But Robertson, like other "strict interpretaters of the Constitution," such as Robert Bork, Reagan nominee to sit on the Supreme Court, deny this and wish to go beyond a "strict literal" reading of the Constitution to gain their own goals: stopping a born woman's right to pursue her liberty in determining the destiny of her property: namely her own body.

Continuing distorting fact in favor of fiction, Robertson claims that the anti-choice/anti-abortion people outnumber pro-choice/pro-abortion supporters. Actual national surveys show the numbers to be reversed. Robertson claims that the Gallup Poll and other polls lie to insure themselves of other commissions.

Robertson does acknowledge that those who opposed the Supreme Court decision on *Roe v. Wade* are so opposed to the "killing of millions of babies" that they have vowed they would kill the justices who voted in favor of the right of a woman's choice to make her own decisions.[17] He cites comments craftily created by Roman Catholic prelates in opposition to the Court's decision — even though over 60 percent of all Roman Catholics in America favor birth control and support abortion — a fact elucidated upon by Maria Schriver in August 1987.[18]

Arguing for a "strict literal" interpretation of the Constitution, Robertson voiced concern that *Roe v. Wade* was equal to the *Dred Scott Decision* and argued that the Supreme Court was empowered only to "settle disputes" on the basis of "this Constitution, the Laws of the United States, and Treaties made"[19] without recognizing that the judges had done just that. Since the days of the Founding Fathers, the Supreme Court has not accepted a staid and ossified definition of the words of the Constitution, but instead used the words as foundation for current needs and intrepreted the message of the Founding Fathers to be relevant for all times — not in a biblical *ex cathedra* sense, strangling human evolution or limiting the development of intellect and the advance of self-actualization.[20]

What Robertson, in truth, is arguing for is a theocracy.[21] This would be a government run by Judeo-Christian ministers in charge of legislation, the judiciary commissioned to render judgment based upon the eternal Judeo-Christian Bible that would never change to meet current or evolving circumstance.

Robertson is against "moral neutrality" in government, arguing that it is the responsibility of government and education to teach morals and values, implying that the lessons to be learned are Christian morals and values as opposed to any other religious beliefs, principles, morality, or valuation.[22] Robertson's churches are to get involved in politics on all levels. "Good Christians" (meaning those who endorse and adhere to a strict biblical literalism in a rigid form of Christian fundamentalism) are to lead the political process,[23] sit in Congress, occupy the White House and judge from the bench of the Supreme Court those who do not conform to the Christian perspective elucidated by Robertson.[24]

In regards to what Robertson would do about abortion if he were to be elected president of the United States, the Virginian has presented his stand in a flier released by "Americans for Robertson" committee of Chesapeake, Virginia. Not only does he see the act of abortion as "murder," but he would stop all federal funds being used to finance an abortion — even if the funding and abortion action was necessary to save the woman's life who was carrying the fetus.

The Reagan Admisnistration has frequently fed federal funds and functions into Pat's spiritual empire, CBN. When the Reagan Administration began its anti-drug campaign, it singled out Robertson's fundamentalist Christian Broadcast Network for a special role in the attack on illegal drugs. Phil Baum, associate executive director of the American Jewish Congress noted, correctly, that Robertson's organization would undermine the effort to involve all churches equally in the effort and would violate the constitutional prohibition against governmental establishment of religion. Baum declared,

> [Reagan's] Task Force . . . saw fit to single out Reverend Pat Robertson's Christian Broadcast Network as a preferred vehicle for this purpose. Endowing a particular religious institution with special status undermines the effort to involve all churches equally. . . . More profoundly, it contravenes the constitutional prohibition against governmental establishment of religion, one of whose essential requirements is that the federal government may not confer special standing upon any one church or denomination or its constituency. By assigning special responsibilities to the Christian Broadcast Network, an integral part of the Rev. Robertson's religious mission, the task force has signaled to the nation that as far as the White House is concerned, Rev. Robertson and his church enjoy a unique place among American religions. The task force has thus placed the imprimatur of the presidency on a particular group of congregants and indicated that the Administration has special confidence in its work.[25]

Taking a cue from Ronald Reagan, who insisted that abortion decisions should be left up to state legislatures,[26] Robertson has publicly declared that abortion of the fetus is strictly a state's rights issue. Furthermore the televangelist argues that the issue of abortion should be determined by each individual state.[27]

A declared states' rightist, Robertson has endorsed HR 1729 (Reagan's Pro-Life bill). HR 1729 is a *national* bill to legislate private morality and abortion *nationwide* — quite out of step with his own stand on state's rights and individual state's right to determine abortion practices and freedom in their own geographical area. Robertson, traditionally, has been inconsistent.

In his cavalier and schizophrenic way, Robertson opposes Grove City legislation (HR 1214), which would require private, religious hospitals that accept medicare/medicaid patients to perform abortions — which Robertson terms the "slaughter of babies" — since its enforcement would be national.[28] Even though this issue is a "local option," since its enactment into law might afford women the individual right of choice to determine whether or not they will maintain the gestation of fetal material in their wombs, Robertson is opposed to it. He is convinced that states' legislatures, primarily composed of men, would continue the mysoginistic chauvinism of the past, and in crazed gynophobia legislate against freedom of choice when it comes to the right of women to determine what happens to their own bodies and the tissues within their bodies.

Interestingly, while opposing the Grove City issue, Robertson supports the Tauke Sensebrenner Amendment that would protect hospitals nationwide from the preceding provision. His erratic stand is justified on the grounds that Robertson is "defending life" — cell or otherwise, and that in this regard his "state's rights" issue is not essential to the case.[29] In short, Robertson argues for whatever issue most dramatically affects his political posturing and his potential to win a presidential race to occupy the White House as a new pharaoh surrounded by Old Testament profits.

Notes

1. Before announcing, Robertson claimed that he was "very reluctant" to do so but justified his announcement, stating "I have been encouraged by at least three United States senators and one former president, who I will not name . . . plus one former national [Republican]

chairman of one of the parties and some other people who are looking at the situation today as sort of an open field." April Witt, "TV Evangelist Ponders Presidency," *The* [Norfolk] *Virginian-Pilot and The Ledger Star* (11 August 1985), sec. A, pp. 1, 16.

2. Robertson, *Answers*, 176-76.

3. *The* [Memphis, TN] *Commercial Appeal* 17 June 1987. Cf. *The* [Memphis, TN] *Commercial Appeal* 18 June 1987.

4. *Roe v. Wade*, 410 U.S. 113; 35 L.Ed.2d. 147; 93 S. Ct. 705 (January 22, 1973).

5. Larry Eichel, "Robertson With An Eye On '88, Tells Abortion Foes That Death Is Their Ally," *Philadelphia Inquirer* (14 April 1986), sec. A, p. 3.

6. Dr. Edwin C. Meyer, chair of Pediatric Neurology of the Medical College of Virginia in Richmond, furthers the details in the *New York Times* (25 February 1985). *See* my *Abortion Handbook: Abortion's History, Practice & Psychology* (Las Colinas, TX: The Liberal Press, 1986; rev. ed. 1987), 20ff.

7. For additional information rejecting Nathanson's eophytic neuro-physiological arguments, see the half-hour documentary by Patricia Jaworski, "Thinking about the *Silent Scream*," first aired in New York City and surrounding communities on Sunday, 18 August 1985. Other information is in my *Abortion Handbook* as cited, above.

8. See the illustrations on brain development in my *Abortion Handbook: Abortion's History, Practice & Psychology* (Las Colinas, TX: The Liberal Press, 1986; rev. ed. 1987), 24.

9. Cf. Marion Deutsche Cohen, *An Ambitious Sort of Grief: Woman, Reproduction & Neo-natal Loss* (Las Colinas, TX: The Liberal Press, 1985). Much of the argument given by Cohen is the result of her own longing to have a living child, as seen in her subsequent books *Shadow of An Angel: Diary of Subsequent Pregnancy Following Neo-Natal Loss* (Las Colinas, TX: The Liberal Press, 1986), and *A Flower Garden: All About It: The Diary of a Woman's Thoughts After Cesarean Birth* (Las Colinas, TX: The Liberal Press, 1987).

10. See my *Abortion Handbook: Abortion's History, Practice &* *Psychology*.

11. Dr. Pasko Pakic, in the *New York Times* (25 January 1985); cp. *Philadelphia Inquirer* (27 January 1985); *Washington Post* (9 February 1985).

12. Larry Eichel, "Robertson: Justices Are 'Despots' on Abortion," *Detroit Free Press* (14 June 1986), sec. A, p. 4.

13. Phil Gailey, "Abortion Foe Sees Hope in Mortality of Justices," *New York Times* (13 June 1986), p. 6.

14. Phil Gailey, "Abortion Knits Religious Right Into G.O.P. Fabric," *New York Times* (19 June 1986), p. 12.

15. Pat Robertson, *America's Dates with Destiny* (New York: William Morrow, 1985), 253ff. Cf. Connie Paige, *The Right to Lifers: Who They Are, How They Operate, Where They Get Their Money* (New York: Summit Books, 1983), 186. Cp. Doris Ludtke, "Robertson Rally: Television Evangelist Spreads His Political Message around The Area," in *The Mellus* [Michigan] *Newspapers* (30 April 1986), sec. F, p. 4; at the Allen Park rally representatives of Robertson's Freedom Council solicited membership among those attending, asking for a donation of $25 per person in exchange for the group's monthly newsletter "which contains 'vital information and instruction to help you become an effective citizen'." This theme is also carried in Remer Tyson's article, "Christian Campaign Rivals Kemp, Bush," in *Detroit Free Press* (4 May 1986), sec. A, pp. 1, 8.

16. Cf. my *Abortion Handbook: The History, Practice and Psychology of Abortion* (Las Colinas: The Liberal Press, 1986: revised edition 1987).

17. *Roe vs. Wade*, 410 U.S. 113 (1973 [January 22]). Summaries, 35 L Ed 2d 147, JANE ROE v. HENRY WADE, 410 US 113, 93 S ct 705, pp. 119f. Cf. Robertson, *America's Dates with Destiny*, 257; and Jerry Falwell, *If I Die Before I Wake* (Nashville: Nelson, 1985), 31-48, for an emotional appeal to a medical fact.

18. Robertson, *America's Dates with Destiny*, 258, in which he cites Bob Woodward and Scott Armstrong, *The Brethren* (New York: Simon and Schuster, 1979), p. 239.

19. *God Is Not Elected*, CBS special, 26 August 1987.

20. United States Constitution, Art. III, Sec. 2.

21. See my *Origins of the (Female) Species* (Dallas: Monument Press, 1986); my *Woman Before History Was Written* (Dallas: Monument Press, 1985); my *Prehistoric Woman* (Mesquite, TX: IHP, 1982). Cp. James Gorman, "Would You Vote For A Man Who Says He's No Kin To An Ape?" *Discover* (December 1986): 25-27.

22. Cf. Patrick B. McGuigan, "The Religious And Political Values Of Dr. Pat Robertson," in *Conservative Digest* (December 1986): pp. 31-38. McGuigan's article's title is quite misleading, as he spends time discussing Robertson's boxing interest, the books Robertson reads, and Robertson's educational development. The title "Dr." which McGuigan accords Robertson is not noted in print as being either (1) an honorary degree, similar to the honorary doctorate conferred on Jerry Falwell, or (2) gleaned from Robertsons' taking a *juris doctoris* degree in law, which is neither a Ph.D or any other form of academic doctorate qualifying Robertson to use the title.

23. Cf. Mark Wingfield, "First Biblical Inerrancy Conference Set at Ridgecrest," *Baptist Standard* 99.5 (4 February 1987): p. 4. Cp. Orville Scott, "Speakers Tell Students: 'Be Radical Witnesses,'" *Baptist Standard* 99.7 (18 February 1987): p. 4.

24. Cf. "1987: A Year Baptists Can Make A Difference," *Baptist Standard* 99.1 (7 January 1987): p. 6. Cp. Ira H. Peak, Jr., "The Theological Case Against . . . State-Sponsored Gambling," *Baptist Standard* 99.13 (1 April 1987): pp. 10, 11; and Ken Camp, "New Bingo Bills Opposed," ibid., pp. 3, 11. Cf. "Strong Argument Against State Run Lottery," *Baptist Standard* 99.2 (14 January 1987): p. 6, and Toby Druin, "Effort Can Stop Gamblers, Says [Phil] Strickland [director of Texas Baptist Christian Life Commission]." *Baptist Standard* 99.11 (16 March 1987): pp. 3, 5; and Presnall H. Wood, "Votes 'Can Be Won': Anti-Gamblers Organize," ibid., p. 9.

25. Robertson, *America's Dates with Destiny*, pp. 302-304.

26. Lexis News Release (27 August 1986). Cp. Ari L. Goldman, "Jewish Congress Assails U.S. Report," *New York Times* (30 August 1986),

27. Reagan's most recent contribution to the growing hysteria over the issue of a woman's freedom of choice in respect to abortion on Saturday, 12 September 1987, when Reagan mourned that *Roe v. Wade* "was another of the court decisions that altered the relationship between state and federal governments." For a digest of various wire reports, see "Reagan: Abortion Decisions Belong to State," *Dallas* [Texas] *Times-Herald* (13 September 1987), sec. A, p. 5.

28. Associated Press (27 June 1986).

29. James Coates, "Abortion Battle Taking on A New Face," *San Francisco Examiner & Chronicle* (15 June 1986), sec. A, p. 3.

Chapter 9
Robertson on The Supreme Court

Robertson is adamantly opposed to any Supreme Court ruling that contradicts his own ideological interpretation of the Constitution concerning human rights,[1] education,[2] god,[3] war and peace.[4] He claims the existing Supreme Court is tantamount to a tyranny[5] that he will, if elected, change either by appointing more than the number currently established,[6] or by praying for the demise of "liberal judges"[7] he has judged to be outside the pale of his god and moral value system.[8] All authority is to come from his god — not from the Constitution.[9]

Since he is quick to condemn anyone, the justices of the United States Supreme Court are an obvious target for his invectives. Robertson's raging hatred against the more conscientious (or, as he calls them — "liberal") judges has led the televangelist into proclaiming that the judges and "a small coterie of liberal activists" will not be satisfied until "the United States is moving in concert with the Union of Soviet Socialist Republics" and a "one-world system" is installed.[10] Not only are the justices charged as being "liberal" with that word being used as an opprobrious epithet, but Robertson has styled them "an elite oligarchy of self-styled rulers,"[11] obviously unaware that a Supreme Court justice is appointed by the president and confirmed by the Senate as required by the Constitution — a constitution about which he speaks volumes but seldom shows a shred of evidence of having ever read.[12]

In a *Washington Post* interview[25] in June of 1986, Robertson heatedly denounced the current composition of the United States Supreme Court. Disclaiming several Supreme Court decisions that countered his own perspectives and interest, Robertson declared that he did not consider Supreme Court rulings the law of the land. Not only did Robertson argue that he would not accept Supreme Court judgments as the official interpretation of law in the United States, but this crafty caretaker of god's word smiled sourly that neither the Congress nor the president of the United States is obligated to follow or enforce Supreme Court decisions.[26]

Robertson is quoted by the Associated Press on Friday, 27 June 1986, as saying:

> I don't think Congress is subservient to the courts. . . . They [the Congress] can ignore a Supreme Court ruling if they so choose. A Supreme Court ruling is not the law of the United States.[27]

Not only does Robertson thus hold openly that "A Supreme Court ruling is not the law of the United States," he has publicly boasted, "I am not bound by any case or court to which I myself am not a party."[28]

Robertson obviously feels that he is above the law, that laws as defined by the Court are not applicable to him — unless he wants them to be, as demonstrated in his personal litigation.

Robertson's attacks on the Supreme Court are clothed in high-sounding phrases, muddled history, and outright misinterpretations of fact. Robertson cites the famous case of *Marbury v. Madison*[13] in formulating his decision not to obey judicial rulings with which he disagrees. Being committed to always call upon a higher power, he asked the dean of his new CBN University Law School for an interpretation on the power of the Supreme Court in order to bolster what he had to say. The dean wrote, and Robertson reiterated, "Neither the Congress nor the president, having not been a party to the case, has a duty to obey a judicial ruling that is contrary to the Constitution."

No one should be shocked at the comment of the dean of CBN's School of Law. This was formerly the law school which Oral Roberts established. It was, then, later moved to CBN. The School of Law instructors have, under both regimes, linked the Bible to legal precedents. They see the two as interchangeable. At CBN the law school begins each class discussion of legal cases and briefs with a prayer that lasts approximately fifteen minutes and calls upon Pat's god to guide the deliberations, directions, decisions, and determinations of both students and faculty. Five of the eight-member faculty at CBN School of Law taught at the Oral Roberts University School of Law.

The CBN School of Law, however, is not accredited by the American Bar Association, and forty-three of the fifty states in the Union, including Virginia, do not allow graduates of unaccredited schools to take bar examinations[14] and practice law in those states.

Reflecting on the CBN stand on the Constitution, the editors of the *Washington Post* noted, "Contrary to the Constitution according to whom?"[15] They continued:

> In a republic where governmental decisions are ultimately enforceable in courts, the answer must be that the Supreme Court determines finally what the Constitution says. Congress may pass a law that it believes to be constitutional; but if the Supreme Court refuses to enforce it on the grounds that it is not constitutional, that's the law of the land. That is exactly what happened in *Marbury v. Madison*, decided 183 years ago.

Beyond the usual Robertson distortions of fact and history, *Marbury v. Madison* has a totally different history than what he gives. William Marbury, one of President John Adam's "midnight appointments," had been named as a justice of the peace in the District of Columbia, but his commission, though duly signed and sealed, had not been delivered to him at the time Adams left the office of the presidency. Madison, as Jefferson's secretary of state, refused to hand over the commission, and so Marbury appealed to the Supreme Court for a writ of mandamus, directing Madison to perform his official duty. Chief Justice Marshall decided that Marbury had a right to his commission, but that the Court had no power to issue the order, in spite of the fact that the Judiciary Act had conferred such a power upon the Court. Marshall argued that the powers of the Court had been defined in the Constitution itself and that Congress could not rightfully enlarge them. Thus, the case was decided in favor of Madison. The significance of the decision is that the Court determined that it had the right to review legislative acts and determine if they were valid in light of the Constitution. This is what Robertson denies.

The original debate centered on the validity, constitutionality, and authenticity of the Judiciary Act of 1801. The Federalists maintained that the Supreme Court had the power of reviewing acts of Congress and disallowing those that conflicted with the Constitution. In part, their arguments were the fruition of one of Alexander Hamilton's *Federalist* papers which argued that the Supreme Court should have such power. The Supreme Court had actually exercised such power as early as 1796, in upholding the law of Congress that was in question. *Marbury v. Madison* was appealed on that basis in 1803. In that case, the Court for the first time declared a congressional act, or a part of one, unconstitutional. Chief Justice John Marshall wrote for the majority:

> It is emphatically the province and the duty of the judicial department to say what the law is. Those who apply the rule to particular cases must of necessity expound and interpret that rule. If two laws conflict with each other, the courts must decide on the operation of each.
>
> So if a law be in opposition to the constitution, if both the law and the constitution apply to a particular case, so that the court must either decide that case conforming to the law, or disregarding the law, the court must determine which of these conflicting rules governs the case. This is the very essence of judicial duty.
>
> If, then, the courts are to regard the constitution, and the constitution is superior to any ordinary act of the legislature, the constitution, and not such ordinary act, must govern the case to which they both apply.[15]

Robertson's attacks on the Supreme Court have not gone unchallenged. People for the American Way, a Washington-based lobbying group, has written to more than 130 television stations that broadcast Robertson's "700 Club" attacks on the Supreme Court, urging them to air spots by former Texas Representative Barbara Jordan and actor Lloyd Bridges under the Fairness Doctrine — a one-time FCC ruling, a ruling that Robertson opposed, publicly labeling the Fairness Doctrine as "satanic."

Bridges declares, at one point, in the television clip on which he appeared, "I don't like people who attack the courts and demand to have only those judges whose minds are made up beforehand . . . judges who wouldn't even qualify to sit on a jury." Jordan enlarges on the point, "You and I and Pat Robertson all have the right to criticize judges and their decisions, but none of us have the right to demand that the courts rubber-stamp our views on political, social or religious issues."[16] Ms. Jordan is not willing to sit in a sterile environment where debate and discussion are prohibited, where one interpretation alone is allowed and dissenters are packed off to unknown destinations and tribulations.

Robertson would have the court homogenized, sharing a single opinion: an opinion that would speak only of Christian values and laws even if the litigants were not Christian and did not agree to or desire Christian justice. Those justices who would be nominated to sit on Robertson's Supreme Court would have to be as conservative as he. Men of Robertson's calibre, who toe the Robertson line, are men who have a colorful conservative past with little judicial experience, like Daniel Manion.

Robertson endorsed Daniel Manion, even though the Judiciary Committee, in a highly unusual move, sent his name to the Senate with no recommendation. Manion had never argued a federal appeal of any kind, nor had a legal article published. He is one of the least qualified of all jurists in America. A staunch supporter of the anti-democratic John Birch Society, Manion won the support of the radical religious right when he urged that the Supreme Court be stripped of some of its powers.[17] Since then he has become the darling of the Robertson camp and of conservative fundamentalists everywhere. He is one who would shape the destiny of the United States if Robertson should be elected president.

In a 17 January 1986 interview in *Christianity Today*, Robertson declared that one of the two qualifications for which he would look in Supreme Court nominees is the individual's commitment to affirming prayer in public schools. The second qualification would be the nominee's committed opposition to abortion.

Those he would consider would be those proposed by "religious leaders and others whose opinions I respect." Those who would offer him their opinions include such reactionaries as Jerry Falwell, Campus Crusade for Christ President Bill Bright, Southern Baptist Convention President Charles Stanley, Black Baptist leader E.V. Hill, and head of the American Coalition for Traditional Values, Tim LaHaye. Each of these men has come out publicly for the death of liberal judges, declared AIDS to be "god's punishment for the sin of homosexuality," degraded women as being of less value than a man, or continued a Christian message of hate towards those who do not accept their strict fundamentalist (and in most cases Southern Baptist) beliefs. Robertson has capitalized on these emotionally charged, unorthodox beliefs, carrying them with him on to the *Phil Donahue Show*.

On that show, Robertson blasted women's rights and gay rights, and preached a primary Christian message more fit for the the inmates of a looney bin than for modern humankind. When he carried his message of subordinating women to men on this particular pseudo-liberal, populist, national television show, the audience of 350 (90 percent of whom were women), audibly groaned.[18] Robertson was not accustomed to being interviewed. As the host of the "700 Club," Pat asked the questions. On this Monday, 29 September 1987, Pat was being interrogated by the populist Phil Donahue, who, backed up by his traditional housewife audience, usually "bearbaits" his guests. There were no polite introductions — just angry questions. Robertson was asked to spell out and confirm his ideas on women staying at home rather than pursuing careers: whether or not he really believed god had told him to run for the presidency of the United States; and, if elected, would he appoint Jews to any top government jobs? Contradicting his autobiography, *Shout It from the Housetops*, and his *Answers to 200 of Life's Most Probing Questions*, Robertson said "yes" to all three.

Robertson defended his attack on women seeking and maintaining careers independent of the home by arguing that "when both parents work, unattended children run the risk of getting into drugs, sex, and crime. . . . Someone's got to stay with the children, . . . [otherwise] we are forfeiting our next generation." He never considered the possibility of the man staying at home and bringing up the children. One had to give him credit, as he tried to fight it out verbally.[19]

A sizeable part of Donahue's Atlanta audience supported Robertson. Coming from the buckle of the Bible Belt, they heralded Pat's stand as being "in tune with the Bible." Many of those wanted to upstage Donahue, the pseudo-liberal New Yorker, drove BMWs and Volvos and support Pat, who was a Southern boy, a conservative, and a born-again Christian. Supporting Pat meant for many the final soul-ution; voting for Pat meant they never had to think again.

Women, won to Jesus by Robertson or through the machinations of other fundamentalists, have agreed to their lesser role and have augmented the Robertson push towards the presidency of the United States. His boasting of the subjection of women was met with praise from his followers. Many are women who willingly accept the male yoke of alleged superiority. They revel in being told that they must work at ending the "liberal agenda" that supposedly promotes the spread of pornography, homosexuality, teenage pregnancy, and abortion. Yet, basically they are motived by hysteria and fear — fear that Robertson's god will visit his wrath upon them if they deny allegiance and support.

A few fundamentalist supporters of Robertson wrote their local newspapers to complain of his treatment at the hands of Donahue, as seen in the "Letters to the Editor" in such media as the *Atlanta Constitution*, where the telecast was broadcast; the primary complaint launched against the journalists who analyzed the show was that they had (allegedly) patronized or defended "underworked women," or alternately, they were accused of being "Feminists for the Protection of Lesbian Rights Among Endangered Whales" [such an organization does not exist]. The letters which were received and published by the *Atlanta Constitution* were written by writers from Minnesota, Duluth, cities as far away as — the distance indicating the possibility that the writers were conscripted to write to the paper without being privy to the actual articles written and published in the *Atlanta Constitution*.

Robertson has secured the support and labor of Carolyn Sundseth, age sixty-four, the White House liaison to the Christian community. Sundseth has told women for Robertson that Robertson's god will tell all those who pray to him which jobs they should assume:[20]

> Maybe he'll want you to walk the district and knock on doors. Maybe he'll want you to baby-sit, so someone else can do that. But there's something for each of us to do and we need to ask God what it is because we *can* change this country.

The women's committee members were enthused, seeing in her another prophetic voice. Ancient Israel under the prophets has been born again in Virginia Beach, Virginia, the United States of America.

There is also always the fear for women that Robertson's god will visit a new plague on them and their children — not the frogs of Egypt, but the "green monkey" disease out of Africa transmitted through Haiti: AIDS. Robertson's god, by Robertson's own admission, wages germ warfare against a selected ground of "sinners" (AIDS victims), and women "who require redemption." A gynephobe, intimidated by women and therefore needing to dominate them, Robertson has dragged out and brushed off the misogynistic line that "women are not to wear men's clothing."[21] He declares that love is a limited valuable only Christian fundamentalists have a right to embrace, enjoy, or share. Sex, Robertson and CBN have argued, is the "diabolic element" in our being. Unless we suppress the "Satanic force" of sex outside of heterosexual marriage, Armaggedon will rain havoc and death upon the world before anyone is prepared.

Of course, Robertson is not alone with the idea that sex, for procreative purposes only, must be performed on the marriage bed. The Roman Catholic church, the Mormons, and other fundamentalist sects share this idea. For this reason he is supported in his utterances. Sex is the chief weapon that the "Prince of Darkness" has used against humankind and most recently to destroy television ministries and empires of both Jim Bakker and Jimmy Swaggart.[22]

The men who can counter the machinations of Lucifer and of designing women and, through some unexplained power, stop the spread of AIDS, Robertson believes will all be good Christians, who will:

> . . . bring unity in the body of Christ, and give Christians a focus of discussion in the councils of leadership in our nation.[23]

These are the only men of the type who would sit on Robertson's Supreme Court. Such "unity," however, would come with a stiff price tag. The mind must devolve into blind acceptance of Robertson's biblical interpretations. Secular legal education, free inquiry, and indvidual ingenuity are to be cast off as perversions.[24]

Until the day that he will be able to select Supreme Court justices, Robertson laments he will have to endure the current court.

With each ruling by the Supreme Court, Robertson becomes increasingly disenchanted. By mid-1986, he was taking his most radical stand in relationship to the Supreme Court and its judgments.

Like a medieval despot, or as if he were *Le Soleil Roi* (Louis XIV), or even the pope, Pat is convinced that he is answerable only to his god. He sees himself as a god — the buddy of Jesus, for he believes that it has been prophesied that he will claim the world for Jesus.[29]

Rather than consult the combined wisdom of lawyers, barristers, judges, attorneys, or Congress, Robertson would consult the oracles and prophets of the Old and New Testament, particularly Revelation.[30] Unlike any mortals since the Delphic oracles in pagan Greece, Robertson's god speaks directly to him: "God has spoken to me. I had learned to know his voice."[31] It will be this voice of his deity to which he will listen in deciding whether or not he would abide by or enforce a Supreme Court decision if he would become president.

Robertson's views on the Supreme Court and the Constitution of the United States are extreme. His attitude on the Constitution is even more extreme.

According to Robertson, the United States Constitution is a "Christian document."[32] It was, again according to Pat, written by and meant only for Christians. The United States Constitution, he claims, was written for the "self-government of *Christian* people."[33] Anyone who disagrees with Robertson is, in Robertson's own words, an "anti-Christian atheist," a "communist" or "Nazi," and he argues that his "Christian laws" are to be made applicable to those who do not believe as he believes. The Constitution is not for Atheists, nonconformists,

144

Jews, Buddhists, or others who have different opinions.[34] Those who demand equal time to rebut his arguments, or the arguments of any other "good Christian," are dismissed as being "of the Devil."[35]

On 16 May 1986, Robertson broadcast that the "Christian people" of America would not allow the "mavericks" of the Supreme Court to "make" laws much longer.[36] Robertson wants the United States Supreme Court to parrot "original intent" of the Founding Fathers, as if their intent, *as they would apply it to present circumstances*, could be known. Supreme Court justices would not be men and women who would define legal issues or interpret laws passed by Congress, in our day and age — they would need to be able to operate Ouija boards to be in communication with men dead for two centuries. Robertson's Supreme Court would issue judgments based solely upon eighteenth-century standards, moot traditions, and the simplistic meaning of words as they were used in general, Caucasian, Protestant-Christian, heterosexual, coastal eighteenth-century colonial society: the only society allegedly known to the framers of the Constitution.[37]

Convinced that the Constitution of the United States of America is a "Christian Document," Robertson has argued at length that nowhere in the Constitution is there a prohibition against a union between church and state.[38] He focuses on the words that "Congress shall make no laws" respecting organized religion. He argues that the constitutional writers meant that the issue of church and state was to be left up to the individual states; that the only prohibition in the Constitution concerning church and state separation is the qualifier that no national church is to be created by Act of Congress. States, however, can establish state churches, fund churches, and work with churches so that the United States would be a Christian nation — according to the Gospel by Pat.[39] Robertson points out that all he needs to change the composition of the U.S. Supreme Court is two more timely deaths: those of Thurgood Marshall, and William Brennan — especially since John Paul Stevens has already resigned.[40]

Notes

1. Gerald T. Straub, *Salvation for Sale*; An Insider's View of Pat Robertson's Ministry (Buffalo, NY: Prometheus Books, 1986), pp. 97-101.

2. Cf. Steve Maynard, "TV Evangelist Talks Like a Real Candidate," *Houston* [Texas] *Chronicle* (11 August 1985), pp. 1, 2.

3. Straub, *Salvation for Sale*, pp. 89-94.

4. Robertson, *On Bible Prophecy*, series of tapes issued by CBN.

5. Cory SerVaas and Maynard Good Stoddard, "CBN's Pat Robertson: White House Next?" *The Saturday Evening Post* 257.2 (March 1985): p. 109.

6. "700 Club" 11 April 1986 and 1 May 1986.

7. "700 Club" 6 June 1985. United Press International wire report carried in the *San Francisco Chronicle* (9 May 1984). Cp. *American United Press Release* 13 May 1987.

8. Cf. Daniel J. Nicholas, "Pat Robertson: Leading a Moral Reformation: A Profile," *Religious Broadcasting* 18.2 (February 1986): p. 66.

9. Pat Robertson with William Proctor, *Beyond Reason: How Miracles Can Change Your Life* (New York: William Morrow, 1985), p. 174.

10. Steve Schlather, "Robertson Waits for a Sign; Says Candidacy Depends on Shift toward Family," *San Antonio* [Texas] *Light* (6 March 1986), sec. A, p. 12.

11. Andrew Mollison, "The Quotable Pat Robertson on Politics, Religion, Himself," *The Orange County* [California] *Register* (17 September 1986), sec. A, p. 21.

12. Cf. United States Constitution, Article III. Section 1 details the establishment of the judicial power and the appointment of judges and their terms of office (for life). Section 2 declares: "The judicial Power shall extend to all cases, in Law and Equity, arising under this Constitution, the Law of the United States, and Treaties made, or which shall be made, under their [the justices] Authority."

13. Jean McNair, "CBN Law School Links the Bible with Legal Precedents," *Schenectady* [New York] *Gazette* (29 November 1986), p. 9.

14. *Washington Post* (14 July 1986), Sec. A, p. 10.

15. 16. Judi Hasson, "TV Evangelist's Attack on Courts Draws Fire," *The Charleston* [West Virginia] *Gazette* (17 June 1986), sec. A, p. 7.

17. Cf. Remer Tyson, "Minister Sees Conservative Brethren as Dividing GOP," *Detroit Free Press* (1 October 1986), *loc. cit.*

18. "Letters to the Editor,"*Atlanta Constitution* (16 October 1986)

19. Gustav Niebuhr, "Robertson Gets Grilling on 'Donahue'," *Atlanta Constitution* (30 September 1986), sec. A, pp. 1, 8. Hubert Mizell, "With Donahue on Mound, Robertson Can't Get to First Base," *Atlanta Constitution* (30 September 1986), sec. B, pp. 1. 11. Cf. Russell Baker, "What's a Commentator to Do with a Man of The Cloth?" *Atlanta Constitution* (24 September 1986), sec. A, p. 19. Cf. Manuel Rico, "Robertson Seen as Opportunist," *San Antonio* [Texas] *Express-News* (26 September 1986), sec. A, p. 8.

20. Kendall Guthrie "Women Mull Table Politics: Christians Plan an Active Roll," the *Virginia-Pilot and Ledger Star* (1 June 1986), p. 83. 21. Deut. 21.

22. Straub, *Salvation for Sale*, p. 70.

23. Marjorie Hyer, "Evangelist Lists Two Topics for Court Qualifications," *Washington Post* (25 January 1986), p. 3.

24. Straub, *Salvation for Sale*, pp. 68-69.

25. David S. Broder, "Robertson Says High Court Not Preeminent; Prospective Candidate Cites Founding Fathers on Equal Power of Judiciary and Congress," *Washington Post* (27 June 1986), sec. A, p. 3.

26. *Albuquerque* [New Mexico] *Journal* (28 June 1986), p. 2.

27. "Rulings 'Not Law of Land,' Robertson says; Evangelist Takes Aim at Supreme Court," *Los Angeles Times* (28 June 1986), pt. I, p. 2.

28. *Los Angeles Times* (28 June 1986), pt. 1, p. 2.

29. Pat Robertson, *Shout It from the Housetops*, pp. 214, 228.

30. Pat Robertson, *Shout It from the Housetops*, pp. 69-79. Robertson declared, "I would often have to rely on just such revelations. . . . To rely on this kind of direct guidance for your life's course, and not to have a clear channel, could lead to immediate disaster." (ibid., p. 70) Most of Robertson "oracles" occurs when he is "flip[ping] through the pages [of the Bible] until I [find] the verse. . . ." (ibid., p. 75) which he details in personal letters to followers, friends, and family: "The letter where I told you God was speaking to me through Luke 12:33" (ibid., p. 77).

31. Robertson, *Shout It from the Housetops*, p. 82.

32. Cf. Robert H. Meneilly, "The Threat to Our Church . . . and Our State," *The Squire's Other Paper* pp. 27.31 (6 March 1986): pp. 1-2. Cp. George F. Will, "Pat Robertson's Mustard Seed," *Newsweek* (3 March 1986): p. 72.

33. "700 Club," 25 September 1984.

34. "700 Club" 25 September 1984. Cf. "700 Club," 19 September 1985 and 16 May 1986. Cp. Robertson, *Answers*, pp. 272-73,

35. "700 Club," 19 September 1985.

36. "700 Club" broadcast.

37. Robertson, *America's Dates with Destiny*, pp. 261-62. Cp. Justice William Brennan, in "Intent of the Framers," *Newsweek* (28 October 1985): p. 97. Cf. *New York Times* (1, 2, 3 July 1979, and 24 March 1981).

38. "Campaign of TV Evangelists Reflects Rightward Shift," *The People* 96.7 (5 July 1986): p. 5. Cp. Joanne Firestone, "No Pat from Backers," *Detroit News* (25 July 1986), sec. A, p. 1, 2; Robert Shogan, "Robertson Could Mobilize Religious Right: Evangelist's Presidential Bid: Test for Church and State,: *Los Angeles Times* (4 March 1986),

pt. 1, pp. 1, 12, 13. Among the many humorous responses to this patent unhistorical statement, see Mike Royko, "God Knows, It's an Easy Error to Make," *Chicago Tribune* (16 October 1986), sec. 1, p. 3; cp. Lewis Grizzard, "I Interviewed God," and his "If God Doesn't Have the Answers about Politics, Then Who Does?" (1986: Cowles Syndicate, Inc.). Not all of Robertson's Protestant co-religionists support his view, as read in the "Letters to the Editor" of the *Denver Post* (30 September 1986), which argued that "Historically, governments that are accountable to a church and not to their diverse citizenry have inevitably led to persecution and injustice." The letter was signed by Episcopal Fr. Marion J. Hammond, Presbyterian pastor Glendon B. Taylor, Roman Catholic priest Leroy D. Burke, C.SS.P., and Unitarian minister James A. Hobart. For a heated discussion on the issue of church and state, see "America: Republic of God?" in the Viewpoint section of the *San Antonio* [Texas] *Light* (16 November 1986), sec. MM, pp. 1, 3.

39. "700 Club," 11 April 1986.

Chapter 10
On Variant Lifestyles:
Feminist, Gay, Non-Conformist, Atheist[1]

Once the United States of America returns to its Christian heritage, laws, and rules, Robertson claims, homosexuality can be eradicated[2] (either by spiritual conversion or force[3]), abortions will be stopped, and education will be Christian-based.[4] Robertson will neither accept the reality that times and situations change nor the heterogeneity of a society that has grown strong and healthy because of its diversity in expression, life-styles, attitudes, and philosophies.

When, two years ago, the Supreme Court of the United States upheld[5] a Georgia law which criminalized oral and anal sex, Robertson applauded since he perceived that the conservative elements had captured the consensus of opinion. In that case, *Bowers v. Hardwick*, the Supreme Court ruled on a 1984 Gerogia statute which provided in pertinent part:

> (a) A person commits the offense of sodomy when he performs or submits to any sexual act involving the sex organs of one person and the mouth or anus of another. . . .
> (b) A person convicted of the offense of sodomy shall be punished by imprisonment for not less than one nor more than twenty years. . . .

The court accepted that a tradition a thousand years old, based on religion, still stood sentry at the bedroom door for millions of American citizens. The court held:

The Constitution does not confer a fundamental right upon homosexuals to engage in sodomy. None of the fundamental rights announced in this Court's prior cases involving family relationships, marriage, or procreation bear any resemblance to the right asserted in this case. And any claim that those cases stand for the proposition that any kind of private sexual conduct between consenting adults is constitutionally insulated from state proscription is unsupportable.

Gay men and lesbians have, according to the Supreme Court's findings, no right of privacy, no right against cruel and unusual punishment, no right to resist arbitrary arrest, and no right to be free from an invasion of their domicile or other properties. The Inquisition was born again in the United States for one-tenth of its citizens on June 30, 1986, the day the decision was handed down. (The Supreme Court let stand a similar decision in a Texas state case,[6] from Dallas, in 1985.)

Many saw this decision as a victory for the religious. Others proclaimed that the court conservatives, again led by Chief Justice William Burger, had announced that the promise of the United States was now "with liberty and justice for some"; that "freedom" was but a password for election or appointment to office and not a key to daily life. They raised their voices to say that once more the High Court based its collective, but not unanimous, decision on tired, trite traditions that no longer speak to the modern world.

Until 1961 all fifty states outlawed sodomy, and in 1986, twenty-four states and the District of Columbia provided criminal penalties for sodomy performed in private and between consenting adults. That is to say that one-tenth of all American citizens engaging in their preferred sexual style lost their chance to experience the same freedom of sexual liberty as the conventional heterosexual hitting only the "right" hole.

Robertson's applause at the demise of sexual rights for gay men and lesbians is but one indication of Robertson's primitive psychology. He would far prefer to live in the distant past, thousands of years ago, during a time he assumes to be homogeneous and harmonious. He ignores the continued controversies, the degenerate life-styles, the violence, the filth, the disease, the poverty, the ignorance, and the sloth. He would rather not live in the current world where the dignity of the individual and the individual's potential to better society for all is more important than an affectional interest or form of love expression. The rise of human worth and the potential of self-actualization pale before Robertson's god. Because Robertson's god is a jealous and petty god, human dignity means nothing, and suffering is a joy to his ears.

Even though the televangelist attempts to justify his stand by citing the glories of the past, these "illuminations" were seldom actual. The legendary *Pax Romana* never existed, any more than did a single god, a single system, a single law, a single interpretation of the alleged single law — there was not even a single judgment agreed upon by all, heralded by all, for democracy in the past was rare, and the few experiments with democracy were met by the armed forces of the church and by preachers who were unwilling to surrender their lives of leisure and consumption for the good of the commonwealth.

Societies and governments have been, and are, heterogeneous. They are in a constant state of conflict both in democracies, where the conflict is aired and public discussion and dissension is permitted, or in oligarchies, tyrannies, and theocracies by any name, where dissent is stifled and discussion follows either along party, sectarian, or denominational lines.

On abortion, a Southern Baptist *cause célèbre*,[7] Robertson faults the "liberal" element for deciding "against the fetus." He claims that the fetus is a living being, even though it is unable to sustain life on its own and has no feeling of pain or pleasure since it is without the necessary apparatus of nerve endings. Robertson has pledged himself to protect this collection of maturing and differentiating cells even if it should cost the woman carrying the cells her life or health. No man — or woman — who supports freedom of choice for an abortion would sit on his Supreme Court.

In the area of religion, Robertson has argued angrily against Supreme Court decisions banning prayer in school, public displays of Christian symbolism, and the utilization of public funds for Christian or any religious events. Such Supreme Court action, Robertson claims, is the product of Atheist, non-conformist, non-fundamentalist agitation which is Communist (i.e., Soviet) inspired. To counter it, Robertson would seek the introduction of a constitutional amendment to "permit" prayer in school, issue education vouchers to families who want their children educated in a Christian, monolithic environment, and "weed" out all secular-humanistic works of literature, history, and science in the public schools. If the Supreme Court did not support his plans for reshaping the United States, Robertson has vowed to increase the number of jurists sitting on the Supreme Court — in much the same manner as Franklin Delano Roosevelt had proposed during the 1930s.[8]

The Supreme Court is to be(come) a "Christian Court." Its judges are to be Christians. The Christian "Judge of all the Earth" is to rule over it, and the judges of the Supreme Court are to make their decisions on legal cases that have come before their collective bench on the basis of Christian doctrine and Pat Robertson's interpretation of the word and command god.[9]

Anything which promotes Atheism, or any individual who would promote it, or nonconformity to Robertson's concept of Christian fundamentalism, or socialism/communism, is to be declared illegal, censured, and stifled. On 8 June 1986, Robertson telecast his most stinging denunciation of freedom of choice in religious matters. He declared, mixing metaphors and massacring historical facts:

> Our liberties are under assault from the very people who said they would take off the shackles of the people during the French Revolution and Bolshevik Revolution in Russia, and then enslaved them. Why is it in America we are trying to establish atheism as our official religion [Atheism is not a religion — ed.] when a recent survey showed 94 percent of all our people [who were polled] believe in God and only six percent had no faith in a Supreme Being?[10]

As odous as Lyndon LaRouche, who sees himself as a savior of the Western world,[11] Pat Robertson has adorned himself with a cape of infallibility, preaching on all aspects of human life.[13] As does LaRouche, Robertson damns the very aspects of morality he has proclaimed he has the ability to cure, protect, and enhance.

Robertson's past is a tapestry of claims that he possesses spiritual healing powers. He insists that he is "the candidate who listens to God," the sole individual who can "bring back" theistic[14] "principles" to the average home in the United States.[15] Robertson uses his "divine gifts" as political, economic, social, and medical blackmail. Only those who accept his god, his interpretation of the Protestant Bible, his Republican ideology, his capitalism-at-all-costs, his orthodox-supine heterosexual-conservative-nonexperimental sex, will he save. He has, in the past, been quick to boast of curing hemmorhoids, headaches, hangovers, and cancers of the throat, breast, and liver, as well as numerours other afflictions, diseases, aneurysms, and clotting, but he — or his god — neither will nor can cure AIDS.

Not only is Robertson physically unable to cure, or even arrest, AIDS — including those who carry the disease and who have flocked to his banner — but he elects to ignore all medical evidence concerning this equal opportunity virus.[14] Robertson has set himself as the spokesman for the future of politics in the United States, and as the judge of those who would be permitted to survive in his brave new world.

Coupled with his love affair with totalitarian pronouncements, Robertson has set himself up as the equivalent of the Old Testament god-of-spite and vengeance. This sour sage has declared that AIDS is not only divine retribution against those who have "sinned" but an ontological judgment against the United States and the nations of the world which have strayed from the Robertson path and his concept of Christian worship and praise.[15]

Rejecting scientific data that point out that the only way that AIDS can be contracted is through the exchange of bodily fluids or the sharing of intervenous needles,[16] Pat Robertson has publicly stated that the AIDS virus not only can survive outside the human body — a view with which medical specialists have strongly disagreed — but "If, say, we're in a room with twenty-five people with AIDS and they're breathing various things into the atmosphere, the chance of somebody catching it has become quite strong."[17]

Robertson argues that AIDS can be transmitted through the air. On 5 February 1987, he argued that AIDS will be cured only when homosexuality is erased and sex takes place within marriage only.[18] He has also gone on public record as saying that AIDS can be spread through dental surgery.[19] While AIDS can be transmitted through blood from a cut in an AID's victim's mouth, the only way that it could infect the dentist is if the dentist had an open cut, sore or wound on his hand (or any other part of his anatomy) if and when the blood reached that opening. To prevent this, the dentist need only wear rubber or other nonporous gloves. Still, in keeping with his character, Robertson ignores this *caveat* and a rejects any warning save his and Lyndon LaRouche's, that the way to fight AIDS is to avoid AIDS victims, incarcerate, quarantine, and ghettoize individuals with AIDS in holding camps. This idea has been reported, however, only microscopically, and then only in papers that attempt to present the full nefarious facets of the televangelist-turned-politician.[20]

Notes

1. Pat Robertson, *Answers to 200 of Life's Most Probing Questions* (New York: Bantom Books, 1984), pp. 271-72, 280.

2. The "eradication" of homosexuality became a popular advocacy in the early 1970s, when Ernest Aron (later known as Elizabeth Debbie Eden) and John Wojtowicz were married in a public ceremony in 1971. Aron/Eden in August 1972 wanted a sex change and tried to kill her/himself with a drug overdose, prompting Wojtowicz and a partner to attempt a bank robbery to get the money necessary for the operation. They took hostages, the partner was killed, and Wojtowicz arrested. Their story resulted in the 1975 movie, "Dog Day Afternoon," starring A1 Pacino.

Wojtowicz served seven years in prison. Aron/Eden got the sex-change operation, legally married someone else from whom she was later divorced. After her divorce, from 1987 on, Eden visited Wojtowicz until her death from complications of AIDS (through pneumonia) 29 September 1987. In this case and those on the "700 Club," the "homosexuals" were not "victims" of "the disease of homosexuality" but were trapped in the wrong gender, which an operation could change to give them a body conforming with their psychology. Christian fundamentalists, however, have denied this reality, and it has become the focus of such groups as the Episcopalian EXODUS, and Colin Cook's Quest Center, that have leagued with psychologically trained homophobes. Cf. Henry Jay March, "Shrink, Shrank, Shrunk: The Stormy Relationship between Gays and the Mental Health 'Experts'," *The Advocate* 483 (13 October 1987): pp. 43-49, and co-related article by Mark Vandervelden, "Proselytizing AIDS Patients," ibid., pp. 10-11, 18, 20, 28-29, 31; cp. Desert Stream Ministries [pseud. for Jonathan Hunter], *Homosexuality & the Christian: Questions Gays Ask Most . . .* (Santa Monica, CA: Vineyard Christian Fellowship, 1986); see my: *Exposing the "Ex-Gay" Christian*, forthcoming, and my *Homosexuals Anonymous: A Psychoanalytic and Theological Analysis of Colin Cook & His Cure for Homosexuality* (Garland, TX: Tangelwüld Press, 1987).

3. Robertson, *Answers*, pp. 174-75, 193; Robertson cites Rom. 1:24-25, and 1 Cor. 6:9-10 and, as usual, has taken both verses out of context, distorting each beyond the meaning inherent in the words. In each case, the opposition of Saul of Tarsus (St. Paul) is to "wanton" life-styles (that is) wholly gratuitous, generic in nature, and is a reference to impersonal activities more in keeping with heterosexual activities than homosexual or lesbian liaisons; see: Plutarch, *Erotikos* 753, which, in the Greek, applies to passive sexuality (*malthacoe*) in heterosexual men. The only inference towards "homosexuality" is in

the issue of male prostitution, but even here the objection is to the intent rather than the physical act: the desire to *sell* sex, not the act of engaging in sex. Interestingly, what Robertson objects to as passages against male homosexuality were, in fact, interpreted throughout the Middle Ages and well into the twentieth century by the Roman Catholic church to be condemnations of masturbation; see: H. Noldin, *Summa theologiae moralis scholarum usui* (Leipzig, 1940): "De sexto praecepto"; cp. Aquinas, *Summa theologiae*, 2.2.154.11, Resp.

The passage in Romans (which is actually found in 1:26-27), reflects primary Pauline plagiarism; cf. Wisd. 12:23-27, Ezek. 7:20, *Testament of Naphtali* (which may have been written as early as the third century before Romans); and then is a condemnation of orgiastic pagan rites in honor of false gods (cf. Herman van de Spijker, *Die gleich-geschlechtliche Zuneigun* [Freiburg, 1968], pp. 82ff.) and is a warning against heterosexual and homosexual immorality of the *kadeshim*, where there is active, emotionally charged physical involvement in ritual worship, such as has become the hallmark of most evangelical pentecostal movements in fundamental Christianity in the United States. Cf. John Chrysostom, *In Epistolam ad Romanos*, Homily 4 in Migne, *Patrologiae . . . Graeca* LX:415-20.

4. Robertson has attempted to equate his stand for Christianizing education in America with that of Ronald Reagan. Reagan's relevant rhetoric concerning "Studying for God" was in the form of a radio address to the nation from Rancho del Cielo on 24 August 1985, at 9:06 A.M., PDT, the White House, Office of the Press Secretary, Santa Barbara, California. It quickly became the catalyst for similar speeches by other would-be politicians, such as that given by Gary L. Bauer, under-secretary of education before the Third Annual National Consultation on Pornography, meeting in Cincinnati, Ohio, on 5 September 1985. His speech, "Educating for Virtue," is reproduced in full in the *American Atheist* (November 1985, p. 6-8).

A word must be said concerning the *American Atheist* magazine published in Austin, Texas. Although it is nearly universally banned from libraries and has few newspapers permitting its advertisements in their journals and records, it is one of the few contemporary magazines that gives entire religious speeches in its pages without commentary or censorship. While the *American Atheist* is customarily censored, it does not censor, for the stated purpose of the magazine and its parent body is the full distribution and dissemination of information. The same is true with the American Atheist book press, which will publish uncensored works, permitting authors the opportunity to fully cite sources and give unbridled analyses, especially in respect to the current upswing of Christian fundamentalism. Cf. "Utilize Texas Baptist Education Survey . . . Voting for Children?" *Baptist Standard* 96.26 (27 June 1984): p. 6.

5. *Bowers v. Hardwick*, 106 S.Ct. 2841 (1986).

6. *Baker v. Wade*, 769 F.2d 289, reh'g denied, 774 F.2d 1285 (CA5 1985) (*en banc*).

7. Toby Druin, "FBC, Euless [Texas] Fights Abortion In Pregnancy Testing Center," *Baptist Standard* 96.34 (22 August 1984): p. 15.

8. "700 Club," 11 April 1986.

9. "700 Club," 6 June 1985.

10. Don Tschirhart, "TV Preacher Calls Believers to The Mission of Politics," *Detroit News* (9 May 1986), p. 12. The St. Louis, Missouri *Post-Dispatch* on 30 September 1986, recorded the quote as

> . . . I do not think that the 94 percent of the people who believe in God in this nation should dismantle their belief for the 6 percent who are atheists.

11. John King, "LaRouche Saw Himself as Savior, Attorney Says," *Fort Worth* [Texas] *Star-Telegram* (18 December 1987), sec. 1, p. 7.

12. Cf. Anson Shupe, "GOP Ignores Reality as Robertson Rolls On," *Fort Worth* [Texas] *Star Telegram* (10 December 1987), sec. 1, p. 41. Shupe is chair of the department of sociology/anthropology at Indiana-Purdue University in Fort Wayne, Indiana.

13. Associated Press (26 December 1987).

14. *The AIDS Epidemic*, ed. Kevin M. Cahill (New York: St. Martin's Press, 1983); *Acquired Immune Deficiency Syndrome*, ed. Irving J. Selikoff, Alvin S. Teirstein, and Shalom Z. Hirschman (Annals of the New York Academy of Sciences, vol. 437; New York: The New York Academy of Sciences, 1984); my *AIDS Hysteria* (Dallas: Monument

Press, 1986).

15. Cp. "AIDS Apocalypse Devastates Africa," *New Solidarity* (19 January 1987), p. 1; Mark Sonneblick, "N[ational Lyndon LaRouche] D[emocratic] P[olicy] C[ommittee] Adviser [Debra] Freeman Speaks in Peru on AIDS Crisis," *New Solidarity* (19 December 1986), p. 1; Warren J. Hamerman, "E[xecutive] I[ntelligence] R[eport] Releases New Computer Study of AIDS Initiative [Quarantine/Concentration Camp] Backers," *New Solidarity* (5 December 1986), pp. 1, 4, are samples of the LaRouche mentality, while Robertson revealed his ignorance in an interview with the editorial board of the *Concord* [New Hampshire] *Monitor* (16 December 1987), an ultra-conservative far-right paper.

16. When New York Governor Mario Cuomo proposed giving free sterile needles to addicts to stop the spread of the fatal AIDS virus among the 200,000 New York City drug addicts, the LaRouche faction came out heavily against the measure, claiming that such compassionate action would make drug abuse easier; see Kathleen Klenetsky, "Cuomo to 'Fight' AIDS by Giving Addicts Free Needles," *New Solidarity* (24 November 1986), pp. 1, 7. Cp. Jeanne P. Bell, "Anti-AIDS Prop 64 [in California] Changed U. S. Politics," *New Solidarity* (10 November 1987), pp. 1, 9; the LaRouche camp's "public health expert" is Dr. Debra Freeman, whose medical expertise is questionable and whose interest in politics is greater than her concern with the truth. Monstrous in her self-elevating claims, Freeman has flown to countries around the world to sprea AIDS hysteria, with the quiet remonstrance that unless the world turns to the fascism of LaRoucherd there is to be no peace, safety, or health. More on the order of Nazi Josef Mengle than legitimate contemporary medical science, Freeman's "medical remonstrances" are sponsored by the United States Lyndon LaRouche political action committee: the National Democratic Party Committee (which has no relationship with or to the National Democratic Party). See: Mark Sonnenblick, "NDPC Adviser Freeman Speaks in Peru on AIDS Crisis," *New Solidarity* (19 December 1986), pp. 1, 3.

17. *Concord* [New Hampshire] *Monitor* (16 December, 1987).

18. Harvey Feit, Gannett News Service (5 February 1987), the exact wording being:

And somewhere down the line, people will tend to demand quarantines, begin to demand some kind of drastic action. What's needed now is not 'safe sex' but old-fashioned abstinence and sex within marriage. Anything beyond that is very dangerous to people's health. We could solve AIDS this year with that particular point of view.

19. *Boston Globe* (17 December 1987).

20. Cf. *Fort Worth* [Texas] *Star-Telegram* (17 December 1987), sec. 1, p. 16.

Chapter 11
Mixing Politics and Religion: Pat on The First Amendment & War with The USSR

Pat's followers jumped at the announcement that the televangelist might run for the presidency of the United States. Hillard Pauley of East Detroit declared, "I'm not afraid of mixing politics with religion. Politics is religion." He was seconded by theocrat Diane Blanchard of Brighton, Michigan, who chortled, "We need someone who knows God in our government and will listen to God's counsel, not the counsel of men."[1] Roman Catholic Marlene Elwell,[2] Robertson's Michigan coordinator for the Freedom Council,[3] concurred and declared that Christians abstaining from the political process allowed liberals to gain power with what she calls anti-Christian agendas — especially concerning the issues of abortion[4] and "humanistic" teaching in public schools.[5]

When Robertson won the Michigan primary fight,[6] he sent out a "Christian letter" that stripped away all of his pretense of working towards "democracy" and fulfilling the American dream. Blatantly anti-Semitic as well as against anyone who does not worship his deity, Robertson gloated, "THE CHRISTIANS HAVE WON!" and promised Christians that they could take over all aspects of Michigan government, turning Michigan, and later the United States, into the theocracy of which he dreamed, with Pat himself sitting in the throne of righteousness with his buddy Jesus.[7]

At last Robertson found those individuals who would do away with privy advisers, Congress, and the basic tools of democracy which insure that the rights of all are maintained. It was now, to many Robertson followers, only a short distance to a Heavenly City where laws would be biblically based, apostates and non-believers consigned to the vengence of the deity, and books that did not praise the Robertson god would be destroyed. Tim LeHaye, a fundamentalist minister, joined the religious battle to fight for a theocracy to be forced upon America, where, according to George Marsden, historian at Wheaton College (an evangelical school in Illinois), Christian fundamentalists would rule against any compromise and stand for a rigid caste system. LeHaye's wife, Beverly, heads the Concerned Women for America, a quasi-inquisition that is serious about sweeping "righteous politicians" into office, and Christianizing the United States and everyone in it — regardless of individual choice.[8]

The book burnings of Nazi Germany will appear to many as a picnic at Sunnybrook Farm if the radical right religionists take over. "Conservative values" are to be entrenched as law, introduced and required to be memorized at school, and to be practiced by all people — regardless of their views, attitudes, choices, or interests.[9] Judgments are to be "utopian" and life is to match Robertson's religious rose garden of dreams and illusions.[10]

Instead of facing the criticisms of his political peers who witnessed Pat's political sideshow, the televangelist basked in the incestuous adulation of his own, while he acrimoniously slashed at the idea of self-expression, and preached about ending individual rights and privacy. The excesses of this self-proclaimed spokesman of god, oriented towards the fullness of suffering for the people his god allegedly himself created, contaminate the entire democratic process. Robertson would have a "Christian America."[11] He reaches out with a hostile harangue against not only all other religious practices, such as those of Jews, Buddhists, followers of Islam,[12] and Confucians,[13] but against Atheists, freethinkers, agnostics, deists, and those who elect to be non-churched or are ontologically or theologically non-compartmentalized.[14] Robertson advocates "another order"[15] not only totally out of tune with contemporary thought but also out of tune with the original intent and writings of the Founding Fathers of the United States who were determined to keep state and church separate.

Robertson's advocacy of a theocracy in our nation is but the resurrection of ghosts of dictatorships past and reinforcement of totalitarian governments present. He is poised to take over diplomacy. Yet, when the legitimate representatives of the people fail to assert the interests of a commonweal as above individual presidential pretensions buttressed by non-accountable security councils and kitchen cabinets, the result is obvious. He approves of low-ranking military figures plotting national destiny and with immunity shredding any evidence of their nefarious actions. If anyone attempts to say them nay, or interfere with the plans of these "born-again" wanderers in this lifetime, Robertson's minions shout down their accusers as being less patriotic than those who broke the law while believing that they were above the law and allegedly having the best interest of their Christian nation at stake.

Robertson salutes such sinister sallies against the democratic process and, with other evangelicals, gives applause and honor to those who create shadow governments within the framework of a legitimately elected government. How easily this can be seen in his admission of talking with Lieutenant Colonel Oliver North[16] about the latter's clandestine and illegal maneuverings.

The Iran/Contra hearings brought out of hiding the basic anti-Semitism and racism of the Contra supporters, seen in the enormous amount of mail that flooded the committees, drilling investigative attorney Arthur Liman and denouncing Senator Daniel Inouye of Hawaii as a "Jap." The lack of tolerance of the born-again fundamentalists who blasted the supporters of freedom bore bad news for a putative democracy, for, as "Citizens for Fairness for North Committee" expressed, if North would be indicted, those who supported "evangelical truth and those in favor of Armaggedon to wipe out Communism" would have to declare martial law and invade the nation's capital; all that would be left would be to trample the Constitution, a goal that Robertson and others of the radical right have pledged to be a part in their scheme to "rewrite" it so that it conforms to their interpretation of "democracy" and is favorable to their Jesus.

Robertson described the Iran-Contra affair as an attempt to free United States hostages being held in Lebanon and to help Nicaraguan "freedom fighters [sic: Contras] . . . liberate themselves from communist domination" and restore the power of the Christian church in Central America. Thus Bishop Bosco Vivas was backed to mediate the first face-to-face encounter between the legitimate government of Nicaragua and the United States-supported Contras. When Robertson's death squads didn't get their way and usurp power in Nicaragua, Cardinal Obando y Bravo was called in to mediate.

Opposed to any equitable division of land and wealth, the cardinal was immediately welcomed by the Contras. Bravo had little time for the revolutionary forces, still smarting from an incident that occurred when the MDN youth prevented a group from the Comunidades de Base from presenting a letter to his bishop while he was but a monsignor.

When the Sandinistas took over and the Somosists were expelled, Bravo's first reaction was to treat the revolutionaries led by Daniel Ortega as subjects of Cuba, fearing the "Cubanization" of Nicaragua. He feared a secularization of parochial education, a reduction in the perquisites of the Roman Catholic clergy, and a lessening of his own authority and voice in political matters. His clergy were not a united front. Many of the clergy sided with the people, preached liberation theology, and condemned the wealth of the church that seldom was used to help the poor. They were more like the martyred St. Lawrence, who was roasted over hot coals chained to a gridiron, than like the wiley cardinal, who was closer in spirit to the fun-loving popes of the Renaissance; one could not say that Orbando y Bravo was a copy of the impoverished Christ — but then, neither Robertson nor Orbando y Bravo would know the poor Jesus if he kissed them on their blood-drained lips, lips far more familiar with threats of damnation than promises of love and assistance. And both mortals had the same disregard for human suffering that Ollie North showed when he sold United States weapons to the terrorists in Iran who made sport blowing up civilian aircraft and military barracks.

Robertson claimed that he met the lieutenant colonel at a Washington airport in September 1985. According to Robertson, North mentioned that he was flying to Iran.

What is not clear is why North felt free to tell the televangelist of his clandestine, covert, and illegal action, yet at the same time did not feel free or comfortable to mention it to Congress. Was it because North, as a born-again evangelical, felt he could only trust a shepherd and not the commander-in-chief?

North's problems crept up quickly following the Robertson meeting. When he was confronted with Robertson's claim, he swore under oath, "I do not recall that conversation." He further attempted to clarify his statements to the Congressional panel investigating the Iran-Contra subversive activities of the Shadow Government, claiming, "I don't believe we actually addressed plans to go to Tehran until February of 1986."

Robertson, on the other hand, rejected North's feeble defense. He reminded those who would listen that he had interviewed Ronald Reagan a few days after his meeting with North. During the 19 September 1985 telecast, Robertson said to Reagan, "We were heartened to learn that Reverend [Benjamin] Weir had been released from Lebanon and word reached us that a member of the White House staff was dispatched Sunday, I believe, to Iran to seek the release of the remaining six — and actually it was seven at the time. Is there any word on that that might give hope to us?"

Evasive as usual, Ronald Reagan drily responded, "I can't really talk about what we are doing, because I don't want to do anything that will endanger the prospects of the others being freed. I can only say that we have explored another avenue. . . ." Evidence now points to this "other avenue" as the sale of arms to Iran — arms that would later be used against United States military personnel.

The web of intrigue was woven to fool the United States citizens. The Constitution was mocked.

North felt it was "a keen idea" to circumvent the foreign policy[17] of the United States that should have been planned by Reagan but guided and watched by Congress under the Boland Amendment. Under such circumstances, no one could ever be sure that those who were determining their individual fates and fortune were truly elected. It became obvious during the Contra hearings that mortal citizens of the United States could not but worry that their destinies lay in the hands of some unaccountable petty, *mala fide* lieutenant colonel or amoral admiral who equally scorned the Constitution and played at empire-building, funded mass murderers enriched by trafficking in narcotics, and sold illegal drugs to the nation which not only supported them but believed that they were decent men. Robertson, of course, terms the Contras[18] of Nicaragua as well as those who work to sustain them: "Christian men."[19]

Pat makes no pretense of his determination to establish a "biblical republic." He regularly uses the Bible to predict, interpret, and analyze foreign policy. He has said on the air that the Bible "specifically, clearly, unequivocally says that Russia and other countries will enter into war and God will *destroy* Russia through earthquakes, volcanoes," and other holocausts and plagues. In one segment of his "700 Club" telecast, aired in 1981, Robertson stood before a map, and with a pointer indicated the Middle East, declaring:

> I believe that the Bible indicates that ultimately Israel will take territory all the way up the Euphrates River, which is north of Damascus. This might well be the trigger that would bring the Soviet Union down on Israel for an invasion that was spoken of in the book of Ezekiel, chapter 38, and I don't think we've got a long time to wait for that.[20]

In fact, Robertson is convinced that the Bible specifically speaks about the United States of America. According to this preacher-who-would-be-president, the United States will engage in a nuclear war to bring "the blessings of Christianity" to the world — even if the world has no interest in receiving such "blessings."

During the same telecast, Robertson lamented the sin of the Soviets: a "sin" which he defined as a mixture of "Communism" and "Atheism" — yet never bothering to define either concept. When his co-host Ben Kinchow (a former Black Muslim) talked about the "Young Lions" who might come to the aid of Israel, and "which many Bible scholars feel is the United States," Robertson nodded in agreement. "The only time where the United States is talked about in the Bible is in connection with this area," came the summation. Then with a distinct smugness, Robertson swung the conversation back to the "sins" of the Soviets, claiming that the United States would have to become involved in a war to help Israel when the Soviets leagued against Israel with other "demonic powers" (Iran, possibly?).

Continuously claiming that his interpretation was accepted by "biblical scholars," Pat failed to tell any of his viewers exactly who the Bible scholars are that "feel" that the United States is the subject of the Robertson-Kinchow dialogue. University of Richmond biblical scholar Alley did not agree with the televangelist. When queried, Alley responded, "The whole idea that the Bible mentions the United States is totally outrageous! . . . This is throwing an irrationality blanket over foreign affairs that is scary."[21]

Alley's denial of the factuality and exegetical exactness of Robertson's fantasies and prophecies discourages no one who worships at the CBN network. A skeleton crew of Robertson disciples is determined to make this ghost of dictatorships past a living promise for tomorrow. All that is needed, they argued, is for Pat to be president and his prophecies will be fulfilled. *Au contraire*, with Pat as president, Armageddon is as close as your 7-Eleven.

Notes

1. Tschirhart, "TV Preacher Calls Believers to the Mission of Politics," *Detroit News* (9 May 1986).

2. Remer Tyson, "Christian Campaign Rivals Kemp, Bush," *Detroit Free Press* (4 May 1986), sec. A, pp. 1, 8.

3. Cf. Hugh McDiarmid, "Link Robertson Bid, Council? God

Forbid," *Detroit Free Press* (23 March 1986).

4. Howard Fineman, "God and GOP in Michigan," *Newsweek* (4 August 1986): p. 17.

5. Chris Christoff, "Political Pastor Pat; Get Involved, Evangelist Tells Christians," *Detroit Free Press* (21 March 1986), sec. A, pp. 14. The article begins on p. 1A. The viability of Robertson's political force was hinted at by John W. Mashek, "Nibbles on a TV Preacher's Hook," *U.S. News & World Report* (9 June 1986).

6. "The Early Line in Michigan," *Newsweek* (21 April 1986): p. 10. Remer Tyson, "Robertson Pulls Out Stops for Delegate Candidates," *Detroit Free Press* (29 May 1986), sec. A, p. 9. "Pat Robertson Claims Michigan *GOP* Win," *Dallas Times Herald* (29 May 1986), sec. A, pp. 1, 6. Radio WXYT celebrated the Robertson coup. "Confusion Reigns after Michigan Primary," *The Orange County* [California] *Register* (7 August 1986), sec. A, p. 19.

7. See below my chapter on anti-Semitism for additional development. The first reporter to carry this story was Hugh McDiarmid, "Robertson's Letter Strips away Myths," *Detroit Free Press* (17 July 1986), p. 1.

8. Cf. Thomas B. Edsall, "Via Satellite, Evangelist Woos Michigan GOP; Pat Robertson Flexes Political Muscle," *Washington Post* (9 May 1986), sec. A, p. 9. Paul West, "Showing by Evangelist Indicates Dramatic Inroads into GOP Structure," *Houston* [Texas] *Chronicle* (1 June 1986), sec. 1, p. 10.See Russell Chancler, "Religious Right Makes Political Arena Its Major Battleground," *Los Angeles Times* (29 March 1986), pt. I-A, p. 7. An interesting analysis is Mary McGrory, "Preachers Are Giving The Politicans Heartburn," Universal Press Syndicate, (12 June 1986).

9. "700 Club," 1 May 1986.

10. "700 Club," 1 May 1986.

11. Pat Robertson, *America's Dates with Destiny,* (New York: William Morrow, 1985), pp. 273-82. Gordon L. Hankins and John Gilman, eds., *My People: A Pictorial History of Washington for Jesus* (Klamath Falls, Oregon: Craft Printers, 1980), p. 25. William F.

Buckley, Jr., "Evangelist Robertson Puts Political Spotlight on Religion," in *Austin* [Texas] *American-Statesman* (20 August 1986), sec. A, p. 7.

12. Pat Robertson, *Answers to 200 of Life's Most Probing Questions*, (New York: Boston Books, 1984), p. 63-64.

13. Robertson, *Answers*, p. 70.

14. Robertson, *Answers*, pp. 87-88, 169-70, 271-72, who will be judged by his god, p. 32, and punished, pp. 90-91.

15. Robertson, *Answers*, pp. 132-34, 194-96.

16. The venality of Lieutenant Colonel Oliver North is exposed in Peter Kornblush, "Ollie's Follies: What North Might Have Wrought," *The Nation* 244.25 (27 June 1987): pp. 871, 887-89. Cp. the editorial "Turning to Teheran," *The Nation* 245.1 (4/11 July 1987): p. 1. Cp. Claudia Dreifus, "Sergio Ramirez: the View from Managua,"
The editors of *The Progressive* 51.9 (September 1987): pp. 14-18, detail how *The Progressive*, as cited, pp. 19-20.
The account of the Robertson-North meeting was carried in the *Des Moines* [Iowa] *Register*, "Probe on North Focusing on Link to Evangelist" (3 September 1987). This information was secreted during the Iran-Contra hearings.

17. Oliver North's argument that he was "following orders" is identical to that of the Nazis tried at Nürnberg following the collapse of the Third Reich. At Nürnberg, international jurists ruled that a subordinate following any order that was against humanity was unjust and that to follow it on the claim that it was the mark of military deference was not only illegal but immoral. See: Ann Tusa and John Tusa, *The Nuremberg Trial* (New York: Atheneum, 1986); the official transcripts of the trial is *Trial of the Major War Criminals before the International Military Tribunal*, Vols. 1 to 22, Nürnberg, 1947; cp. Joe Heydecker and Johannes Leeb, *The Nuremberg Trials*, trans. E. A. Downie (London: Heinemann, 1962); Taylor Telford, "The Nuremberg War Crimes," *International Conciliation* p. 450 (April 1949).

18. David Corn and Jefferson Morley, "Schools of Scandal: A Guide to Iran/*Contra* Theories," *The Nation* 245.3 (1/8 August 1987): pp. 74,

88, 90-92.

19. Jonathan Kwitny, "Money, Drugs and the *Contras*," *The Nation* (29 August 1987): pp. 145, 162-66. Jonathan Marshall, Peter Dale Scott and Jane Hunter, *The Iran-Contra Connection: Secret Teams and Covert Operations in the Reagan Era* (New York: South End Press, 1987).

20. Cf. Robertson, *Answers*, p. 152: "The regathering of Jews to Israel is a clear sign, in both the Old and New Testaments, that our age is just about over." He argues that the 6 June 1967, Jewish takeover of Jerusalem is a signal "for the approaching end of Gentile world power." Cp. ibid., pp. 146-47.

21. Myra MacPherson, "The Pulpit and the Power: '700 Club's Pat Robertson, Preaching Gospel & Eyeing the White House," *Washington Post* (18 October 1985), sec. D, p. 8.

Chapter 12
Ego, Good Looks, The Presidential Quest, The McCloskey Letter, and Sundry Other Matters

To achieve the presidency, although Robertson was not an officially declared candidate before 1 October 1987,[1] Southern Baptist minister[2] Pat Robertson organized a PAC (Political Action Committee) euphemistically styled "American Friends of Robertson." The stated purpose of Robertson's "American Friends of Robertson" was to raise a required three million signatures endorsing his candidacy and pledging to work for his election.[3]

Running as a candidate for the presidency of the United States is costly. Such a run requires enormous quantities of cash, grueling hours, hostile critics, numerous chicken dinners, cold hamburgers — but worse for Robertson's personal television empire was that he was compelled to resign from "The 700 Club." A few followers even argued that they might gather popular support to compel the Southern Baptist minister to resign his ordination[4] — although there is no constitutional requirement in the Baptist Convention that he do so if he were to be elected.[5] Nonetheless, to cement his candidacy, he did resign.

The financial burden of running for the presidency of the United States would not be any major drain on Robertson's existing wealth. A man of substantial means, Robertson's 1987 salary, according to federal court documents, was $140,000. Unlike the working woman who takes home, according to Robertson, only $1,800 a year of her salary, Robertson takes nearly the entire $140,000 he earns to the bank. He has few expenses.

It must be remembered that Pat's father, Absalom Willis Robertson (died 1 November 1971), left a sizeable part of his estate to his son, the televangelist. Assets distributed to Marion G. Robertson on 10 April 1973 included 176 shares of American Telephone and Telegraph (AT&T), 206 shares of Standard Oil of New Jersey, 110 shares of Continental Corporation, 100 shares each of Philips Petroleum, SOCCNY, Mobil Oil, Manufacturers Hanover, and American Smelting and Refining. Other shares included Colonial American National Bank (55), Union Carbide (50), Harrisonburg Telephone (34), Virginia National Bank (32), and 12½ each of Continental Corp, and First National Real Estate Trust. Additionally Pat received a cash disbursement of $25,634 on 12 May 1973, and $6,000 on 28 June 1973. (Rockbridge County Circuit Court, Va., Book 89. pp. 6-9. The will is dated 11 September 1970.) Also, it was his mother who had the wealth in the family. Her will was not available to the author at the time of this writing.

Robertson lives in a rent-free house. He has the use of a private jet. Other perquisites are equally lavish and include secretarial help, grounds keeping, and constant gifts ranging from clothing to food.

Publicly, Robertson has, in the past, claimed his income to be "only" $60,000. He says he donates this $60,000 back to the ministry — although CBN records of accounts show his salary more than double that amount.

The televangelist star of the "700 Club," Robertson boasts that he supports himself and his family with book royalties, speaking fees, and investments.[6] Yet the sales of his books have been "sluggish," with bookstores returning 30,000 unsold copies — out of an initial printing of 120,000 — to the books' publishers. Robertson also estimated, in May of 1987, that he could generate $750,000 on speaking tours to promote his newest book *America's Date with Destiny*, and would produce a series of tapes on "the secret of financial success," as well as to write a new autobiography.[7]

With his "uncertain" income, Robertson polishes the brass that holds together the rivets of his campaign quest to win the American presidency. He has little to worry about as he is the toast of most evangelical soirées and seances from Pennsylvania to California, New Hampshire to Florida, with powerful political brokers in the Republican Party eager to throw their strength behind him — provided that he "lowers taxes," ends minimum wage, and keeps "laborers in their place."

Since Robertson's earliest overtures towards the Republican Party, offering himself as a candidate for the presidency of the United States, he has been busy attempting to gather information on his own standing in popular opinion. Robertson could not afford to offend the fat cats of the Republican Party, and he could not jeopardize the "grass roots" middle class that he would need to have cast their votes for him.

Robertson has, according to record, toyed with the idea of running for the presidency since the early days of 1985,[8] speaking at Baptist churches around America.[9] He has declared that "there is overwhelming evidence of support, especially in the South, for someone with the values that I share. . ." and, as such, is convinced that he is an electable candidate.[10] First, in 1986, and later in 1987, to ascertain that his candidacy was the "will" of his god, Robertson broadcast that he would need to see a list of no less than three million[11] signatures, each signature promising to support him "if" he should run.[12] With god on his side, one wonders why he would have needed the signatures.

Even before the Robertson presidential race began, Pat stumbled. Carelessly he tripped over his own past, his own claims, his own books.

Although Pat had boasted of serving his nation as a "Marine combat officer in Korea,"[13] he never saw actual combat and spent a lot of time in Japan. When the truth came out concerning his fabrication of his military career, Pat's political posturings and presidential aspirations almost wilted.

The quest for the presidency polished by Robertson to a rich patina was tarnished when United States Indiana Democrat Representative Andrew Jacobs made public in October of 1986 a letter written on 4 August 1986 by former Congressional California Republican Representative Paul McCloskey suggesting that Robertson had relied on his father, A. Willis Robertson, then a Democratic senator from Virginia, to keep him out of combat[14] — in direct contradiction to Robertson's press releases that stated he saw combat duty during the Korean conflict.[15]

There is a strong foundation for McCloskey's statement. Pat's father was in frequent correspondence with Gen. Lemuel Shepherd, Jr., commander of the Marines in the Pacific, as his letters archived in the College of William and Mary Library, in Williamsburg, Virginia, testify.[16]

The Robertson-Shepherd letters show that Shepherd, who commanded 200,000 men in the Pacific, took a personal interest in Pat and sent the senator periodic reports of the future televangelist's well-being.[17] At the same time, Senator Robertson wrote letters urging that Shepherd be promoted to commandant of the Marine Corps. Shepherd was awarded this political plum and took the oath of office for the Marine Corps's highest position in December 1951 — when Pat was safe in Japan where he would not be subjected to enemy fire, as McCloskey and Jacobs would be.[18]

McCloskey was wounded in Korea while leading a bayonet charge up Hill 566. He was awarded the Navy Cross, the Silver Star, and the Purple Heart.

Andrew Jacobs went to Korea while his father was a sitting member of Congress from the district that he now represents; Jacobs was wounded by shrapnel. For his suffering, Jacobs is legally entitled to a 10 percent disability benefit. He has refused to collect it after his election to Congress in 1964.

Both McCloskey and Jacobs faced other men armed with rifles who were attempting to kill them.[19] Robertson faced no armed enemy.

Robertson never saw battle, and the only war wound he received was in "non-combatant duties." It is hard to earn any medal for valor when wounded by opening beer cans.[20]

When Pat Robertson pulled out all the legal stops to silence McCloskey and Jacobs by taking them to court, charging them with libel and seeking $35 million in damages from each,[21] the televangelist met with adamant opposition from various quarters. He was no longer a hero to all who went to Korea or served in combat.

McCloskey's argument was supported enthusiastically by former Marine John Gearhart of Los Angeles, who told the *Los Angeles Times* that he was with Robertson in 1951 when Robertson called his father from Japan. Gearhart, telling that he, Robertson, and two other Marine officers were pulled off the ship and assigned to a base in Japan, noted, "It was generally understood we were pulled off because of the good fortune of Pat's influence."[22]

In an interview, Gearhart on 24 September 1986 testified that McCloskey's allegations were correct. Robertson, according to Gearhart, did make the now-Robertson-denied telephone call to his father.[23]

Gearhart remembers walking with Robertson from their ship, the *U.S.S. Breckinridge*, into Kobe, Japan, "and into a U.S. Special Services facility where they had telephones with radio connections available for servicemen. And we each made separate calls to our parents." The next day, Gearhart, Robertson, and four other lieutenants, including Edwin Davis, now a history professor at the University of Arizona, were transferred from the detail going to Korea and war combat, to safe duty in Japan. Even Davis admits, "We might have received preferential treatment," and confesses that Robertson "wasn't hesitant about letting people know his father was a [United

States] senator."

The McCloskey story and Gearhart account were further acknowledged to be true by Huntington, New York, lawyer Pierce Power. Power served with Gearhart in Korea in 1951.

When Power was questioned concerning Gearhart's possible motives in supporting McCloskey's account and releasing his own testimony when Pat was prepared to take the plunge into presidential candidacy waters, Power noted that "Gearhart has no ax to grind. He considers Pat Robertson a friend."[24]

The only combat Robertson saw, according to the McCloskey letter, was in fighting for liquor for officers. "His major duty was . . . to fly to Japan once a week and bring back booze for the officers' mess."[25]

Only when reporters pressed Robertson did the televangelist admit that he was "not in the trenches with his hand on the trigger." Robertson's claim that he saw combat duty was but a "technicality" determined by himself as an assistant adjutant at First Marine Division headquarters in Korea.

> The technical definition of "combat" used by the entire Armed
> Forces of the United States is that anybody who is attached to
> a combat unit in what is called the battle zone is in combat,

Robertson explained.[26]

Regardless of his rhetoric, Robertson has been cartooned as a "conservative war wimp who now talks tough to the Commies," but who "found a safe haven when the Commie bullets were flying."[27] Robertson did the drawing himself.

Problems with the McCloskey letter[28] arose when Jacobs forwarded the letter to syndicated columnists Rowland Evans and Robert Novak, known supporters of New York Congressional Representative Republican Jack Kemp,[29] who printed it in their September column.[30] After the McCloskey-Jacobs debacle denouncing Robertson's alleged patriotism and combat service during the Korean Conflict, Robertson was determined to learn how his popularity fared.[31] To that end, he subpoenaed both CBN and A.C. Nielsen Co. for information about the number of people who view his religious talk show, "The 700 Club."[32] In both situations Robertson was refused access to the ratings, on the grounds that Robertson would use the information for himself and to enhance or determine his political possibilities — especially after the McCloskey revelation.[33]

To punish McCloskey and Representative Andrew Jacobs of

Indiana, Robertson filed twin $35 million libel suits on 21 May 1986, allegedly in defense of his father and for making "wanton and reckless statements denigrating my role with the U.S. Marine Corps while serving in the Korean conflict."[34] If McCloskey's account could not be discredited, one additional lie would have surfaced in the Robertson cartoon.[35]

Another aspect of the case came to the attention of the media with the seventy-eight page deposition given by retired Tulane University professor of language Paul W. Brosman. In the deposition, Brosman stated that Robertson was an inconsiderate young Marine who "messed around with prostitutes." Robertson, it appears, delighted in terrifying the teenage Korean girl who cleaned his barracks, in spite of the fact that "she pleaded with him to stop." Brosman who shared quarters with Robertson said he would not stop. "Pat used to fool around with her all the time, that is pinching her and carrying on. That would terrify her." Robertson's rejoinder was to say, "I never said I didn't show some wild oats. I've sowed plenty of them."[36]

Later Robertson was forced to drop his libel suit, he said, because the hearing was set on Super Tuesday, the day he expected to take America by storm.[37] It was necessary, then, that he pay the court costs of between $10,000 and $20,000 to McClosky.[38]

To extract himself from the buffoonery of his Korean sit-com, Robertson has turned to a most unique *Weltanschauung*. If Robertson were to become president, he has pledged himself to take his politics from Jesus,[39] Mother Teresa of India, Henry Ford, and J. C. Penney.[40]

Education,[41] social intercourse, business, the military-industrial complex, and all other facets of American life are to be "Christian" even if the participants are not Christian. Christian ethics and values are to become the staple sustenance of society, to be rotely memorized and blindly followed by Jews, Buddhists, followers of Islam, and all other peoples with or without any religious affirmation.[42] Those who disagree, like "Communists" — especially the Soviet Union — are to be "eliminated" . . . "not contained."[43] Robertson's call for elimination of a people is truly reminiscent of another "solution" proposed in the first half of the twentieth century in Germany.

Conservative strategists questioned if Pat's "exploration" for the presidency was the will of god — or his own.[44] Several saw Robertson as a divisive individual who would scare people away from the GOP.[45] However, Sen. Paul Laxalt (Rep. - Nev.), in his official capacity as general chair of the Republican party, answered the call of Paul Weyrich, head of the committee for the Survival of a Free Congress, and met with a dozen Christian evangelical leaders to assure them that they and their followers were welcome in the GOP.[46] Others questioned Robertson's religious "calling" — wondering if his religiousness was but a front for personal political aspirations.[47]

Robertson's supporters see the televangelist's candidacy as one filled with political clout. This clout, according to Ed McAteer, a religious right activist who helped start the Moral Majority, and now heads Jerry Falwell's Religious Roundtable, meant that Robertson had his election to the presidency guaranteed: "Pat Robertson has his handsome face in 60 million homes every week. That's clout."[48] Many voters in the United States do cast their ballots based on the candidate's physical appearance — or the candidate's Hollywood-type role. Style frequently has meant more to voters than the candidate's substance or political stand.

Robertson maintains his televangelist "star image." He refuses to allow photographers on the "700 Club" set to take candid pictures. Candid pictures might be "unflattering" to him.[49]

Robertson also refuses impromptu interviews. He might say something he regrets.

To avoid saying anything that cannot be used to his advantage, Robertson preplans interviews. He maintains a prepared, class-B script. It is always nearby — along with his canned smile and transparent sincerity.[50]

Robertson's political goals are as plastic as he. His plans for the United States are as brittle as peanut candy.

Although some consider Robertson attractive enough to win the necessary votes to push him into the White House, not all of Robertson's supporters are as convinced as is McAteer. To stem any possible loss of momentum, media time and space are purchased to build the momentum of Pat's political ministry.

The cost of running for president is high. It is higher than running with Jesus.

To meet the price that must be paid to run a winning election bid, Robertson has come down from his ivory tower at CBN. Instead of praising Jesus, Robertson now willingly sells Jesus.

Jesus is to be the key to open the coffers of the rich, the not-so-rich, and the poor — to pay for Robertson's campaign. He has learned to grovel like other mortals before the money lenders in the temple of politics, to eat the barbecue of the Hunts, to share rice with the Southern Baptist Jesse Helms,[51] and to take a chicken leg on farms, a hamburger too rare or overdone in the cities.

On 16 May 1986, Robertson hosted a high-stakes fund-raiser at the Washington Sheraton. Tickets were sold for various amounts between $1,000 and $25,000 a couple.

Since federal election laws forbid a couple to give more than $25,000 to a prospective presidential candidate, Robertson put the maximum allowed by law ($5,000) into his political war chest, styled the "Committee for Freedom."[52] He "contributed" the rest to his Freedom Council.[53] Robertson did this to avoid a tax investigation. It was nothing more than legal fiction.[54]

Among those who attended were conservative Republican Senator Jesse Helms of North Carolina and radical right publisher of the *Saturday Evening Post* Cory SerVaas, along with Lee Buck, a retired executive of the Mutual Insurance Co., and current chair of Robertson's Committee for Freedom, who succeeded retired Army officer Jerry Curry. The latter wanted to inject martial fervor into the campaign.[55]

Robertson's Freedom Council apparently used unreported donations for political purposes. Council members attempted to justify their evasion of the tax law by claiming that they were "confused" about the technicalities of the council's tax status. Yet the financing of Robertson's Freedom Council amounted to tens of thousands of dollars a month in its first years and more than $200,000 a month by late 1985.

To claim that Pat Robertson was "confused" by the tax law makes his alleged degree in corporate tax law a joke, at best. Robertson personally handled the council's finances and set its policies. According to record, Robertson was familiar with the tax law he and his council circumvented, for the 1984 CBN tax filing shows a loan of $821,000 payable to the council. The council's return shows no donations over $5,000.[56]

Notes

1. "Robertson to Run for President; Evangelist Says He Will Make GOP Candidacy Official on Oct. 1," *Austin* [Texas] *American-Statesman* (16 September 1987), sec. A, p. 3. Cp. *Dallas* [Texas] Times-Herald (16 September 1987), sec. A, p. 6. Cf. Associated Press (October 1986).

2. See my *Evangelical Terrorism: Censorship, Falwell, Robertson & the Seamy Side of Christian Fundamentalism* (Irving, TX: Scholars Books, 1987), index.

3. Joe Drape, "Pat Robertson Hopes to Enter Race by June," in the *Dallas* [Texas] *Morning News* (3 March 1987), sec. A, p. 16.

4. *Rocky Mountain* [Denver, Colorado] *News* (12 April 1987), p. 44.

5. Robertson severed his ties to the ministry on 27 September 1987, two days before he became an official GOP candidate. See press reports of 29-30 September 1987, and Steve Stone, "Norfolk Church OKs Robertson Resignation," Norfolk, VA *Ledger-Star* (7 October 1987).

6. April Witt, "Robertson Reports '87 Pay of $104,000," in Norfolk, VA *Ledger-Star* (6 May 1987), sec. D, pp. 1, 5.

7. Witt, *Robertson Reports*, sec. D, p. 5.

8. Chris Christoff, "Pulpit Politician" Get Involved, Evangelist Tells Christians" in *Detroit Free Press* (21 March 1986), sec. A, pp. 1, 14. Cp. Robert S. Boyd, "Evangelist Considers Race for President," in *Detroit Free Press* (14 March 1986), sec. A, p. 6. Kate DeSmet, "Rev. Mr. President? Pat Robertson Admits He's Considering Race," *Detroit News* (10 October 1985), sec. A, pp. 1, 13. Booth News Service, "700 Club Host for President? Drive May Be under Way," the *Flint* [Michigan] *Journal* (28 September 1985), sec. A, p. 12. David E. Anderson, "Will Robertson Seek Office? He's Praying for An Answer," the *Houston* [Texas] *Post* (7 September 1985), sec. G, p. 11.

9. Staci Elder, "Robertson Says He Expects to Announce Candidacy by June," in *Carrollton* [Texas] *Chronicle* (4 March 1987), sec. A, p. 12.

10. Boyd, "Evangelist Considers Race," loc. cit.

11. Little Rock *Arkansas Gazette* (14 April 1987) gives the required number as three million. This is also the number carried in the article by Annette Wannamaker, "Pat Robertson Addresses Enthusiastic Supporters," in the Staunton, Virginia *Daily News Leader* (22 July 1987), giving the date of 17 September as the point in time when the magic number needed materialize if Robertson would declare his candidacy. Robertson called for 3 million in his 17 September 1986

speech "A New Vision for America" given at Constitution Hall in Washington, DC; in the typescript, it apears on p. 5.

12. Cf. Carl P. Leubsdorf, "Dole Courting Iowa Evangelicals, Fundamentalists," *Dallas Morning News* (14 September 1987), sec. A, p. 3, with the Robertson *putsche* carried in columns 1, 2. Cp. Remer Tyson, "Efficient Organization Lifts Robertson Early," *Austin* [Texas] *American-Statesman* (18 September 1987), sec. A, p. 24. T. R. Reid, "Robertson's Bid Powered by Faith, Self-Assurance; 'Prophet' Struggles with Secular Role," *Washington Post* (11 September 1987), sec. A, pp. 1, 10.

13. Pat Robertson, *Shout It from the Housetops*, p. 14.

14. Amy Wilentz, "Combat Zone — Pat Robertson Sues for Libel," *Time* (3 November 1986): p. 29.

15. Cf. *New York Times* (3 June 1987) in *Des Moines* [Iowa] *Register* (3 June 1987), sec. A, p. 7. Robertson's official response was given in a press release dated 2 June 1987.

16. Jack Nelson, "Dad's Letters Contradict Robertson's Combat Claims," *Austin* [Texas] *American-Statesman* (28 October 1987), sec. A, p. 9.

17. "Senator Knew Son Would Leave Ship; Dad's Letter: Robertson, Pal to Debark in Japan," *San Antonio* [Texas] *Express-News* (20 January 1987), sec. A, p. 2.

18. Andrew Petkofsky and Peter Hardin, "Robertson Letters Emerge; Evangelist's Father Wrote General about Son," *Rocky Mountain* [Denver, Colorado] *News* (12 December 1986), p. 124.

19. Jack Newfield and James Ridgeway, with the research assistance of Jeff Salamon and Kris Jacobs, "Robertson," *The Village Voice* [New York] (16 September 1986): pp. 16ff.

20. Pinching the buttocks of young local girls and various prostitutes he slept with after "sowing wild oats."

21. T. R. Reid, "Robertson's Honesty to Go on Trial," *Washington*

Post (11 September 1987), sec. A, p. 10.

22. United Press International release carried in *The Orange* [County, California] *Register* (26 September 1986), sec. E, p. 9. Robertson's Marine general dismissed McCloskey's claim, telling the *Los Angeles Times* that he had no personal recollection "of receiving any communication" similar to that detailed by McCloskey and Gearhart; however, to admit to being subject to a senatorial whim would be disastrous to the general's career, as he noted.

23. Phil Gailey, "Robertson Sues 2 Over War Record; TV Evangelist Says 'Liberals' Are Out to Discredit Him," *New York Times* (22 October 1986).

24. "Ex-Marine Backs Charge Pastor Avoided Combat: Robertson Again Criticized on Military Record," Toledo, Ohio *Blade* (25 September 1986), p. 3.

25. *San Diego* [California] *Union* (22 October 1986), sec. A, p. 2.

26. Fruhling, *Robertson, Religious Zealot*, sec A, p. 4.

27. Mike Royko, "Robertson Fighting Mad; Battles War Wimp Image," syndicated column (24 October 1986).

28. Cf. *Houston* [Texas] *Post* (22 October 1985), sec A, p. 2.

29. Cf. Mark Shields, "The Anti-Robertson Coalition; Some Will Say It Is a Miracle," the *Washington Post* (6 October 1986), sec A, p. 15.

30. Rowland Evans & Robert Novak, "Did Pat Robertson Use Clout to Avoid Combat?" *Chicago Sun-Times* (6 September 1986), p. 17. McCloskey wrote that "Pat was affable, garrulous and candid. He spoke frankly of his desire to avoid combat and to have his father, Sen. Willis Robertson of Virginia, intervene in his behalf. When (on Feb. 14) we went ashore at Yokosuka (Japan), I believe most of us thought he was joking when he told us he was going to call his father and request transfer off the ship."
Robertson "did make the call," but didn't say if he contacted his father. He returned to the ship and sailed to Kobe, Japan. That resulted in "good-natured ribbing of Pat" about "a six-minute life expectancy for

platoon leaders in combat. . . . My single distinct memory is of Pat, with a big grin on his face, standing on the dock at Kobe (on Feb. 15) after his second phone call . . . telling us that his father had gotten him out of combat duty."

This letter is interesting, especially in light of McCloskey's final comments, which concluded that he and other 1st Division veterans "share a laugh . . . occasionally over the reborn Pat Robertson, who would now lead us against the dread communist menace" when he would not lead them against the Korean communists during the war in 1951.

31. Cp. The comments of Rev. Rene Ouelette of First Baptist Church, Bridgeport, Michigan, in the *Detroit Free Press* (14 April 1987), sec A, p. 3.

32. Caroline E. Mayer, "Religious Broadcasters: Beyond Pray TV," *Washington Post* (5 February 1984), sec F, pp. 1, 8. Cf. Jeffrey K. Hadden and Charles Swann, *Prime Time Preachers: the Rising Power of Televangelism* (Reading, MA: Addison-Wesley Press, 1981).

33. April Witt, "Robertson Seeks Ratings Information," in *The* [Norfolk, Virginia] *Ledger-Star* (28 April 1987), sec. D, p. 2.

34. *Rocky Mountain* [Denver, Colorado] *News* (22 May 1986), sec. S, p. 2. Phil Gailey, "Robertson Sues 2 Over War Record; TV Evangelist Says 'Liberals' Are Out to Discredit Him," *New York Times* (22 October 1986).

35. Jack Nelson, "Doubts on War Record Hound Pat Robertson," *Austin* [Texas] *American-Statesman* (24 September 1986), sec. A, p. 6. Cf. Bill Peterson, "Robertson May Find Libel Suit Becoming a Political Land Mine," *Des Moines* [Iowa] *Register* (7 April 1987), Opinion page.

36. Laura King, "Robertson's Sexual Past Discussed; Deposition Tells of Visits to Korean Prostitutes 36 Years Ago," *Fort Worth Star-Telegram*, 4 December, 1987, sect. 1, p. 3; Thomas A. Fogarty, "Robertson Ducks Reporters Questions on Prostitutes' Story." *Des Moines Register*, 5 December 1987, Sec. A. p. 3.

37. David Willman, "Robertson Drops Libel Suit," *Austin American-*

Statesman, 2 March 1988.

38. "Robertson May Drop Suit If He Pays Court Costs," *Austin American-Statesman*, 5 March 1988.

39. Robertson continues to claim his sole message "is Jesus," yet couples this with others. See "TV, Radio Evangelism in Midst of a Boom," *Los Angeles Times* (25 February 1980), pp. 3, 15.

40. Deborah Wiley, "Robertson Takes Cue from Jesus, Ford," in *Des Moines* [Iowa] *Register* (19 April 1987), sec. B, p. 3.

41. For a more detailed discussion on Robertson's ideas on education in America, see the chapter on education in this book.

42. *Times-Advocate* [Escondido, CA] (7 April 1987), sec. A, p. 3. Cp. David Yepsen, "Robertson: A Political Enigma, but Shepherd to an Enormous Flock," in *Des Moines* [Iowa] *Register* (6 February 1987), sec. A, p. 8.

43. Yepsen, loc. cit.

44. John Dart, "Evangelist Opposed as Candidate," *Los Angeles Times* (8 March 1986), pt. II, p. 5.

45. Boyd, "Evangelist Considers Race," loc. cit.

46. "Laxalt Tells Evangelicals They Are Welcome in The GOP," *Washington Post*, 1 October 1986.

47. Eric Kinkopf, "Evangelist Robertson's Calling May be Political," *Detroit Free Press* (22 June 1986), sec. K, p. 6.

48. Hill, "Pat Robertson: A Serious Presidential Contender?" p. 36.

49. Another problem that Pat faced with his "700 Club" image was that of the unusual to preposterous claims of one of his stars: Danuta Soderman. A polished story teller, Danuta struck out at logic with the same insensitivity that the Grand Inquisitor Torquemada did in medieval Spain when interrogating any infidel. Her stories, frequently bizarre, were delivered with unusual warmth. Her charm spellbound

her listeners until she threw the warped ideas of her Jesus to the listener not for his psychological analysis, but to force the ideas into the individual's mind hoping that all independent thought and reason would be washed down the gutter of despair that comes in religious life.

A classic example of Danuta's style is her speech on how she met her husband. Robertson's god called Danuta to the Christian broadcast system and the "700 Club." Then, he not only craftily told her that she was to marry, but who she was to marry — by giving her a sign. The miracle of god's choice came one night, quite late, when god rang her wind chimes.

Nearly deified in her own right as a goddess, her smile was seen as therapeutic to the pain of — a hysterectomy. Old women saw her as "Christ-like." They explained, "That means she's like Jesus."

Danuta's cult grew daily. Her worshippers multiplied. To many she became more important, and certainly more real, than Jesus or his father.

Robertson cashed in on her popularity. He never rebuked any of her idol worshippers. See: Lynell Mickelsen, "Christian TV's Talk Show Queen," *Detroit Free Press* (22 May 1985), sec. B, pp. 1, 2.

50. Cp. Rod Gragg, "Partisan Conversation," *Southern Partisan Magazine* VI.1 (Winter, 1986): pp. 39-42.

51. On Helms' link with the fundamentalist movement, see *Southern Baptist Advocate* V.6 (July/August 1984): pp. 1, 10. Helms is equally committed to "Christianizing" America.

52. Joel J. Smith, "Political Mission Mounted; Evangelist's Group Sows Seeds in State [of Michigan]," *Detroit News* (1 May 1986), sec. A, p. 11.

53. Dudley Clendinen, "Pat Robertson Looks to South and Evangelicals as Key to 1988," *New York Times* (24 June 1986), p. 8.

54. After the initial demise of the Freedom Council, Hugh McDiarmid wrote a celebration of what he hoped to be the end of an era; see: Hugh McDiarmid, "Goodbye to a Fiction: Freedom Council," *Detroit Free Press* (30 September 1986), sec. A, p. A3.

55. Thomas B. Edsall, "High-Stakes Fund-Raiser Benefits Robertson," *Washington Post* (17 May 1986), sec. A, p. 6.

56. Jeff Gerth, "Tax Data of Pat Robertson's Groups Are Questioned," *New York Times* (10 December 1986).

Chapter 13
Pat's Platform and Style

Robertson's political platform is laid bare in his book *Answers to 200 of Life's Most Probing Questions*.[1] Robertson, however, goes on to label Marx a "satanist priest."[2]

Karl Marx is credited by Robertson as being responsible for the "massacre of tens of millions of people." Robertson also argues that Marx is singularly responsible for the "persecution of innocent people in the gulags of the Soviet Union and other communist countires."

Marx died in 1883, scores of years before the Soviet Union existed. He died in England, never having visited Imperial Russia. Marx said that communism would appear in highly industrialized nations. Russia (now the Soviet Union) was not industrialized until after World War I. Robertson's knowledge of history is as marginal as his comprehension of economics.

Communism Robertson describes as a "hideous" philosophy[3] which, he later argued on 21 July 1987 at an Augusta fund-raiser, is spread in the United States by "teachers' unions with leftist tendencies." To counter Communism in the classroom, Robertson vowed, earlier in the day, that he would eliminate the U. S. Department of Education.[4]

Judgments are easy for Robertson; capital punishment is a "necessary corrective to violent crime." He does not spell out what a "violent crime" is. But, the state alone should have the power to take human life. Abortion is "tantamount to murder."[5] Robertson seemingly has an usual understanding of human life. He would risk the life of a living woman for the potential of one not born.

If we take Robertson's insistence that all crimes be based on the Judeo-Christian bible(s), a violent crime includes incest, rape, murder, self-mutilation, masturbation, and most nonsupine sexual acts. Thus a man who engages in cunnilingus with his wife could be executed for initiating the violence of the crime of oral sex — prohibited in the ancient Israeli codes. A man could also be put to death if he touched another man's penis — as could a woman be sacrificed on the altar or sexual irrationality.

Other forbidden acts include seeing a parent naked (the "sin" of Noah's children), speaking disrespectfully or hatefully towards a parent, stealing grapes, working on a holy day, failing to feast during a festival, or rescuing an ox that had fallen into a well during the Sabbath.

The first to be charged with crimes of violence could be gays, Atheists, nonbelievers, tax-dodgers, angry children, sullen wives, and incorrigibles. The latter group is open to any number of variant forms.

Robertson defends his support for capital punishment claiming that an execution of a social deviant would act as a deterrent to others who might have like proclivities and propensities. Yet to cut off the hand of a man caught masturbating will not stop other men from engaging in this form of sexual self-gratification. Castrating or killing homosexuals will not end homosexuality. And depriving a shrewish wife of life or limb has never stopped other angry wives from demanding equal and fair treatment from born-again Christian husbands and fathers.

A perennial whipping boy, homosexuality is condemned by Robertson as being responsible for the fall of civilizations. Even Edward Gibbons, in his *The Decline and Fall of the Roman Empire*, rejects such rank homophobia and historical illiteracy. Rome and other civilizations have fallen when currency is debased, government spending gets out of hand, intolerance is allowed to spread toward and against minorities, and any single religion becomes the sole church of the state. As Yale professor John Boswell pointed out in his *Christianity and Social Tolerance*, homosexuals allowed to function freely as equals in a society benefit the society in the arts, letters, sciences, and military.

Robertson's claim that homosexuality is a "sign that a society is in the last stages of decay"[6] — is absurd and self-contradicting, for homosexuals work at Robertson's CBN, in spite of the fact that Robertson has a policy dictating that those who discover a homosexual employee are to turn the homosexual in to the "law enforcement agents at CBN." Robertson's "enforcement agents" are a covert gestapo every bit as dangerous as the SS in Nazi Germany.[7]

Homosexuals, as people, are to be presented to the world at large only if "they" return to "the straight life,"[8] confess Jesus with their mouths, and worship Pat.[9] They must testify that their homosexuality is evil, bad, degrading: they are ordered to call "sin a sin."[10]

Love is to be "measured with physical punishment."[11] Love hurts. It is not wrong to beat a child or wife. The man is the vicar of Christ and acts for Jesus at all times in all things.

Marriage and marital love is subordinate to the love of god. According to Robertson, marriage is more of an obligation than a love union. Robertson reminds his followers: "Wives, submit yourselves to your husbands."

Wives who submit themselves to their husband's yoke can feel that "he is looking out for her." Being dutiful to her "lord of the house," the Christian evangelical woman will not insist on her "rights." Robertson does not see wives as having rights exclusive of the husband. He is the head. She is but one part of the family unit subject to the man's authority.

Any proclamation of equality or a demand to share in the household decisions "will destroy the marriage" and make the husband "apprehensive about following the Lord."

To save her husband's soul the obedient wife resists temptation and has "voluntarily surrendered a portion of her autonomy to her husband when she marries."

Women are to be subordinate to men, especially in matters of the soul and individual faith.[12] A wife must submit to her husband's decision "even though she may disagree with it."[13] Women are to be like Dede Robertson: without will, equality, or spirit, totally subject to their husbands.

Capitalism is the system "most closely related to the Bible."[14] Since capitalism is the song of the angels, Communism is the death march of the Devil.[15]

Robertson argues that capitalism is synonymous with Christianity. Communism is satanic and ushered in to a civilization by Satan.

People should avoid taxes by contributing to Christian or charitable causes.[16] Tax evasion is a sin[17] — unless you are CBN, Robertson, or his Freedom Council.[18]

Taxes are like a cross that Christians resign themselves to carry. Robertson exhorts Christian fundamentalists to pay their taxes as a way of obeying god's word. His defense of others paying their taxes is that payment of duties to a state makes the Christian stronger in the Christian faith. Seldom do any of his coreligionists realize that Pat doesn't pay his fair share.

While Robertson says people should pay their taxes if they live in the United States, he notes that in "America, when there is a waste of mammoth proportions, and when money is being used for programs that are abhorrent to Christians, the Christian should do everything he can to bring about change and reform. He must help to curtail the excessive spending of government, the growth of government and he must protest the improper use of his money."

The greatest virtue is to lie to the IRS. It is wrong that "God gives — and the IRS takes away."[19]

Pat likes to fulfill scripture. The IRS is not responsive to the teachings of Jesus as Pat defines them. Pat's problems with the IRS came to a head by December of 1986. The extent of his involvement in tax evasion is unknown.

There were at least three tax-exempt organizations founded and directed by Robertson that gave both incomplete and false information to the IRS. This action Robertson excuses as being an act "for Jesus." Robertson has refused to issue any additional comment on the tax problem.

The best way to avoid an audit is to claim that all monies received were for charitable reasons. To prove this, Robertson formed his Freedom Council. Although this Freedom Council was initially formed for the purpose of "prayer, education and action," the Council quickly decided, with Robertson's concurrence, "to get involved in politics." In spite of the fact that by 1983, the Freedom Council had both a staff and a physical headquarters, its 1983 Federal Tax Return showed neither revenue nor expenses, and no donation of services or monies — information required by federal tax law.

Interestingly, the Freedom Council operates under Section 501(C)(3) of the Federal Tax Code. This section severely restricts political activities. Only donors to a 501(C)(3) group are entitled to a tax deduction. Any group covered by this restrictive part of the code is prohibited from donating to a group that operates under a less stringent provision unless the donor group controls the use of the money and receives a full accounting to assure it was not used for political purposes.

The "improper use of" the Christian's money, according to the televangelist, is paying for any service or contributing to any charity that doesn't recognize Jesus as lord, or reflect Robertson's concept of proper Christianity and christian mission. According to Robertson, it is a sin to support any institution, hospital, or cause that stands for women's independence from men, opportunity to express a personal feminist opinion, or obtain a safe and therapeutic abortion. It is equally wrong to support non-Christian candidates running for public office; it is acceptable to Robertson's god to send money to candidates who are Christian, but far better to send money to born-again evangelicals who have vowed their determination to bring about a religious theocracy in the United States. It is also Christian to send monies to murderers if the murderers are born-again Christians, such as is the case with the Contras, or even right-wing dictators of the stature of Pinochet in Chile, or the corrupt governments in El Salvador and Honduras.

Jews have to become Christians.[20] Unless Jews confess Jesus as their "lord and savior," they cannot be "saved" or expect to prosper.[21]

Robertson is the instrument of the Christian god. To counter Pat is to go against god, for, as Pat told Norman Lear, taking on Pat is like trying to "box God" — and Pat was a boxer in his youth who had won "Golden Gloves" in his early career.[22]

To avoid giving equal time to other presidential aspirants, under the aegis of the "equal time" doctrine — an FCC policy prior to Fall 1987, and one which Pat had labeled as being "of the Devil"[23] — Robertson did not announce his candidacy until after he resigned from the "700 Club." Later, he first elected to pass up federal matching campaign funds,[24] then changed his mind and took $4.5 million from the U. S. Treasury.[25] At the same time, Robertson's disciples question whether or not they should give him political contributions.[26] His plea for an additional $21 million to "see CBN through the next seven months," issued in May of 1987, was met with skepticism by many who worried whether or not their donation would line his political pockets instead of helping to defray network costs.[27] The escalation in operating costs and the expansion of CBN have made Robertson's network appear to many as the "Video Vatican of Christian broadcasting."[28]

Notes

1. Robertson, *Answers to 200 of Life's Most Probing Questions* (Nashville: Nelson, 1985). A paperback edition is published by Bantam Books (New York, 1984), from which all references are taken.

2. Pat Robertson, *Answers to 200 of Life's Most Probing Questions*, p. 188. Hereafter, this work is cited as *Answers*.

3. Robertson, *Answers*, p. 118. Cf. *News Virginian* [Waynesboro, Virginia] (22 July 1987), pp. 1f, records Robertson as wanting to see the "elimination of communism from the face of the earth, including the Soviet Union," and implying that he would not be averse to a first-strike, or preemptive attack against the Soviet Union. Robertson, *Answers*, pp. 198-99. In August of 1987, Robertson appeared in Staunton, Virginia, at a press conference held at the Holiday Inn. There he suggested that the only solution to the Soviets was to eliminate them; see the report of Arnold L. Via and Wilson Fleming, Jr., to the Society of Separationists dated 3 August 1987; typescript in the archives of the American Atheist Center, Austin, Texas.

4. Dan McCauley, "Robertson Blasts 'Scandal': GOP Hopeful Speaks at Augusta Fund-Raiser," in Harrisonburg, Virginia *Daily News-Record* (22 July 1987), pp. 1, 9.

5. Robertson, *Answers*, pp. 175-76.

6. Robertson, *Answers*. p. 174.

7. Gerald T. Straub, *Salvation for Sale*: An Insider's View of Pat Robertson's Ministry (Buffalo, NY: 1986), pp. 104, 108-9.

8. Robertson, *Answers*, p. 175.

9. Cf. Robertson, *Answers*, p. 193. Robertson also objects to homosexual parents.

10. Straub, *Salvation for Sale*, p. 97.

11. Robertson, *Answers*, pp. 23-24.

12. Robertson, *Answers*, pp. 195-96.

13. Robertson, *Answers*, pp. 194, 118.

14. Robertson, *Answers*, p. 186

15. Robertson, *Answers*, p. 187. Robertson cites Rom 13:1-7; as is Robertson's custom, these passages are taken out of context and twisted to support his thesis on taxation. The text concerns itself with

the position of "powers" and the discussion is on "tribute" and not taxes. The "tribute money" is actually a temple tax (cf. Matt. 17:24, and by law the temple tax could only be paid in Tyrian coins (the most common means of exchange was the two-drachma piece known as the *didrachma,* which was minted in Tyre, and was worth between one and two dollars in 1980 currency valuation). This tax brought about a flourishing business for "money changers" who charged a hefty 4 percent commission changing Greek and Roman coins that were the common currency in Judea into Tyrian drachmas. This temple tax was paid every year by all adult Jewish males, with only the priests being exempted.

The actual concept of paying taxes to the state is in Matt. 22:21: "Render unto Caesar the things that are Caesar's . . ." Cf. Alexander Sizoo, *Die antike Welt und das Neue Testament* (Konstanz, 1955).

16. Robert S. Boyd, "Evangelist Considers Race for President," *Detroit Free Press* (14 March 1986), sec. A, p. 6. Provisions within the tax code read that tax-deductible charities are barred from "carrying on propaganda or otherwise attempting to influence legislation . . . including the publishing or distributing of statements [supporting] any political campaign on behalf of any candidate for public office." The Freedom Council's *Newsletter* is a continuing misapplication of fact, with an initial statement that tax donor "contributions are now tax deductible," and then qualifies the statement later by adding, "We expect official approval shortly." Johnell Hunter of the IRS has opined that organizations "cannot say donations are tax deductible until they get their [new] tax status"; and any organization or individual who would make the claim that such a group was deductible or that any contribution to the organization was deductible would be in error and that the contribution to such an organization would be disallowed. If this becomes an official statement of IRS policy, it could have serious and significant consequences for CBN and Robertson. For an interesting analysis of this question, see: Thomas B. Edsall, "Fund-Raising Methods of Pat Robertson Council Questioned," *Washington Post* (6 June 1986), sec. A, pp. 1, 12. Cp. Jeff Girth, "Robertson Groups May Have Filed Faulty IRS Papers; Misstatements either evasion or sloppiness," *The News Tribune,* [Tacoma, Washington] (11 December 1986), sec. A, p. 11. Girth points out that CBN tax returns do not include the required listing of gifts or relationships, nor do the council's filings list the donations and relationships on how money was raised and spent. Furthermore, no tax returns were filed from 1982 through

1985 (when it was dissolved and immediately reorganized by Pat). It is unlawful to knowingly file false statements of a significant nature with the IRS. Failure to file such a return can result in a fine of up to $5,000 for each officer and director.

17. Robertson, *Answers*, pp. 146-47. Cf. Robert Shogan, "Evangelist's Presidential Bid: Test for Church, State," *Los Angeles Times* (4 March 1986), pt. 1, pp. 12, 13.

18. Robertson, *Answers*, p. 147. Robertson cites Rom. 11:1-32. The text is in direct opposition to Robertson's claims. The first line reads: "I say then, Hath god cast away his people? God Forbid. For I am also an Israelite, of the seed of Abraham, *of* the tribe of Benjamin." The only passages that could be construed to be primarily anti-Semitic are verses 21-24; the "prophecy" that the Jews will become Christians is a bad translation of verse 26. Neither claim was made by Jesus. Both promises were pledged by Paul, and it is a statement of his neat legalistic thinking (cf. Romans 7:4), and is a continuing paraphrase of Old Testament prophecies against worshipping false — non-Israelite — gods (cp. Gal. 2:14).

19. Robertson, *Answers*, p. 239. Robertson recognizes Deborah as a prophetess in the Old Testament, yet distorts the New Testament by inanely declaring "nowhere in the Bible is there an example of a woman pastor who actually directed the spiritual lives of a congregation of believers." Robertson should be less selective in his reading of his Christian scriptures and turn to Rom. 16. As for woman serving as priest/pastor, with full Greek-Syriac and Hebrew-Latin texts from the early scrolls/scriptures, with critical analysis and commentary, see my *Woman as Priest, Bishop & Laity*, as cited, index.

20. Robertson, *Answers*, pp. 165-66; cf. "700 Club," 18 January 1983.

21. Robertson, *Shout It from the Housetops*, p. 14.

22. Monies not paid to the IRS are, according to Robertson, to be channelled into "mission" work: "Christian or charitable causes": see: Robertson, *Answers*, p. 188.

23. "700 Club," 19 September 1985.

24. Escondido, California *Times-Advocate* (31 May 1987), sec. A, p. 3.

25. Norfolk, Virginia *Ledger-Pilot* (16 May 1987), sec. A, pp. 1, 3.

26. "Robertson War Chest Second Only to Bush," *Des Moines* [Iowa] *Register* (16 October 1987); "Robertson Receives More than $11 Million," *Times-Advocate* [Escondido, California] (16 October 1987), sec. A. p. 3; Mike Sante, "Robertson Has Change of Heart, Takes Federal Campaign Aid," Austin [Texas] *American-Statesman* (1 January 1988) sec. A, p. 4; "12 Candidates Get $28.7 Million in Matching Funds," *Minneapolis Star & Tribune* (5 January 1988) sec. A, p. 3; Charles R. Babcock, "Robertson Reverses Course, Will Accept Matching Funds," *Washington Post* (1 January 1988).

27. Mayer, "Religious Broadcasters," p. F8f. Robert Kassis, founder of the National Christian Network, argues that the solicitation for funds "has degraded the thrust of the Gospel." ibid., p. F9.

28. Carolyn Mayer, "A Quiet Giant in Virginia," *Washington Post* (5 Febrary 1984), sec. F, p. 8.

Chapter 14
Robertson on Democrats and Democracy

Robertson's attitude toward the Democratic party is simple. Democrats are bad, evil, and amoral to immoral.

James Muffett, associate pastor of the Maranatha Christian Fellowship in East Lansing, Michigan, summarized the viewpoint of the new religious right. Reflecting on his own past before he "got saved," he claimed, "I was a Democrat, a leftist and a cocaine addict."

As a "saved" man, Muffett, like Robertson, supports prayer in schools, the quarantine of AIDS victims, and the takeover of local county Republican conventions "for our Lord Jesus Christ."

Muffett opposes Jewish politicians. He longs to see a continuing increase in defense spending. At the same time he calls for a cut in taxes and a balanced budget. After Reagan's supply-side economic disaster, and the abortive Gramm-Rudman Act, a balanced budget would truly take one of the Christian miracles to make it occur.

Muffett's reasons for wanting the balanced budget is not to lessen the tax burden on the United States citizen. Instead, like Robertson, he believes that once the budget is balanced, the newly generated surplus can be spent on fighting "Communists" and "Atheists." This fight, especially in Nicaragua, is to be a "Christian Crusade" financed by the federal government to help the civilian-slayers who make sport out of destroying villages, schools, orphanages, convents, and small farms in the name of "freedom-fighting," as Pat boasts, being as they are, "good Christians."[1] These "freedom fighters" — naive Nicaraguan peasants led by retread Somosista gangsters who had preyed on their fathers before them — have spent more time pushing cocaine into the

U. S. black market than working for the overthrow of the Sandinista government legitimately chosen, supported, and elected by the people.[2]

Robertson has no concern for the democratic process that brought Daniel Ortega[3] to power in Nicaragua.[4] Instead, he pleads for a continuation of the Contra killings. He justifies the slaughter of the innocents on the grounds that Ortega's Sandinistas pose a "Communist threat" first to his personal economic aggrandizement and second to the alleged stability of the western hemisphere.[5] He refuses to mention, much less discuss, the Contra attacks on civilians, Contra rape of nuns and small children, Contra destruction of small farms, Contra theft of farm equipment, and Contra kidnapping of peasant farmers. The Contras kidnap young men to fill their military machine more as cannon fodder than as soldiers. Robertson sees nothing wrong in this.

He styles the Contra mass murderers as leaders "deeply committed to democracy." With a passionate plea, Robertson asserts that the Contras are also "deeply committed to Christ."[6]

Robertson's hatred of anything to which he is opposed, such as the Sandinistas and Ortega, clouds his thinking. His animosity to opposition narrows his perspective and crushes his ability to reason or accept the possibility of alternatives.

Robertson argues for a freeze of Nicaraguan assets in the United States. At the same time he rejects any similar retaliatory tactic by the Sandinistas against the U.S. government.

It is all right for the government of the United States to mine Nicaraguan harbors. It is wrong, in Robertson's eyes, for the Nicaraguan government to take necessary steps to insure the safety of their seaports and retaliate against U.S. mining operations and other covert operations.

It is "Christian," Robertson responds, for the United States government to take up collections of monies to aid those who would slay civilians, but it is wrong for Ortega to seek weapons to fight the murderers of his people. As long as the Contras give lip service to his god, Robertson will back one of the most vile and venal armies[7] that have ever existed in the Northern Hemisphere.

Robertson refuses to "turn the other cheek" or accept the concept that what is right for one is also right for the other. At the same time Robertson praises right-wing dictators, who like the religious fundamentalists, will tolerate no dissent.

Robertson was quick to sing the praises of Ferdinand Marcos of the Philippines. In his hymn celebrating the Marcos regime, Robertson scored Marcos as completing a sacred act for having "brought order and even greater freedom to his people out of chaos and danger on the streets." Never once did he mention the thousands of civilians who disappeared as Marcos' troops advanced, of land confiscated from opponents, or how the Roman Catholic Church in the Philippines ignored the pleas of the masses for justice and democracy and instead chastized those priests who proposed a redistribution of land and wealth, and asked for aid to impoverished islanders.

Robertson draped a holy shroud upon the shoulders of Marcos of the Philippines. Anointing Marcos with the oil of his speech, Robertson declared that the Philippine dictator "was welcomed by the people, *especially the middle class and the owners of small businesses*" (emphasis mine). Grudgingly, Robertson admitted only late in the Marcos era of infamy that Ferdinand and his wife were consumed by greed.

Governments, no matter what their nature, which "stand against terrorism and insurgency by the Communist guerrillas," Robertson argues, deserve the support of all Christians. No act commissioned or executed by a Christian is to be considered profane if the act is done in the name of stopping "godless Communism" and protecting the barons of capitalism.

Robertson lumps the Communist-hating Khomeini and Islam with Nicaragua's popular president, Ortega. He couples both extremes with the Libyan madman Gadhafi, as if the three men were all one and the same.

Blind to the atrocities of right-wing dictators, Robertson found little hesitation in attacking socialist or populist states where the people count for more than right-wing born-again bureaucrats and evangelical ideologues. At the same time he launched verbal assaults on left-wing governments, issuing some surprising statements that are not borne out by facts nor can be proved with any ease by serious analysts or political experts. Even after agonizing over his statements for hours, professional political scientists remain at a loss to explain some of the more fanciful rantings of the rate-conscious televangelist.

Pat's political pronouncements punctuated 1987. The year 1988 became even more a target for the angry arrows of Robertson's verbal assault on foreign governments.

In February of 1988, preacher Pat declared that there were Soviet missiles based in Cuba. Robertson quoted second-hand information, citing the 1967 U.S. Senate subcommittee's hearing on missiles in Cuba. He cited the testimony of Paul Bethel — a U.S. State Department official from Miami who said Cuban refugees had told him of seeing missiles — and one of the refugees, identified only as Mr. Apud, told him that Cuban soldiers had allowed him to know about the missiles' existence, telling Apud that they were aimed at Washington, D.C.

In spite of this evidence and testimony contradicting his own statements, Robertson continued to unleash a flurry of funny facts — and his supporters continued to believe in him. A master of prevarication of the turth, Robertson's concern is not so much for the existence of non-existing missiles, but is tuned to turning a martial ardor on within the hearts and minds of his zealous followers — looking for that moment, if he should become president of the United States, that he can launch a full-scale invasion of Cuba and invite a nuclear holocaust.

The televangelist condemns the "terrorism, human rights violations, and military proliferation" in Iran and other totalitarian dictatorships that lie politically to the left. Pat refuses to see that the same occurring in Chile, the Union of South Africa, and other despotic rightist regimes that support the West.

When news of Robertson's claims concerning missiles in Cuba became known in the State Department, U.S. government officials immediately rejected the televangelists' twisting of the truth. The government spokesmen noted that the Cuban military does have some surface-to-surface missiles in its inventory, but none of these missiles have nuclear warheads, nor has any missile the physical capability of reaching the United States or its island possessions even if such warheads existed.[8]

When Robertson was not claiming Cuba has missiles poised at the United States, like a wounded babbling child, the televangelist demanded that the United States government escalate its war appropriation and that United States industries produce more sophisticated weapons of destruction — toys with which he can play if he should become president. Robertson's anticipated toys are to be used — not just admired — however; and if Robertson's statements to the press are accurate, preacher Pat plans to employ their destructive energy almost immediately — if his "presidential demands" are not met by nations or individuals who do not share his philosophy — a philosophy he deludes himself into believing that other United States citizens share.

Among the nations which are to feel the Robertson wrath, if the televangelist is installed in the White House, are Nicaragua and Libya.

According to United Press International, Robertson has called for a U.S. military quarantine of these offending nations. He openly advocates that the United States military invade Nicaragua, and hints at the invasion of other nations who defy his precepts of government.

In his magazine *Policy Review*, published by his conservative Heritage Foundation, Robertson demands a war — using "surgical strikes" to "ferret out" the enemy — and thus cure the "problems" of the United States. The "problems" that are to be cured by a first-strike war against the "enemies of the United States" include secular humanism, Atheism, homosexuality, premarital sex, pornography, aggressive women, Jews, and a host of other actions or causes that defy his concept of truth and justice and the Christian way of life. Those who cause problems are worldwide — they are the "unsaved." Part of the unsaved are Iran's Ayatollah Ruhollah Khomeini, Libya's Col. Moammar Gadhafi, and the Nicaraguan Sandinistas. Never once did Robertson suggest that those who differ from his thinking may be reflecting their own national interests; instead, Robertson labels such dissenters as "tools" of Soviet expansion.

Robertson is a firm believer that is alright for any nation to be the political tool and economic pawn of the United States and United States interests. However, it is not acceptable to Robertson to allow nations who decline to follow U.S. dictates to align with nations who opposed U.S. policies and programs. Robertson sees his econo-political ideas as being the only right way to approach economics and politics. This is especially true in the case of Nicaragua.

Increasingly vocal about his opposition to the Sandinistas, Robertson has taken a public stand demanding that the United States invade Nicaragua. He told an appreciative audience composed mostly of Nicaraguan Somosista exiles on 12 November 1987, that he would not only launch an invasion of Nicaragua if he were president of the United States, but that he would encourage Nicaraguan exiles to set up a government in exile.

Speaking at a Nicaraguan steakhouse in Sweetwater, Florida, the televangelist to a cheering gathering of fifty supporters that not only would he set up a Nicaraguan government in exile, but that he would immediately "withdraw recognition of the Sandinista government." He would "invoke the Monroe Doctrine and tell the Soviets, Bulgarians, Cubans . . . this is our hemisphere and they should get out of it."

Shortly after Robertson's speech he met with reporters who hungered for additional details of Pat's plan to punish the Sandinistas. Without flinching under the weight of his ominous prophecy of international war, Robertson spelled out his opposition to all Central America peace plans. He was especially hostile to the peace plan put forth by Costa Rican President Oscar Arias — a plan that was signed on 7 August 1987 by all five Central American presidents.

Discarding world opinion and thumbing his nose at international law, Robertson again proposed a quarantine of Nicaragua, the establishment of a Nicaraguan government in exile to be headed by retired Samososista butchers, and invited the United States to invade an independent sovereign state. The televangelist termed the conditions of the Arias peace plan as "an illusory peace that leaves a communist dictatorship in power."

When Robertson was reminded of the link of drugs in the United States flowing from his Contra connections, Robertson turned fact into fiction. He denied that the Contras were behind the illegal drug trafficking. Illegal drugs in the United States were the result of "militant homosexuals" and those who had not been born again. Robertson minced, "I have no intention of surrendering the streets of America to the militant homosexuals and the drug pushers. If it's a fight they want, a fight they'll get. But we are not going to give over the greatness of this nation to the forces of decay and disintegration."[9]

To stop the decay Robertson sees flooding across the United States, the televangelist promised his faithful that he would "do anything" — even if such action were patently unconstitutional. Justifying his concept of going beyond the Constitution and, if necessary, defying Congress, Robertson lauded the Reagan Administration and Lieutenant Colonel Oliver North, praising their covert actions as being in line with the purpose and destiny of Christianity. He derided those who talked of the Iran-Contra connection as being a scandal. "That's no scandal," the televangelist tripped tartly. "The scandal is the fact that the Congress of the United States and the nations' press[es] don't want to do anything to take communism away from Nicaragua."[10] Congress and the United States press support Communism! Robertson reiterated.

As a Christian, Robertson could not allow the United States Congress or the national press to permit communism to enter the Western Hemisphere. He would join a small group of elite who would lead the Christian revolution against those who wanted communism or lived under it. There was nothing that Robertson would not do to end communism — even if it meant selling United States military supplies to fanatical Shi'ite Moslems in Iran — weapons that have been turned against the United States military and U.N. peacekeepers stationed in the Middle East.

For Christianity no price is too high to pay, no crime too odious to commit, no falsehood too vile to say. Those who stretched the truth, sold their heritage for a bowl of porridge, and went above the law were "heroes." The North-Poindexter shadow government, operating out of the basement of the White House, was actually fulfilling the will of Robertson's god: "Negotiating was certainly proper . . . that was in the best interest of the United States."[11]

North and Poindexter had to act, Robertson justified, because the United States government was not taking a firm step against communism in the Western Hemisphere. When the government fails to meet Robertson's standard of quality it is to be dispensed with and a new government created. According to Robertson the true government of the United States would fight communism, support Christianity and see to the Christianizing of all people, even if it required the United States to act dispassionately, break international laws, abandon human rights, and discard justice. Lybian and Nicaraguan assets are to be seized, and when confiscated, given to those displaced by "hostile regimes." Bombs are to be dropped, for in the name of Jesus all acts of violence and terrorism are justified — even if "bombing raids . . . are risky and endanger civilians."[12]

Bombs dropped on the "enemies of Christ" are the manifestation of Robertson's god's love for Christians. Bombs for Christ would insure that the political-economic factors of any nation are such that contributions to wayward ministries would flourish. If communism is allowed to grow it would become a cancer to Christianity. The communist political-economic mess is a menace that is to be seen as "infected with a deady disease." It is to be "quarantined," like gays, Atheists, Jews, and nonbelievers are to be singled out, and kept away from "innocent people who do not wish to be contaminated."

If political quarantines do not work and the native people of Iran and Nicaragua do not rise up against their governments, diplomatic relations are to be severed. Commerical trade is to be terminated.

Any action, no matter how barbaric and unjustifiable, would be justified. A "Christian president" would intercede with the Christian god, explaining that such acts were done in the name of spreading the word of Jesus.

Negotiations with "the enemy" is for sissies, perverts, and "bad people." A true Christian does not negotiate until there is a sign from the Christian god that negotiations are at a propitious time.

Negotiations with Nicaragua, Iran, or other states that are not overly zealous in fawning adulation, are to be initiated only when the Soviet Union leaves Afghanistan and tears down the Berlin Wall. Christianity is to be restored in Russia and throughout the remainder of the Soviet Union and other communist nations before the United States is to extend any aid or formal recognition. Until Christianity is restored there can be no "true civil rights," for without the controlling influence of Christianity, women will suffer the illusion that they are equal to men, freedom of choice will prevail, and education will become analytic and critical — requiring empirical evidence before anything is taken as fact.

The same human rights violations and military proliferation that exist in "Communist countries" have become a part of the daily life in the United States of North America, South Korea, and Honduras — but Robertson is blind to that. He is passively silent concerning the engorged U.S. military. His silence is even more chilling when he is reminded of the waste of tax dollars on items that could be purchased for a fraction of the charges the Pentagon pays major industries, if they were bought at local stores.

The televangelist refuses to speak out against the terrorism of Winston Wilder, who advocates violence in the name of Christianity. Pat says nothing about the radical right's movement against those who would defend an individual's right of choice, since their leaders are clergymen. At the same time, he adopts an inquisitorial callousness in his advocacy of censorship and the forced Christianization of our nation.[13] Pat supports those who will help him achieve power. He endorses those measures that will keep him in power. A twentieth century Machiavellian, Robertson rings the bells that peal "might makes right," and "the end justifies the means."

Notes

1. Cf. James R. Pierobon, "Robertson Promises . . ." *Houston Chronicle* (18 September 1986), sec. 1, p. 2. Cf. Peter Brown, "Seize Libyan, Nicaraguan assets, Robertson urges," *Rocky Mountain* [Denver, Colorado] *News* (26 January 1987), p. 36.

2. Robert S. Boyd, "Evangelicals Try to Increase Power in Political Arena," in *Detroit Free Press* (7 June 1986), sec. A, pp. 9, 14; see George Gallup's definition of an evangelical, synthesized by Boyd, on p. 14A. Cf. Jonathan Kwitny, "Money, Drugs and the *Contras*," *The Nation* (29 August 1987): pp. 145, 162-66. See also: my, *Tomorrow's Tyrants*, chap. 1.

3. Playboy Interview, "Daniel Ortega," *Playboy* 34.11 (November 1987): pp. 59-60, 64-66, 69, 71-74, 77-78, 130. Cf. *The Central American Crisis Reader*, ed. Robert S. Leiken and Barry Rubin (New York: Summit, 1987).

4. Steve Baker, "Robertson Hits Inaction in Nicaragua," *The Tennessean* (13 February 1987).

5. Pat Robertson, "Dictatorships and Single Standards: Restoring Confidence in American Foreign Policy," in *Policy Review* 39 (Winter 1987): pp. 2-9. His ideology is the same demagoguery dictated by Jeanne Kirkpatrick in her attacks upon the popularly elected Nicaraguan government. See my *Tomorrow's Tyrants: the Radical Right & the Politics of Hate* (Dallas: Monument Press, 1985), pp. 6-10, 51-58.

6. April Witt, "Robertson Heckled by Peace Activists," *The* [Norfolk, Virginia] *Ledger-Star* (21 March 1986), p. A5.

7. Robertson has called members of the armies that bring "vengeance" on "lawbreakers" (anyone in opposition to an existing regime) "ministers of God"; see: Robertson, *Answers*, p. 207. Repeatedly Robertson has argued that the Contras are the "legitimate government" of Nicaragua, and that the Ortega regime is not only usurping governmental powers, but, being Communistic, is outside of the protection and blessing of god. To this end, Robertson, as detailed in Straub, *Salvation for Sale*, has gone to Contra camps, praising their murderous actions as "god-sent" and "god-given."

8. *Santa Rosa* [California] *Press Democrat* (12 February 1988), sec. A, p. 6.

9. Associated Press (13 November 1987); Harvey Feit, Gannett News Service (5 February 1987).

10. Steve Baker, "Robertson Hits Inaction in Nicaragua."

11. Peter Brown, "Seize Libyan, Nicaraguan Assets, Robertson Urges," (Denver, Colorado) *Rocky Mountain News* (26 January 1987), p. 36; David Holtz, "Robertson Blames Congress, Press for Iran Scandal," *Flint* [Michigan] *Journal* (20 March 1987), sec. A, p. 3.

12. *Escondido* [California] *Times-Advocate* (4 October 1987), sec. A, p. 3.

13. Robertson, *Dictatorship and Single Standards*, p. 9. Cp. his "A New Vision for America," a speech delivered at Constitution Hall, Washington, DC, 17 September 1986, p. 3.

Chapter 15
Robertson on Education

Education should be "Christian based." Education should be "Christian taught."

It does not matter to Pat if the child-student is a non-Christian or a nonbeliever: an Atheist, agnostic, or freethinker. Pat is convinced that given "the opportunity to hear the word of Christ," the child will accept Christian mind control, convert to Christianity, and exuberantly experience the cold plunge beneath the icy waters of the baptismal font.

If public schools will not permit the child to be "raised [*sic:* reared] and educated as a Christian," the government must afford "parents the maximum opportunity to choose education for their children." This is doublespeak in support, generally, of tax vouchers for parochial schools. But, he wants the churches to have their cake and eat it: He opposes any "voucher plan that would allow any government at any level within the United States" to "interfere with private religious schools" or religious instructions.[1] Robertson endorses a voucher plan for tax money if such a system supports parochial education in church-related schools.

In time Robertson hopes that church schools will replace public education, since, Robertson argues, public education is "anti-Christian."[2] Public education isn't "real education," according to Christian standards.

The curriculum has been judged by Pat and other fundamentalists to be "humanistic."[3] Humanistic education teaches there are more gods than the Christian god. This "anti-Christian revelation" the televangelist "discovered" in the diary of a young Jewish girl, Anne Frank. A victim of the Nazi pogrom, Anne Frank wrote in her diary, "it doesn't matter which god" a person believes in "as long as you believe in something." That was tantamount to declaring for "no god" — according to Pat.

"Humanistic" education, Robertson continues, teaches that there are a variety of social values and expressions as well as numerous political and economic structures. Women have to be women: feminine, soft, weak, passive, obedient, subordinate. Men have to be masculine: hard, aggressive, passionate, strong, arrogant, controlling, condemning, and rigid. There is not to be any merging of the sexes except in a supine conjugal missionary sexual position, in Christian wedlock. I.E., CALVINIST GUNNY SACK SEX

In "humanism" there is no single "way" or plan, program, pronouncement, or philosophy which is given as an absolute. Such neutrality, objectivity, and equality is "unChristian," "anti-Christian," "godless" and "satanic."

To the horror of Robertson, "the tenets of humanism" state that all things are equal. Scholars are invited to sample the various offerings in order to make the best, rational judgment that they are capable of making. Such uncontrolled, uncharted independence and opportunity for self-judgment of issues is tantamount to total free will. To the chagrin of Robertson, such action, freedom of thought, and independence of inquiry might lead to the realization that there is no need for a priestly class of pulpit pounders preaching which way an individual is to go, what the individual is to do, or where an individual might find self-actualization, personal contentment, and a sense of self-pride. Such a catastrophic calamity as individual selection, Robertson argues, is the result of a public education system that "excludes Christianity's contribution" to America's past and present.[4] For that reason, public education is to be either abandoned or "Christianized."

To stem the flow of the intellect into open channels of learning, and in an effort to continue to enchain the human mind to an antiquated system of inquiry and blind faith, Robertson has created the National Legal Foundation (NFL) as a part of his CBN network. The NLF was created to challenge "secular humanism" in the courts: initially in Tennessee and Alabama,[5] where "born-again" Christian fundamentalist judges would preside — both of whom would find for evangelical plaintiffs.[6]

The raw, un-American denunciations of learning leveled at public education exploded the evangelical rage of Vicki Frost in Tennessee. (MRS. SHIT-FOR-BRAINS)

Her attack on the public school curriculum came as a chilling blast against reading material she considered "unChristian." Her holy war boiled over into what was described by the media as a contemporary Scopes trial. Once more, to their joy, evangelicals found themselves sparing with Satan. Pat Robertson's National Legal Foundation could have chosen scores of incidents as a basis for litigation. It chose but one which came to be known nationally. Since that case represents Robertson's values, it is necessary to look at it in depth.

Vicki Frost took her daughter out of the Hawkins County public school system because she did not want the child to read from "anti-Christian" books, she declared. She didn't want anyone else's daughter to read from them, either — whether they desired to do so or not. She had to fight the "great Satan," "secular humanism," to save mankind.

Frost won her first battle when Frost took her daughter out of the classroom. She insisted on teaching the child, herself, in the school library. This interfered with the learning of others. The disruption made reading difficult for those who sought the library as a place for quiet study. If she could keep others from reading "anti-Christian" books, she could save them from "secular humanism" and "Satan."

When Frost was asked to leave the public school library, she refused. She was arrested for trespassing. Humiliated, she sued for "false arrest."

Overnight Frost became the darling of the radical right evangelical fringe. Robertson spoke of her in glowing terms. Her fight was "god's fight."

Subsequent notoriety pushed Frost into the limelight. She had become a prophetess of god. She was a born-again Ruth, following Robertson around as her Boaz — angry at the world, spitting out god's denunciations on those who worshipped the false god of secular humanism, and vowing to tear down the altars raised to free inquiry and academe.

Robertson jumped immediately into the fray. His foundation filled the coffers of the new Christian crusaders and his lawyers aided with the case while Beverly Le Haye and her Concerned Women for America lent support.

Robertson had to support Frost. She stood as a Christian martyr for purity. Her purity was the substance on which he could capitalize — in his political quest and in the continued building of his televangelist empire commandered by his son, Tim.

Pat Robertson is a firm supporter of censorship. The First Amendment of the United States Constitution means nothing to him — unless

Robertson has little hesitation in speaking out against what he considers to be either "unAmerican" or "unChristian." He praised U.S. District Judge W. Brevard Hand's ruling banning forty-five textbooks from Alabama, speaking at the convention of the National Association of Evangelcials meeting in Buffalo, New York, in 1986.

Robertson claimed that the forty-five textbooks banned in Alabama had to be thrown out because they promoted a godless religion he called "secular humanism." On Thursday, 5 March 1987, Robertson minced, "The ultimate thrust of the new textbooks and the new learning is to move the United States into an international alliance with the governments based on the socialist model of the Soviet Republic." He added, "In Alabama, we took a stand and said, 'No more.' " His religious network helped not only pay the expenses of the evangelicals who brought the suit, but acted as a friend of the court.

Alabama, like Tennessee, had become a new holy land where purity of thought and limitations on expression promised to herald in a new earthly paradise where the only literature would be "biblically sound." Hand had achieved the stature of Vicki Frost, and the new Christian notoriety was on the ascent.

All of Robertson's empire would sheath themselves for the onslaught of secular humanism. To maintain their ardor Hand and Frost would be placed on pulpit pedestals as the new Joan of Arc and St. George.

Swords were drawn: the spiritual saber of the evangelicals to clash against the blades of scholarship. Frost stood on one side. Academe was poised on the other.

Battle lines were drawn.

Ranting against "Atheistic" books, Frost spouted that "capitalism is ordained by god." Like Robertson, Frost ignores the last lines of both Acts 2 and 4 that detail the Communistic community in which the early Christians lived.

Fearing the descent of the evil witch from the liberal northeast, Frost objected to witches being portrayed as good and pointed out that Cinderella could lead "innocent minds" away from Jesus.

But Vickie Frost and Robertson had forgotten the number of witches that exist in their Bible. Saul turned to one in battle.[7] Jezebel had betrayed her lord; and women were turned from their presumed lot of subservience to bring down the wrath of an every watchful and avenging Yahweh. Others were considered near-prophetesses. All were damned for being too involved in secular life, clamoring for recognition from men.[8]

Frost also objected to both the magic and supernatural in Cinderella. To have pumpkins change into coaches denied the Protestant work ethic. The Mad Hatter, in Lewis Carroll's *Alice Through the Looking Glass*, was judged as a reprobate. Too many hats provided an excuse for vanity. The Queen of Hearts encourages gluttony. Sin lurks behind each child's fairy tale and impregnates the words and colored pictures by the forces of darkness. All a child needs to read is the Bible. Yet, Frost had no comment on the countless biblical stories maddened with lust, sex, violence, and perversion.

While Frost discounts and discredits the myths of wonderland and fantasies, she fervently believes in miracles and faith healing: religious terms for the magic and superstition conjured up by those who would control the minds of the ignorant people who need an angry god to silence their own fears of the unknown. Frost condemns the pleasures of Cinderella, yet reads to her children the legend of Solomon's palace; she rejects the suggested sexuality in Shakespeare, and yet opens her Bible to read of Solomon's harem of thousands of wives and his many sexual murders,[9] Absalom's rape of his father's concubines,[10] Lot's bedding down with his daughters,[11] and the rape of Jethro's daughters.[12] Frost rejects pumpkins being changed into coaches, yet she believes that a man could walk on water; she rejects a woman descending into hell (Persephone), yet confesses that a man did so and then rose into heaven (Jesus). Frost, like the typical evangelical, is a woman full of contradictions. It is her inability to separate fact from fiction, allegories from reality, that led her to attempt to torpedo the ship of education in the United States which alone can help young minds to cross the ocean of ignorance to a land of knowledge.

Vicki Frost stood up for Robertson's concept of public education. The splinter group, Concerned Women for America, quickly funded Frost's fight.

Robertson's cult hoped that Vicki's standard would be unfurled throughout the United States. With Vicki's flag held high, Robertson was convinced that it was but a short time until "secular humanism" would be destroyed. He preached again the nineteenth century Know-Nothing party's gospel to his twentieth century Club members in the United States and invited them to take a stand for Jesus.

Robertson's "700 Club" membership is an odd assortment of religious zealots who would have biblical lunacy the law in the classroom.[13] With their checkbooks they have vowed a fight to the finish. Calling the faithful to take up arms, grab their pens, and write checks to his crusade, Robertson encouraged his army of believers to help "Vicki win."

The campaign began to eradicate non-Christian education in the public schools of Tennessee. More monies were needed to be raised to fight god's holy war in Alabama.

Alabama public education was to be just the beginning. Next the nation! Then the world! Not one of Robertson's supporters believed that their cases would ever be overturned.

Some of the monies Robertson raised would go to further the evangelical crusade to install Christianity in the classroom. Other monies would be raised to broadcast Robertson's general agenda across the nation.

Robertson's plan for public education promised to take "public" out of learning. Not only was Jesus to be enthroned in the classroom, but the crucified carpenter would first guide Pat to the White House, and then others who confessed their faith in the Galilean and the man from Virginia Beach televangelist.

By cleaning up "godless" literature and dispensing with "anti-Christian" books, Robertson pledged to end inequality among all *Christian* people. His argument against "secular humanism" appeared to many as a statement of Robertson's interest in equal Christian education for the different races.

Regularly, on his talk show, the "700 Club," Robertson argued that "Blacks deserve a better education" than they were receiving under "the liberal Democrats." Playing on human emotions, and bleating about "little lost black sheep," Robertson directed this rhetoric towards Black families.

Pat lamented that Black children would be forever confined to, and contained in, segregated ghettos as long as they suffered public education. The "wealth" of Black families, Robertson declared, is in their children. The extent of the "wealth," Robertson cautioned, can only be found in educating their children in "Christian environments."

Educating a Black child in the "love of Jesus" is to be the first priority for the Black family, Robertson warned. Federal assistance programs for anything other than educating the Black child in a Christian environment would be wasted. Welfare, without Christian education, would only continue the impoverishment of the Black family.

Impoverished Black families are not to receive federal, state, or local assistance in the form of welfare payments for food, shelter, medicine, or medical attention. Such payment might be used to insure the health and mental acuity of the Black child; and, Robertson admonished, the payments could be misused to further enslave the Black child to the existing socio-economic system — especially one that ordained a secular education for all.

To counter the continuing secularization of Black education, Robertson proposed that the Black family be given education "vouchers." These vouchers would be good only in paying for the Black child's educational experience.

With the Robertson tokens the Black parent could select a school, preferably a parochial school, outside of the school district in which the potential student lives. Since Robertson sees the current school districts in which Blacks live as being "ghettos" for prostitution, drugs, crime, and a lack of faith, Robertson condemns them as "anti-family, anti-human, anti-life."

To get the child out of the ghetto, Robertson suggests removing the Black child from his home. By removing the Black child from his parental and familial environment, Robertson hypothesizes, the Black youth will no longer be prone to teenage pregnancies, crime, suicide, prostitution, or other vices brought on by neglect, violence, and want. On what the Black is to do once he or she has been taken out of the ghetto, Robertson has remained silent. He offers no concrete solutions.

Robertson merges his philosophy on Black education with a "Christian" injunction to the family to tie love, work, and cooperation together.[14] This "tie" would only be valid if Jesus is accepted, and the Black family commits itself to work for the Christianization of the United States — along evangelical lines.

Education, under a Robertson presidency, would not be as it has been known for generations. History is to be rewritten to give it a "Christian" flavor. Non-Christian works are to be relegated to the trash bin, or glossed over. Books are to be censored. The fate of the great library at ancient Alexandria could easily become the fate of school libraries from Maine to Hawaii.

Robertson has taken to rewriting the history of the United States. He has the "first Thanksgiving" being celebrated at Cape Henry, Virginia, by 149 men, on 29 April 1607, who lined the railings of the ships sent by the Virginia Company. He has the Reverend Robert Hunt as the instigator of the alleged religious observance carrying to shore "a much-treasured Bible in his hands." He forgets that the men were already ashore, dining on roast oysters left by Indians who fled at the sight of the white men. This fantasy and abuse of history he has "captured in an original oil painting" that hangs on the second floor of his CBN Center. It is the beginning of doublespeak and the erasure of reality. Robertson is determined to create a past that will agree with his own ideas and myths.[15]

Robertson promises to do the same with the violence and corruption carried throughout the Old Testament[16] and New Testament[17] as he would with history, science, literature, and other disciplines. The economic plans of Charles, Lord Baltimore, are excused as "zeal for the cause of Christ,"[18] while the Puritan's vicious gynephobia against Anne Hutchinson is translated as godliness. The massacre at Henrico is seen as a martyrdom, while the plight of the Indians who had been rousted from their lands, murdered, and in cases enslaved is ignored. Everything that is done by the European white Protestant is holy. All acts by naked aboriginal natives is condemned as satanic.

The vile vituperative utterances of the narrow-minded, uncharitable, and calloused Christian cleric, Jonathan Edwards, are lauded as a "calm, resonant voice" that spoke "the wrath of God like great waters that are damned for the present." The concept of Hell is capitalized, and the legendary "basic sinful nature of man" is driven home with an inquisitional ardor that would have made the murdering clergy at Smithfield or Toledo gasp with envy.[19]

History is turned upside down. Fiction is made to appear as fact.

The ancient record of myths, legends, and superstitions in the Bible is presented as a current guide to life and an authentic record of a distant and legendary past: Old Testament laws that were plagiarized by a wandering people from various locations and climes, from ancient Babylon to nomadic communities huddled in the Chaldees. These forgeries are made to appear divinely inspired and relevant for all times. The laws of the Old Testament on which Robertson wants to base jurisprudence in the United States are complete with prohibitions against eating shellfish[20] and pork;[21] limits on what work can be done;[22] denunciations of select sexual and conjugal acts "committed" when the woman is menstruating.[23]

The terror and tyranny of the established churches, from the early Christian to the Roman Catholic, Eastern Orthodox, and various sects of the Protestant Revolution are applauded as being helpful to the settling of the New World. Robertson fails to see that these same churches imprisoned, sold into slavery, tortured, killed, and abused American Indians, white and Black women, children, and scholars.

Robertson claims that America's Founding Fathers were all Christians. They were not. America's Founding Fathers, were, for the most part, deists or freethinkers.

 Yet Washington and the other Founding Fathers of the United States are baptized after their death by Robertson into becoming Christian apologists and thinkers.

Robertson's bastardization of political science is poison to conscientious scholarship. Our Congress is depicted as a Christian institution. Our Constitution is seen as an extension of the Christian Bible.

Eighteenth century congressional proclamations are surreptitiously given Old Testament antecedents and referenced to biblical passages and pseudohistorical movements.[24] Thomas Jefferson, in laying the groundwork for Congressional acts, is praised as being not only a Christian, but a man committed to establishing a Christian nation in the New World.

Thomas Jefferson has been libeled by Robertson. Jefferson rejects Robertson's claims for him bluntly in his letters now nearly two centuries old.

Thomas Jefferson commented:

> I am a Christian, *in the only sense* in which he [Jesus] wished anyone to be; sincerely attached to his doctrines in preference to all others.[25]

Any other claim is taken out of context and meaning.[26]

Leading the fight for the disestablishment of the Anglican church as the official state religion in Virginia, Jefferson's argument was a discussion on ethics — not an organized faith. Jefferson had little if any time for any organized religion — a fact which upset many evangelical fundamentalists in his own eighteenth century era. They feared that their churches would become temples of reason and that people would break out of the suffocating religious stranglehold, stop lining the pockets of clergy with their hard earned money, and reject the superstitions the church had forced upon them for centuries.[27]

Jefferson wrote:

> The day will come when the mystical generation of Jesus, by the Supreme Being as his Father, in the womb of a virgin will be classified with the fable of the generation of Minerva in the brain of Jupiter. But we may hope that the dawn of reason and freedom

of thought in these United States will do away with this artificial scaffolding, and restore to us the primitive and genuine doctrines of this most venerated Reformer of human errors.

Thomas Jefferson was a disciple only of the ethical doctrines reported to be those of Jesus. At no time and in no place did he articulate or write that he was a disciple of Jesus or that he believed in Jesus or Christianity.[28]

Jefferson's attitude on the establishment of an organized religion as the official church of the United States was like his attitude towards Christianity — he held them both dangerous.

Jefferson's wisdom was both heralded and endorsed by Thomas Paine. Paine wrote:

> I do not believe in the creed professed by the Jewish Church, by the Roman Church, by the Greek Church, by the Turkish Church, by the Protestant Church, nor by any Church that I know of. My own mind is my own Church.

Jefferson was not slow to give his opinions at the time.

> It does me no injury for my neighbor to say there are twenty gods or no God. It neither picks my pockets nor breaks my legs.

President John Adams was less subtle. He came out boldly, declaring in a flourishing penmanship:

> The divinity of Jesus is made a convenient cover for absurdity. Nowhere in the Gospels do we find a precept for Creeds, Confessions, Oaths, Doctrines and whole carloads of other foolish trumpery that we find in Christianity.

Several generations later, Abraham Lincoln confessed:

> The Bible is not my Book and Christianity is not my religion. I could never give assent to the long complicated statements of Christian dogma.

Even Benjamin Franklin would repent of earlier Christian confusion and craftly chord in written form:

As to Jesus Christ . . . I have, with most of the present Dissenters in England, some doubts as to his divinity.

President James Madison commended his readers to reason. Arguing against superstititon, Madison mounted his campaign:

During almost fifteen centuries the legal establishment known as Christianity has been on trial, and what have been the fruits, more or less, in all places? These are the fruits: pride, indolence, ignorance and arrogance in the clergy. Ignorance, arrogance and servility in the laity, and in both clergy and laity, superstition, bigotry, and persecution.

Madison wrote, on 24 January 1774, to "Mr. William Bradford Junr. at the Coffee-House Philadelphia":

Union of Religious Sentiments begets a suprizing confidence and Ecclesiastical Establishments tend to great ignorance and Corruption of all of which facilitate the Execution of mischievous Projects. . . . Poverty and Luxury prevail among all sorts: Pride ignorance and Knavery among the Priesthood and Vice and Wickedness among the Laity. This is bad enough but it is not the worst that I have to tell you. That diabolical Hell conceived principle of persecution rages among some and to their eternal Infamy the Clergy can furnish their Quota of Imps for such business.[29]

All of these statements are ignored as distortions, partial truths, innuendos, suggestions, and outright lies about history that have become part and parcel of the Robertson baggage he would bring to the White House if elected president. Within his verbal valise Robertson has the instruments of religion and those who would swing them to force his unscientific and inaccurate ideas on the young of the nation.

Robertson's Southern Baptist denomination was among the most outspoken defenders of slavery. When Dr. George B. Ide, pastor of First Baptist Church in Philadelphia, attempted to convince his coreligionists that slavery was wrong, Dr. Spencer H. Cone, a prominent Baptist minister from New York City, attempted to isolate the slavery issue from the Convention's policies. Dr. Richard Fuller, a Baptist minister of South Carolina, urged the Convention to restrict itself solely to missionary enterprises, and to forget slavery — he owned several slaves himself. After the debate the resolution was withdrawn, and Ide offered a noncommital policy on the institution of slavery, urging the Convention to cooperate in the work of foreign missions, disclaiming "all sanction either expressed or implied, whether of slavery or anti-slavery," but to allow individuals the freedom to express themselves and promote either view.

Ide's actions renewed the fears of Southern Baptists. The "solution" was to couple the issue of emancipation or continued enslavement with the Baptist mission to the Indians.

While Robertson distorts the history of the United States, attempting to cover over the crimes of Christianity against native American Indians, women of all races, Black slaves,[30] gays, and non-European peoples, Robertson has not been able to gloss over or hide the wisdom of Thomas Jefferson, who spoke laconically in his final days: "I do not find in orthodox Christianity one redeeming feature."

Notes

1. Americans for Robertson, p. 3.

2. "700 Club," 13 May 1984.

3. "700 Club," 13 May 1984, 4 February 1986.

4. "700 CLub," 4 February 1986, 1 April 1986.

5. Cf. "Robertson Says Books' Goal Is Soviet Alliance," *Toledo, Ohio Blade* (3 March 1987), p. 3.

6. Stan Hastey, "Textbooks Banned; 'Secular Humanism' Cited," *Baptist Standard* 99.10 (11 March 1987): pp. 3, 4. "Schools Begin Removing Banned Texts," *Escondido* [California] *Times-Advocate* (6 March 1987) sec. A, p. 3. "Robertson Says Books' Goal Is Soviet Alliance," *Toledo* [Ohio] *Blade* (6 March 1987), p. 3. "In Alabama, We Took A Stand and Said, 'No More'," *St. Petersburg* [Florida] *Times* (6 March 1987), sec. A, p. 20. *Minneapolis* [Minnesota] *Star & Tribune* (23 February 1988), sec. A, p. 3, refused to hear the last appeal of seven evangelical Christian families who say Tennessee public schools violated their children's religious freedom by requiring them to read textbooks that contradict their faith by teaching "occultism, secular

humanism, evolution, disobedience to parents, pacifism, feminism," and depicting other religions without stating that their own was the only correct one.

7. 2 Sam. 28:13.

8. 2 Kings [4 Kings] 9:22; Micah 5:12; Nah. 3:4; Deut 18:10.

9. 2 Kings [4 Kings] 15-21, 23-25; Solomon's sexual jealousy is graphically related in 2 Kings [4 Kings] 22:2; cp. 1 Kings [3 Kings] 2:31-32. Solomon was the son of David who is one of history's most unique murderers: slaying the husband of one of his lovers: Bathsheba, in 2 Samuel [2 Kings], 15f, as well as coveting Jonathan, and others.

10. 2 Sam. [2 Kings] 16:21-22: "A shameful public spectacle was arranged for this act so that it happened before the eyes of all men according to [counsel's] advice." See Arthur Frederick Ide: *Absalom's Rape Feast: The Hebrew Text with Translation and Commentary* (Toronto: Historical Examination Press, 1974).

11. Gen. 19:31-34. Lot was able to impregnate both young women the same night: Gen. 19:36-38. This was not a "single incident" for he had grown fond of his daughters and later gave birth to the Ammonite tribe through one of them: Deut. 23:18.

12. For further discussion of sex and violence in the Bible, see: Arthur Frederick Ide, *The Descent of Man from the Animal: A Study of Sex and Violence in the Bible*, forthcoming.

13. Melinda Beck with Ginny Carroll, Lynda Wright and Barbara Burgower, "A Reprise of Scopes," *Newsweek* (28 July 1986): pp. 18-20.

14. M[arion] G. Robertson, "The Wealth Of Black Families," *Conservative Digest* (June 1987): pp. 35-[40].

15. Robertson, *America's Dates with Destiny*, pp. 25-27.

16. Cf. Ben Edward Akerley, *The X-Rated Bible* (Austin: American Atheist Press, 1985).

17. W.P. Ball, G.W. Foote, John Bowden, Richard M. Smith, and others, *The Bible Handbook* (Austin: American Atheist Press, 1986).

18. Robertson, *America's Dates with Destiny*, pp. 31-32. Cp. Arthur Frederick Ide, *Woman in the Colonial South* (Mesquite: IHP, 1983), index.

19. Robertson, *America's Dates with Destiny*, passim.

20. Lev. 11:10.

21. Lev. 11:7; Is. 66:17.

22. Lev. 23:3, 7-8, 21, 25-28, 35, 36.

23. Ez. 18:6; Lev. 12.

24. Robertson, *America's Dates with Destiny*, p. 63f.

25. A. Koch and W. Peden, eds., *The Life and Selected Writings of Thomas Jefferson* (New York: Modern Library, 1944), p. 567.

26. Robertson, *America's Dates with Destiny*, p. 65.

27. Straub, *Salvation for Sale*, pp. 306-309.

28. Cf. Henry S. Randall, *The Life of Thomas Jefferson*, vol. 3, (New York: Derby and Jackson, 1958), p. 451.

29. *The Papers of James Madison*, ed. William T. Hutchinison and William M. E. Rachel vol. I, (Chicago: The University of Chicago Press, 1962), pp. 105-6, note on p. 107. Madison warns of the power of the clergy in his letter of 1 April 1774; ibid., pp. 112-113, and on 19 June 1775, warns that some members "of the ministry" might attempt to sit in Congress "before they make their ultimate appeal to the Sword." ibid., p. 152.

30. See: Mary B. Putnam, *The Baptist and Slavery: 1840-1845* (Ann Arbor, MI: G. Wahr, 1913), pp. 37-38. Cf. my chapter on the history of the Baptists, in *Evangelical Terrorism*, index.

Chapter 16
War & Peace:
Robertson's Military-Theocracy Complex

Pat's promise of the United States of America's "turning back to God" is but another way of saying that he would turn our nation into a theocracy[1] if elected president of the United States. He has had little difficulty in justifying to himself the use of monies raised for ostensibly religious purposes being diverted into political and terroristic channels. Money is essential if the United States, and the world, are to be converted to Jesus.

Robertson has developed close connections and friendships with terrorists. He not only supports and visits the Contras in Nicaragua, but has come out in favor of Major Saad Haddad, who has been carefully and closely linked with the Israeli slaughter of Palestinians in Lebanon refugee camps.

Robertson has defended the $25,000 a month "contribution" of his religious network, CBN, to the political "Voice of Hope,"[2] a radio station that the United States Department of State contends has been Major Saad Haddad's mouthpiece for threats against Lebanese civilians and United Nations' peacekeeping forces. Haddad's response was to praise Robertson as a "Christian and a patriot."

Haddad and other Lebanese "Christians" have claimed that the blood that has been shed in Lebanon's ever-escalating war against the Palestinian Liberation Organization (PLO) and splinter terrorist groups is at the commission and injunction of their god. Haddad's Jesus, like Robertson's god, believes in the divine qualities and permissibility of war, murder, bloodshed, rape, pillage, terror, sodomy, and torture. Haddad's war is identical to the "holy acts" (in Arabic known as *jihad*) of Islam. Both Haddad and Khomeini, like Robertson, defend barbaric bloodletting as a spiritual commissioning. Those who kill for their god win not only future rewards in paradise but an immediate recognition as "true believers."

Haddad has not alone praised the "Christianity" of Robertson, but this Lebanese Christian has appeared as an honored guest on Pat's "700 Club," his appearance being made possible by means of an interview beamed by satellite from the Middle East.

The Haddad interview was conducted by Pat's son, Tim. Tim is a youth who has his own aspirations for an empire similar to his dad's. It's an easy life. There is wealth, fame, and power in being a televangelist. By fall 1987, Tim had stepped into his father's shoes as a talk host on the "700 Club," while Pat put on his sneakers to run for the presidency of the United States.

Tim is another story. Yet he is every bit as dangerous to democracy as is his father, for he, like Pat, is quick to varnish over venality in fellow Christians and to applaud those who would slay the innocents in the name of their joint deity who demands a rather singular economic, religious, and political system. Tim is a master of distortion. He praises terrorism and justifies murder as part of "God's plan."

Tim so idolizes Haddad that he rushes to praise this brigand as being a near-deity who cannot be questioned by any true Christian.

Even when irrefutable evidence was presented that Haddad had, during the middle of September 1982, ordered the massacre of hundreds of Palestinian civilians, primarily women and small children ghettoized in two camps (Chatilla and Sabra), Pat and his son, Tim, denied any culpability on the part of Haddad. Tim proudly beamed "this good Christian's" ready denial of a fact that has been accepted even by the United States Department of State.

Tim sees Haddad as the epitome of a patriot. Haddad is thus labeled not only as a "good Christian" but a man who would defend his Christian nation against all odds. Tim's god rejoices when babies are butchered.

Haddad, commander of a ten-mile-wide border strip he calls "Free Lebanon," has been labeled a "deserter" by the Lebanese army and has been branded a "renegade" by the United States Department of State.[3] Tim responded to these charges that the United States Department of State was out of touch with reality.

Far from being a "defender of peace," Haddad is an instigator of war. Peace is as distasteful to Haddad as it is to the god who would commission Armaggedon. Haddad certainly would be more than happy to please this god of Armaggedon and launch the nuclear warheads that would wipe out those who dissented from his view and politics. How closely Haddad matches the Robertsons!

Nuclear war is just one of the many ideas that bring excitement to the blood that flows in Haddad's veins. Opening the veins in others is even as thrilling to this Lebanese Christian.

Haddad has been soundly accused of the cold-blooded slaughter of numerous women and children, noncombatants who had no involvement with the Lebanese civil war. It has been questioned whether or not Haddad plays the role of an ancient Herod slaying the newborn in Judea, or if he styles himself a born-again pharaoh determined to wipe out the infants of his enemies.

The United States Department of State has judged Haddad as a sinister force with which it must deal in the bloody conflict raging in Lebanon — an armed turmoil and rebellion which Haddad merrily keeps going as he defends his own religious broadcast station "Voice of Hope." The hope that Haddad has is to exterminate his opposition.

Haddad's "Voice of Hope" cost $500,000 to construct. Robertson's CBN network contributed $150,000 towards its completion.[4]

Instead of Haddad's broadcasting real messages of hope on his religious network, he fills the Lebanese airwaves with religion closer to the fanaticism enunciated by crazed Iranian *mullahs* and the Ayatollah Khomeini. He threatens violence against those who oppose him and, in a Robertson manner, shells the populated areas that do not accept his brand of religion, thought, and politics. Those areas which he most frequently threatens, with a strange mixture of hatred and religion, are Lebanese civilian suburbs, United States military personnel quarters housing those who serve with the United Nations' peacekeeping forces in the area, and United Nations' security posts.

Tom Homan, of the United States Department of State, has branded this "savior" so idolized by Robertson and the Christian fundamentalists as "a creature of the Israelis." The Department of State has charged that Haddad was armed by the Israelis to liquidate the PLO — a judgment that Robertson rejects. But, Robertson is a member of the Board of Regents of Haifa University in Israel and in addition Robertson has his own radio station, WYAH, in Israel. Robertson can't imagine his friend Haddad acting capriciously without religious reasons. Certainly the State Department has to have been wrong.

Troubled over this report that Haddad had been in the pay of the Israelis, Robertson called into question any State Department pronouncement; he had no choice. The State Department paper went counter to his own political interpretations and plans.

While condemning the State Department as not being "Christian" enough in its dealings with Haddad, Robertson at the same time continued to deny the escalating evidence against Haddad. He elects to overlook Haddad's bulging record of murder, mayhem, rape, pillage, plunder, torture, and other crimes against humanity — even though the accounts of Haddad's atrocities read graphically as if they had been cut out of a page of Nazi war crime records.

On 18 April 1980, Haddad "allegedly" captured and murdered two Irish members of the U.N. security forces. From 28 February 1981 until 3 March 1981, Haddad shelled the city of Sidon in an effort to force the Lebanese government to give his "Christian" troops "back pay." One of the shells that he lofted on 3 March 1981 hit the girls' evangelical school in Sidon. Robertson read the reports of Haddad's work. But, concerning this unwarranted aggression, Robertson chose to remain silent.

On 5 March 1981, Haddad's troops wounded nine children who were at school in the town of Hasbayya — but they were not Christians.

Eleven days later, Haddad attacked a Nigerian battalion of the U.N. force. His "Christian act" killed three and injured eleven Nigerians. They were all Black — they were not Christians either .

In July of 1981, Haddad resumed his radio broadcasts. Agitated, he threatened the Lebanese citizenry "in another attempt to extort payment" for his troops, according to the United States Department of State. Robertson had no word of caution, warning, or disapproval for Haddad. Haddad was fighting the war for Jesus. Instead, Robertson blasted the State Department, questioning its credibility in attacking his friend.

Anything done in the name of Jesus is acceptable to Robertson. Commenting on the State Department's paper on Haddad, Robertson puffed out, "Major Haddad is a patriot. His people were facing massacre: 100,000 Lebanese *Christians* have been butchered in the last, say, five or six years over there. His village was shelled on Easter Sunday morning as they were preparing to go to church."[5]

The slaughter of Christians is inexcusable to Robertson. But Robertson does not lament the loss of non-Christian lives since the massacre of non-Christians is part of god's "just war." If Christians are killed as they prepare to go to church to worship Robertson's god, that is evil, inexcusable, wrong, and barbaric. If Moslems are killed as they prepare to go to mosque to worship their god, Allah, that is good, righteous, and just. Robertson forgets that when Haddad massacred the PLO women and children that was a Friday, their day of preparation for Islam.

Even when Robertson was confronted with the naked revelation that the Israeli government of Begin acknowledged the slaughter of the PLO women and children, Robertson remained quiet. Sidestepping the question on the legitimacy of Haddad's actions, Robertson could only reply, "I'm talking about broad policies. Specific details — it's up to the Israelis to determine."[6]

This follows a pattern, for generally Robertson believes that he has to concern himself with the "big picture" in politics, theology, and war. His god will take charge of the little details.

It must be remembered and emphasized that Robertson's god commissions violence so that there can be peace. War is an essential part of Robertson's god's plan. Peace is not. Pacificism, according to this televangelist, is "not biblical."[7] War is. Yet Robertson fails to explain why he was not engaged in active combat during the Korean crisis; he downplays the cushioned job his father found him beyond the actual physical combat, although definitions, by military machinations, can give the legal fiction that he was in the "combat zone" — just nowhere near the actual fighting.

With no war record and no combat experience, Robertson argues that he is qualified to be commander in chief of the United States armed forces and lead the United States in combat with the the "malevolent power "Communism" that over the last four decades has resulted in the death of 250 million [??] human beings."[8]

Robertson throws statistics around with the same careless ease as he inflects commentary on systems concerning which he has little to no knowledge, while he praises mass murderers, such as Haddad, for fighting "satanic" forces. Robertson's rabidness against "Communism" is similar in nature to Ronald Reagan's theatric denunciation of the "Evil Empire."[9]

The vengeance, anger, hostility, and bloodthirstiness of Robertson's god can be seen most graphically in the televangelist's philosophy on Iran and the Iranian revolution. Publicly Robertson has declared that the Iranian crisis "is not of the devil, it is of God himself. He [god] is shaking the world."[10]

Instead of Americans mourning the loss of American lives in Iran, or lamenting the rise of the totalitarian Khomeini government and its accompanying horrors, Robertson encourages United States citizens to rejoice in the overthrow of the Shah. Robertson has dictated that Americans "ought to be praising God for bringing prophecy to fruition." To moan over the United States' hostages who are incarcerated and possibly being tortured by the Iranians is, in Robertson's view, equal to disapproving of "god's plan" for the universe in general, the United States in particular, and specifically for the possible rapture of Christians who live in the United States.

Haddad is only helping to fulfill the will of his god, as is Khomeini, Gadhafi, and other terrorists. At the same time, Robertson is unable to explain how the Soviets' entrance into Afghanistan isn't a part of "god's plan." But he prophecies that a new world war will see the Soviets defeated[11] as Mideast oil supplies are cut off and some of the Soviet wells catch fire "and flare forever."[12]

Notes

1. Cf. "Pietism and Politics; TV Evangelist Robertson Shakes Up The GOP," *Asbury Park Press* (20 June 1986), sec. A, p. 18.

2. Caroline Mayer, "A Quiet Giant in Virginia," *Washington Post* (5 February 1984), sec. F, p. 8.

3. Lisa Ellis and Pete Rowe, "Maj. Haddad Innocent, Says Pat Robertson," Norfolk, Virginia *Ledger Star* (24 September 1982), sec. A, p. 8.

4. Ellis and Rowe, loc. cit.

5. Ellis and Rowe, loc. cit.

6. Ellis and Rowe, loc. cit.

7. Robertson, *Answers*, pp. 190-91. Cf. *Time* (17 February 1986): p. 66.

8. *Time* (17 February 1986): p. 66.

9. Ronald Reagan is not a religious man. His father was a Roman Catholic. His mother belonged to a Disciples of Christ church. Reagan has never shown any passionate commitment to any one church or to institutionalized religion in general. All that is known is that he does attend, generally, Episcopalian Easter services. He does not have religious services conducted at the White House, as did Richard Nixon

and Lyndon Johnson.

Reagan's 1979 federal tax returns show that Ronald donated less than 1 percent of his income to *all* charitable causes, including religious activities and organizations. This is significantly less than the 10 percent tithe many Christians, including Robertson, consider to be an acceptable minimum contribution.

As for being a stalwart champion of the pro-life movement, Reagan, as governor of California, signed into law the first abortion bill in the United States, one that allowed 60,000 abortions to be performed from the time he signed the bill in 1967 to the day he left office as governor in 1975.

Divorced from actress Jane Wyman, his friends included AIDS victim Rock Hudson. He was himself an actor, although not of any noticeable talent by any standard, for years. Reagan has never publicly professed Christianity and much of his image has been created by Jerry Falwell and manipulated for political reasons by Pat Robertson. See my *Idol Worshippers in 20th Century America* (Dallas: Monument Press, 1985); my *Tomorrow's Tyrants: The Radical Right and the Politics of Hate* (Dallas: Monument Press, 1985); and my *Reagan & Woman* (Dallas: Texas Independent Press, 1984). Cp. David Briggs, "The Packaging of a Christian President," *Buffalo* [New York] *News* "This World" (2 November 1986), p. 17.

10. William A. Henry 3d, "Pat Robertson and The 700 Club," *Boston Globe* (2 January 1980), p. 17.

11. *Time* (17 February 1986): p. 66.

12. William A. Henry 3d, "Pat Robertson and The 700 Club," loc. cit.

Chapter 17
Pulpit and Politics:
Pat on Buttressing The Power of
The Clergy in The U. S.

In the company of Christian fundamentalists, Pat Robertson styles himself a minister of "the Word." Outside of this selective circle of religious rightists, Robertson quickly drops his self-styled label of preacher, and defines his role in life and United States society as being "a professional broadcaster."

I'm the head of a major television network. I'm trained as a lawyer. I'm a communicator on world affairs."[1]

Robertson plays down his faith-healing past. Publicly Robertson doesn't talk "in tongues."

Pat preaches that he no longer believes (as he once told his followers) that the Bible predicts a nuclear war.[2] His previous prophecies that the beginning of the end of the world would occur in the 1980s is played down.[3]

Robertson *is* conscious of the general attitude in the United States to be wary of clergy. Those who fled the shores of European nations for refuge in the colonies that hugged the North Atlantic seaboard came to the North American continent to be free of any obligation or ritual *outside of their own beliefs.* Of course, once they got to the shores of what was to be our nation, they became just as intolerant of other belief systems as had been those who prosecuted them.

There was no single sect of faith in the early colonies, as long as one accepted Christianity. Only in the New England area and Virginia was it mandatory to be a member of a church. But belief was a matter of law. The very famous "Toleration Act," passed in Maryland in 1649, indicates the state of affairs:

> . . . that whatsoever person or persons within this province and the island thereunto belonging shall henceforth blaspheme God, that is, curse Him, or deny our Savior Jesus Christ to be the Son of God, or shall deny the Holy Trinity — the Father, Son, and Holy Ghost — or the Godhead of any of the said three Persons of the Trinity or the unity of the Godhead, or shall use or utter any reproachful speeches, words or language concerning the said Holy Trinity, or any of the said three Persons thereof, shall be punished with death and confiscation or forfeiture of all his or her lands and goods. . . .

Only a few brave individuals, like Anne Hutchinson and Roger Williams, rejected church obligations and turned against the clergy who would control them. They spoke out against the ministers who paraded the same intolerant religious demagogy from which they had fled England and Europe. No church had the right, these early heroes claimed, to impose its narrow philosophy upon a divergent people.

To avoid the powerful political hand of the church, Hutchinson accepted banishment. Williams went on to Rhode Island to establish a commonwealth freed from religious tyranny.

Unlike any of the other colonies, Maryland was founded as a haven for Roman Catholics, yet offered hospice and protection to all Christian religious dissenters. Only when the Protestants outnumbered the Roman Catholics was the above edict of toleration withdrawn, and a colonial state church allowed to emerge.

Robertson wants the rigid past resurrected. He sees his chance to be a "soldier of god" by bringing a narrow-focused Christianity to the United States. He carries with him a yet invisible yoke to place upon the neck of the men and women he would have subject to his capricious and insensitive religious whims.

Notes

1. John J. Failka and Ellen Hume, "Pulpit and Politics: TV Preacher, Possibly Eyeing the Presidency, Is Polishing His Image; Pat Robertson Now Stresses His Success in Business; The GOP's Jesse Jackson? — Finances of a Faith Healer," *Wall Street Journal* CCVI.77 (17 October 1985), pp. 1, 23.

2. Pat Robertson, *On Bible Prophecy* series of tapes issued by CBN.

3. Robertson, *Shout It From the Housetops*, pp. 214f, cf. my comments above with citations. Cp. Straub, *Salvation for Sale*, pp. 290-91; and Robertson, *The Secret Kingdom*, pp. 214-23. The actual prediction for a nuclear holocaust is in *Pat Robertson's Perspectives* now secreted in the CBN University archives. Nuclear war was to occur in 1982. See also, Marcus Stern, "Does Evangelist Robertson Have Presidential Call?" *San Diego Union* (8 December 1985), sec. C, pp. 1, 7.

Chapter 18
Preacher or Politician?

To transmogrify the United States into a theocracy, Robertson is astute enough not to proclaim himself too loudly to be a preacher. In June of 1986, Robertson played down his religious rank, pompously prevaricating, "I am not an evangelist, never was."[1]
Robertson recognizes:

> There is an antipathy in America to the involvement of clergy in politics, and there is not that antipathy toward a Christian businessman. It's a decided plus.[2]

Therefore, to win the presidency of the United States, Robertson has taken up the screening cloak of business — declaring that he is a businessman,[3] emphasizing his "business acumen" as chief executive officer of the multi-million dollar Christian Broadcast Network, the fifth largest cable television channel in the country, Robertson claims that he has the economic savvy to run a corporate United States.

Despite his rhetoric, Robertson is *the* salesman for Jesus. He will market this ware like any tinker treading the dusty streets of small communities, crossing cobblestoned avenues in colonial settings, and walking through weeds west of the Mississippi. He will bask in the shade of orange groves and enjoy the fruits of sunny California and Florida, doing what is necessary. It is a fraud; the products he hawks are Jesus and Christianity.

Robertson's facade is transparent. As a Southern Baptist minister and now chairman of People for the American Way, John Buchanan points out Robertson "has a real knack for reasonably stating extreme views and sounding sophisticated and nice while taking a posture closer to that of a more strident [Jerry] Falwell or [Jimmy] Swaggart."[4]

Buchanan was targeted for defeat by conservative evangelicals at the end of his eighth (and last) term in Congress. The evangelicals objected to Buchanan's defense of a pluralistic society. As Buchanan defined his defeat later, "One of the basic values of our society is diversity and plurality. These folks think of themselves as *the* Christians and do not accept disagreement with their political agenda."

To counter the People for the American Way, New Right leader Paul Weyrich announced on 19 July 1986 the formation of the American Election Commission — a watchdog group to protect the prerogative of the conservative candidates to talk religion on the campaign trail. The new five-member commission is headed by South Dakota Governor Bill Janklow and includes Rabbi Seymour Siegel, professor of ethics and theology at Jewish Theological Seminary of America in New York, and Maurice Dawkins, a Black businessman and minister who ran unsuccessfully for lieutenant governor in Virginia in 1985.[5]

Robertson states one absurdity, such as nuclear holocaust, at one time, denies it at a second session, and reaffirms it later.[6] On 26 January 1987, Robertson called for a military blockade of Libya and the United States supported overthrow of the Nicaraguan government. It is impossible to tell exactly where his mind is, for Robertson is confirmed in his belief that he is a prophet of god and his god will fight his battles for him with the same intensity of purpose that his god will launch a nuclear war to wipe out the Soviet Union.[7]

Buchanan has significant reason to be worried about Robertson and the evangelicals taking control of the government of the United States. Buchanan recalls how "the Moral Majority beat my brains out in Christian love."

Although an ordained Southern Baptist minister, the evangelicals took no notice of Buchanan's religious credentials but went door-to-door portraying Buchanan's opponent as being "god's candidate" and Buchanan as being "on the other side."[8] What cost Buchanan his seat in Congress was his statement:

> For the sake of freedom of conscience, there should be a wall of separation between church and state. Once people take the posture that, "I am the Christian in this situation," then we're in trouble.

Evangelicals see themselves as the sole and singular possessors of truth and righteousness. No one else, evangelicals affirm, can know the will of "god," do "good for the United States," or "love their country" to the extent they believe that they can. Robertson also used this line in attacking the "unChristian" policies of U. S. Secretary of Education William S. Bennett.

Having a monopoly on god gratifies evangelical egos. They can ignore laws if they wish. They don't have to pay taxes if they feel that such a payment is contrary to god's will or would work a hardship on the deity's ministry. Pat refuses to pay taxes.

Pat loves evangelical thinking.[9] He gives lip service to the phobias of his congregants; his "believers" then reward Pat hailing the televangelist as a second Jesus.[10]

Pat is above sin. Nothing he can do is evil or wrong.

If the government interferes with Pat or his ministry, it is the government that is in error. For the federal (or any state or municipal) government to bring suit against Pat is, to many, the government's declaration of being leagued with the Devil. To a man — or woman — Pat's brigade will raise barriers to protect their sovereign earthbound minister of god.

Quick to avoid taxes and unwilling to meet his civic financial obligations — which Pat sees as being a part of a Satanic revival in the United States — Robertson has become entangled with the law. He has been sued by both the state of Massachusetts for taxes due on commercially profitable shows aired on his Boston station WXNE, and the city of Boston. The suit was filed since Massachusetts state law requires all charities (non-profit organizations) to disclose their finances. Pat refused to do so. Then, the entire legal matter was held in abeyance. Nothing further has been heard. One can only presume that god saved the day for his buddy Pat.

The state of Massachusetts and Boston were not the only taxing bodies to sue Pat and his corporate empire. Another suit was filed by the local Virginia Beach tax assessor who decided that part of CBN's vast holdings were subject to a property tax since CBN had begun to produce commercial shows and lease out part of Robertson's luxurious television studios to independent commercial producers.

This was more than Pat's god would accept. After all, didn't Pat's god initially set up his empire, bankroll "his buddy," and speak directly to the ruggedly handsome son of a former Virginia senator? One can't tax god! Can one?

Robertson fought back. Angered at the thought that he could be taxed he turned to his legal counsel. They pointed out that the network had created hundreds of jobs locally, and "suggested" telling the taxing authorities that if the levies were filed, CBN could move its holdings to another more hospitable — non-taxing — locality.

The fact that Robertson's "700 Club" is surrounded by commercial shows is "irrelevant" according to the televangelist. Robertson claims that the main message of CBN is Jesus. The other shows only paid the freight to get the Jesus message across; at least that was the official CBN line.

To tax his network or gainsay his answer, Robertson argued, was tantamount to denying religion access to the airwaves and denying Jesus' First Amendment rights. Jesus is not only a citizen of the United States, but this son of a Galilean carpenter is also a Republican and a "buddy" of Robertson.

To tax the CBN network would be equal to bludgeoning Robertson's chance to save the United States from godless "secular humanism," "Communism," "Atheism," and the Democrats. If his network were taxed, the work of Jesus would suffer a setback. This would not only keep "children from praying," but open the door to perversion, license, and crime. Nothing further has been heard from the local Virginia Beach taxing authorities.

Once he was left alone by tax collectors, Pat turned back to the issue of prayers in school. Prayers were to stop secular humanism and public education could be forged into parochial prayer. "Kids need to pray." Jesus' prayers are to be pushed in schools, so that crime can be conquered and all people saved for the rapture.

To keep children morally pure, Pat also plays his thinly worn record against any form of sex outside of marriage and not between opposite genders. Homosexuality is to be outlawed[11] because Robertson's Bible says it is evil.[12] Pat overlooks that the same Bible also forbids a man to trim his beard, get a haircut, or have sex with a menstruating woman.[13]

So that there can be enough kids to pray, never shave, cut their beards, or have sex with menstruating women (assuming that these "kids" are male), abortion is to be banned. Again, Robertson's reading of his scripture says so.

The instrument that is to enforce all of Robertson's wishes is to be a federal government that doesn't tax Pat or his empire. If the federal government does not step in so that Pat, as Big Brother, may purify the morality of the United States, then Robertson has concluded, the states are to "resume" their "natural rights of state sovereignty" and enforce the Judeo-Christian concepts his alabaster tyrant-god dictates. Only then can "kids . . . pray."

Law enforcement agencies are not only to be the instrument of seeing that biblical laws are kept. Law enforcement agencies are to obey the Robertson will — for as he announced on his television soap the "700 Club," if he "couldn't move a hurricane [Gloria]" he "couldn't move a nation."[14] (All that Robertson's god required the televangelist to do to stop Gloria was to command, "In the name of Jesus, we command you to stop where you are and move northeast." The "we" was never defined.)[15]

If local law enforcers are unable to maintain biblical purity, Robertson has a solution. Strengthen the FBI and the CIA. Make sure Big Brother's teeth are sharp.

Robertson pledges to strengthen the Central Intelligence Agency (CIA) when he becomes president of the United States. According to Robertson the CIA has been weak since Watergate.[16] The CIA is to be given *carte blanche* in foreign affairs, and although he promises to strengthen the United States' ties with "Godless and Communist" mainland China, he sees the action as being Jesus-inspired since it will give him the "potential in evangelizing Asia."[17]

Strong international police power will enable Robertson not only to "evangelize Asia" but assure a rebirth of "morality" in the United States. Bringing about "Christian morality" is to become one of Robertson's programs when (and if) he is elected president.

Delighting in talking about sex, which he has equated with "cult abuse," he interrogates numerous women and girls who appear on his shows about their sexual lives. It has not been uncommon for Robertson to ask graphic questions about their sexual activities. He has asked, at various times, the women and girls who have been guests on his shows if they had fornicated in their "old lives of sin"[18] — and how many times! He likes to hear all the unseemly aspects of sex so he can pardon the sinner, satisfy his prurient interests, and increase his TV ratings. Porn sells not only in *Hustler* magazine but is good at attracting new viewers and financial supporters to Robertson's "700 Club."

Tantalizing his viewers with details of past fornications and adulteries, without mentioning his own, Robertson also relishes going into detail concerning the sex lives of gay males. He not only condemns fellatio, analingus, and sodomy, but delights in damning nocturnal emissions as a "dread curse,"[19] all the while fulminating against actual homosexual orgasm.[20] Would he have us believe that he has never masturbated?

Homosexual love is, according to Robertson, a spiritual death penalty.[21] To escape eternal execution (being burned forever in a firey pit) Robertson recommends that gay men and lesbians marry a member of the opposite sex, seek and accept Jeus, and publicly testify to their past sins of loving someone gay.

Any interpretation of Robertson's *sermo* is ranked as heresy, and heretics are to be dispatched so that they cannot contaminate life as he wishes it to be lived on earth in his unique usurpation of Christianity for personal political purposes.[22] His arguments against heresy are paraphrases of the fifteenth century Inquisition. Dissent is not allowed. Total submission to his interpretation of biblical law is to be requilred of all citizens of the United States — and some day n the future — of the world. This Robertson would accomplish by having his coreligionists elected to Congress to pass Christian laws and have the same enforced by born-again Christian judges.

Notes

1. Andrew Mollison, "Robertson Redefining Self in Presidential Terms," *Austin* [Texas] *American-Statesman* (14 September 1986), sec. D, p. 9.

2. Ibid., sec. D, p. 9.

3. David Waymire, "Don't Judge Me Only on Faith, Robertson Asks," *Grand Rapids* [Michigan] *Press* (23 September 1983), sec. A, pp. 1, 2.

4. DeSmet, "Rev. Mr. President?" sec. A, p. 13.

5. See: "Candidates Have Right to Claim God's Endorsement, Group Says," *Atlanta Constitution* (21 July 1986), p. 2; See: Pat Aufderheide, "The Next Voice You Hear," *The Progressive* (September 1985): p. 34.

6. See his article, "Dictatorships and Single Standards," *Policy Review* (January 1987). For a summary, see *Los Angeles Times* (27 January 1987).

Former colleague Gerald Straub, author of *Salvation for Sale*, told United Press International, that he feared Robertson could start a war, nuclear, as well as conventional.

7. DeSmet quoting Buchanan, "Rev. Mr. President?" sec. A, p. 13.

8. Kate DeSmet, "Pat Robertson Isn't God's Candidate, Minister Says," *Detroit News* (27 September 1986).

9. Cf. Jay Merwin, "Robertson Visits With His Flock," *Concord* [New Hampshire] *Monitor* (11 February 1987), sec. A, pp. 1, 12.

10. Jay Merwin, "Robertson Visits With His Flock," sec. A, p. 1.

11. Straub, *Salvation for Sale*, pp. 106-8.

12. Lev. 17, 18, 19, 20.

13. Cf. Lev. 20:18.

14. "700 Club" 11 June 1986. For an analysis of the hurricane account given by Robertson, see: Jim Fitzgerald, "Holy Diversion? Detour Might Come in Handy Too," *Detroit Free Press* (29 September 1986), sec. F, p. 16. Cf. Larry Peterson, "Robertson: Congress Harder Than a Hurricane to Deal With," *Orange County Register* (6 February 1987), sec. B, p. 4.

15. Andrew Mollison, "The Quotable Pat Robertson on Politics, Religion, Himself," *Orange County* [California] *Register* (17 September 1986), sec. A, p. 21.

16. William A. Henry 3d, "Pat Robertson and the 700 Club," *Boston Globe* (2 January 1980), p. 17.

17. William A. Henry 3d, "Pat Robertson and the 700 Club," *loc. cit.*

18. William A. Henry 3d, "Pat Robertson and the 700 Club," *loc. cit.*

19. Straub, *Salvation for Sale*, p. 180.

20. Straub, *Salvation for Sale*, pp. 104, 106-8.

21. Straub, *Salvation for Sale*, p. 108.

22. Jim Baker, "Network Preacher Rides Divinity Into Politics," *Buffalo* [New York] *Courier-Express* (2 July 1980), p. 10.

Chapter 19
Saving The Alcoholic for Jesus

Robertson has a lot of fun with sin.[1] He labels almost every mortal pleasure a sin,[2] frequently in direct conflict and contradiction with his Bible.

Robertson's concept of sin is nearly universal in scope. He defines sin as sex, non-religious music, alcohol, amusements, and public education.

Sex outside of marriage is always bad. If it doesn't have procreation as its motive — sex is sin. But Mary, the mother of Jesus, was one-half a sinner since she conceived outside of marriage. Worse yet, she lived with a man she never married.

Religious music can be passionate ballads. Religious music can also be erotic. The classic "Jesus Christ Superstar" includes anger, vice, lux, and sexual propositioning as well as doubt, violence, and other emotions found in non-religious music.

The amusements of holy people in the Bible include war, rape, pillage, and seduction of both sexes. Israelites are ordered to kill all harlots and witches. Jewish soldiers are permitted to take booty during pillage. Dancing is common, as is singing and personal adornment. The ancient Hebrews were not on their knees night and day, unless it was for a sexual act such as that between David and Jonathan. Drinking intoxicants was not only pleasant and exhilarating — and definitely *not* forbidden.

Public education is condemned because it is secular and objective. The brutality in the Old Testament is exposed and analyzed as history and literature — not as a given eschatological command. And the biblical accounts are compared with other historical literature of the day, such as the Persian epic *Gilgamesh* and the Babylonian *Code of Hammurabi* which have the same stories and contain the same laws as are found in the various "historic" versions of the Old Testament. What is especially disquieting is that the pleasures Pat puts down are not biblically condemned when srutinized. Even the consumption of alcohol is approved.

While Robertson maintained a bar (he was fond of whiskey) in his private quarters in a chauffeur's lodge where he and his wife, Dede, initially lived,[3] he became opposed to alcohol when he found Jesus.[4] Generally Robertson chooses to ignore that the Jesus figure, as defined and discussed in Robertson's Bible, changed water into wine[5] — not grape juice.[6]

The preacher's paranoia concerning intoxicants crept more rapidly into his mind cells than the consumption of alcohol formerly made it cruise through his veins. It quickly changed into a genuine cancer of self-abasement which destroyed his power to reason.

Determined to save others from a fate he had not himself avoided — the swilling of booze — Robertson has turned CBN into a "model community." Liquor, in any form, is forbidden. If an individual would apply for a job, he or she could expect not to be hired or quickly fired if Robertson learned that the applicant or new employee had consumed alcohol — even if it were only wine at a meal.[7]

Spirits of any nature were the "corrupting element" that the Mephistophelian Prince of Darkness put in the way of good citizen's plodding toward paradise. If our citizens cannot individually put away alcohol, then the government must do see that it is done, to save each person's individual soul from everlasting damnation. Robertson totally ignores that the apostles of his god commanded all people — including government officials — to "drink a little wine for the stomach's sake."[8]

Robertson's pontifications on alcohol won him the immediate adulation of prohibitionists, many of whom lurk in Christian fundamentalist groups and associations. Their praise of Pat's anti-alcohol stand sent his already inflated ego soaring higher — and brought additional contributions to his war chest. They cared little for what the Bible actually said, or what might be desired by the citizenry. Their goal is to reign over the "social values" of the people of the United States restoring the prohibition at any price.

Notes

1. Robertson. *Answers*, pp. 77-78, 83-85, 123, 202, 213, 215-16, 259-60.

2. Robertson, *Answers*, p. 202.

3. Robertson, *Shout It From the Housetops*, pp. 13, 27.

4. Robertson, *Answers*, pp. 223-24.

5. John 2:9.

6. Pat only reluctantly admits this. See: Robertson, *Answers*, p. 224. He does so, however, by suggesting that alcoholism was "not a problem" in the days of Jesus. This, again, is Robertson's distortion of fact. For immediate reference, see: C. Saltman, *Wine in the Ancient World* (London: Routledge, 1957) F.R. Cowell, *Life in Ancient Romes* (New York: Capricorn Books, 1967), pp. 86-88.

7. Straub, *Salvation for Sale*, pp. 101-2.

8. 1 Tim. 5:23.

Chapter 20
Pat on Congress

The height of Robertson's autocratic arrogance came in 1980 when he attacked Congress's makeup as "anti-God" and "anti-family," arguing for the election of those who were pro-school prayer, anti-abortion, anti-ERA, anti-homosexual, pro-family, and anti-Communist. Tenaciously, this televangelist took on some of the most seasoned veterans in Congress, declaring that liberals were not "Christian."[1] Robertson frequently attacks the "liberal mindset," but never declaims against the "Christian mindset." While the former is considered by Robertson to always be evil, the latter is praised as "godlike" and necessary to establish and maintain "traditional values." These arguments helped the religious right to defeat liberal lawmakers such as Democratic Senators Dick Clark of Iowa and Thomas McIntyre of New Hampshire, who were replaced by two ultra-conservative Republicans: Roger Jepsen of Iowa and Gordon Humphreys of New Hampshire. Jepsen would be defeated after his first term in the Senate in part because of the revelation of his membership in a "swinging singles" club in Iowa.

Among those Pat picked to pound was born-again Baptist Republican Senator Mark Hatfield of Oregon.[2]

Hatfield responded punctually to Pat's prattlings. He argued that Robertson's notion that liberal politics is anti-Christian "is a throwback to the Middle Ages."

At the same time, Robertson rhetoric reached to block the equal-rights amendment in various states from Virginia to Nevada. Opponents to women's rights, such as Phyllis Schlafly, argued that the

ERA would lead to unisex bathrooms and the downfall of the family, a misstatement of fact that won over the Oklahoma legislature and cost the ERA that state's vote of ratification.[3] Anita Bryant also benefited by the base homophobia of preacher Robertson. Her meteoric ascendency in Florida led to the defeat of a Miami gay-rights ordinance, which spilled over into other areas, including several states which enacted laws to protect church-related schools from public interference and augmented anti-gay statutes out of an hysterical fear that gay teachers would recruit non-gay students to become gay men and lesbians.

These statutes were but a prelude to the downfall of basic civil rights that would come with the 1980s election when Falwell, Robertson, and other far-right preachers bleated that Jesus was a Republican and that to vote for any Democrat was to vote against god. Illinois Senator Adlai Stevenson termed the theological thundering of the televangelist "the ultimate hypocrisy."[4] The Senate was purged of "liberals" and a pogrom against accustomed civil rights was begun. Schools were permitted to discriminate on the basis of color,[5] non-profit organizations were permitted to discriminate on the basis of gender,[6] and individuals could be fired from public school or civil employment on the basis of personal opinions and expression.[7]

When Robertson and his fellow Christian cohorts saw their goals "not fully met," although their teflonized "champion of Christ's cause" [Ronald Reagan] won the presidency, Robertson pledged that Reagan would correct this "injustice" of liberal domination of the U. S. Congress. This would begin in the U. S. Senate.

In Illinois the Robertson faction works under the acronym "United Republican Fund of Illinois," which held a Dr. [sic] Pat Robertson rally "on Our American Political Heritage," 12 March 1986, at the Continental Regency Hotel in Peoria, and sent out fliers with the February 1986 issue of *Time* featuring Robertson on its cover as the art for the flier. Objective observers at the rally had a difficult time telling who was for anything positive, outside of the repeated pontifications that the "Christians" would lead America back to its "Christian roots." Most of the program featured attacks on minority groups. "Voting" and "Christian responsibility" were regularly interchanged and intermingled, with the speakers implying that a "good citizen" was a "Christian" who "voted" while those who would "destroy" America were not "Christians" and thereby were not "good citizens" and should not be allowed to vote.[8]

Pat was enraged and he promised that when he became president the goals of evangelicals would be fully met. This goal of being president, about which he had dreamed since 1977, would please Jesus.[9] The satisfaction that his savior would savor would turn into limitless blessings and rewards for those who voted for Pat. And, with his occupancy of the White House, he would push the United States closer to an Armaggedon that would cleanse the world by annihilating all unbelievers.[10]

Notes

1. See Eddie Vela, "Evangelist Attracts Voters: Republican Robertson Decries 'Liberal Mindset'," [The University of Texas at Arlington] *Shorthorn* 67.82 (11 March 1986): pp. 1, 2.

2. See my *Reagan and Woman* (Dallas: Texas Independent Press, 1984).

3. See my *Idol Worshippers in 20th Century America* (Dallas: Monument Press, 1985).

4. See "Preachers in Politics," *U.S. News & World Report* (24 September 1979): pp. 37-42.

5. Baker, "Network Preacher," loc cit. 6. Brian J. Kelly, "Major Network Planned: Evangelist Plugs into TV Power," *Chicago Sun-Times* (16 November 1977), p. 36.

6. *Grove City College v. Bell*, 465 U.S. 555, 104 S. Ct. 1211, 79 L.Ed.2d. 516 (1984).

7. *Roberts v. United States Jaycees*, 468 U.S. 609, 104 S. Ct. 3244, 82 L.Ed.2d. 462 (1984).

8. *Adler v. Board of Education*, 342 U.S. 485, 72 S.Ct. 380, 96 L.Ed. 517 (1952), aff'd 342 U.S. 951, 72 S.Ct. 624, 96 L.Ed. 707 (1952).

9. Cp. Manuel Rico, "Robertson Isn't Guided by Providence," *San Antonio* [Texas] *Express News* (30 September 1986).

10. For Pat's Congress see his *Answers*. pp. 190-199.

Chapter 21
The Anti-Jew Stance of Pat Robertson
& His Hatred of Other Refuseniks of Christianity

By June 1986, the nation's capital in Washington, D.C., was set for an onslaught. "The Christians are coming! The Christians are coming!" was the cry of many.[1] (I.E. "THE WHITE IRANIANS ARE COMING!!! "—EGAD!)

On his "700 Club" Robertson reveled, "No society should have to dismantle its entire religious framework to accommodate the one or two percent [of Jews] who are disbelievers [in Jesus Christ]." He couples Jews, whom he refers to as "non-Christian people," with Atheists, and exclaims that the two together are "destroy[ing] the very foundations of our society."

Robertson is determined to resist giving any liberties or freedoms to Jewish people. As he said on a "700 Club" broadcast, the duty of "good Christians" is "to insist that the Jewish pressure groups desist in their efforts to strip [the Christian] religion from public life in America."[2]

Robertson's anti-Semitism was fully unveiled in his 17 September 1986 telecast. It was on that date that Pat announced that he would run for president of the United States if he were able to marshall three million signatures.

Duane Rash of Aloha, Oregon, expressed the common sentiment of those who witnessed Robertson's telecast. Robertson was to be "the Christian's candidate." Robertson neither could nor would represent all Americans. Robertson would represent *Christians*. As Rash relished, "When all the Christians find he's running, they will back him."

In a similar vein, Dana and Teresa Taplin of Portland, Oregon, argued for Robertson's election. Robertson would get the Christian "messages of the church into the schools." No reference was made of getting Jewish, agnostic, Buddhist,[3] Islamic, Atheist, or any other "messages into the schools." The message was to be as singular as Robertson's candidacy: Christianity for everyone regardless if everyone was Christian.

A litany of lamentations against Robertson rose, here and there.

A new crusade was to be launched. The politico-religious war machine guided by Robertson promised to steam ahead overrunning the United States and leaving behind it the crushed freedoms lost by Jews and non-believers.

Like Pope Urban II, Robertson nearly screamed, *"Deus volte! —* God wills it."* The swords of the Christian crusaders were to be swept from their sheaths to find a home in the naked bosom of civil liberties. Individual freedoms were to be dashed to pieces like the skulls of so many non-believers.[4] The rights of innocents with few or no convictions were to be trampled by the followers of the new hoards. Crosses were to be swung against synagogues and temples. Christianity was to triumph. The anti-semitism of Robertson's political posturings was polished to a tinsel patina while his followers pledged that truth would be their first victim.

All Jews who held public office were to be attacked. Only conservative Robertson and Republican Christians were to sit in congress.

Little cover was given to the rank anti-Semitic stand of Rob Scribner, a lay minister in the Church of the Four-Square Gospel in Los Angeles. Claiming that god called him to run against Democrat Congressional Representative Mel Levine, a Jew, Scribner chortled in a controversial letter that Levin "[is] diametrically opposed to nearly everything the [Christain] Lord's church stands for in this nation."[5] Damning anything "not Christian," and intimating that "non-Christian people" should be removed from the United States, the angry anti-Semitism of Scribner is but one bead in the bloody rosary of the radical religious right — a group of strict fundamentalists who work ceaselessly for Robertson's campaign — moving toward his goal to Christianize the United States.[6]

The Scribner letter, dated 22 April 1985, read:

> I too am a [Christian] pastor. You know how much you love and value those in the congregation you lead. That's how much I treasure my flock. However, a year ago God did a rather unique thing — he called me to run for Congress in California's 27th District. I do not believe every pastor has or will have this call; however, as you know, when God requires a thing of you, you must obey. Therefore, as a future congressional representative

and as a pastor, I am asking for your support. Here's what is needed: . . .

2.) Wherever you are located, be it in this district or not, encourage your congregation to vote. Teach them to vote wisely. Teach them to vote based on the relationship of the issues and the Word of God. Teach them not to vote according to party or personality, but according to the candidates integrity before God. You can do this by showing incumbent voting records. Christian Voice, as well as other Christian groups, will make available prior to national elections, the voting records and view of those running. . . .

4.) Influencing people in society (politics) means money. Where your treasure is, there will your heart be also. I hope you will consider this opportunity. . . .

In the 1984 race for Congress, 27th District, I ran against the incumbent, Mel Levine. Mr. Levine received a zero rating in the Christian Voice index [Levine is a Jew]. He is diametrically opposed to nearly everything the Lord's [Christian] Church stands for in this nation. . . .

I recently relayed these things to Dr. Pat Robertson of the 700 Club and his gracious response was to come here on behalf of the campaign and speak in November of this year. . . . For me, . . . I hope you will agree to link arms with us as we literally "take territory" for our Lord Jesus Christ.

The nationwide *putsche* of the radical Christian right is anti-Judaic in the most terrifying way — a terrorism that Congressional Representative Carl Levin was to learn in Michigan. The campaign against Levin was bitter. The anti-Judaism was thinly veiled by the evangelicals who called upon local pastors to "put a good Christian" into Congress, and "remove" the incumbent who did not "confess Jesus."

This same insensitivity so characteristic of the Christian fundamentalist movement became the hallmark of the venal and bigoted antics of Intelivote in Texas.[7] Not only did the Texas Intelivote field Christian candidates for local, countywide, statewide and national offices, but its officers, headquartered in Garland, sent letters ranking candidates on their responses to "Christian" questions. Many candidates, such as Dottie Lynn of Arlington, were "judged" without even having returned Intelivote's questionnaire.

Organized by Garland lawyer Wyatt W. Lipscomb, who demands an hourly fee if he is to be interviewed, Intelivote's first meeting was held in the First Assembly of God church in Mesquite, Texas, with over two hundred ministers and lay people present. From 25 February to 26 March 1985, Mesquite ministers menaced those who did not toe the fundamentalist line on life and politics: being against abortion, homosexuality, and general human rights.

First Baptist Church of Mesquite pastor Don Bradly boasted to the local media that it was important to know the private thoughts of those in politics, especially on "certain moral questions." One candidate targeted was Mesquite Mayor Brunhilde Nystrom.

Nystrom was sent an Intelivote questionnaire. She refused to complete it or return it, claiming that the group's rating of candidates on moral and religious issues made Mesquite look "stupid and backward."

Although she survived the first onslaught of Intelivote in 1985, in spite of having a score of only 4.73, based on a scale of 1 to 15 (though she did *not* respond to the questionnaire), Intelivote's opposition to her running Mesquite was so strong that she was defeated in 1987. The storm troopers of Intelivote, celebrated uproariously.[8]

The same groups, flaunting the "Christian charity" that bludgeoned Nystrom from office, went after the Arlington City Council. City Councilwoman Jen Barney was given a "D" — she refused to answer any questions from the group. Councilwoman Dottie Lynn, visibly upset by evangelical pandering, issued the strongest statement against the gestapo maneuvering of the group, condemning its totalitarian tactics, declaring that its questionnaire was an invasion of a person's privacy totally foreign to the principles of American democracy, and demanding that it be sent "back to Mesquite from where it came."[9]

The perfidious plundering of political offices grew stronger as Intelivote enlisted evangelicals from a wider area. Tom Carter was put up against Congressional Representative John Bryant. Bill Clements was endorsed over incumbent Governor Mark White. While Bryant was able to defuse the Intelivote assault directed against his campaign, White was routed by the organized religious intolerance. His upset gave new ground to the radical right religious group and inspired other evangelicals nationwide.[10]

Rabbi Arnold Scheinberg of Congregation Rodfei Sholom, in San Antonio, Texas, noted that:

> . . . if the impression I have is correct that he [Robertson] wants to make the United States a Christian country, I believe that would be a disaster for democracy.[11]

Levi Olan of Dallas, five years earlier, had warned against the rise of Robertson and his "Christian crusade" as being "exceptionally dangerous to the Jew in the United States."

Robertson has never been neutral. He has never embraced the traditional American attitude and consensus towards religious and ethnic pluralism. If he can unseat Jews and other non-Christians he shouts the praises of his god while digging the grave for democracy.

That Robertson plays a key role in the anti-Judaic *putsche* in the United States among the religious right can hardly be questioned. He has consistently been able to turn out more supporters than his rivals in the GOP expect.

Robertson calls his covert operation the "Hidden Army." He vows to score upset victories at the polls where non-Christians will be outvoted and where non-Christian politicians will be handed a Christian defeat. Thus, a fundamentalist Baptist preacher in Oregon drew 43 percent of the vote in Oregon's GOP primary in an attempt to unseat Senate Finance Committee member Bob Packwood.

The move to the political right is staggering. Christian fundamentalists see no option but to take over the system and turn the objective political process in the United States to Christian subjectivity and intellectual oppression.

The Presidential Biblical Scoreboard was making its rounds of the United States early in 1988. The *Manchester Union Leader* reported on a forty-page edition which appeared before the New Hampshire primaries. Pat Robertson fared well on the favorite issues of the radical religious right: anti-abortion, pro-capital punishment, pro-school prayer, pro-Strategic Defense Initiative, anti-Equal Rights Amendment, and support of Nicaraguan "freedom-fighters."

The Scoreboard[12] tried to rally its readers:

> We could elect a president no matter how objectionable he was to the liberal, humanist media. We could ensure that the majority of congressmen took a strong moral stand. We could pass godly legislation. A BIG — REAL BIG DANGER!

It cautioned against the enemy, which included the American Civil Liberties Union, the National Education Association, the National Organization for Women, and the Planned Parenthood Federation of America — all of which are "in a struggle to remove Judeo-Christian values and influence from American life." Politically, it beat on the

Democrats, characterizing the "Rainbow Coalition" of Jesse Jackson as:

> Predominantly composed of radical elements — militant Black Panther Party members, Student Nonviolent Co-ordinating Committee elements, Black Muslims, homosexuals, Marxist-Leninists and others.

From his video vatican of Christian broadcasting, Robertson has pushed his image as a protestant pope capable of theological theorizing and political pontificating. There is no room in Robertson's Christian enchained mind[13] for any social perspective or political system that differs from what he enunciates as "inspired views."[14] Peggy Shriver writes in her book *The Bible Vote: Religion and the New Right*:

> Pat Robertson chats with successful beauties who love Jesus, with congressmen who share his sense of the End Times coming but who also seem unafraid, and he invites those who are troubled to call him and pledge their dollars for God's bountiful multiplication.[15]

Woe be to the Jew, the Atheist, the non-believer, or any believer in any god(s) that are not the selected singular god of Pat Robertson.[16]

Pat's anti-Judaism dangles threateningly over the heads of Jews like the sword of Danocles every time Pat preaches "Jesus is Coming soon."[17] Those who aren't Christians are to feel the retribution of his god.[18]

Interestingly enough, the Jews who are to be damned by Pat's god are to be thrown into a *Christian* hell that no self-respecting Jew accepts anyway. The Christian concept of life eternal, of rewards/punishments, is directly opposed to Jew's Old Testament.

While Pat delights in citing 2 Peter 3:10 (which states that the earth will perish),[19] the Jews read Psalm 78:69 (which states that the earth was established to last forever). While the Jews accept the verdict of 1 Kings 8:12, which has god dwelling in thick darkness, Robertson points to 1 Timothy 6:16, a passage that claims that god dwells in unapproachable light. Did Robertson's god move?

While the accounts of Christ's alleged birth and life on earth are engorged with contradictions, Jesus' resurrection is laden with even more, including the threadbare message of the Galilean's "Second Coming."[20] In a "believe it or not" scenario there has, along the way, even been speculation as to how a video recording could be made of the prognosticated "Second Coming" so that Pat could air it on his "700 Club," and thus scoop every other network.

To Pat's regret, Jesus didn't cooperate in G.S.P. — God's Secret Plan — to win souls — and money for Pat.[21] Of course then, Pat's god doesn't always play by Pat's rules. God is seldom fair and usually quite a bastard when it comes to doing anything substantively good.[22] The truth is that the god to which Robertson refers is not only the author, according to the Bible, of numerous atrocities, but also countless absurdities.

This god allows fathers to sell their daughters into slavery in order to pay a debt.[23] One of this deity's many messengers ("angels") was commissioned to slay 185,000 Assyrians,[24] and permitted 14,700 Jews to die in a plague because they rebelled against the autocracy of a religious dictator.[25] Using this form of rationalizing, it is but a short hop to defending the pogroms of the Nazis in the 1940s, since Robertson's god commanded the beheading of 24,000 Israelites for sleeping with unacceptable women and worshipping a "foreign" god,[26] and then struck dead another 50,070 innocent Jews whose only crime was to glance up in an effort to see the Ark in which god allegedly lived and slept.[27] Another 120,000 Israelites were inhumanely dispatched by the same tyrannical god, being murdered in a single day by King Pekah, who, like Robertson after his Michigan victory, claimed that he stood for the godhead, and was instructed by god to wreak vengeance upon "unbelievers."[28]

One might wonder if Robertson will be given the same power as allegedly was forced upon Elisha, another wild-eyed biblical messenger who moved god's wrath against those who offended the deity of the burning bush. Elisha's reputation was certainly questioned in his own day; he damned those who refused to follow him and instead found sport in laughing at his bald head. To punish his detractors, Elisha had two bears eat forty-two of those who laughed at him. All forty-two of those consumed by the bears — in the name of Elisha's god — were children.[29]

Although Robertson does not yet have dominion over wild bears, he is as intolerant of those who question or disagree with his cornucopia of misstatement, mutilation of facts, and pseudobiblical exegeses. Through his *700 Club* Robertson has twisted any positive messages for life that might have existed into floods of judgments and verdicts of guilty.

Even if Jews, Atheists, agnostics, or believers in any gods other than

Robertson's fanatical, fundamentalist, capricious god, live quality lives, are faithful to their own religious or humanitarian beliefs, sacrifice for the good of others, and are kind, honest, and caring persons — if they do not belong to a "spirit-filled" Christian (usually read as Southern Baptist) church and generously tithe to televangelistic ministries, those men and women will be marched into hell. "Salvation only comes from the savior-god Jesus."[30]

Exactly what this "savior-god" saves has never been fully or adequately discussed, described, or detailed. Robertson and his henchmen, however, are sure that part of their ministry is to save those Jews who are "capable" of being saved.

Being "capable" of achieving "salvation" means the ability of the Robertson cultists to craftily connive against unsuspecting Jews, while elaborating on the merits of Christianity. The Robertson faithful delight in going after especially strong religious Jews, confronting, badgering, and baiting them as if the conversion of Jews to Christianity was a test of Christian skill.

The "capability" ploy is used by Robertson's cultists when they encounter a conservative or orthodox Jew. Cornering him, the evangelicals place a slick pamphlet in his hands. This pamphlet "speaks" of the Christian god "who so loved the world" that he butchered his own son — a Jew.

Seldom is the Jew converted. All that occurs is a pious Christian littering of highways, causeways, walks, and markets.[31] This angers the pious pretenders, to the point that the evangelical vows an even more energetic campaign to convert the people of Israel.

Seldom do evangelicals see that the plastic god of Robertson has become more brittle, less colorful — more of a mental dildo than a sustaining breath of life. They see their Jesus as still set on saving those who do not wish to be saved.

The Christian response to the Jewish aversion to this outreach of Jesus by his bully-boys is to reiterate Robertson's message of "love" — a sweat-soaked shirt of spiritual suicide: a set against freedom of choice. The Jew must accept Jesus or nuclear war will erase the unbeliever in Christianity from the threshold of the living. Robertson has written that Jesus knew of nuclear holocaust and will use it against those who defy Robertson and his prophets:

> The second New Testament Greek word that we translate "power" is *dunamis*. *Dunamis* carried the concept of resident strength or explosive force. The English word *dynamite* comes

from *dunamis.*

A U. S. President has *exousia* over the nuclear arsenal. The atomic bombs in the arsenal have *dunamis.*

Before He ascended to heaven after His resurrection, Jesus commanded His followers not to leave Jerusalem until they received *dunamis.* He told them, "You shall receive *dunamis* when the Holy Spirit comes upon you. . . ."

He then cites Acts 1:8.[32] Not only is the scriptural passage out of context, but the translation of the text is faulty at best. The actual context speaks to a celebration of the "resurrection," for which reason the ancient church established "Whitsunday," which was described in the fourth century *Peregrinatio Etheriae.* It's only law forbade any fasting during this "fiftieth day" period of time.[33] It had no reference to either the dispatch or conversion of Jews.

A good deal of Robertson's anti-Semitic views are screened away by his constant profession of the Christian faith. Yet in each of these pronouncements, Robertson's hatred of Judaism is apparent, for he speaks continuously of the superiority of Christians and Christianity — as if either has a monopoly on virtue, truth, value.

In one of his crisscross crusades through Michigan in 1986, Robertson proclaimed, "*Christians* in Michigan can say we stand for values, we stand for family, we stand for God and country, we stand for liberty and freedom." Robertson's rhetoric was tantamount to the televangelist's saying, "Jews do not stand for values, Jews do not stand for family, Jews do not stand for God and country, Jews do not stand for liberty and freedom." Into this message any non-adherents or non-Christians can be lumped as failing to meet the patriotic criteria *pro Deo et patria.*[34]

Being "for god and country" however, has a shredded veil. Scarcely cloaked, Robertson's evangelical call is for the truth of the testimony of Jesus and a Christianized United States.

The final veil that hid Pat's rabid anti-Semitism was torn off with the release of his letter to his faithful followers who stormed the political process in Michigan, handing him a coup over the aspirations of Jack Kemp[35] and George Bush[36] who equally lust after the Republican nomination for the presidency. Not only did Robertson declare that "THE CHRISTIANS HAVE WON," but he took aim at the GOP politics in Michigan, saying that if enough followers were elected in the August 5 primary, they would "have within their grasp" the power to name GOP nominees for various state offices as well as "delegates to the 1988

National Convention."

Cannonading at the wall that separates state and church, Pat zeroed in on Michigan's Christian fundamentalists. He noted that they had gained the tools they needed to forge out a Christian revolution against unbelievers. He would lead an "army of god" against the unbelievers.

Pat's army of god came from evangelical churches. All are violently opposed to "Jesus' slayers" — the Jews, and to other non-believers. These fundamental Christians gave Robertson the final margin for victory. Their ministers were the generals leading the charge against the Constitution of the United States. They gave Robertson the ammunition he needed to launch a rapid-fire attack on the opposition. The shells that were aimed at the political polling place, striking down freedom of or *from* religion were the names of "politically aware" church members.

Each of the individual's whose names had been supplied to Pat were contacted by their church leaders. Once they were contacted, they were drafted into the army of the religious right to spend a month of "eighteen hour days" learning the Robertson rhetoric.

Intensely indoctrinated into political fundamentalism, the draftees returned to their congregations to take fellow church members through the same basic training of the how and why each should plunge into the alien thicket of local politics.[37] Such maneuvering tactics, Associate Pastor James Muffett admitted, were "like mining for gold."[38]

Robertson's "Freedom Council" claimed that it had recruited 4,500 people to become political bullets for Robertson. They would report loudly against the enemy — humanism.

This continuing attack on "secularism" by whatever name, won over many a convert who lusted for a taste of a holy war. They looked to a battle that was to be won so that dissenters against their brand of Christianity would fall on the field of annihilated freedoms.

Humanism was seen as "Atheistic" and "Communistic" — even though humanism is a respect for that which is, and is not a respecter of particular times, climes, personalities, theories, economic determinations, or other renderings labeled as humanism by the conservative fundamentalist element. But using an arsenal of words honestly and carefully, with a full appreciation of their meaning is foreign to Robertson. To attempt to be just with words might cost Robertson a modicum of the precious time he needs to subject the United States to his will.

The hysteria and hyperbole of Robertson over "humanism" found allies in an unexpected quarter. Roman Catholic Archbishop Edward

McCarthy of the Miami Catholic Archdiocese joined Robertson in his attack on secular education.

Originally from Cincinnati, Ohio, McCarthy blasted the Supreme Court's reaffirmation of the separation of state and church when the Supreme Court struck down an Alabama law that required a moment of meditation or silent prayer in public schools. Tunnel visioned, McCarthy feared that the Supreme Court was "making children schizophrenic" because they are "agnostics in school, believers at home."

Metaphysically beating his breast, McCarthy continued,

> Freedom of religion seems to be shifting to freedom *from* religion and our nation seems to be adopting a new "national religion" — namely, secular humanism.

The Roman Catholic prelate was wording his attack as a defense of Christianity being *the* religion in the classroom, of the state, and of the nation, for there are few Jewish teachers in public schools, and few if any public schools give time to Jewish considerations.

An unscrupulous henchman for the Vatican, McCarthy's veiled anti-Semitism is not unique among "Christian leaders." The reference the primate pounded into the heads of those who would listen to his prattling was clear. Children had to offer "Christian" prayers to a "Christian" god.

McCarthy had no consideration of the pluralism in education. In keeping with his Roman Catholic tradition, he rejects the plethora of faiths as well as the absence of faith in any deity by men.

The Miami prelate's hatred for freedom of choice, as well as freedom of and from religion, is bitter. Bashing freedom of choice has become reminiscent of the aims of those who stoked the fires for heretics. McCarthy dropped himself to the ranks of those tyrants of yesteryear. His mind remains shut to any sense of brotherhood or charity. Void of compassion, he would return to the era of that senator from Wisconsin who terrorized the United States thirty years earlier.

McCarthy's stand on Christianity in the classroom is anti-Semitic, which can be understood easily. He is subject of the Vatican — an agent for a foreign power which has a history of persecuting the Jews and those "separated brethren" outside of the Roman Catholic fold: from the bloody days of the crusades through the Inquisition fired by the hatred of Dominican and Franciscan monks more interested in learning the sexual habits of their accused than the orthodoxy of their beliefs, to the current moment when John Paul II declared during his 1987 tour of the United States that dissent is not permitted in the Roman Catholic Church any more than freedom is in Christianity.[39]

McCarthy continues to live in the dark ages of religious superstition surrounded by the trappings of pontifical monarchy and clerical absolutism. There is no democracy in his thinking nor is he a champion of the rights of the people.

Always a potential candidate for the papacy, McCarthy would sell his democratic heritage to sit upon the despotic throne on Vatican Hill. Rather than being a part of a nation of laws, he would make laws for a small nation nestled in the very heartland of the City of Rome.

The sectarian statements of McCarthy match those of Robertson, the only real difference between the two men is their goals and aspirations. Roman Catholic McCarthy can dream of being pope. Protestant Pat works toward his dream of ruling the United States.

Neither tolerates dissent. Both want to control people with absolute authority. Theirs are those that would be willingly accepted by others.

Rabbi Henry Michelman, executive Vice President of the Synagogue Council of America, hailed the Supreme Court's recent decision[40] which upheld a previous case outlawing prayer from the public schools as maintaining the historic separation of state and church. He denounced Robertson's ill-hidden anti-Judaism, when the televangelist condemned the Supreme Court's decisions on prayer in the school, text books used in public schools, and other basic state/church separation issues. Lynn Taylor, professor of religious studies at the University of Kansas and executive director of the National Council on Religion and Public Education, concurred. The Supreme Court ruling, Taylor underscored, "took school-structured religion out of schools. Children can still pray in school — privately."

Taylor emphasized that the Supreme Court merely reaffirmed its 1962 decision against school sponsored prayer.[41] The new ruling was new only in time, not purpose or intent.

Regardless of the intent of the Supreme Court ruling on prayer, Robertson vowed, it would not happen again. Robertson told his people the day the 6-3 decision was reached that he would see to it that the ruling was overturned, Christianity put into the classroom, and Christian prayers said to a Christian god. It was a promise he means to keep. He repeated it often throughout the following year as he planned for his day of decision in Michigan. All he needed, Robertson affirmed, was a few loyal people who would follow "god's word," as he interpreted it, and work to the final resolution. Robertson needed robots willing to do his will without thinking, discussion, or inaction. His followers had to be completely loyal to him. Their lives, energies, and monies had to be pledged to him. There could be no dissent.

Candidly Robertson admitted that his people operated systematically, almost robotically. In his letter of jubilation following the Michigan upset, he chuckled:

> What a thrust for freedom! What a breakthrough for the kingdom!. . . . We saw the hand of God going before us in Michigan, affirming our every step. We went to city after city, and everywhere I found thousands of believers jumping to their feet, ready to work, ready to pray, ready to give — thrilled that their time had finally come.

Robertson's crusade knows no bounds or limits. The Jew, the non-Christian, the Atheist, agnostic, and free-thinker are to be put to the "thrust" of the spiritual sword. The minority are to rule the majority.[42]

What was needed was the slaughter of the innocence of democracy. Robertson's knights, greedy fundamentalist clergy thrust religious rapiers against those who failed to "give," slashed at those who disagreed.

Using unreported millions of dollars, the spiritual convictions of the self-righteousness, and their self-aggrandizement, all at the expense of the non-believer, Robertson gave battle in the secular arena against the non-believer. He seeks to destroy the liberty that generations have taken for granted.

Those who disagree Pat labels as:

> Those who do not stand for any absolutes and who do not believe in right and wrong. . . . If that attitude continues, it will destroy our families . . . and it can lead in this country to anarchy and chaos.[43]

Over and over Robertson canonizes the absurd: the selection of born-again fundamentalists as being the only patriotic people, asking for their election to public office, although seeing them not necessarily as thought-conscious. Indirectly, as it may be, Robertson repeatedly labels Jews and other non-adherents to his way of thinking as anarchists, nihilists, and intellectual vandals. ROBERTSON IS THE VANDAL

On 20 March 1986, Robertson declared in Mount Pleasant, Michigan, that those who protest his words and aspirations are influenced by "Marxist thinking."[44] As if he were W. A. Criswell of First Baptist Church, Dallas, Robertson is quick to throw the haunting shadow of hammer and sickle over any opponent. He brands those who speak out against him as "Communists."[45]

Notes

1. David S. Broder, "Religious Activists' Influence Will Be Felt," *Houston Chronicle* (1 June 1986), p. 2; this was originally entitled "Murmur from Michigan: 'The Christians Are Coming,'" as it appeared in the *Richmond* [Virginia] *Times-Dispatch* (1 June 1986), sec. F, p. 7.

2. See the American Jewish Congress newsletter, Fall 1987, pp. 1, 2.

3. Robertson, *Answers*, p. 70.

4. Phil Manzano, "Robertson Hailed in Portland," Portland, Oregon *Oregonian* (18 September 1986).

5. Marsha Blakemore, "Religion Shows Clout in GOP," *St. Petersburg* [Florida] *Times* (24 August 1986), sec. B, p. 1

6. William F. Buckley, Jr., "Tirade against Robertson Challenges Religious Enterprise," Universal Press Syndicated column carried in the *Dallas* [Texas] *Morning News* (21 August 1986), sec. A, p. 29. Among those working for Robertson are former cowpokes Dale Evans and Roy Rogers, who joined the National Committee to Draft Pat Robertson, see *Dallas* [Texas] *Times Herald* (20 August 1986), sec. A, p. 3; Robert S. Boyd, "Rogers, Evans Stump for Pat Robertson," *Detroit Free Press* News Tribune (20 August 1986), sec. A, p. 4; the commercial that the cowpersons are making for Robertson is discussed in the Associated Press release carried in the *Tacoma News Tribune*, [Washington] (20 August 1986), sec. A, p. 11.

7. See my *Unholy Rollers: Televangelism and the Selling of Jesus* (Arlington, TX: Liberal Arts, 1985), index, especially "Mary Lassiter."

8. See my: *Demons & Demagogues: Political Fanaticism In The Longhorn State* (Las Colinas, TX: Liberal Press, 1985), pp. 124-28.

9. Arlington, Texas *Daily News* (17 April 1985), sec. A, pp. 1, 6.

10. See my forthcoming, *Twisting the Cross*, as cited.

11. J. Michael Parker, "S.A. Clergy Balks at Robertson Run," *San Antonio Express-News* (19 September 1986), sec. A, p. 9.

12. Steve Daley, " 'Biblical Scorecard' Rates The Candidates," *Arkansas Gazette* (29 February 1988).

13. Straub, *Salvation for Sale*, pp. 302, 303.

14. Straub, *Salvation for Sale*, p. 19.

15. Peggy Shriver, *The Bible Vote: Religion and the New Right* (Princeton, NJ: Pilgrim Press, 1981).

16. Straub, *Salvation for Sale*, p. 120-21.

17. Straub, *Salvation for Sale*, pp. 113-14f.

18. Straub, *Salvation for Sale*, pp. 56-57.

19. II Peter 3:10: The text reads that Jesus "will come as a thief in the night;" this line is of pagan origin and part of a priestly hell created for the economic benefit of the clergy, since it was indicative of an "unredeemed" death (cf. Romans 6:21, 23) where the deceased would either be denied burial or special prayers to comfort the living: the *poena damni* — or the exclusion of the presence of god — more than a *poena sensus*, denoting external agents of torment. Cf. death as a divine scapegoat, in: H. Usener, "Italische Mythen," *Rheinisches Museum* N.F. 30 (1875), p. 914, with ceremonies discussed by Th. Vernalcken, *Mythen und Bra'uche des Volkes in Oesterreich*, p. 293 *sq*; Strackjan, Aberglaube u. Sagen aus dem Herzogthun Oldenburg, II, p. 39, No. 306, with the theft of the soul in Bastian, *Die Seele und ihre Erscheinungwesen in der Ethnographie*, p. 36.

20. Robertson, *Answers*, p. 32.

21. Straub, *Salvation for Sale*, pp. 160-62.

22. Straub, *Salvation for Sale*, pp. 166-67.

23. Exod. 2:7-11.

24. II Kings 19:35.

25. Num. 16:41-49.

26. Num. 25:4, 9.

27. I Sam. 6:19.

28. II Chron. 28. Cp. Lev. 26 and 33 for other examples of the mercy of Robertson's draconic deity who will not suffer a Jew to challenge him or question him. These stories of religious violence make mayhem on television seem like infantile pranks.

29. II Kings 2:23-24.

30. Straub, *Salvation for Sale*, p. 79.

31. Straub, *Salvation for Sale*, p. 81.

32. Robertson, *Beyond Reason*, p. 168.

33. J. A. Jungmann, S. J., "Pfingstoctav und Kirchenbusse in der römischen Liturgie," in *Miscellanea Liturgica in honorem L. Cuniberti Mohlberg*, i (Bibliotheca Ephemerides Liturgicae, xxii; 1948), pp. 162-82. G. Kretschmar, "Himmelfahrt und Pfingsten," in *Zeitschrift 'fur Kirchengeschichte* 146 (1956), pp. 209-53.

34. Thomas B. Edsall, "Evangelist's Tax Status, Gifts Raise Questions," loc. cit.

35. Since the Michigan Robertson *coup*, Kemp, realizing the need for political expediency, leagued with the televangelist in an effort to derail Bush. See: James Risen, "Kemp-Robertson Alliance Chips Away at Bush," *Los Angeles Times* (1 April 1987), pt. I, p. 28.

36. Bush ordered a restructuring of his political machinery in Michigan after the Robertson win. See: Remer Tyson, "Shake-up

Ordered in Bush's Campaign," *Detroit Free Press* (4 August 1986), sec. A, pp. 3, 11; cp. Michael Tackett, "GOP Hopefuls Watch Michigan as '88 Yardstick," *Austin American-Statesman* (4 August 1986), sec. E, p. 22. Bush, initially, had the support of Jerry Falwell and Jimmy Swaggart — televangelists who later deserted his political tent to trip towards Robertson's rally round for a Christian takeover. See: Dennis B. Roddy, "Swaggart Opposes Robertson Bid for President," *Pittsburgh* [Pennsylvania] *Press* (18 August 1986), sec. B, p. 4.

37. Paul Taylor, "Networking in Churches Pays off for Pat Robertson in Michigan," *Des Moines* [Iowa] *Register* (30 May 1986), Opinion Page 1.

38. Paul Taylor, "Churches Were the Way To Robertson's Recruits," *Washington Post* (29 May 1986).

39. Jim Jones, "Dissent Is Wrong, Pope Says," *Fort Worth* [Texas] *Star-Telegram* (17 September 1987), sec. A, pp. 1, 10.

40. *Wallace v. Jaffree*, 105 S.Ct. 2479, 86 L.Ed.2d 29 (1985).

41. Adon Taft, "Religious Leaders Split on Prayer Ruling," *Miami Herald* (7 June 1985), sec. B, pp. 1, 4.

42. Hugh McDiarmid, "Robertson's Letter Strips Away Myths," loc. cit.

43. April Witt, "Robertson Heckled by Peace Activists," *The Ledger-Star* (21 March 1986), sec. A, pp. 1, 5, especially A5.

44. April Witt, "Robertson Heckled," op. cit. p. 15.

45. April Witt, "Robertson Heckled," ibid.

Chapter 22
Penthouse, Playboy,
Sex, Censorship, and Pat

Robertson has had a difficult time with human sexuality. Pat is convinced that any form of sex that isn't procreative, in a marital supine position, is evil and sinful. He has blasted any printed material that isn't a medical guideline, and has condemned such popular magazines as *Playboy* and *Penthouse*, arguing that these magazines lead to sexual promiscuity.

Robertson, taking the censor's hood as his cap, labels any pictorial presentation of human nudity or sex as a perversion leading to mental breakdown and socio-family disintegration. According to the televangelist, heterosexual marriage, and supine sex within marriage, is the only way to avoid a total disintegration of human morality which would, of course, deprive the offender of immortality.[1]

To insure the continuation such specific sexual practices, Robertson endorses censorship of any sexual publications as being "anti-family." He has applauded the unscientific findings of the notorious Meese Commission on Pornography, which "blackmailed" several retail chains into removing what it considered "offensive material" — such as *Playboy* and *Penthouse* magazines.[2] Even the Library of Congress was forced to withdraw *Playboy*, fearing Congressional reaction against it.[3]

Among the darlings who merit Robertson's support is Andrea Dworkin, one of the most colorful figures who appeared to testify against "pornography." Primarily she protested that pornography is a form of sex discrimination. In January 1986, at the New York City seating of the Meese Commission, Dworkin complained that pornography "creates a vast hopelessness for women, a vast despair."

Dworkin's actual objections, although covert, were against heterosexual depictions of human intercourse. As a lesbian, Dworkin has authored erotic-to-pornographic prose so graphic that few dare to review it or include it in public library collections. In her autobiography, she wrote:

> N is easy to love. Devotedly. She is very beautiful, not like a girl. She is lean and tough. She fucks like a gang of boys. Women want her. So do men. She fucks everyone. It is always easier for her to than not. She has a perfect courtesy and rare grace. She is marvelously polite, never asking, never taking, until licensed by an urgent request. Then she is a hooligan, all fuck and balls. . . . She is a rough fuck. She grinds her hips in. She pushes her finger in. She tears around inside. She thrusts her hips so hard, you can't remember who she is or how many of her there are. The first time she tore me apart. I bled and bled.

Not only does Dworkin glorify lesbian sex, but sexual violence — the two objections she finds in the heterosexual "debauching" of women.[4] Interestingly, and in the usual spirit of evangelical contradiction, Dworkin has little to say about the "sexual enslavement" of men by "pornographers." Her arguments on women and pornography are not accepted by major psychiatrists or psychologists, and are not supported by facts.[5]

Like Dworkin, Robertson's position on human sexuality is in direct confrontation with scientific fact and laboratory research. Since incipient genital responses are quickened by initial viewing of erotic materials, orgasm is desired; however, if viewing erotic material or reading "pornographic" literature is continued, genital response declines proportionate to the visual injestion period of the material.[6]

When the Reagan Administration set up a panel of "experts" on pornography, Robertson felt that the day had come when "evil" books, pictures, videos, and movies would be expurgated from the nation. With the publication of the Meese commission's report, Robertson was, however, openly disappointed: the commission had not gone far enough in censoring what a citizen of the United States could read, view, or hear.

Among the many "oversights" of the Meese Commission, Robertson argued, are the concerns of the media, its use of pornography and the message pornography gives. This televangelist is convinced that the mere existence of erotic material destroys the human mind, endangers the family, turns heterosexuals into child molesters and rapists, and transforms Christians into Atheists, agnostics, Jews, and other "non-Christians."

Medical science, pregnant in psychological studies, does not support the Robertson thesis. Slides, movies, and other visual erotica offer only temporary arousal.[7] Books, tapes, and other "non-visual" or "non-graphic" materials offer even shorter periods of human sexual excitement.[8] Non-explicit story lines, in fact, offer greater arousal to women, while tales of raw violence without any mention of sex or pandering to human sexuality, encourage men to feel penile stimulation.[9]

Studies show that reading select passages in the Christian Bible dealing with violence, bloodshed, and "divine retribution" actually have aroused men more than the nudity in *Playboy* or *Penthouse*, and fostered sexual aggressiveness for longer periods of time.

The constancy of sex, violence, and obscenities in the Bible's parade of legends and stories[10] have created greater sexual problems for modern men than have all *Playboy*, and similar magazines.[11] The Bible, in fact, not only glorifies rape[12] but mutilation;[13] murder is sexual, and voyeurism common therein. Pat's Bible spends many of its pages on sex, sexual arousal, sex perversions, and sex-related violence.[14]

Interestingly, the name of god (*El*) is the root for the nickname of the penis *El-hhemameh*, which literally translates as "dove" and which became the symbol for the Holy Ghost who announced (John 3:16) that Jesus was the "beloved son" of god.[15]

Since the King James Version of the Bible "condemns" homosexuality, so does Pat. Robertson's signet against homsexuality has been the traditional totem raised by such clerical charlatans, as Colin Cook of Reading, Pennsylvania.[16] To argue that homosexuality is the result of "pornography" shows not only a gross misunderstanding of homosexual development, but of the entire process of human sexuality, not to mention a microscopic mentality in the area of knowledge of eroticism and its affect on the human psyche.

Masturbation is high on Pat's list of "no-nos" although masturbation is normal. Contrary to Christian fundamentalists, masturbation does not lead to insanity.[17] Masturbation does not make a person homosexual any more than masturbation makes a person heterosexual, asexual, or bisexual.[18]

Masturbation is a sin in Robertson's concept of Christianity, as it is in many Christian cults, but masturbation is neither a disease nor a sign of mental dysfunctioning. It is a normal process in life. It is practiced by nearly everyone throughout individual existence.

There is no "cure" for masturbation, even if the male is castrated or the woman subjected to a clitoridectomy.[19] Masturbation can take place physically as well as mentally. Theologians tend to masturbate the minds of their flocks into a united orgasmic outflow of non-intellectual "Amens" and "Hallelujahs." Under Christian coercion a constant fear of the normal settles where the fluid of inquiry and self-development once was oiling the engine of the human mind.

Human awareness of sexual differences between male and female, as well as the proclivity to type of sexual expression, begins early.[20] An attempt at the coital act is often experienced by the age of five. It is but an infantile investigation of possibilities and a primitive first attempt at accumulation of knowledge for later reference.[21]

Some sexologists claim that actual sexual knowledge and interest (proclivity and/or orientation) is generated in human behavioral evolution to a point of ultimate development by the time the individual has reached the age of three.[22] Sexual experimentation, commonly called "games," quite frequently becomes more modest due to social prohibitions and objections to the natural process, both of which affect the soundness of mental development, creating sexual phobias and sexual restrictions that are not normal in the evolution of each human life.[23] Proscribing, limiting, defining, and denying human sexuality in any of its multifacets can lead to actual mental malaise, as well as socially unacceptable actions.[24] If human sexual development is arrested too early, the individual may be unable to experience the pleasures of sexuality within the framework of any meaningful relationship.[25]

Human sexuality is also limited by curtailing, suspending, or forbidding sexual fantasies, regardless of age or condition. Myths, fairy-tales, and tales of supernatural people forbidden to fundamentalist children can lead to sexual dysfunctionings, since fantasies are not only a healthy part of the process of maturation, but conducive to mental development.[26] A *caveat* that needs to be noted by any parent is that the child must not believe that these supernatural events took place or that myths are real. A belief in myths as being real arrests psyche development.

Myths are any tales that are told about physical actions that deny physical properties: giants, such as Atlas, who can carry the world, men who walk on water, miraculous beans that can grow up to the sun, and the like.

The only aspect that has a more limiting and destructive impact on the mental development of the individual is unwilling and uninvited incestual invasion of the vagina or anus. There are numerous police reports of this becoming increasingly common in Christian fundamentalist homes. This is especially true when the born-again parent discovers his children sexually investigating his or her own body or the body or bodies of siblings and/or peers.[27]

Evangelical fundamentalist daddies who molest their children are defended by co-religionists who see the sexual abuse of children as being biblically proper and in keeping with Lot's rape of his daughters, and David loving Jonathan. Child molestation by born-again daddies has been condoned as manifesting "the will of god" with the usual citation of Lot "going into his daughters," after the alleged fall of Sodom;[28] father-daughter incest being the most common reported cases.[29]

Fathers who commit incest usually come from unhappy homes. They have experienced poor relationships with their parents. A common characteristic is that these men were overly concerned with spiritual matters to the exclusion of secular psycho-physical development.[30] The extent of the control that a continuing literal reading of the Christian Bible has on men in the United States was, in part, the subject of "Born Again: Life in a Fundamentalist Baptist Church" [in Massachusetts] aired on the Public Broadcast System on 23 September 1987. According to that program, evangelicals accept "no other way" than the precepts of their Bible, declaring that all things are done not by their own strength, intelligence, ambition or the like, but by Jesus. It is Jesus who "pays" for their trucks, determines who they are to marry — and if a child marries against the will of the parent who stands in the place of Jesus — it is Jesus who forbids the child to return home. If sex takes place between parent and child, this, too, is the will of the dastardly deity.

Women who discovered that they are in an unhappy marriage, blamed this same god. Girls who are violated by their fathers define the violation as the will of god or they curse god. God becomes the only thing that controls the will of the people — a god is defined and interpreted by the minister, said Ron Marshall who appeared on the show.

Marshall was trained by Jerry Falwell, at Liberty Baptist Bible College, in strict fundamental adherence to the Bible.

In keeping Old Testament restraints, Ron rides rough-shod over family liberties. He is an absolute tyrant, and dictator. Brainwashed as they are, his family members swear blind, unwavering allegiance to him as the führer over their lives. Ron's wife, Geri, argued before the cameras that it "is very easy for a wife to be submissive" to her husband. She swore that the Bible commanded the wife to do so.[30]

Wives who object or attempt to stop their husbands from sodomizing and raping their children are chastized as "harlots" and "fallen from the Lord Jesus." Yet incest is only one part of evangelical philandery. Eighty-four percent of the fathers who had incestuous relationships with their daughters had engaged in extramarital affairs. This is not only true among evangelical laity but among fundamentalist clergy.[31]

Incestuous fathers, for the most part, drink too heavily. Their drinking helps them to endure self-imposed bondage to authority figures, ideas, and goals. Authoritarianism is stressed strongly in religious fundamentalism. Common authority figures are spouses and employers who lecture continuously on the sin of human sexuality and emotions, and on the need to obey.

The word *incest* is used guardedly. *Incest* is a legal term. Many victims of incest actually are quite willing to participate in the act regardless of social customs, norms, or religious teachings or prohibitions.[32] Those committing or commissioning incestuous relationships seldom consider the act to be "incestuous" at the time it is done. The psychological effect of incest on the "victim" depends on the age of the victim and whether or not the child/youth/adolescent/adult was truly "victimized."

Incestuous acts have no direct correlation to "pornography." Where "pornographic" materials are accessible, there has been a decline in sexual license, action, and violence.[33] Where censorship occurs, the reverse has been the case.

That which has been forbidden has historically been that which has been desired, sought out, secured by any means, used, utilized, and abused. This was graphically noted when the federal government of the United States prohibited alcohol.

Prohibition didn't work. Censorship will never work.

Even if all the "pornographic" materials are denied, banned, and burned, the idea of what it contained, how it was expressed, and when it occured, will remain in the minds of those who desire it. Eroticism will develop new expressions within the same pornographic parameters for those who have such an interest.

It is human nature to be interested in the human body and the sexual act. Such an interest has been recorded in detail in the world religions and their literature. It is a common theme that runs through all secular classics and is a part of gothic and contemporary romances.

Much of the interest today in pornography, among evangelicals, is the result of the fundamental religious double standard and the current clerical conniving to take over the United States and change it from a democracy to a theocracy. The double standard declares that women have one role[34] and men have a different role. An archaic idea, it is one of the foundation blocks of the Robertson rhetoric,[35] his campaign, and a continuing message of his hate broadcast.—WITNESS JIMMY SWAGGART'S PROBLEMS

While 82 percent of those recently surveyed believed it was acceptable for a man to engage in premarital sex, only 77 percent felt it was acceptable for a female to enjoy sex before marriage.[36] Even preacher Pat, his military friends relate, playfully practiced this male right of passage, pursuing teenaged girls and prostitutes while serving as a marine in the Orient.[37]

While these statistics seem generous, the woman has greater difficulty in satisfying her sexual needs. Women are adversely conditioned early in life from enjoying sex outside of the traditional Judeo-Christian marriage.[38]

Christian fundamentalist aversion to human sexuality is set in the *rigor mortis* mold of the "Protestant Ethic." If an individual wants to go to the Christian heaven, that individual has to be chaste in body and mind.[39] Nothing is to be enjoyed unless one longs for it, strives for it, works towards it, amidst various forms of self-denial, self-deprivation, self-denunciation, and self-abuse (albeit, not masturbation which has historically been seen as "manual pollution"[40]) all self-applied.[41]

Scientific findings and psychological evidence show that pornography has no adverse affect on people who view or read it.[42] It is considered a problem only when one individual elects to censor the reading and viewing habits and patterns of another without the consent or choice of the other.[43]

When an authority figure, such as Robertson, argues that he speaks for god and that his god does not wish an individual to view what Robertson defines as pornography, the viewer — if a Robertson adherent — can suffer a guilt complex, or attempt unacceptable social behavior[44] — such as committing suicide.

Consumers of "pornography" are no more deviant than non-consumers.[45] The enjoyment of viewing, reading, or listening to "pornography" does not lead to pathological behavior.[46]

Robertson, like other fundamentalists, simply has no idea what he is talking about. PAT ROBERTSON, LIKE ALL OF HIS KIND, NEED A ONE-WAY TICKET TO IRAN!

1. *Dallas Voice* (13 June 1986), p. 3.

2. Kurt Vonnegut, "God Bless You, Edwin Meese!" *The Nation* (25 January 1987): pp. 65, 81-82. Cf. Philip Harper, "7-Eleven to Halt Sale of Playboy," *Dallas Times Herald* (11 April 1986), sec. A, pp. 1, 14. Hugh M. Hefner, "The Blacklist," *Playboy* 33.7 (July 1986): pp. 2-3. Cp. my *Evangelical Terrorism: Censorship, Falwell, Robertson & the Seamy Side of Christian Fundamentalism* (Irving, TX: Scholars Books, 1986), introduction.

3. *Dallas Times Herald* (29 August 1986), p. 4A.

4. See: Penthouse Interview, "Andrea Dworkin," *Penthouse* 18.8 (April 1987), pp. 51-52, 56, 70, 72. Cp. her *Woman Hating: A Radical Look at Sexuality* (New York: Dutton, 1976); and her *Intercourse* (Chicago: Free Press, 1987).

5. As for Dworkin's argument that women's freedom is abridged by erotica and its publication, filming, see: Susan R. Estrich and Virginia Kerr, *Our Endangered Rights* — The A.C.L.U. Report on Civil Liberties Today, who argue that "women in America now enjoy an unparalleled measure of freedom."

6. A. C. Kinsey, W. B. Pomeroy and P. H. Gebhard, *Sexual Behavior in the Human Male* (Philadelphia: Saunders, 1948), p. 509. A. C. Kinsey, W. B. Pomeroy, C. E. Martin and P. H. Gebhard, *Sexual Behavior in the Human Female* (Philadelphia: Saunders, 1953). If masturbation or other means of emission occurs, the testosterone level in the man declines, resulting in general penial flacidity. Testosterone production in men reaches its peak when the man is between twenty and thirty-five, with the refractory period of the penis lengthening with age. Women do not undergo this same change.

7. Gunter Schmidt and Volkmar Sigush, "Sex Differences in Response to Psychosexual Stimulation by Films and Slides," *Journal of Sex Research* 6 (1970): pp. 268-83.

8. G. Schmidt, V. Sigusch and S. Schafer, "Responses to Reading Erotic Stories: Male-Female Differences," *Archives of Sexual Behavior*

2 (1973): pp. 181-89.

9. Ibid.

10. Robertson acknowledges. He cites certain "baffling" aspects of his Bible and their historical "incompleteness"; see: Robertson, *Answers*, pp. 237-54.

11. See my *Evangelical Terrorism*, pp. 139-58.

12 Gen. 19:35-36.

13. Deut. 22:25ff. Judges 19.

14. Judg. 19. Lev. 20:11-12. Cf. Gen. 34.

15. See my discussion in *Evangelical Terrorism*, pp. 159ff.

16. See my *Homosexuals Anonymous: A Psychoanalytic and Theological Analysis of Colin Cook & His Cure for Homosexuality* (Garland, TX: Tangelwuld Press, 1987).

17. E. H. Hare, "Masturbational Insanity: the History of an Idea," *Journal of Mental Science* 108 (1962): pp. 1-25. Cp. the Christian fundamentalist stand, as noted by John Vehon, "100% Morality — Go for It!" *Dallas Times Herald* (17 July 1986), sec. A, p. 33; and, David H. Pence, "Revival of Moral Standards," *Dallas Times Herald* (9 July 1986), sec. A, p. 29.

18. Glenn V. Ramsey, "The Sex Information of Younger Boys," *The American Journal of Psychology* 56 (1943): pp. 217-33.

19. J. Duffy, "Masturbation and Clitoridectomy," *Journal of the American Medical Association* 186 (1963): pp. 246-48; See J. Michael Clark, *Reflections on Pink Triangles* (Arlington: Liberal Arts Press 1987)

20. Floyd M. Martinson, *Infant and Child Sexuality: A Sociological Perspective* (St. Peter, MN: Book Mark, 1973), p. 31.

21. Carlfred B. Broderick, "Sexual Behavior among Preadolescents,"

Journal of Social Issues 22.2 (1966): pp. 6-21.

22. Floyd M. Martinson, *Infant and Child Sexuality*, p. 39.

23. Ibid, p. 40; Boston Women's Health Center, *Our Bodies, Our Selves* (New York: Simon & Schuster, 1976), p. 40f.

24. Tamara Jones, "Did Mother's Demands, Nude Dancing, Spark Girl's Suicide?" *Kansas City* [Missouri] *Star* 106.254 (6 July 1986), sec. A, pp. 1, 4.

25. *Anorgasmia* is the medical term for "frigidity." It is a problem when a woman cannot experience orgasm yet wishes to do so. In most cases the situation develops because of suppressed sexual feelings or the indoctrinated belief that sex and a woman's sexual fulfillment are wrong. Most cases of *anorgasmia*, where indoctrination is determined, have been the result of overly zealous religious fundamentalists who wish to keep women "pure" either for a male spouse or for Jesus (in the case of nuns in the Roman Catholic church). Cf. A. M. Zeiss, G. M. Rosen, and R. A. Zeiss, "Orgasm during Intercourse: a Treatment Strategy for Women," *Journal of Consulting and Clinical Psychology* 45 (1977): pp. 891-95. It is equally true in the world of Islam where women are sequestered. *Islam & Woman* (Dallas: Monument Press, 1985).
Lesbians tend to experience orgasm more frequently than do heterosexual women. In part this is because, by acknowledging their lesbian proclivity and orientation, gay women have rejected at the same time the religious fundamentalist prohibitions on human sexuality under which they were reared.
Gay and heterosexual women who are not encumbered with an archaic attitude toward human sexuality tend to experience orgasm more frequently and with greater force than do women who are in fundamentalist families. Women, in general, can experience multiple orgasms, where few men can do the same. See: Lewis M. Terman, "Correlates of Orgasm Adequacy in a Group of 556 Wives," *Journal of Psychology* 32 (1951): pp. 115-117.

26. Cf. Barbara Hariton, "The Sexual Fantasies of Women," *Psychology Today* 6.10 (1973): pp. 39-44. Gordon D. Jensen, *Adolescent Sexuality in the Sexual Experience*, ed. N/B. J. Sadock, *et al.* (Baltimore: Williams and Wilkins, 1976), pp. 144f.

27. John H. Gagnon, "Female Child Victims of Sex Offenses," *Social Problems* 13 (1965): pp. 176-92; James McCaghy, "Child molesting," *Social Behavior* 1 (1971): pp. 16-24. Incest affects approximately 4 percent to 13 percent of today's youth; see: J. H. Gagnon, W. M. Pomeroy, and Cornelia V. Christenson, *Sex Offenders: An Analysis of Types* (New York: Harper and Row, 1965).

28. Florence Rush, *The Best Kept Secret: Sexual Abuse of Children* (New York: McGraw-Hill, 1980). Susan Brownmiller, *Against Our Will: Men, Women & Rape* (New York: Simon and Schuster, 1975), pp. 277-82.

29. Father-daughter incest accounts for 78 percent of the cases reported to law agencies. However, psychological research shows that brother-sister incestuous relationships may outnumber father-daughter interludes. See: David Lester, "Incest," *Journal of Sex Research* 8 (1972): pp. 262-85. Cp. Morton Hunt, *Sexual Behavior in the 1970s* (Chicago: Playboy Press, 1974).

30. This distortion is addressed by Nancy Hardesty, Lucille Sider Dayton and Donald W. Dayton, "Women in the Holiness Movement: Feminism in the Evangelical Tradition," in *Women of Spirit: Female Leadership in the Jewish and Christian Traditions*, ed. Rosemary Ruether and Eleanor McLaughlin (New York: Simon and Schuster, 1979), pp. 225-254.
Early Gnostics in the Christian movement noted that the word "female" meant lust — and lust was any inordinate desire to possess that which would not come voluntarily; cf. Hennecke and Schneemelcher, *New Testament Apocrypha*, vol. I (Philadelphia: Westminster, 1965), p. 166f. The fundamentalists base their objections to the equality of women on a misinterpretation of I Corinthians 9:5, and the "veiling" of women. This argument is rejected by B. Bayer, "Uxores Circumducere" (I Kor. 9:5), in *Biblische Zeitschrift* 3 (1959), pp. 94-102; cf. my *Woman as Priest, Bishop & Laity.* Most of the early missionaries were couples, and women were equal (cf. Phil. 4:21f). Many were prophets (Acts 2:17f, and 21:9). Some were clearly superior and controlled men (3 John; Acts 18:2ff, and 18:18, 26); cp. *diakonos* in I Cor. 3:5, 9, and II Cor. 6:1, 4). The condemnation of women is a reflection on the pagan education of Saul of Tarsus who was familiar with the priestesses of Delphi and other cities, a priestship he introduced into Christianity

along with numerous other non-Christian antecedental adiaphorous items: from dietary to personal hygiene, actions, rejection of political involvement and the like. History of the Christian church rejects this fundamental evangelical interpretation and action. See: K. Beyschlag, *Simon Magnus und die christliche Gnosis* (Tübingen: Mohr, 1974), pp. 134-64; G. Lüdemann, *Untersuchungen zur simonianischen Gnosis* (Göttingen: Vandenhoeck & Ruprecht, 1975), pp. 55-81.

31. "The Jessica Hahn Story," *Playboy* 34.11 (November 1987): pp. 82-89, 178, 180, 182, 183-86, 188, 190, 193-94, 198 (pt. 1); Jessica was told that by fellaioing Bakker, she "saved PTL" (p. 183); the second part, serialized in *Playboy* 34.12 (December 1987), recounts the mind control of religious right-wing Christian fundamentalist ministries, brainwashing by the PTL, and declarations of demonic possession coupled with "hush money" (bribery) to keep Hahn quiet concerning the assault by Bakker.

32. David Lester, "Incest," *Journal of Sex Research*: pp. 270ff.

33. Berl Kutchinsky, "The Effect of Easy Availability of Pornography on the Incidence of Sex Crimes: the Danish Experience," *Journal of Social Issues* 29 (1973): pp. 163-81; cf. *Kama Sutra*.

34. 2 Cor. 11:2, Titus 2:5, I Pet. 3:2.

35. Robertson, *Shout It from the Housetops*, pp. 27, 31, 82, 90 (Dede's comment, "I take orders only from my husband"), 92ff.

36. Morton Hunt, *Sexual Behavior*.

37. T. R. Reid. "Robertson Corrects Details of His Life," *Washington Post* (October 1987) sec. A, pp. 1, 6. San Francisco *Chronicle* (9 October 1987). New York *Times* (9 October 1987) p. 11.

38. The reactionary statement, indicative and typical of the nineteenth century, initially elucidated by A. Hayes, in *Sexual Physiology of Women* (Boston: Peabody Medical Institute, 1869), p. 227, who argued that "a modest woman seldom desires any sexual gratification for herself," has been carried over to the current century by the near-anonymous "J," in *The Sensuous Woman* (New York: Lyle Stuart, 1969), p. 28, who writes that a woman "should settle for less

than the best," or spend the rest of her life in self-enforced chastity. Part of this is because of the conditioned male concept that women cannot experience sexual fulfillment, seeing male ejaculation as equal to a woman's fulfillment that men call "orgasm." See the satire of Bette-Jane Raphael, "The Myth of the Male Orgasm," *Village Voice* (25 October 1973), reprinted in *Psychology Today* 7 (1974).

39. Numerous pre-1960 "sex manuals" urged women to "fake" an orgasm "to please their husbands." See the Christian writings of E. R. Novak, *Gynecology* (Baltimore: Williams & Wilkins, 1952), p. 572; cp. Ellen B. Vance and Nathaniel N. Wagner, "Written Descriptions of Orgasm: A Study of Sexual Differences," *Archives of Sexual Behavior* 5 (1976): pp. 87-98.

40. Early denunciations of masturbation include the medieval *Lex Visigoth* III.5.7, and Peter Damian, *Liber Gomorrhianus* 7. S. A. Tissot, a Lausanne physician, in 1760 declared that masturbation was "psychological[ly] damag[ing]" in his *On Onanism, or a Physical Dissertation on the Ills Produced by Masturbation* — a work and thesis upheld by the Vatican in 1976, when the encyclical *Declarations on Certain Questions concerning Sexual Ethics* was released. The ancient Greeks saw masturbation as a "safety valve" — although they believed it to be used primarily by women who were "without men." See: Herondas, "The Two Friends," in his *Mimisibus* 6.

41. William Simon and John Gagnon, "Psychosexual Development," *Transaction* 6.5 (1969) reprinted in *Human Sexuality*, ed. E. S. Morrison and V. Borosage (Palo Alto, CA: Mayfield, 1977); P. E. Slater, "Sexual Adequacy in America," in *Intellectual Digest* (December 1973): pp. 132-35; and, George W. Albee, "The Protestant Ethic, Sex, and Psychotherapy," *American Psychologist* 32 (1977): pp. 150-61.

42. J. L. Howard, M. B. Liptzin, and C. B. Reifler, "Is Pornography a Problem?" *Journal of Social Issues* 29 (1973): pp. 133-45.

43. J. Mann, J. Sidman and S. Starr, "Evaluating Social Consequences of Erotic Films: An Experimental Approach," *Journal of Social Issues* 29 (1973): pp. 113-31.

44. Donald L. Mosher, "Sex Differences, Sex Experience, Sex Guilt and Explicitly Sexual Films," *Journal of Social Issues* 29 (1973): pp. 95-

112.

45. Harold Nawy, "In the Pursuit of Happiness? Consumers of Erotica in San Francisco," *Journal of Social Issues* 29 (1973): pp. 133-45.

46. Keith E. Davis and G. Nicholas Braucht, "Exposure to Pornography, Character and Sexual Deviance. A Retrospective Study," *Journal of Social Issues* 29 (1973): pp. 183-96.

Chapter 23
Pat Robertson on War

Pat Robertson believes in war.

War, according to Robertson, is inevitable.

If Robertson should become president of the United States, the televangelist has stated that he would feel it to be his Christian duty to initiate a nuclear holocaust. Pushing the button that would lead to international conflagration is the will of Robertson's god, who demands we must all rigidly adhere to his divine timetable. This is especially, now, more critical than ever since none of the past prophecies penned into ancient scriptures have come true: Jesus has never returned, although generations have watched and waited for the advent of the millenium[1] for nearly two thousand years, while peace has ever been elusive.

Robertson justifies nuclear genocide by citing his Christian Bible. His "authority" in defense of war is Jesus. As has been his custom, Robertson takes the biblical passage[2] out of context, as he does his coordinate reference.[3]

In both instances[4] Robertson's references are to *rumors* of war and wars that existed at the time of the gospels' writing. Still, this televangelist pounds home the "necessity" of and for a war to end all wars — to usher in the final reign of a physical Christ.[5]

Robertson is convinced that his concept of "freedom" can be won "through the use of military force."[6] This military use of force is defended by citing Old Testament accounts of military battles and blood purges of entire nations.[7] Pat's arguments favoring nuclear war are not only out of tune with biblical Christianity, and in direct opposition to his own Baptist roots, but divert if not abandon completely any stable psychological thinking.[8]

The war-deity whom Robertson worships can't bring about universal peace in the world. Putting aside disclaimers and the outraged cries of his coreligionists, Pat posits that the United States must send military forces into those areas out of step with his god's wishes.[9] On Friday, 16 October 1987, Robertson seethed against an arms agreement with the Soviet Union. His disgust with Reagan administration figures, the Joint Chiefs of Staff of the United States military forces, and First Lady Nancy Reagan (whom he implied was too eager to accommodate the Soviet Union),[10] was thinly veiled.

With an arsenic smile, Robertson minced Ronald Reagan as being emasculated in foreign military affairs by Nancy. Continuing his attack on Nancy and measuring her against his own obedient wife, Robertson, alluding to the well-known desires of Nancy, huffily proclaimed:

> I will set your mind at ease. She [wife Dede] has never suggested that I should make an accommodation with the Soviet Union in order to win the Nobel Peace Prize.[11]

Indeed, Robertson has no interest in peace at all if he is not its architect and if his god is not forced upon all who would suffer under Pat's pacification program. Robertson reiterates what he announced years earlier on his video tapes: if he is elected president of the United States, he will see that "all arms and material supplies we can make available" will be there for anyone who is fighting "god's enemies."[12]

As for peace, Robertson is equally opinionated. Peace will envelop the earth only when Jesus returns to reign — a Second Coming that has been anticipated and prophesied since the first century of this era.[13] But until this lethargic and much awaited *Logos* appears on earth, Robertson is convinced, war must occur. It is as if nuclear bombs will have the strength to shake his sleeping god awake and roust the deity to dress and descend to reign over a world purged of unbelievers.

The United States must take up instruments of war against his god's foes and initiate the first strike. Not only are non-believers, Atheists, and non-evangelicals to be roasted in the raw heat of thermonuclear destruction, but the United States must ready itself to wage war against the Soviet Union which, Robertson repeatedly harrangues, will come when the Soviets invade Israel.[14] Jubilant over the prospect of nuclear holocaust, Robertson sets up a presumed future scenario wherein the United States comes to the rescue of religion — and Israel[15] — by launching all its nuclear warheads into the Soviet Union, sending troops into Central America, and training "Christian soldiers" to police the streets of the United States. This army will be composed of a new breed of Christian babies born twice to bolster Pat's control — unlimited babies generated to a "pay future bills" of his administration, "and to stave off" the decline of his concepts of culture and values.[16]

To push Armaggedon, Robertson declared on 16 October 1987 (during a speech given to faithful Republican fundamentalists and party loyalists in Seattle, Washington) that he would appoint a secretary of state who would "stand up for America." A fanatical patriotism was to be enjoined on all who would serve their nation. He glorified the misdeeds of Ollie North, and vowed that his future secretary of state would not be afraid to use force, violence, or war to achieve Robertson's global goals. Furthermore, Robertson promised, he would appoint military leaders "who have learned to fight rather than to accommodate."[17] Robertson's distaste for the current crop of United States military leaders has never been secret. All who opposed him in Congress or any bureau or agency of government will be swept away.[18]

Arbitration or mediation in an effort to achieve peace, where all sides have equal representation and opportunities to be presented, with all points of views considered, and discussed by these equals, is anathema to Robertson. Robertson would be more comfortable in a dictatorial role regally dictating the terms other people and nations must bring to the United States in their quest of the holy grail of world harmony.

Peace, according to Robertson, is not only a Soviet plot, but a ploy used by Atheists and non-Christian fundamentalists to drag evangelicals into hell where the Devil was banished after unsuccessfully challenging Robertson's god in a war in heaven — a myth that became the structure ofthe blind English poet John Milton's epic, *Paradise Lost* — and has little biblical foundation.

Any good Christian will not give peace a chance. Those who do not support war and armed invasion of nations, who do not ape the United States and its leaders' interpretations of "peace" are to be cut off from Robertson's Jesus.

Jesus, after all, came "not to bring peace, but to bring a sword."[19]

Notes

1. The primitive Christian church believed Christ's Second Coming (known as *parousia*) was imminent, and this hope has been revived numerous times since. See: F. Tillmann, *Die Wiederkunft Christi nach den paulinischen Briefen* (Biblische Studien, xiv, Hftt. 1-2; 1909); J.

Jering, *La Royaume de Die el sa venue. Étude sur l'esperance de Jesus de l'apôtre Paul (Études d'histoire et de Philosophie religieuses*, xxxv; 1937); Bernard of Clairvaux, *Epistolae*, in *Patrologia Latina*, ed. J.-P. Migne (Paris: Tarnier Freres, 1879), cols. 67-220. Charles Dejob, *La Foi religieuse en Italie au XIVeme siecle* (Paris: Albert Fontemoing, 1906). Carolly Erickson, *The Medieval Vision* (New York: Oxford University Press, 1976); Angela of Foligno, *Le Libre des visions et instructions*, trans. Ernest Hello (Paris: A. Tralin, 1914).

2. Matt. 24:6, as cited in Robertson, *Answers*, p. 32.

3. Mark 13:7, cf. Robertson, *Answers*, p. 43.

4. Robertson, *Answers*, pp. 37, 192.

5. Robertson, *Answers*, p. 191.

6. Robertson, *Answers*, p. 191.

7. Robertson, *Answers*, pp. 32, 191. He repeats II Chron. 20:20-23 — in this case the battle was won by Jehoshaphat when he sent his people into battle singing; it was their voices that sent the opposing forces fleeing "in confusion": there was no conflict of arms. Robertson also draws upon Joshua 16:15-19, but in this case, again, the god of the Israelites did the fighting; no armed conflict occurred until after the war when Joshua was ordered by YHWH to kill all the Canaanite children as a testimony of Joshua's obedience and love for YHWH.

The Old Testament is riddled with raw destruction and bloodshed fought in the name of Robertson's deity and always for the sake of the priestly class. Robertson's extremist views are not totally endorsed by his coreligionists, such as Jimmy Draper, who, although a biblical literalist, acknowledged that YHWH is a cruel and vengeful deity demanding that children be slaughtered in ancient Israel, and concluded that the present god would not be a party to such a blood bath. *See:* Joe Edwrd Barnhart, *Southern Baptist Holy War* (Austin: Texas Monthly Press, 1986), p. 116.

Robertson elects to forget that New Testament biblical Jesus admonished people to "put away the sword," and praised "the peace makers"; cf. Matt. 5:9. Robertson also fails to note that the early Christians were pacificists to such an extent that many accepted death rather than serve in the military. Cp. Justin, *Apologia*, 5, 6; 11, 12;1

Martyrdom of Polycarp 3, 8-10; various *passiones* in the *Acta Sanctorum*; and, my *Martyrdom of Women*, index.

8. "Martyr's" Synod (20 August 1527) led Hans Denck to join the Anabaptists, and Hans Hut to defend radical pacifism. Hut argued that the Bible proved that the world would come to an end in 1528.
Both Northern and Southern Baptist Conventions recognized pacifism during World War II, although 1,064 Southern Baptist chaplains and 547 Northern Baptist preachers served in clerical ranks in the United States armed forces; cf. Southern Baptist Convention, *Annual 1941*: pp. 38-39, and Southern Baptist Conventions, *Home Mission Digest* 2 (1945), p. 17.

9. Robertson, *Answers*, pp. 191-92.

10. San Francisco *Examiner* (18 October 1987) sec. A, p. 6.

11. Various wire reports (17/18 October 1987).

12. *Dallas* [Texas] *Times Herald* (18 October 1987), sec. A, p. 15.

13. Robertson, *Answers*, p. 190. Cf. my *Woman In The Age of Christian Martyrs* (Mesquite, TX: IHP, 1982).

14. Robertson cites Ezek. 37-39 as "proof" that the Soviet Union will invade Israel. Contrary to his interpretation, there is neither linguistic, stylistic, or prophetic proof in this passage of or concerning the Soviet Union and its military forces. The Soviet Union, in fact, did not exist in the days of Ezekiel. It rose only after the Russian Revolution of 1917. Interestingly, Robertson rejects his own admonition for peace, which he suggested in his book *The Secret Kingdom*, p. 204, (although Robertson gives the context of Jesus stilling natural elements; cf. Mark 14:39).

15. Robertson, *Answers*, p. 32.

16. *Des Moines* (Iowa) *Register* (24 October 1987) sec. A, p. 4. Wayne King, "Robertson Urges Policy to Increase Birth Rate," *New York Times* (24 October 1987) p. 9.

17. *Dallas* [Texas] *Times Herald* (18 October 1987), sec. A, p. 15.

18. Wayne King, "Robertson Plans Asking for Purge." *New York Times* (24 October 1987), and *Des Moines* [Iowa] *Register* (26 October 1987). Robertson's statements in favor of a nuclear war and holocaust were reported in the *Des Moines* [Iowa] *Register* (1 November 1987) sec. C, p. 3.

19. Robertson, *Answers*, p. 185, and discussion above. Cf. Charles W. Sutherland, *Disciples of Destruction* (Buffalo, NY: Prometheus Books, 1987), pp. 109, 203.

Chapter 24
Robertson on Premarital Sex

Pat Robertson's political rhetoric has focused on "morality." Throughout his "unannounced" (pre-October 1987) and his "announced" (post-October 1987) campaign, Robertson has condemned premarital sex,[1] although he suggests he participated in sexual liaisons prior to his own marriage that came a few short months before son Tim was born.[2] One of the set lines of Robertson's speeches has been:

> We must encourage our children to take the institution of marriage very seriously and to bring back the old-fashioned concept of moral restraint and abstinence before marriage.

Preaching righteousness has been one of the focal points of Pat Robertson that has made him popular — among evangelical fundamentalists, celibates, blue-noses, and those who hate any form of human sexual expression.

Pat's pronouncements promising to punish those engaging in pre-marital and extra-marital sexual activity read like a judgment from an Islamic Court in Iran, and have become rallying cries for the "anti-pornographers," moralists, and Mary Lassiter types who have harbored hope of turning the United States into a sterile, asexual monastery, or a home where supine sexualilty is portion-controlled and uninterestingly listless. "Sowing wild oats" is to be done only in the fertile fields of the Midwest by debt-riddled farmers who have taken oaths of loyalty to their spouses that any oats sewn would be only of the grain variety. Any other "oats" sewn, sings savior Pat, is sinful and unclean — unless they were his own oats sewn in a variety of feminine fields where not all of the women with whom he consorted with were truly laid back in supine (prayerful?) supplication.[3]

Robertson's rank hypocrisy is nothing new to those who have made a study of preacher Pat.[4] Like most evangelical-fundamental theologians, Robertson terms premarital sex as "fornication."[5] Pat, like others of his ilk who have turned their collars backwards, has reveled at various times in this same depravity, now deemed to be "fornication."

Not until 1987, during the heat of his campaign for the United States presidency was Robertson confronted with his own "youthful indiscretions." The press presented evidence that his son Tim had been conceived 26 weeks before Pat married. When accused of hypocrisy, Robertson, like his clerical colleagues, excused it by saying that such actions took place before he found god — unlike his personal protégé, Jimmy Bakker, who continued his carefree abandonment of "moral principles" throughout his television ministry, and his political supporter Jimmy Swaggart, who was discovered to have paid visits to prostitutes to watch them undress and perform "other sins" for his entertainment.

When confronted with tiny Tim's birth record, Robertson royally spouted indignation. Theatrically he protested, "I have never been held to this standard of precision before." What Robertson's words meant, as sagely pointed out by Molly Ivins of the Dallas *Times Herald*, was that Robertson has not before been faced with the truth.

Truth, like justice, is something for which Robertson has little respect, and even less interest in presenting, practicing, believing. Televangelist Pat prefers to be seen as nearly divine, or superhuman. It is painful for him to "lower" himself to the stature of other mortals who are human, fallible, *sexual*, and interested in experiencing that which he would deny *everyone* if he were to become president of the United States.

As president Pat would push his brand of morality on all residents of the U. S. of A. Although Pat likes to determine morality, he does not care to practice what he preaches.

Pat's ivory tower has had the drawbridge of human reality drawn up too long. With his entrance into the political circus, his tower has been exposed to be *papier mâché*. Pat's anticipated "bring[ing] back the old-fashioned concept of moral restraint"[6] is a line out of a gothic romance. He has become the new Sir Galahad. Robertson's problem is his inability to stay on any horse long enough to ride it.

Pat's ploy promising to restore "abstinence[7] before marriage"[8] captures headlines but does nothing to explain or lay to rest his own interest in premarital sex and how it has been brought back to him.

In the 1940s, Kinsey concluded that 71 percent of all males had premarital intercourse by age 25. Only 31 percent of all females had similar sexual experiences.[9]

Kanter and Zelnick found in 1971 that 46 percent of all women surveyed had premarital sexual relations by age 19.[10] Hunt reported in 1972 that 67 percent of all women had had premarital sex by age 25.[11] Hyde continued the research, and in 1979 released her findings that 91 percent of all men, and 81 percent of all women surveyed, had engaged in premarital sex during an engagement period; 86 percent of the men, and 74 percent of the women surveyed, registered approval of premarital sex between any couple that was in love, even if they were not engaged to be married, and 84 percent of all men and 69 percent of all women stated that they had engaged in premarital sex even without love or commitment.[12] What Robertson failed to note is that when sexual impulses are repressed, aggression takes over and aggressive thinking dominates. This domination leads to crimes of violence against property, physical being, and life.[13]

Robertson's fear that premarital sex is rampant today is irrational. Men, typically, have about six premarital partners — hardly "rampant sexuality."[14] Those who do engage in numerous premarital heterosexual encounters do so, for the most part, in an effort to prove their heterosexuality as society buckles under religious fundamentalist intolerant protestations against homosexuality or a form of sexual exchange that could lead to the development of new friendships and alliances.[15] The "guilt trip" that televangelists, such as Robertson, force upon the minds of those who watch their airwave antics has not met universal acceptance. 77 percent of all married women who have had premarital relations see no reasons to regret this natural occurance, and consider such theatrical theologizing on sexuality to be absurd.[16]

Robertson has defined premarital sex as "a sin against the body."[17] The televangelist has written that those tempted to tarnish their immortal soul by engaging in premarital sex should "flee fornication as a sin against self and God."[18] He, of course, did neither.[19]

It took the *Washington Post*[20] to reveal that Robertson had been legally married only ten weeks before the birth of his first child — a son. Robertson lied to the *Post* when he told them that he was married on 22 March 1954 — five months earlier than he actually was — a ceremony hastily performed on 27 August 1954.

Robertson's attempt to justify his fornication (pre-marital sex) by claiming that he, and his wife, Dede, considered themselves married at the time that the fetus was conceived, was issued only when he was trapped politically. His rhetorical reasoning is a monstrous machination, a maneuvering of facts, to have the public believe Robertson only engaged in premarital sexual intercourse with Dede once, and then at the moment conception occured. Such an argument is patently absurd, for science has calculated the extraordinary exception it must be to have a conception take place in an initial intercourse no matter how well planned: it would be like inserting a small .177 calibre pellet rifle (a BB gun) into a swimming pool which has one gold fish and expecting to hit the gold fish with the first shot.[21] Such an argument has more foundation and support in pagan mythology[22] and Christian *pseudoepigraphia*[23] than it has support in traditional Christian scripture — or medical science.

Interestingly, according to the writings of Robertson, premarital sex is always the entrapment of the male by the sinful female[24] — even though he admits that he "sowed plenty" of his own "wild oats" before his marriage.[25] He did not reveal which "fallen woman" "forced" him into the sin of premarital sex, although in his biography he acknowledges that his Roman Catholic-reared wife, Dede, played a significant role in shaping his life-style before he "found Jesus." Still, records exist aligning the televangelist with a plethora of prostitutes in Korea — without mentioning the joys of Japanese Geishas and common street women of Tokyo.

More than likely it was Dede, pregnant with Tim (who in the Fall of 1987 went on to "pray for the sins" of others when he took over his father's televison soap, the "700 Club"), who forced Pat into marriage. Pat sighed that "even in marriage I was burdened with the futility of life," so that he not only contemplated suicide,[26] but sought an escape from his responsibilities to Dede and the infant Tim by fleeing either to the golf course and alcohol[27] or to the woods.[28] Could it have been that Pat saw Dede as the temptuous evil and sin-inspiring Eve? After all, according to Pat, woman was the original "source" of sin, and is now the "instigator" of continuing sin![29]

Repeatedly Robertson argues that not only does the woman lead the man into the sin of human sexuality (this sexual sin is defined by Robertson as any sexual act committed or experienced prior to marriage), but the woman also damns both of their immortal souls to hell.[30] This damnation of the "soul," according to the televangelist, did not apply solely to those who lived at the time of Saul of Tarsus,[31] but also to the twentieth century. He declares that premarital sex is "a sin that will keep millions of people out of heaven."[32]

When questioned by Ted Koppel on *Nightline* (8 October 1987), Robertson objected to "the media" making inquiries into his "private life." The hypocrisy of Robertson's protestations is venal at best in light of the numerous times that he has castigated and condemned others for the same actions that he has taken.[33] He called the questions of Koppel and the media "outrageous" for trying to "resurrect some skeleton" that was in his closet, quite out of tune with his eagerness to unearth the buried remains of any sordid pasts of those who oppose him.[34]

This would-be arbiter of national morality was not as moral as he pretended to be. His morality, or lack thereof, is as much a fiction as his fabricated education at the University of London which he claimed was an in-depth study of economics, whereas it had only been an introductory arts course for students from the Unites States.[35] While Pat protested against other preachers pandering for votes, Pat in his race for the GOP nomination for the presidency of the United States openly broadcast that he had a "direct call and leading from God to run for president."[36] Pat Robertson's words ring hollow as he protests, "I would ask a little mercy. There's something in the Bible that says, 'Judge not that ye be not judged'."[37]

Notes

1. Robertson, *Beyond Reason*, p. 34.

2. Wayne King, " 'Wild Oats,' Robertson Says of Late Marriage," *New York Times* (9 October 1987) p. 11. Randall H. Balmer, "Robertson and The 'Character Issue,' " *Des Moines* [Iowa] *Register* (20 October 1987). Jim Leggett and Rita Ross "How Reverend Pat Robertson Lied About His Pregnant Bride," *Star* (27 November 1987).

3. T. R. Reid, "Robertson Says His Son Conceived Out of Wedlock," *Dallas* [Texas] *Times Herald* (8 October 1987), sec. A, pp. 1, 16.

4. Molly Ivins, "Righteous Robertson Destroys Credibility Outside His Flock," *Dallas* [Texas] *Times Herald* (11 October 1987), sec. H, p. 3.

5. Robertson, *Answers*, p. 171.

6. The unnatural state of celibacy was condemned in the early Church, with many early councils in the Eastern Orthodox church asserting or implying that the clergy had a right to be married and engage in sex, with the act of sex not necessarily having been restricted to a time after marriage. This position was stabilized by the Council of Trullo in A.D. 692 (canon 13). The proposal that all clergy give up cohabitation with their wives, issued at the Council of Nicea (A.D. 325), was rejected, although celibacy in bishops was made mandatory provided that they were not married at the time of their elevation to the dignity.

The earliest canonical enactment of clerical celibacy occurred at the Council of Elvira (c. 306; canon 33), but became a directive only by papal action when Pope Siricius issued a decretal in 386 ordering celibacy for "priests and levites"; a stand repeated by Innocent I (402-417), and somewhat tempered by Leo I (440-461). Clerical concubinage remained rife throughout the church, even to the time of the sixteenth century Protestant reformation. Thomas Aquinas noted (*Summa Theologica* II, ii, q. 88, a. 11) that celibacy was not a law of god, but a church law, which later popes cited in permitting priests who married to stay both married and priests. This was the case with Pope Julius III who recognized priests who married during the reign of Henry VIII (in the Church of England, celibacy of the clergy was formally abolished in 1549, so that Archbishop Thomas Cranmer's marriage was legalized), and Pope Pius VII, who accepted priests who married during the French Revolution. Details of this are in Henry C. Lea, *History of Sacerdotal Celibacy in the Christian Church* (New York: University Books, 1966), pp. 305, 396, 402, 413, 485, 543; F. X. Funk, *Kirchengeschichtliche Abhandlungen und Untersuchungen*, 1 (1987), pp. 121-25: "Coelibat und Priesterehe"; E. Vancandard, *Etudes de critique et d'histoire religieuse* (1905): pp. 69-102: "Les Origines du celibat ecclesiastique."

7. Originally abstinence was a penitential practice intended to apply to food, since food, ancient philotheologians argued, made people sexual and interested in sexual activity during periods when the female was not fertile. Prior to the advent of the organized church, abstinence was known as fasting. Leviticus 11 gives elaborate food prohibitions which became a part of Jewish life, but was tempered (Acts 15) in the early Christian movement. Sexual abstinence was never considered holy or viable without the food prohibition. See related articles in *Dictionnaire de Theologie Catholique*, ed. A. Vacant, E. Mangenot,

and E. Amann (15 vols.; Paris, 1903-1950), vol. I, cols. 261-77. To suggest sexuality as reason for abstinence negates the basic and primary psycho-physiology of human motorskills, functions, instincts, and traits, devolving the human to robotic standards that are not mentally sound since such action places the body into a noncorruptable, eternal presence, which is physically impossible. Robertson's arguments are more reminiscent of Tertullian (*On the Resurrection of the Flesh*, 7) than Ambrose (*De Noe* 18, *De Officils* I, 83, 220).

8. "Old-fashioned" is ambiguous and relative. Such "moral restraint" was seldom practiced before the middle of the nineteenth century; see: David J. Pivar, *Purity Crusade: Sexual Morality and Social Control 1868-1900* (Westport, CT: Greenwood Press, 1973). Then it was centered on the regulation of prostitution ("illicit" or "subterranean," or basement sex), which was feared as the source of mental dysfunctions and moral malaise; see: John Chynoweth Burnham, "The Medical Inspection of Prostitutes in America in the Nineteenth Century: The St. Louis Experiment and its Sequel," *Bulletin of the History of Medicine* 45 (1971): pp. 203-18; Benjamin Scott, *A State Iniquity: Its Rise, Extension and Overthrow* (London: Kegan, Paul, Trench, Trübner & Co., 1890); Vern L. Bullough, *The History of Prostitution* (New Hyde Park, NY: University Books, 1964), pp. 127-30 focuses on Christian thought regarding prostitution and marriage; Emil Oberholtzer, Jr., *Delinquent Saints: Disciplinary Action in the Early Congregational Churches of Massachusetts* (New York: Columbia University Press, 1956); Kai T. Erikson, *Wayward Puritans: A Study in the Sociology of Deviance* (New York: John Wylie and Sons, 1966), with his introductory chapters of especial value on the concept of social deviance; cp. Daniel Defoe, *A Treatise Concerning the Use and Abuse of the Marriage Bed* (London: T. Warner, 1727), who has a counterpart in Benjamin O. Flower, "Some Causes of Present Day Immorality and Suggestions to Practical Remedies," *The National Purity Congress: Its Papers, Addresses and Portraits*, ed. Aaron M. Powell (New York: Caulen Press, 1896), which is more in keeping with Robertsonian rhetoric.

9. A. C. Kinsey, *Sexual Behavior in the Human Male* (Philadelphia: Saunders, 1948).

10. John F. Kanter and Melvin Zelnik, "Sexual Responses of Unmarried Women in the United States," *Family Planning Perspectives*

4.4 (1972): pp. 9-18.

11. Morton Hunt, *Sexual Behavior in the 1970s* (Chicago: Playboy Press, 1974).

12. Janet Shilbey Hyde, *Understanding Human Sexuality* (New York: McGraw-Hill, 1979), p. 244.

13. Daniel Offer and Judith Baskin Offer, *From Teenage to Young Manhood: A Psychological Study* (New York: Basic Books, 1975), pp. 32, 97.

14. Hunt, loc. cit.

15. Robert R. Bell, *Premarital Sex In A Changing Society* (Englewood Cliffs, NJ: Prentice-Hall, 1966). Conflict in societal attitudes is the subject of Albert Ellis, *The American Sexual Tragedy* (New York: Grove Press, 1962), cf. p. 29.

16. A. C. Kinsey, W. B. Pomeroy, C. E. Martin, and P. H. Gebhard, *Sexual Behavior In the Human Female* (Philadelphia: Saunders, 1953).

17. Robertson, *Answers*, p. 171.

18. Robertson, *Answers*, p. 171.

19. Fort Worth, Texas *Star-Telegram* (8 October 1987), sec. 1, p. 8. Cf. Joanne Jacobs, "Actions Speak Louder Than Words," ibid., p. 31.

20. *Washington Post* (8 October 1987).

21. This analogy was refined by James Ehle of Grand Prairie, Texas, in his comments on conception.

22. Cf. Pausanias VIII 42 1-2, VII 4 4, VIII 23 5, III 16 10: in *Pausaniae Graecia descriptio*, ed. H. Hitzig and H. Bluemner (3 vols. in 6; Leipzig, 1896-1910); Kallimachos, *Hymnus in Jovem*, in Kallimachos, *Callimachus*, ed. Rudolph Pfeiffer (2 vols., including the scholia; Oxford: Oxford University Press, 1949-1953) pp. 10 ff; Carl Kerenyi, *Dionysos: Archetypal Image of Indestructible Life*, trans. Ralph Manheim

(Bollingen Series LXV.4; Princeton, NJ: Princeton University Press, 1967), ch. II.

23. Cf. *The Gospel of the Birth of Mary* 3:5, 11; *Protevangelion* (or *Gospel of James*) 5:5; *Gospel of the Infancy of Jesus* 1:15ff

24. Robertson cites I Cor. 6:15-16, which is, as is his custom, out of context.

25. Associated Press (9 October 1987).

26. Robertson, *Shout It from the Housetops*, p. 15.

27. Robertson, *Shout It from the Housetops*, p. 27.

28. Robertson, *Shout It from the Housetops*, pp. 31-33. Note especially his negation and neglect of familial responsibilities on p. 33, and his assignation of those responsibilities to his god: "I can't leave. God will take care of you."

29. Cf. Lev. 17-26, especially 20:11-21; I Sam. [I Kings] 20:30; cp. I Cor. 7:3-6 for a contradiction, which is distorted in Augustine of Hippo, *De Civitas Dei* 14:16, 21, 23, and 22:17, with his repulsion of the human body in *De Civitas Dei* 14:17-18, that is continued in Boethius, *Consolation* 2:5, and book 8. See for comment: W. E. H. Lecky, *History of European Morals* (2 vols.; London, 1905) II:107ff; and, Frank Bottomley, *Attitudes To The Body in Western Christendom* (London: Lepus Books, 1979).

30. Robertson, *Answers*, p. 171.

31. Robertson cites I Cor. 6:9-10, and in his reference to the Tarsusian's letter attempts to join Jesus to his sexual phobia, citing I Cor. 6:15-16. Jesus had no statement on premarital sex any more than the Nazarene had any comment on homosexuality; at most, the man from Galilee damned only the sale of the body (prostitution) and infidelity, and even these lines are subject for discussion.

32. Robertson, *Answers*, p. 171.

33. Robertson, *Shout It from the Housetops*, pp. 179, 196, 243, cf.

92, 27; Robertson, *Answers*, pp. 32, 90-91, 87-88; and, above, Straub, loc. cit.

34. Various wire reports, carried in the *Dallas* [Texas] *Times Herald* (9 October 1987), sec. A, p. 14.

35. In his biography, *Shout It from the Housetops*, Robertson claimed that his god told him that a minister should never get involved in elective politics, p. 195. In part, Pat's reluctance to support his father in his reelection bid was because of the future televangelist's aspirations towards and lust for a "million-watt TV station" (p. 196) and his personal goal for empire. He desired to become enriched and electronicommunicatively powerful (pp. 111, 229, 242, 254). Power and money became the secret deity of Robertson, the denouncer of mortals who openly sought financial gain and a better life on earth, without fearing what might be or might not be after death.

36. *Dallas* [Texas] *Times Herald* (9 October 1987), sec. A, p. 14.

37. Robertson forgot to state that this line is Matthew 7:1, a common error in spite of the fact that he puffs himself up to be an authority on the Bible, and cites it, continuously in a distorted manner in his books.

Chapter 25
Defeat?

On 1 October 1987, in the slums of Brooklyn, New York, where Pat had served but a short time as pastor to a Baptist congregation, a profession he has not practiced in any parish pulpit the last twenty-five years since, Robertson officially declared himself a candidate for the Republican nomination for the presidency of the United States.[1]

While heckled by those who saw him as the antithesis of that for which the United States stands, Pat pushed his statement of his presidential ambitions with a frenzy. At no point did he acknowledge the possibility that he might not be the candidate, or that if he were the GOP standard bearer, he might be defeated. God was on his side. God had singled Pat out. No one would dare to run against Pat, nor would the people risk the wrath of his god and vote against the prophet from Virginia Beach.

What if Pat should lose a race that god told him to run, promising Pat he would win? Pat summarized it sharply in 1985, "That's the most dreadful suggestion I've heard all day."[2]

Robertson is convinced that he can be defeated only by the hand of Satan. This hand would be exercised by those who failed to listen to his interpretation and his reading of his Bible.

Pat firmly believes that "god-fearing" people will vote for him. He argues, repetitively, Romans 13:1-2: "the powers that be are ordained by God . . . they that resist shall receive to themselves damnation." He takes these select verses out of their context.[3]

The third verse continues: "For rulers are not a terror to good works, but to the evil. Wilt thou then not be afraid of the power?"[4] The biblical injunctions are *against* "men of god" going into politics to rule; it is not an admonition for people to vote for a preacher. Jesus was emphatic about mixing religion and politics: they are two separate spheres that are not to be joined by anyone.[5]

Determined to win the office of the presidency of the United States, Robertson on 29 September 1987 declared that he would cut all ties to his TV ministry, and resign as a Southern Baptist minister. While the former decision was "one of the most painful I have ever been required to make,"[6] the latter was, at best, a joke. Although a Southern Baptist minister, Robertson's "ministry" has been one of obeisance to power, passion, political play, and pay. He seldom exhibited any interest in the Southern Baptist cult. He wrote in the early 1980s, "the church government I feel most closely parallel[s] that of the New Testament is the Presbyterian [denomination]." The Southern Baptist "form of church government . . . is handicapped . . . [since Southern Baptist] congregations can dominate the pastor who should be God's servant [not man's]. Without a true spirit of prayer and humility, the only remedy left in such a situation is a power struggle, a suit in a secular court, or a messy church split [between an autocratic pastor and those congregants who believe in democracy]."[7]

Robertson laments that the Southern Baptist ministers do not have absolute mind control over their congregants. He believes that shepherds of any cult should coerce and control the voting patterns of their flock. Such mental enchainment is essential if Robertson is to capture the White House and dominate social and personal life in the United States.

To vote against Robertson, is to vote against Robertson's god. Robertson and his god are one. Robertson has written:

> More autocratic forms of church government have the advantage of a great sense of historic continuity, plus the ability to mobilize coordinated resources and to control both purity of doctrine and the practice of the clergy . . .

— and the faithful.[8]

Robertson and his god have nothing in common with any Bible of any religion. His interpretation is but a ruse.

Luckless individuals who might be tempted to cast a vote against him should remember that his god does not tolerate or prolong the lives of those who counter his prophet Robertson's cautionary and instructive words.[9] This pseudo-preacher warns that those who vote against him would be sealing their own doom to an eternity[10] in the fiery bowels of hell.[11]

In this regard, Robertson typifies the tyrants that Thomas Jefferson warned the United States about, ". . . in every country and in every age the priest has been hostile to liberty."[12]

Notes

1. All news services noted that Pat's proclamation of his candidacy roused little interest. It did not generate spontaneous or universal enthusiasm. Several of his former congregants openly questioned the televangelist's sincerity for the democratic process.

2. Andrew Mollison, "The Quotable Pat Robertson on Politics, Religion, Himself," loc. cit.

3. Rom. 13:1-2.

4. Rom. 13:3.

5. Cf. Luke 20:25.

6. Associated Press. 29/30 September 1987.

7. Robertson, *Answers*, pp. 133-34.

8. Robertson, *Answers*, p. 134.

9. Robertson, *Answers*, pp. 240-41. Robertson's god "shuts off rebellion" against his rule, for fear that some mortal might overthrow the immortal and become a new god. On the totality of dedication and blind obedience to this "god" of Robertson, see: ibid., p. 201.

10. Cf. Robertson, *Answers*, pp. 35-36, for his comments on eternality.

11. Gary Miller, "Querying Robertson's Campaign," *Connellsville* [Pennsylvania] *Daily Courier* (3 September 1986), p. 13. Cp. Robertson, *Answers*, pp. 35-36, 62, 87-88, 240-41; cf. ibid., p. 160.

12. Cf. Rusell Baker, "It'll Be Hard to Go against The Parson, but

Then, All That Money. . . ." syndicated column from the *New York Times* carried in the *Austin* [Texas] *American-Statesman* (24 September 1986), sec. A, p. 15; *Dallas* [Texas] *Times Herald* (18 September 1987), p. 1; *Fort Worth* [Texas] *Star-Telegram* (19 September 1987), p. 1; *Waterloo* [Iowa] *Daily Courier* (18 September 1987), p. 1.

Chapter 26
The Final Stretch

As 1987 slipped into 1988, Pat began throwing off his various disguises. Revelation followed revelation with apocalyptic horsemen riding roughshod over both civil liberties and the concept of separation of state and church that the colonial fathers on the North Atlantic seaboard had toiled to hammer out on the forge of early democracy.

At the end of December 1987, Robertson became more emphatic concerning the role fundamental Christianity was to play in the United States once he became president. Robertson's quixotic behavior repeated his earlier lapse of stability, as detailed in his 1984 book *Answers to 200 of Life's Most Probing Questions*, where he admitted to having been a potential suicide, and being brought to depression's ultimate expression when he came to the conclusion that he had been attacked by demons.[1]

Strengthening previous arguments telecast on his "700 Club," Robertson repeated that the civil government of the United States should be subordinated and subservient to the will of his god. Democracy is to be tolerated, only because democracy has become so engrained in the general psychology of the United States citizenry that to attack it could spell political suicide for the evangelicals of the Robertson camp. As Pat prattled, democracy is "next best" to "government controlled by God."[2]

As polling places were readied for introductory caucuses and party meetings, Pat preached an altered tune. Robertson was reported to have said, "Christians are the only ones really — and Jewish people, those who trust the God of Abraham, Isaac and Jacob — are the only ones that are qualified to have the reign [government], because hopefully, they will be governed by God and submit to him."[3] This same insensitivity towards non-Christians and those who are not Abrahamic Israelites was repeated in July 1986, when Robertson declared that Christians are not only more patriotic than non-Christians, but that Christianity alone could keep the nation together and restore "traditional values."[4]

A strong states-rightist, Robertson would subordinate the general commonwealth to the vested interests of local governments. His stand against federal government again is supported by his interpretation of the Judeo-Christian Bible.

The Bible should be, Robertson claims, the new constitution of the United States. Laws and judgments are to be rendered according to Biblical precedence — as the ancient Jews experienced more than 4000 years ago.[5] The Bible is to be "the principle for protecting the environment, ensuring racial and sex equality, supporting workfare over welfare, improving labor-management relations, providing for industrial safety and opposing coercion and a strong central government."[6]

To insure states rights and the advance of evangelical Christianity, Robertson would increase the number of Christian slogans used on coinage, stamps, stationery, flags, and general literature. Robertson's quest to impress Christianity on every United States citizen, and to incorporate the symbols of Christianity into civil and private materials, is based upon his overriding belief that "Jesus is coming soon."[7]

When Jesus returns, Pat has prepared an "invisible army" to lead the dead Nazarene to the headquarters of the Robertson government.[8] Robertson's "army" are those evangelicals currently carrying Robertson's message to coreligionists.[9] The most fervent followers of the preacher are young people whose zeal is to find a niche in his spiritual kingdom since jobs have declined, costs escalated, and security vanished over the past eight years, leaving the United States impoverished, weak in science, with a poorly educated people,[10] a trade balance that collapsed from a $17 billion surplus in 1980 to a $139 billion deficit in 1986, and "pink slips" for one to two million domestic manufacturing workers each year. More than a third of them remain indefinitely out of work; more than half the rest have taken pay cuts of 30 to 50 percent in new jobs that cannot make use of their experience; a feebler productivity growth (0.4 percent yearly from 1979 to 1986; the weakest net investment effort in our postwar history (averaging 4.7 percent of GNP from 1980 to 1986); a significantly higher level of federal spending in 1986 (23.8 percent of GNP) than we had in 1979 (20.5 percent of GNP); and the United States has gone from a creditor nation to a debtor nation since Reagan and the radical right took office.

Robertson's anticipated restoration of the Kingdom of Jesus, and the physical, bodily return of the crucified Nazarene, has taken a major toll of his thinking and life preparation.   Robertson even ordered Gerald Thomas Straub to help him plan a way to televise the Second Coming, not only to have the journalistic jump on a major event, but to strengthen his own television network and raise additional capital to promote his concept of a god-centered empire. The alleged Second Coming is to take place soon after Robertson has been sworn in as the President of the United States, for Jesus "had it up to here and the hour of His wrath has come."

Robertson continued, "Now if I'm hearing Him right, things are starting to happen. What is started over in the Middle East is not going to stop short of a war. I believe in the next two years, I would put it at '82, but dates are risky, there is going to be a major war in the Middle East. . . . I mean, from now on it's going to be bloodshed, war, revolution and trouble." When this Armaggedon begins, obviously not in the forecast year of 1982, Robertson would assist Jesus in protecting, Christians, exclusively.[11]

As Robertson spilled into 1988, his political stand, based on his interpretation of the Bible and his covert conversations with Christ, became increasingly exotic. Jesus has taken such an increased significance for Pat that he has come to the point that he has cried, "Even in hell I'll praise him."[12]

Robertson, in the 1988 campaign, became increasingly less coherent, avoided realism, and lapsed into inconsistency.[13] His record, writings, television pronouncements, and public posturings show neither truthfulness nor candor.[14] While statistically Mississippi is among the five least adequate, most understaffed, poorest paid places to obtain an education in the United States, Pat proclaims that he will make Mississippi education the model for the nation. Like other demagogues, Robertson elects to forget that which is discomforting or will expose his own fascist thinking and disregard and distaste for democracy.[15] Robertson has publicly stated that he would limit democracy, preferring a republic where his god will control a confederation of states similar to the Southern Confederacy prior to the emancipation of slaves.[16] Initially he refused to accept matching federal campaign funds[17] but later reversed his decision and took the available money—getting the second biggest check from the treasury in the amount of $4.5 million.[18] Robertson had received more than $11.7 million in contributions, collecting more than all other hopefuls with the exception of Vice President George Bush.[19] He has repeatedly condemned premarital sex, and yet spawned his own son Tim out of wedlock.[20] He spoke of salvation for "Christians only" and then permitted Jews to consider themselves among the elect to be saved.[21] Robertson has declared that if he is elected President of the United States, his administration will allow all people access to him, yet, he has said that Atheists would not be tolerated in his administration.[22] Although he has labeled himself an evangelist in his books, and has preached with a Southern Baptist license, on Monday, December 14, 1987, Robertson attempted to distant himself from his theocratic past by claiming that he had never been an evangelist, and was but the head of the fifth-largest cable network in the United States.[23] His personal selfishness is legendary, from the time he abandoned his wife Dede, to questioning his concept of faith healing when his wife contracted cancer and required surgery — a practice in which he has stated little belief.[24]

Because Robertson is a preacher, the news media and other journalists have been terrified of attacking him. Their fear is not so much over the alleged wrath of god, but the reaction of fundamentalists who buy advertising space in their papers and magazines, and the possibility that those who are evangelicals will cancel their subscriptions. As in most political situations, electors vote their pocketbooks and their homes, not only at the polls but in their marketing and selling.[25] While Robertson's support is narrow,[26] The few conservative Jews who do support the Robertson candidacy, do so in hopes of Robertson establishing "traditional values" and morals based upon Old Testament YHWHist literature;[27] thus little is said about his machinations and movement to destroy the basic fabric of democracy and choice in the United States.

Notes

1. *San Francisco Chronicle* (January 8, 1988).

2. Wayne King, "The Record of Pat Robertson on Religion and Government," *New York Times* (December 27, 1987) p. 1.

3. "700 Club" (January 11, 1985).

4. Susan F. Rasky, "Robertson Talks Issues and Results Are Mixed," *New York Times* (8 January 1988), p. 8; Richard Cohen, "Will The Real Robertson Own up?" The [Cleveland, Ohio] *Plain Dealer* (1 January 1988), p. 9-D. Cf.: "Pat Robertson Holds Houston Rally, January 23," *Something Better News* (January 1988), p. 1; King, "The Record of Pat Robertson," p. 30.

5. Lee Bandy, "Robertson Running His Campaign by The Book," [Long Beach, California] *Press-Telegram* (January 30, 1988), p. A1.)

6. Bandy, "Robertson Running His Campaign by The Book," p. A4.

7. Cf. Tim Miller, "Prayer, Politics Merge in Robertson Camp," *Dayton* [Ohio] *Daily News* (January 24, 1988), 1A, 15A.

8. Mary McGrory, "Robertson Relies on 'Invisible Army.' " *Des Moines* [Iowa] *Register* (23 January 1988), p. 12A.

9. Kenneth Pins, "Robertson: Faith Issues Won't Detour Bus Tour," *Des Moines* [Iowa] *Register* (19 January 1988), p. 3M.

10. On the decline of the economy, see: Peter J. Peterson, "The Morning After," *The Atlantic Monthly* (October 1987), pp. 43-69. Peterson notes: "Six years after the radical reforms of Reaganomics. Americans are about to wake up to reality."

11. King, "The Record of Robertson," p. 30.

12. King, "The Record of Pat Robertson," p. 30.

13. Randall H. Balmer, "Robertson Has Credibility Problems," *Des Moines* (Iowa) *Register* (January 7, 1988),p. 8A.

14. "Robertson Vows to Pump Dollars into Mississippi," *he Mississippi Press* January 12, 1988), p. 3A.

15. John B. Judis, "Republican Consternation and Aversion in Orlando," *In These Times* (November 25-December 8, 1987), pp. 6, 7.

16. Wayne King, "Minister Robertson vs. Candidate Robertson: A

Comparison," *Des Moines* (Iowa) *Register* (December 27, 1987), p. 5A; cf. Thomas A. Fogarty, "Robertson Woos the Right with Unorthodox Program," *Des Moines* (Iowa) *Register* (November 21, 1987), pp. 1A, 3A.

17. Charles R. Babcock, "Two Causing Stir in Election Commission," *Washington Post* (December 30, 1987), p. A3; "Robertson to Refuse Refund?" *Pittsburgh Post-Gazette* (January 30, 1987),p. 4.

18. Associated Press release in the *Minneapolis Star-Tribune* (January 5, 1988), p. 3A. By October 16, 1987.

19. Escondido, California *Times-Advocate* (October 16, 1987), p. A3; Mike Sante, "Robertson Has Change of Heart, Takes Federal Campaign Aid," *Austin* (Texas) *American-Statesman* (January 1, 1988), p. A4; Charles R. Babcock, "Robertson Reverses Course, Will Accept Matching Funds," *Washington Post* (January 1, 1988).

20. "Wild Oats," Time (19 October 1987); Ellen Goodman, "Rev. Pat's Birth Policy a Misconception," Escondido, California *Times-Advocate* (November 3, 1987), p. 6B.

21. Wayne King, "Robertson Takes Back Remarks as Minister," *New York Times*, reprinted in the *Detroit Free Press* (December 28, 1987), pp. 1A, 14A.

22. *United Press International*, in *Detroit Free Press* (September 21, 1987); cp. Bob Secter, "Robertson's Base Shallow: Support Still Limited to Religious Right, Poll Says," *Austin* (Texas) *American-Statesman* (January 24, 1988), p. A9.; Lee Bandy, "Robertson's Politics Rooted in Religion," *Detroit Free Press* (January 31, 1988), pp. 1A, 9A.

23. John Ellement, "Robertson Says He's Never Been an Evangelist," *Austin* (Texas) *American-Statesman* (December 15, 1987), p. A11.

24. Lee Bandy, "Wife's Cancer Challenges Robertson's Deepest Values," *St. Paul* (Minnesota) *Pioneer Press Dispatch* (January 3, 1988), pp. 1D, 7D.

25. "The Teflon Twins of 1988," *Time* (January 11, 1988), p. 30.

26. Bob Secter, "Little Robertson Support Found Beyond Faithful," *Los Angeles Times* (January 23, 1988), sec. 1, pp. 1, 22.

27. See: Herb Brin, "Jewish Fundamentalists See Eye to Eye with Preacher," *San Diego* (California) [Jewish] *Heritage* (October 16, 1987), pp. 1f.

Epilogue
Analysis of The
Authorized Biographies

For sheer slick stick writing, one can't beat *Pat Robertson: The Authorized Biography* by John B. Donovan.[1] The book, a composite work of Donovan and three assistants, is based on "forty-five hours of interviews with Robertson, his wife, Dede, and many close personal and business friends."[2]

Donovan consulted no secondary works or opponents of Robertson to round out the picture. There is *no* analysis of Robertson's writings — yet Donovan liberally quotes or grossly paraphrases them at times without giving a citation to the actual source. Such is the case when Dede Robertson objected to Pat's abandoning his family to trek into the woods as a wounded messiah.[3]

Similar statements Robertson made on various issues affecting the citizens of the United States on his "700 Club," or any public posturings put on by Robertson in his quest of the presidency of the United States, are left uncharted, without analysis, but instead given near hagiographic proportions. The book suggests Robertson's immortality — if not his divinity. It is as if Robertson were already sitting at the right hand of Jesus. But then, *Pat Robertson: The Authorized Biography* is exactly that: It is an "authorized biography," a pleasant pat on the back with one "attaboy" and another "good ol' boy" compliment after another. It is soulless, meatless, and without any critical apparatus. It is a fairy tale filled with half-truths and regular distortions, political prevarications, and posturings. And it will sell because it gives a rosy picture of a pastoral United States that Christians, born-againers, evangelists, fundamentalists, and charismatics wish to believe. It would be ego-devastating to have their golden calf exposed to be a skeleton covered with the dung of dangerous demagoguery and crass, callous disregard for individual liberties.

According to his publishers, Donovan is "a journalist with experience in Vietnam and Washington, D.C. He founded and heads the Senior Corporate Writer's Group in Larchmont, New York." The only recognized publication that is on record by Donovan is his authorship of *The Family Book of Bible Stories*, published in 1986 by Morehouse-Barlow of Walton, Connecticut.

Petty biases that favor televangelist Pat come through loud. A "born-again Christian," author Donovan salutes Pat's theocratic aspirations while downplaying the reality of Pat's own life, and his attempts to suffocate human freedoms and personal choice.

Quick to distort fact for fancy, Donovan details how Pat grew up in near poverty:

> My father's salary was $10,000 a year, a modest sum. But in the Depression we had the cook we paid seven dollars a week, and a maid we paid five dollars a week, so twelve dollars a week was awful hard to get. For a family with an income of no more than $10,000 we lived very well. And in our lives we didn't experience the Depression. We drove a Dodge or a Plymouth. In those days, a Dodge or a Plymouth cost $700 or $800. Everything was relative in the economic sense. . . . Those prices were so low and services so cheap.[4]

While Pat's quote appears as meaningless ramblings, it does tell the reader a great deal. Pat does not understand the gravity of the Depression. He shows not only an ignorance of, but a lack of appreciation for the suffering, that existed elsewhere. This is in keeping with his general character. (The twenty room mansion in which he grew up is illustrated elsewhere in this book.)

As for Robertson's father's salary of $10,000 being modest, the 1929 National Bureau of Economic Research reported that "forty-four million people had [annual] incomes of about one thousand dollars each, or less than one-half of one percent of the separate incomes of those at the top." Slightly more than 500 individuals had an income of over $1 million each — out of a total population of 121,767,000.[5] In 1929-1930 $10,000 had a purchasing power, based on 1967 buying base standards, of $19,500; based on today's standards, the Robertson's had the purchasing power of $29,000. They were definitely not "impoverished."[6] This is even more graphic when one compares what a dollar would buy during the depression to its buying power in 1988. The Dodge that Pat's father purchased in 1930 cost approximately $700; a similar stripped-down car today, made by Chrysler, retails for approximately $12,000 (base price).

Pat's father was underpaying both the cook and the maid. Based on national averages and per capita income, Pat was raised on "sweat-shop" labor. Average monthly *relief* benefits ranged from $4 a month to $14.27 (October 1933), while the average *salary* was around $20 per week.[7] Pat's family was considered to be "better off than most" of the people at the time.

The myth of the impoverishment of Pat's family, and later of himself, has continued, and is played big both in Pat's autobiography, *Shout It from the Housetops*, and in Donovan's *Authorized Biography*. In both cases it is a blatant lie. It is the usual myth of the poor man making good, thus holding out this unattainable dream to the average man. Robertson's story is meant to stir the hearts of those on marginal subsistence to vote for a man who has had little to no time for the poor and destitute save to preach to them. Rather than working to alleviate the plight of poverty so that they do have an income, Pat urges the poor to "offer it up" in hopes for a better life in the hereafter.[8]

One cross Robertson had to bear during his early pastoral sufferings, is the woman for whom Donovan has a difficult time disguising his dislike. Actually, the tone of the book indicates that Donovan more than dislikes Dede Robertson. He portrays her as an initially unsupporting shrew. Scornfully Donovan notes that Dede wanted the "children to grow up in a normal home."[9] While giving credence to such absurdities of Pat's as his chancing across random scriptural passages that are allegedly the Christian key to present reality — even though these verses have existed for more than a thousand years and during those thousand years the same claims were made by equally emotionally emasculated men and women[10] — Donovan ignores the helpmate status of husband and wife contained in the very tales he spouts as Scriptures.

Even though Donovan castigates Dede as being "hard-hearted," Dede wrote earlier that she "stood by" her man, whom she found unique: "I don't think I have ever known a more honest man [than Pat Robertson]."[11] This, too, is a cover, for she, like Donovan, fails to note that Pat's academic *vita* for years has been a lie at worse, at best an extension of the truth and his marital history has been altered to hide a shotgun wedding.

311

Donovan totally ignores the fact that Robertson did not study at the London School of Economics. He continues the base lie from which the Robertson camp has made profit in touting the televangelist in official biographies and pamphlets. Both CBN and Donovan credit Robertson with insightful economic analysis. Donovan claims that Robertson has an uncanny perception of "the baleful impact of a spendthrift mentality on the overall economy" that has been perpetuated by government spending conditioned by the Great Depression.[12] Donovan also choses to ignore Robertson's call for a general debt cancellation every fifty years, and argues that Pat is behind a "flat tax."[13] To insure that this will revitalize the economy, Donovan claims that Robertson would "give industry back some of the privileges it [Congress] took away from them [sic: it] in the Tax Reform Bill of 1986." These "privileges," Donovan ignores, includes everything from gross beneficial tax loopholes, to minimal deductions for three-martini lunches, in addition to numerous other perquisites. It also ignores the issue of ever-increasing and expanding trusts and the merger of businesses to the detriment of the individual consumer.[14] Robertson's idea of abolishing debt every fifty years would lead to havoc. Restoring tax loopholes for businesses would add additional economic burden upon consumers.

Neither Robertson nor Donovan shows any grasp of the 1929-1939 era in the history of the United States, nor any understanding of what occurred economically that led to the rise of the era of Franklin Delano Roosevelt.[15] Donovan apparently sides with Robertson in rewriting history, using the doublespeak of *1984*, which is more in keeping with totalitarian dictatorships than with the principles of democracy. Yet even this is justified by "returning to the Bible" and drawing out chance passages to prove personal perspectives, and propensities.

Robertson's total dependence upon chance biblical readings to determine his life pattern and the destinies of those over whom he has charge is skeletonized by Donovan. In a cursory reading of Donovan's book, one notes that Pat sold all the Robertson furniture "since he [god] told me through Luke 12:33 to sell the furniture and give all the money to the poor."[16] Then, following additional biblical injunctions chanced upon in hlis blind bibliolatory, Pat forced himself and his family upon another family whom he expected would take care of the Robertson clan: "Yep. . . . I've given all the money away and moved in here with Dick and Barbara."[17]

Donovan notes that Pat bases his entire system of thought on the Bible. Robertson is quoted as saying that the Bible:

> . . . is a practical book with a system of thought and conduct
> that will guarantee success, true happiness, true prosperity, not
> the fleeting, flashy, inconsistent success the world usually settles
> for.[18]

According to Pat, the Bible is more than a "holy book" or a register
for future ideologies. It is Pat's guide for the United States and the
world. If the Bible demands that the United States drop a nuclear bomb
on the Soviet Union, Pat as President would do so if that line of
Scripture should chance upon his reading.[19]

One theme that trumpets throughout this story of Pat Robertson is
Donovan's recognition of the immeasurable role money has played in
the televangelist's past and present. One can barely get past a page
without being faced with Pat's quest for gold[20] or need to further enrich
himself and his campaign to transform the United States into the
theocracy he envisions. When Pat's god told the preacher to buy a
station, Pat turned to RCA. He offered $37,000, "provided the station
was free from all debts and encumbrances" — and he wanted a six-
month option on that purchase price. The owner, Tim Bright, told
Robertson that the tower alone cost $100,000, and requested earnest
money. Robertson declined, causing Bright to respond, "I don't like
God's way of doing business." Robertson countered by requesting that
Bright show him how to operate the station. Throughout the
negotiation, Pat failed to tell Bright that there was no money in the
bank.

Going to RCA, Robertson continued his negotiations with Sam
Twohig. Twohig was not against the acquisition but insisted that
Robertson pay Bright's obligation of $44,000.[21] It was more than
Robertson could pay for the entire project. To cover himself,
Robertson pleaded that he was negotiating for god — who wanted the
entire project for the $37,000 with no obligations added. Twohig was
not impressed.

Fearing that he had lost the station, Robertson returned. Chastizing
himself, Robertson moaned, "Mr. Twohig, I believe I represented the
Lord very poorly in our talk this afternoon. Twenty-five thousand
dollars is just too big a price to pay on these old obligations."[22] Pat's
god remains the "good businessman" that Pat would have the deity
play; he bargains, cajoles, threatens, pleads, persuades, and pressures
to get the best deal possible so that Pat can have crumbs to feed to
his flock:

Bright scratched his chin and asked how much God was willing to pay. Robertson replied that the offer was $37,000 [*en toto*], provided that the station was free from all debts and encumbrances.[23] . . . Robertson didn't mention that he was going to fail in his commitment to put on the show that day . . . . "We'll never make it, Pat. You've missed God. You're too early." . . . ."[24]

Pat tends to be "too early" for most things. Donovan's apology for Pat in Korea is to take Pat's word for the preacher's activities (or lack thereof) while in the militarized zone.[25] Donovan repeats Pat's pronouncements, which he used to file a libel suit against McCloskey, and which refute the sworn affidavits gathered by McCloskey concerning Pat's less than honorable conduct in the Korean theater. The extent of Donovan's coverage of the Robertson affair in Korea is to argue that McCloskey covertly conspired to libel the Southern Baptist preacher.[26] He gives no legal arguments for his claims, cites no facts, proffers no proof. Instead he calls upon John Warner, now a Republican senator from Virginia, who was Robertson's "college buddy," for a testimonial as to the worthiness of Robertson. All Warner added was that, "They brought up some cases of liquor so we could have a party. I remember getting roaring drunk" and questioning "the meaning of life."[27]

CBN is labeled a "family network."[28] Donovan says nothing about CBN's consistent condemnation of the equality of the sexes, of the right of choice, or of human liberties. Robertson's hostility towards sexual freedom of choice Donovan buries by noting Robertson's insistence that morality is the main business of government. He would have legislation determine public morality and enforce his Christian code.

Ironically, Donovan castigates one of the most radical far-right newspapers in the United States: the *Dallas* [Texas] *Morning News*. The *Dallas Morning News*, a bastion of conservativism, the editorial policies of which border on fascism, questioned Robertson's motives in attempting to legislate personal morality, inviting Donovan to state that the *Dallas Morning News* editorial "was clearly hostile to Robertson."[29] For the *Dallas Morning News* to be opposed to any totalitarian concept or radical Republican idea is unusual at best, for not only does this journal of conservative thought bask in the light of the Hoover Foundation writers, but brings out the big guns of Jeane Kirkpatrick and most of Reagan's henchmen as near-gods and arbiters of public opinion.

Robertson has never denied his interest in determining how people live, act, work, love, and labor. Robertson can be quoted as saying that "No government is neutral. All law ultimately represents somebody's values." As for Donovan's anemic argument that Robertson is merely attempting to assure the freedom of religion, Robertson's own writings declare that he is opposed to anyone who attempts to dissuade religion in the United States.[30] Regularly he attacks the American Atheists, agnostics, and non-Christians. Robertson claims:

> If you do not teach the Judeo-Christian or some other religiously based morality in schools, you will ultimately teach humanism or atheism.[31]

Yet this sweet-sounding sop to the various denominations, cults, and religions of the world is little more than an empty phrase. Robertson's own hostility to any religion other than pentecostal Southern Baptist theology is clearly stated in his *Answers to 200 of Life's Most Probing Questions.*

Not only does Robertson attack the Church of Jesus Christ of Latter-day Saints (Mormons), claiming that Mormons have little in common with (his interpretation of) Christianity,[32] but he flatly states that "when it comes to spiritual matters, the Mormons are far from the truth."[33]

Robertson ridicules Jehovah's Witnesses as being "different from Christians" and states that "many of their [other] doctrines are not biblical either."[34]

He attacks the Unification Church of Reverend Sun Yung Moon as an institution that brainwashes its young, and that does not permit its adherents to "reflect on the lies they are told."[35]

Hindus cannot receive the "Spirit of God."[35]

Unitarians cannot be distinguished "from humanists and atheists," Robertson writes.[37] Ejaculating his pent-up anger, Robertson emotes "any other church that" preaches "unity" and throws out biblical fundamentalism is racing towards a contemporary tower of Babel ripe for the wrath of the Christian god.[38]

Robertson is convinced that it is his obligation, under orders from his tyrannical deity, to restore "right religion" to a United States already raped by religion.[39]

Donovan notes that Robertson has said:

We have in this country freedom of religion. But nobody ever intended freedom *from* religion,

— the emphasis is his.[40]

Tim Robertson, the new heir-apparent to the CBN empire and rapidly becoming the radical right's Torquemada, is given credit for turning Pat to the GOP.[41] Allegedly, Tim told teacher-dad that the Republican party has a great interest in preserving individual liberties although this same political force has rallied against the passage of the Equal Rights Amendment, has attempted through senatorial action to undo the Civil Rights laws passed in the 1960s, seeks to overturn *Roe vs. Wade*, and continue the basic theme of "one nation under God," with the "liberty and justice for some" which has become the hallmark of the Rehnquist court, the Reagan administration, most evangelical circles, and the platform of most domestic demagogues, from the Aryan Nation to the separatist Black Muslims of Chicago, the Christian Knights of the Ku Klux Klan, the mushrooming American paramilitary groups such as the Lejun of Doom spawned at Paschal High School, Fort Worth, Texas,[43] the emerging segregationists in New York. While Donovan makes no claim to be clairvoyant about the future, he does note Robertson's past pronouncements on the right of women to chose an abortion, and he continues the distortion over the issue of choice.

On the campaign trail, 1988, Republican presidential contender Pat Robertson charged on February 2, 1988, that the long-range family planning goal of international Planned Parenthood, was to create a "master race." Speaking in a room overflowing with opponents of choice, Pat Robertson told a New Hampshire legislative committee that he strongly opposed a bill to repeal old state anti-abortion laws and to codify the United States Supreme Court ruling legalizing abortion into state law.

Distorting facts and creating fantasies, Robertson libeled Margaret Sanger, the founder of Planned Parenthood. He charged that she:

> . . . was an advocate of what was called eugenics. She and her disciples wanted to sterilize blacks, Jews, mental defectives and fundamentalist Christians. I don't really favor getting myself sterlized. And I certainly don't favor the programs of the Nazis.[42]

The Christian Broadcasting Network's "counseling" is a feigned excuse to proselytize fundamentalism, to convert people from one faith to Pat's cult, and to prognosticate problems that will lead to an enriching of the Robertson treasury. Pat and his cult give air time to "people who have life-after-death experiences," cold-blooded assassins who "kill Commies for Christ," and to today's tyrants in El Salvadore, Chile and elsewhere.[44]

A patronizing polemicist, Pat's official biographer has bolstered the claims of the radical right, raped legitimate reporting, and roasted the concept of democracy over the glowing coals of clerical corruption and demagogic despotism. The Bible is to become the blueprint of a United States government leading the righteous to world domination and control. Those who would defy Pat are to be leveled as were the walls of Jericho:

> John Gimenez heard the prophet's ancient call and began to dream of what might happen to America if its people, too, were called to return to righteousness. He pictured a mass of people assembling in the nation's capital to pray, to confess, to and to call the nation back to her spiritual roots. . . . . John's dream captured me, and together we began to tell others about our emerging plan for an April 29, 1980, mass rally and march on Washington. . . . [it] was the beginning of a spiritual revolution.
> . . . [45] IT WAS CALLED "CAUCASIAN SAND NIGGERS FOR CHRIST"

It is only at our peril, in Robertson's eyes, that we attempt to construct political or ethical systems that are not soaked in the spirit and sometimes the letter of Scriptures. . . .[46]

History for him [Pat Robertson] also includes events that are still to occur, at least if the American people are adequately aware of these views and agree with them. . . .[47]

The book is as chilling in what it says, as in what it leaves unsaid.

While Donovan's book is a bad joke, Harrell's *Pat Robertson: A Personal Political and Religious Portrait* is worse. Harrell's book rejects all principles of sound scholarship and deifies personal prejudces — for profit. But then it does meet one "need": Harrell is "published" again.

Harrell elects to ignore nearly all aspects of Robertson's past and present political involvements. He offers no comment on Robertson's support for U. S. counterinsurgency operations. He is silent on Robertson's 1982-1983 funneling of aid to Guatemala's born-again dictator, Gen. Efrain Rios Montt, under whose tenure the Guatemalan military massacred thousands of Quichét Indians. Harrell remains silent on Robertson's May 1985 "700 Club" telethon to raise money for the contras and for Guatemala's then-dictator Gen. Mejia Victores. There is no mention of Robertson personally delivering $1 million worth of material to Mejia Victores, nor is there any record of Robertson's CBN being the largest single private donor to the contras, giving between $3 and $7 million to the contras and their families bivouacked in Honduras.

Harrell is stony-silent on the cameo appearances of contra leaders Adolfo Calero, Enrique Bermudez and Steadman Fagoth on Robertson's faith-healing money-raising talk show. Harrell says nothing about Robertson's lauding Roberto d'Aubuisson, head of El Salvador's fascist ARENA Party.

Harrell is equally quiet concerning Robertson's rabid support of the segregationist South African government, which Robertson sees as doing the work of god. Harrell stonewalls with silence Robertson's son Tim's characterization of the African National Congress (organized to promote racial equality in South Africa) as a band of Soviet-inspired killers. Segregationist tones color most of his comments, being more of a throwback to yesteryear than a candle to light up the present or shine into the future.

There is no mention of Robertson's 1980 stand to organize every Congressional district into a "secret army" to give the United States "a Christian President and a Christian government." Harrell offers no critique of Robertson's proposed "Christian government" that is to have faithful and non-faithful alike report all details of their personal lives to sanctified clergy, as well as to receive permission before dating or marrying. Pastors who support Robertson's goal of "Christianizing America" have ordered parents to "train" their children by using heavy doses of corporeal punishment. These same ministers were in the frontlines of Jim Jones whose authoritarian standards were not dissimilar to that of the televangelist, yet Harrell bypasses all this information as if it had been scripted for a Hollywood 1984 tale of horror and is not a part of Robertson reality.

Harrell does not recognize Robertson as a nuclear-war advocate, even though Robertson's own tapes on Armaggedon prove the lie. But then Harrell did not bother to go to any of Robertson's real critics — not even to magazines such as the *Sojourner*, a progressive Christian magazine, which in October 1985, released details of Robertson's assistance to the Nicaraguan contras. The televangelist has never challenged the veracity of the article, yet revealed that both Israel and South Africa were aiding the contras along with William Casey and the

CIA. And, Harrell says nothing.

All Harrell's sanitizing biography will do is earn him money from born-again evangelicals. If freedom of the press should continue in the United States, Harrell's book won't have much of an academic following and is worth less than the paper on which it is printed. But if Robertson does get his way, becomes President, and institutes his brand of censorship, Harrell's book will become bible, and doublespeak will have come into its own.[47]

Notes

1. John B. Donovan, *Pat Robertson: The Authorized Biography* (New York: Macmillan, 1987 [c 1988]).

2. Publisher's comment on jacket of the *Authorized Version* (c. 1988).

3. Donovan, *Pat Robertson*, p. 34, quotes Dede as saying that she recognizes Pat's "schizoid tendencies," yet Donovan fails to cite Robertson's biography, *Shout It from the Housetops*, p. 28: Dede's plea for a "normal environment" Pat was denying her and his family; see also, *Shout It from the Housetops*, pp. 26, 27, and my comments above.

4. Donovan, *Pat Robertson*, pp. 11-12.

5. Gifford Pinchot, "The Case for Federal Relief," *Survey Graphic* (Washington, DC: U.S. Government Printing Office, January 1932), pp. 348-49.

6. *Facts and Figures on Government Finance* (Chicago: The Tax Foundation, 1986); *Survey of Current Business* (Washington, DC: Department of Commerce, Economic Analysis, Census Bureau, September 1987).

7. FERA (Federal Employment Reconstruction Act) *Monthly Report* (June 1935): p. 31.

8. Donovan, *Pat Robertson*, pp. 39-40, 189-90.

9. Donovan, *Pat Robertson*, p. 33.

10. Donovan, *Pat Robertson*, p. 33.

11. Donovan, *Pat Robertson*, pp. 35-36.

12. Donovan, *Pat Robertson*, pp. 133-34.

13. Donovan, *Pat Robertson*, pp. 187, 188.

14. Donovan, *Pat Robertson*, pp. 133-34.

15. Leah Hannah Feder, *Unemployment Relief in Periods of Depression: A Study of Measures Adopted in Certain American Cities* (New York: Russell Sage Foundation, 1936). "Reports from States: Outdoor Relief," *Proceedings* National Conference of Charities and Correction, 1909. Rose Porter, *The Organization and Administration of Public Relief Agencies* (New York: Family Welfare Association of America, 1931). Josephine Chapin Brown, *Public Relief: 1929-1939* (New York: Henry Holt and Co., 1940).

16. Donovan, *Pat Robertson*, pp. 38-39.

17. Donovan, *Pat Robertson*, p. 39.

18. Donovan, *Pat Robertson*, p. 150.

19. Donovan, *Pat Robertson*, pp. 184, 19, 142-44, 190, 99-200, and my comments above.

20. Donovan, *Pat Robertson*, pp. 1, 2, 11, 12, 17, 21, 22, 29, 30, 45, 46, 47, 48, 50, 51, 52, 53, 54, 56, 57, 58, 59, 60, 62, 65, 66, 67, 69, 70, 71, 74, 75, 77, 79, 80, 81, 83, 84, 85, 86, 87, 88, 89, 90, 91, 105, 109, 110, 111, 115, 133, 135, 140, 160, 161, 164, 165, 166, 169, 171, 172, 177, 191, 198, 199, 200, 201, 203, 205, all give dollar figures, while Robertson articulates archaic ideas on taxation on p. 187 and general economic foundations on pp. 184-86. These pages should be read in light of his own book, *Answers to 200 of Life's Most Probing Questions*, pp. 184, 186; his relationship to money is detailed in his biography *Shout It from the Housetops*, pp. 183, 187-90, 198, 201-25.

21. Donovan, *Pat Robertson*, pp. 50-51f.

22. Donovan, *Pat Robertson*, p. 53.

23. Donovan, *Pat Robertson*, p. 50.

24. Donovan, *Pat Robertson*, p. 59.

25. Donovan, *Pat Robertson*, pp. 22-24.

26. Donovan, *Pat Robertson*, p. 23.

27. Donovan, *Pat Robertson*, p. 23.

28. Donovan, *Pat Robertson*, p. 114.

29. Donovan, *Pat Robertson*, p. 193.

30. Robertson, *Answers to 200 of Life's Most Probing Questions*, pp. 192-94.

31. Donovan, *Pat Robertson*, pp. 191, 208.

32. Robertson, *Answers to 200 of Life's Most Probing Questions*, pp. 136-37.

33. Robertson, *Answers to 200 of Life's Most Probing Questions*, p. 137.

34. Robertson, *Answers to 200 of Life's Most Probing Questions*, p. 137-38.

35. Robertson, *Answers to 200 of Life's Most Probing Questions*, pp. 139-40.

36. Robertson, *Answers to 200 of Life's Most Probing Questions*, p. 142.

37. Robertson, *Answers to 200 of Life's Most Probing Questions*, p. 138.

38. Robertson, *Answers to 200 of Life's Most Probing Questions*, p.

143.

39. While Donovan ignores Robertson's claim that "god" told him to run for the presidency of the United States, see my citations above. Donovan skirts this issue on pp. 175-208.

40. Donovan, *Pat Robertson*, p. 194. Robertson considers any objection to Judeo-Christian religion to be a "rebellion against God" and thus a grave threat to society, safety, and the earth. See, Robertson, *Answers to 200 of Life's Most Probing Questions*, pp. 20, 27.

41. Donovan, *Pat Robertson*, p. 173.

42. "Robertson Links Abortion, Nazis" St. Louis, Missouri *Post-Dispatch* (3 February 1988), sec. B, p. 1.

43. See my *Demons and Demagogues: Political Fanaticism in the Longhorn State* (Las Colinas, TX: The Liberal Press, 1986).

44. Donovan, *Pat Robertson*, pp. 199-200, 152, 155-57, 19, 142-44, 151.

45. Donovan, *Pat Robertson*, p. 152.

46. Donovan, *Pat Robertson*, p. 153. The extent of the "spiritual revolution" can be seen in Southern Baptist preacher Jerry Falwell's threat that the fundamentalist vote will sway the 1988 vote; see, Jim Jones, "Religion to Sway '88 Vote, Falwell Says," *Fort Worth* [Texas] *Star-Telegram* (1 February 1988), sec. 1, p. 3. Earlier, Jackie Koszcuk reported in her article, "'Robertson Returns to Religious Roots among Ex-peers," *Fort Worth* [Texas] *Star-Telegram* (31 January 1988), sec. 1, p. 5, that Robertson would made the Religious Right's agenda the blueprint for a takeover of United States government: "We must bring God back into the public school system," Robertson said, and schools must teach history according to fundamentalist interpretations and desires regardless of how it happened. His popularity soared when Robertson took 80 percent of the delegate strength in Hawaii the first week of February 1988.

47. *Pat Robertson: A Personal, Political and Religious Portrait* (New York: Harper & Row, 1988) by David Edwin Harrell, Jr. (chair of the

Department of History at the University of Alabama).

"AIMS AND PURPOSES"
(as recorded in documents of incorporation)

AMERICAN ATHEISTS ARE ORGANIZED:

(1) to stimulate and promote freedom of thought and inquiry concerning religious beliefs, creeds, dogmas, tenets, rituals, and practices;

(2) to collect and disseminate information, data, and literature on all religions and promote a more thorough understanding of them, their origins, and their histories;

(3) to advocate, labor for, and promote in all lawful ways the complete and absolute separation of state and church;

(4) to advocate, labor for, and promote in all lawful ways the establishment and maintenance of a thoroughly secular system of education available to all;

(5) to encourage the development and public acceptance of a humane ethical system, stressing the mutual sympathy, understanding, and interdependence of all people and the corresponding responsibility of each individual in relation to society;

(6) to develop and propagate a social philosophy in which man is the central figure, who alone must be the source of strength, progress, and ideals for the well-being and happiness of humanity;

(7) to promote the study of the arts and sciences and of all problems affecting the maintenance, perpetuation, and enrichment of human (and other) life; and

(8) to engage in such social, educational, legal, and cultural activity as will be useful and beneficial to members of American Atheists and to society as a whole.

"DEFINITIONS"

Atheism is the *Weltanschauung* (comprehensive conception of the world and of total human life value systems) of persons who are *free* from theism — *i.e., free from* religion. It is predicated on ancient Greek Materialism.

American Atheism may be defined as the mental attitude that unreservedly accepts the supremacy of reason and aims at establishing a life-style and ethical outlook verifiable by experience and the scientific method, independent of all arbitrary assumptions of authority or creeds.

Materialism declares that the cosmos is devoid of immanent conscious purpose; that it is governed by its own inherent, immutable, and impersonal laws; that there is no supernatural interference in human life; that man — finding his resources within himself — can and must create his own destiny. Materialism restores to man his dignity and his intellectual integrity. It teaches that we must prize our life on earth and strive always to improve it. It holds that man is capable of creating a social system based on reason and justice. Materialism's "faith" is in man and man's ability to transform the world culture by his own efforts. This is a commitment which is in *every* essence life-asserting. It considers the struggle for progress as a moral obligation and impossible without noble ideas that inspire man to struggle and bold creative works. Materialism holds that humankind's potential for good and for an outreach to more fulfilling cultural development is, for all practical purposes, unlimited.

American Atheists is a nonpolitical, nonprofit, educational organization. Another of its functions is to act as a "watchdog" to challenge any attempted breach of what Thomas Jefferson called "the wall of separation between state and church," upon which principle our nation was founded.

Membership is open only to those who are in accord with the "Aims and Purposes" indicated above and who are Atheist Materialists. Membership in the national organization is a prerequisite for membership in state, county, city, or local chapters. Membership fee categories are reflected on the reverse side of this sheet (American Atheists Membership Application form).

A complete copy of the Constitution and By-Laws of American Atheists is available upon request. Send $1.00 for postage and handling to:

Constitution and By-Laws
American Atheists, Inc.
P.O. Box 140195
Austin, TX 78714-0195

Membership Application For American Atheists

Last name: _________________________ First name: _________________________
    Companion's name (if family or couple membership)
Last name: _________________________ First name: _________________________
Address ____
City/State/Zip ____

This is to certify that I am/we are in agreement with the "Aims and Purposes"* and the "Definitions"* of American Atheists. I/we consider myself/ourselves to be Materialist or Non-theist (*i.e.*, A-theist) and I/we have, therefore, a particular interest in the separation of state and church and American Atheists' efforts on behalf of that principle.

I/we usually identify myself/ourselves for public purposes as (check one):

☐ Atheist   ☐ Objectivist   ☐ Agnostic
☐ Freethinker   ☐ Ethical Culturalist   ☐ Realist
☐ Humanist   ☐ Unitarian   ☐ I/we evade any reply
☐ Rationalist   ☐ Secularist   to a query
☐ Other: _________________________

I am/we are, however, an Atheist(s) and I/we hereby make application for membership in American Atheists. Both dues and contributions are to a tax-exempt organization and I/we may claim these amounts as tax deductions on my/our income tax return(s). *(This application must be dated and signed by the applicant(s) to be accepted.)*

Signature _________________________ Date _________________________
Signature _________________________ Date _________________________

Membership in American Atheists includes a subscription to the monthly journal *American Atheist* and the monthly "Insider's Newsletter" as well as all the other rights and privileges of membership. Please indicate your choice of membership dues:

☐ Life, $500
☐ Couple Life, $750 (Please give both names above.)
☐ Sustaining, $100/year
☐ Couple/Family, $50/year (Please give all names above.)

☐ Individual, $40/year
☐ Age 65 or over, $20/year (Photocopy of ID required.)
☐ Unemployed, $20/year
☐ Student, $12/year (Photocopy of ID required.)

Upon your acceptance into membership, you will receive a handsome gold embossed membership card, a membership certificate personally signed by Jon G. Murray, president of American Atheists, our special monthly "Insider's Newsletter" to keep you informed of the activities of American Atheists, and a subscription to *American Atheist*. Life members receive a specially embossed pen and pencil set; sustaining members receive a commemorative pen. Your name will be sent to the chapter in your local area if there currently is one, and you will be contacted so you may become a part of the many local activities. Memberships and subscriptions are nonrefundable.

☐ I am/we are enclosing a check or money order for $ _________ payable to: American Atheists
☐ Please charge my/our charge card for $ _________ . ☐ Visa or ☐ Mastercard
Card # ____
Bank No./Letters ____
Expiration date: ____
Signature ____

Return form to:
American Atheists, Inc., P.O. Box 140195, Austin, TX 78714-0195

Don't Miss The
American Atheist

Founded by the first lady of Atheism, Dr. Madalyn O'Hair, the *American Atheist* is the magazine of the modern Atheist.

From the latest deeds of Atheist activists to the last antics of the religious right, its articles run the gamut of issues important to Atheists. Skirmishes in the state/church separation battle, the life-style and history of Atheism, religious criticism, current events are all included in the focus of this journal. The nation's hottest topics — school prayer, abortion, creationism — are all covered in its pages from the Atheist's viewpoint.

This magazine's writers bring readers a unique spectrum of viewpoints from literally all over the world. Examples? One columnist offers glimpses into the religions of India. Another highlights the pain of women in the Arab world. Jon Murray, president of American Atheists, spotlights the progress of Atheism (and religion) in the United States.

So why miss any more of this fascinating magazine? Though it is free to members of American Atheists, it is also available to nonmembers on a yearly subscription basis. Go ahead: Check off a box below and head into the wonderful world of Atheism.

□ Regular subscription, $25   □ Sustaining subscription, $50
□ Foreign subscription, $35   (tax-deductable)
□ Sample copy, $2

Last name: _________________ First name: _________________

Address: ____

City/State/Zip: ____________________________________

□ I am enclosing a check or money order for $ ___________ payable to American Atheists.

□ Please charge my credit card for $ __________ . □ Visa or □ Mastercard

Card # ____

Bank No./Letters ___________________________________

Expiration date: ____________________________________

Signature ____

Return form to:
American Atheists, Inc., P.O. Box 140195, Austin, TX 78714-0195